February 11, 2001

Happy Birthday
Marcie !

Cynthia

MY GOLDEN SPOON

MY GOLDEN SPOON

Memoirs of a Capital Lady

Eleanor Davies Tydings Ditzen

MADISON BOOKS
Lanham • New York • Oxford

Copyright © 1997 by Madison Books

Published by Madison Books
4720 Boston Way
Lanham, Maryland 20706

12 Hid's Copse Road
Cummor Hill, Oxford OX2 9JJ, England

British Library Cataloguing in Publication Information Available

Library of Congress Cataloging-in-Publication Data
Ditzen, Eleanor Davies Tydings, 1904–
    My golden spoon : memoirs of a capital lady / Eleanor
Davies Tydings Ditzen.
        p.   cm.
    ISBN 1-56833-096-0 (cloth : alk. paper)
    1. Ditzen, Eleanor Davies Tydings, 1904–   . 2. Tydings, Millard
E. (Millard Evelyn), 1890–1961. 3. Legislators' spouses—United
States—Biography.   4. Davies, Joseph Edward.   5. Statesmen's
children—United States—Biography.   6. Washington (D.C.)—
Biography.   I. Title.
E748.T93D58   1997
973.9'092—dc21
    [B]   96-50353
                                                                          CIP

ISBN 1-56833-096-0 (cloth : alk. paper)

Distributed by National Book Network

♾ ™ The paper used in this publication meets the minimum requirements of American National Standard for Information Science—Permanence of Paper for Printed Library Materials, ANSI Z39.48—1984. Manufactured in the United States of America.

Contents

v

Prologue

My Dear Grandchildren:

Today is Millard Tydings's birthday. He has been gone for two months now, and for the first time in my fifty years, I am completely alone in this big old house, without the three people I loved the most: Father, Mother, and Husband. Only the ghosts of the people who lived on this land before us are here. I can feel the presence of the Susquehannock Indians, whose arrows our children found where our shores run along the Chesapeake Bay. Captain John Smith wrote in 1608 that the Indians were seven feet tall and very handsome. Attractive ghosts? Maybe. I prefer those of my Revolutionary War ancestors or of other forebears like Col. John Thompson, who landed at St. Mary's in southern Maryland in 1634 and lived to be 106. Or my Bohemian ancestor named Augustine Herman who came to New Amsterdam (New York City) about that time and was sent to Maryland as ambassador from the Dutch to argue the ownership of Delaware with Governor Leonard Calvert. He made a good map of Maryland for Calvert and was made "Lord Proprietor" of 30,000 acres in Maryland, which he called "Bohemia Manor."

The Stumps, a distinguished Baltimore family, are also descendants of Herman and built the old part of this house where they lived for about 100 years. Your grandfather Senator Millard Tydings bought it in 1935 for me, his bride. These ghosts would be no comfort to me as I sit here, looking back on twenty-six wonderful years with Senator Millard Tydings. His life ended with encephalitis and mental illness that can be traced to a poison gas attack during World War I.

There is a room in this house, crammed with memorabilia of our life together: photos and clippings, letters and diaries. There are also letters and photos of my father, Joseph Davies, the statesman-lawyer who served as adviser to three presidents and as ambassador to Russia before and during World War II. He was instrumental in preventing the Soviet Union from making a separate peace with Germany in 1943. One cannot live on memories, however. So, my dear grandchildren, I am going to write an account of a life that spanned the transition from Victorianism to the modern age, and intersected with some of the most important lives and events of the twentieth century. My story is part history, part romance, and part tragedy, based upon letters, diaries, and memories of life in most of the twentieth century. It is the story of a girl who rebelled against strict Victorian rules, but was a virgin when she married, and never indulged in the "postmarital" affairs so common today. My story contains no prolonged descriptions of the sex act. I do not think there is anyone left today who needs instruction. If you wish to hear about my romantic and political adventures, you can "read all about it!" as newsboys once shouted on city street corners.

Love,
Grandmother
Oakington House, Havre de Grace,
Maryland
April 1961

Part I

Chapter 1

My Golden Spoon, 1904

Grandmother Nellie Knight looked down critically at me, her first newborn grandchild in her arms.

"Well, little Eleanor," she said rather disparagingly, "you certainly are no beauty at this moment! Let us hope that in time you will acquire the beauty of your mother and the rest of the women in our family and develop from an ugly little duckling into a satisfactory swan! You must feed her something with the golden spoon, Emlen, and that will bring her good luck and good fortune, I hope!"

I wailed loudly and she handed me over to my father's loving arms.

"You can't say she doesn't have nice big eyes!" he said, kissing the top of my head. I blinked then and stopped screaming and have loved him devotedly ever since.

"Let us hope that she will grow up to be as beautiful as her grandmother Nellie and her lovely mother." His wish for me and my golden spoon came true for me for many wonderful years.

Although I have been a Marylander and Washingtonian most of my life, I was born in Watertown, Wisconsin, into two families that were very different. My father, Joseph Edward Davies, was the son of Edward Davies. Edward and five brothers followed their father to the United States from a farming community in North Wales in 1850. Edward Davies owned a Conestoga (covered) wagon factory in Watertown. He met and married Rahel Paynter, a remarkable and gifted young woman, an ordained Protestant minister from the Island of Anglesey in North Wales. She had left parents who were landed gentry to come to preach in this country. When their son was a child, Edward Davies died on a visit to Rahel's sister in Wales. The boy refused to stay in Wales as his aunt's heir and his mother returned to Watertown where she continued to preach. Young Joseph graduated from public school and the University of Wisconsin with honors. He won many oratorical contests and was urged to go to New York to be an actor by an important producer. David Belasco had seen him play the lead in a play at the university. Joe Davies chose to practice law in Watertown and was elected district attorney of his county. He had met Miss Emlen Knight at a prom at the university in Madison and they were married after he was elected.

My father was the first of the men I have deeply loved and who had the greatest influence upon my life. He was handsome, brilliant, and possessed great charm.

It seems to me, as I look back to the time when the century and I were young, that I have always been in the happy state of being "in love" with people and places, with ideas, and with all that is beautiful. By "being in love," I mean loving enthusiastically and joyously. Sex doesn't always enter into that happy state. I adored my father. He could recite poetry by the yard and he told me his Uncle John had encouraged him to memorize a new poem every morning when he washed.

Emlen was the beautiful blond daughter of Colonel John Henry Knight, a Delawarean who fought in the Union Army in Delaware's only regiment, "The Blue Hens Chickens". He survived two battles of Manassas and at Antietam, Maryland, and Lookout Mountain, Tennessee. After the war he commanded Fort Douglas (now Salt Lake City) when the eastern and western railroads were first joined together there in 1869 to form the first transcontinental railroad. His letters home described the place (now Salt Lake City) as "a dirt cross-roads with a hotel," actually a bar and a "House of ill repute," he wrote. "Men fought and shot each other daily and the women were worse than the men! J. C. never crossed the Missouri River," one woman said! Travelers were frequently attacked and killed outside the place by savage Indians.

My grandfather resigned from the Army to practice law in Wisconsin with a U. S. senator who had been his school friend at Albany Law School. The colonel acquired land and built lumber mills, which made him a fortune. He was elected mayor of the town of Ashland, on Lake Superior in the heart of the lumber country where he built and owned two hotels. He was defeated for the U. S. Senate by one vote in the Wisconsin legislature. He married my grandmother—Nellie Clark, of a distinguished Delaware-Maryland family—and moved to Madison, the capital of Wisconsin. My mother,

Mary Emlen, was one of three daughters. Nellie's mother, Mrs. Susan Boulden Clark, and sister, Miss Elizabeth Kettle Clark, lived with them.

My parents moved from Watertown to Madison when I was two. Daddy had built a pretty house on the lake shore and they did their best to make a proper little Victorian out of me. They gave me a very happy childhood and I loved them dearly.

The Knight mansion in Madison occupied several acres beside Lake Mendota, about six blocks from the state capitol. It was a handsome gray stone house with a square cupola on top, which fascinated me as a child. From this vantage point I could see all of the five lakes surrounding the city. My grandparents' lawns bordered one and there were servants' quarters and stables. Like the Clarks's home at the Anchorage, once outside (now inside) Wilmington, Delaware, the Knights lived in style. There were four house servants, two laundresses, a gardener, a groom, and a coachman. In the stables were handsome carriages, a pair of "matched grays," and silver-mounted harness.

The Knights entertained elaborately. I quote from a letter written by my great-grandmother describing a luncheon given by my grandmother Nellie in honor of President Cleveland's wife: "The luncheon yesterday was a success in every respect. Eighty-two ladies came and 30 sent regrets. Your mother sent to Milwaukee, New York, and Chicago for flowers and some of the refreshments. The luncheon menu consisted of ten courses! The ladies sat down at twelve and didn't get up from the table till five o'clock!" (It's a wonder they could get up at all!)

"Compliments were showered on us. One lady said, 'The luncheon was a perfect poem.' Mrs. Hobbins, whose father was minister to the Court of St. James, said that it was true 'Southern hospitality.'"

Chapter 2

Wisconsin Childhood

In the summer, we went to Grandfather's Nississhim Lodge on the Brule River in northern Wisconsin. In the winter, when I was little, I rode in splendor on the frozen lake in a beautiful little sleigh, bundled in white furs. Daddy pushed me on his ice skates, but Mother refused to go on the ice. She had once suffered a shattering experience as a young lady skating with a gentleman (not my father). Her underpants had slipped their moorings, fallen down to her ankles, and become entangled with her skates! She was forced to sit down upon the ice and allow her companion to extricate her. She would never even see him again!

There was little if any crime in Madison and I could walk the few blocks to Grandmother Nellie's house. It was full of wonderful things. There was a large, carved, wooden Swiss chalet with a clock in it on the mantel shelf, and a stereopticon through which we saw pictures of the Grand Canyon and Niagara Falls in three dimensions. There were also big, red plush albums full of photographs of long-dead relatives. Most of the men wore beards of different styles. One man was totally hirsute, as I recall, with just a small area shaved off to show the dimple in his chin!

For the first five years, I was the only child on either side of the family. My parents were strict when necessary. Pouting, whining, and screaming were not tolerated. I was never a screamer or a whiner, although my younger sisters were. I was never spanked because it simply wasn't necessary. Daddy was firm with me and the punishment of being banished to my room was seldom meted out because one stern look from my father's big dark eyes could reduce me to a heartbroken pulp. He impressed me with the importance of once giving one's word, never breaking it. I never did.

My adventures during these first years of my life were mostly imaginative. I spent a great deal of time with my nose in a book (I still do). I lived with Peter Pan, Dorothy and the Wizard in the land of Oz, and at King Arthur's Court. The lawn beside our house ran down to Lake Mendota where big willow trees leaned out over the water. Along the shore was an uneven line of giant boulders. Daddy said a glacier dropped them there long ago. One of these rocks was shaped like the prow of a ship, pointing out over the water. On this mighty galleon, I sailed the Spanish Main, fought pirates, and discovered exotic new lands. Perched high in a tree, I was Peter Pan. Even at this early age, I dreamed of a knight in shining armor or a handsome prince on a white charger who would eventually carry me off to a beautiful castle to live happily ever after.

At the age of four, I attended a small private French school, but at five my parents decided to send me to a good public school around the corner from our house. There were no slums in Madison, but there were some "poor people" who lived some blocks away on the other side of the streetcar tracks. Several children were from a German family who lived in this "undesirable" neighborhood. At school I was shocked at their lack of warm winter clothing. I told my mother, and she promised to do something about it. She belonged to a group of young ladies called the "Attic Angels", like the present-day Junior Leaguers. However, I could not wait for her group to act. In an excess of sympathy for these poor children, I packed my beautiful doll carriage full of my best toys and proudly delivered them myself to the house beyond the streetcar tracks. I was warmly received and properly thanked and lionized. I returned home in a glow of self-approbation! The glow didn't last long. Mother scolded me and I was sent back to retrieve my doll carriage and my beautiful dolls, Bessie and Rebekah, whom I had sacrificed in my wave of generosity. The fact that this time I bore a load of warm winter garments for the children did little to reduce my embarrassment. My mother, realizing that I had been punished enough, did not tell my father what I had done.

My little sister Rahel was born in our house when I was five, and I was sent to stay overnight with my Great Aunt Elizabeth Kettle Clark. It was my first time away from home.

I loved her and her little house. It had a small red staircase leading up to three bedrooms with huge four-posters and a bathroom. In the parlor there was a magnificent stuffed parrot on a stand, which was supposed to talk when wound up, but didn't work. I didn't care. I loved that parrot. Best of all was the marvelous tin tub in the bathroom. It had a long sloping back, which Aunt Bess would soap and I would perch on the wooden ledge at the top, then slide down into the water with a splendid splash!

Aunt Bess introduced me to the Bible, as well as the Baptist Church, and I would read it aloud to her. My favorite part was the description of the Holy City in Revelations, which almost outdid the description of the Emerald City of Oz! She also gave me my interest in history, and I gobbled up her books about France and England. Aunt Bess was a dedicated Christian. She was a true believer, not only in the Lord and the Hereafter, but also in the existence of the Devil himself. When she was sixty-five, she fell down the cellar stairs in her house and broke her hip. She always stoutly maintained that the reason she fell with such dire results was that she saw the Devil standing at the foot of the stairs! There was no question in the minds of any member of the family that she truly believed this.

One thing in her house that I did not like was the large engraving over the bed in my room. It gave me a terrifying nightmare that first night away from home, and continued to do so for years.

I was a Christian maiden, awaiting my turn to join the Christians being mauled and eaten by wild beasts in the Roman Colosseum. The roar of the crowd almost drowned out that of the wild beasts in the arena. Through it came the piercing screams of the Christians. My childhood friend, a young Centurion, was clinging to my arm, begging me to renounce my faith and marry him—Caesar would pardon me! I told him nobly that this I could not do! I loved Jesus Christ far more than I could ever love the Roman or his gods. I turned my thoughts resolutely to my noble and beloved parents. They had already gone to their martyrdom and I hoped to join them in our Christian Heaven.

"Dear God, let it be quick!" I prayed, as the guards tore me away from my friend and pushed me through the great gate into the arena. I held my head high and marched bravely ahead. The heat and the stench of the animals struck my senses like a blow. I closed my eyes against the sight of lions mauling and chewing on shrieking human beings. The shouts of the Roman spectators rose in crescendo as they saw me standing there in my simple white robe. "Thumbs up, Caesar! Save the pretty Christian maiden!" But there were also evil cries of "Thumbs down! Let the lions have her!" I heard an awful growl and looked up to see a huge beast, jaws dripping with blood, stalking toward me. I woke up screaming in the big old four-poster bed, clasped to the warm, capacious bosom of Aunt Bess. Over the bed was the large framed engraving of the Christian girl facing the lions. "There, there, child! It was only a bad dream," crooned my Aunt, rocking me in her arms. "Hush now, Auntie's Little Blossom! We'll have some nice warm milk and you can sleep with Auntie in her bed if you wish." I was only too glad to leave the four-poster and the awful picture that hung over it. For years afterward, I had that nightmare.

After the arrival of my baby sister and a little boy cousin, I discovered that it was almost as much fun to write stories for them as it was to read. I wrote fairy tales and animal stories and even extremely bad poems, all for their entertainment. My father was pleased and had them all typed and bound.

Grandmother Knight took me to Chicago with her when I was six. We went to that glorious store, Marshall Fields, with its fabulous children's playroom full of toys and a lovely tea room with ice cream and hot chocolate. This was all a great thrill, but the highlight of the trip was the play we went to see. My enthusiasm was so great that Grandmother told my mother that most of the audience was watching me instead of the actors on stage! Sadly, she died soon afterward, at the age of fifty-two. She had a severe internal infection but would never allow a male doctor to attend her.

While I was sailing my imaginary ships across Lake Mendota and flying airplanes in my backyard swing, my father was becoming more and more involved in state politics, and his law practice was becoming highly successful. He was a member of the Democratic National Committee of Wisconsin and soon to become chairman of Democratic Western headquarters. Our house was large enough to entertain in, and my mother came from a long line of Delaware and Maryland hostesses. She "set a fine table!" and the governor, senators, and other state bigwigs were frequent guests in our home. I would be proudly trotted out, wearing my best bib and tucker, my blue silk sash and a matching "Dorothy Dainty" hair bow atop my head, to curtsy politely and perhaps recite a poem. Sometimes I was even expected to sit upon some man's knee and even give him a kiss! I was a fairly docile and biddable child and endured it all sweetly until one fine day I rebelled and flatly refused to sit upon the plump knee of William Jennings Bryan. I was never again expected to do more than curtsy.

Father was an idealistic, liberal Democrat, but this never prevented him from fraternizing with prominent Republicans. Among those was the governor of Wisconsin, who lived nearby and would walk uptown to the Capitol Square most mornings with my father. The governor was a simple old man who spoke English with decided Norwegian overtones. Father had a great gift of mimicry and could imitate almost any accent perfectly. I have heard him tell this story about the Governor many times:

One morning the *Capitol Times* had a lead story that the president had offered our governor the post of U.S. ambassador to Uruguay. As usual, Father was walking with him to Capitol Square and was enthusiastic in his congratulations.

Davies: This is a great honor, sir, not only to you but to our entire state of Wisconsin! What a great thing to represent, in your person, the mighty United States of America! To be Ambassador Extraordinary and Minister Plenipotentiary of this great state and nation!

The Governor (shaking his head sadly): Vell, I tell you, Yo (Joe), I don't really vant the yob (job). You know, I got me a fine hardvare store and a nice house back in Boscobel and I vant to go back ven my term is up. My hardvare store ain't doing so goot, she go to hell, Yo, and I vant to go home. Trouble is my vife and my daughters got dis gottam social boog up dere schnoots. Dey vant to go to Churugvay—be big shots! But I got to go back to my hardvare store, Yo, or she go bust! (A moment's silence) And vare the hell is Churugvay anyvay, Yo?

Chapter 3

Politics Takes Us To Washington, 1911–1920

As the presidential election year of 1912 approached, my father became interested in the potential Democratic candidacy of the governor of New Jersey and former president of Princeton, Mr. Woodrow Wilson. On a business trip East, he met Wilson and spent some time with the Wilson family. The latter entertained him in their home and were as charmed by him as he was by them. So much so that Miss Margaret Wilson, the eldest of the three Wilson daughters, came to Madison to visit us that summer. After a week at our house in Madison, we took her up to visit my Grandfather Knight's lodge on the Brule River. The Brule is a beautiful, crystalline trout stream in the forests of northern Wisconsin. It tumbles into rapids and falls and widens into small lakes on its way to join Lake Superior. I spent many summers there. The Indian chief of the local tribe, who had been my grandfather's top guide, was a big man named John LaRoque. He taught me to paddle a canoe and to pole it up the rapids when I was six years old.

Many nights after dinner at the camp, children and grown-ups would gather around a roaring campfire in a clearing among the pines. We children would toast marshmallows and listen with bated breath to our elders' stories of "the Early Days" when the white men arrived on the Brule River and before that when the river country belonged to the Indians. One evening by the campfire, John LaRoque told us about a terrible Indian war long ago, when his tribe had fought against an intruding tribe. John's ancestor had been chief of their tribe, and so he had been told that the Brule River had run red with the blood of that terrible Indian war. He said the Indians would sometimes send out spies who would communicate with their forces by means of birdcalls, such as that we were listening to at that moment—the call of the whippoorwill. One night during a lull in the fighting, John's ancestor was sitting right where we were, eating a mighty haunch of venison for his supper, when he heard a whippoorwill off in the woods. The chief unhesitatingly jumped up and hurled the big venison bone in the direction of the sound. The next morning his braves found the body of an enemy Indian spy. The chief's bone had struck him dead!

Grandfather's friend, Grover Cleveland, was the first president to fish at our camp, and Dwight Eisenhower was the last. One of the in-betweens was Calvin Coolidge. Mother found his signed photograph hidden behind the kitchen stove on which John LaRoque's wife, Lizzie, did the cooking. Big John had spent days with President Coolidge, leading him to the best spots where trout lurked under fallen logs, trying to instruct him in the gentle art of fly casting, which Cal could never master. John, who received not a cent in tips from Mr. Coolidge, was hoping his services would be rewarded with a parting gift of a least one of the many fine rods that well-wishers had sent the President. Instead, he was given this autographed picture, which his wife promptly disposed of behind the stove. "He was a 'worm man,' " John told us in disgust.

In June 1912, my father attended the Democratic National Convention in Baltimore as the Democratic National Committeeman from Wisconsin. He and the other Wilson supporters were pleased with the choice of this Maryland city. Wilson was a Southerner and had many friends in Maryland. When the first session opened in Baltimore's armory on June 25, 1912, the leading contender was James Beauchamp ("Champ") Clark of Missouri, speaker of the House of Representatives, with 435 votes already in his pocket, and Wilson had only 248. A two-thirds majority was needed to win the nomination.

The immediate task confronting Father and the Wilson team was to block Clark. Their best hope of achieving that was to strike up an alliance with other candidates. Among the many were Oscar Underwood of Alabama, chairman of the House Ways and Means Committee; Governor Judson Harmon of Ohio; and Thomas Marshall. The man my father suspected would step forward after all his rivals had annihilated one another was William Jennings Bryan of Nebraska, still the kingmaker among the Democrats, although he had lost the presidency to the Republicans three times.

Joe Davies had a lot to do with the nomination of Woodrow Wilson. The convention was deadlocked for some time between William Jennings Bryan and Champ Clark. My father helped to put together the coalition that nominated Woodrow Wilson. Many years later I met the great newspaperman Henry L. Mencken and asked him if he had met my father at the Baltimore Convention of 1912. Mencken said he had been greatly impressed by Daddy's brilliance and good looks, but mostly by the magnificent shirts he wore.

After frantic days at the convention, my father won over William Gibbs McAdoo and secured the California delegation for Wilson. The forty-sixth count of delegates brought 903 votes for Woodrow Wilson, enough to win the nomination of the Democratic party. My father was made chairman of the Democratic National Committee of Western headquarters in Chicago, and Wilson was elected president of the United States. In the past, any man holding the position that my father held had been rewarded by the new president with a cabinet post. The newspapers speculated that he might be secretary of state. My parents rented their Madison house, packed up, and took me and my little sister to Washington, D.C.

On our way to our new lives in Washington, we stopped overnight at a New York hotel. I can still see the magnificent crystal chandeliers dimly reflected in the shining wood of the dance floor, the little gilded tables, and array of matching chairs that I had come upon while exploring down the narrow back stairs. "You may go down to the library, Eleanor," Mother had said when I showed signs of restlessness. "Perhaps you can find a book to occupy you." In the corridor I had found a door marked "Keep Out—Service Only." Naturally, I opened it and tiptoed down the narrow, dark stairway. Another door to be opened and I discovered the marvelous ballroom. My eyes were popping out of my head when, from nowhere, a waiter appeared.

"What are you doing here all on your own, little lady?"

"I've never seen anything so beautiful. What is this place? Where am I?"

Eyes twinkling, he smiled down at me. "Don't you know? This is Fairyland."

I took him at his word. "I think it must be."

"Well, now, hadn't you better be getting back to your mother?"

I nodded and ran.

The glimpse of this wonderful room was a prelude to what lay ahead. In the morning, we would be leaving to complete our railroad journey to Washington, D.C., where I was to spend most of my life.

Chapter 4

Eleanor Davies Grows Up in Washington

Just after dark the next day, we arrived in the nation's capital. Our train pulled into the splendid new Union Station, which was only as old as my three-year-old sister, Rahel. I was impressed by its size and the colossal statues of giant Amazon women lining its interior walls. Special trains steamed in on every track, unloading tourists and politicos, soldiers and suffragists, and more trains departed. In long lines around the terminal, automobiles were far outnumbered by horse-drawn victorias, hansom cabs, and hotel buses. Outside on the big plaza, the great white Capitol building and its beautiful big dome loomed against the dark sky in the white light of electric beams. I had never seen anything so majestic. It looked like a gigantic white wedding cake. Our handsome capitol in Madison was a mere cupcake in comparison. I caught my breath and Daddy put his arm around my skinny little shoulders and smiled down at me. "Beautiful, isn't it?" he said. "That is the seat of the government of our great free country, where the representatives of all of us make our laws."

"What about the president then?" I asked him. "Isn't he the king of our country?" I then received my first lesson on the checks and balances that make our United States the greatest democracy in the world. My father's eyes sparkled as he explained the functions of the Congress and the presidency and the courts. He described the United States Senate and I thought he would like to be a member of it.

As we waited for a bus to take us to the Shoreham Hotel, he continued to instruct me about our form of government. I was to remind him of this twenty-six years later when my husband was leading the fight in the Senate against the president's Supreme Court packing bill.

The day before President-elect Wilson took the oath of office, the suffragists literally "stole a march" on him. Women did not have the right to vote, and with the change of administration from conservative Republican to liberal Democratic, they hoped for an era of change. Accordingly, they staged a huge parade to press for women's suffrage. An army of women from all walks of life marched; factory hands, shop girls, and serving maids, and even some society ladies were in that parade. There were floats with billboards demanding a constitutional amendment to enfranchise women. I thought this was only right. Twenty years later, this same issue would be the subject of my first argument with my new husband, Senator Millard Tydings.

We had front-row seats at the inaugural ceremony and the parade. I admired the uniformed cadets from West Point and Annapolis who cordoned off the mobs pressing toward the president. I saw Mr. Wilson give a signal and tell a guard to "let the people come forward!" and the cadets wheeled right and left to let the crowds through. My father said the president had thus coined a phrase for the policy he was to call "the New Freedom." The president took the oath of office on his wife's Bible. He had opened it accidentally the night before at the beautiful 119th Psalm: "So shall I keep the law continually for ever and ever and I will walk at liberty for I seek thy precepts."

Mother was one of the few Washington ladies who were not disappointed when, for the first time since the presidency of James Madison, there would be no inaugural ball. President Wilson had called it off because of his financial circumstances, which ruled out any extravagance. The new president had actually been compelled to take out his first bank loan to move into the White House and outfit himself, his wife, and his three young lady daughters. His most expensive gift to Mrs. Wilson at that time was a small diamond pendent that his older daughter Margaret (she asked me to call her Aunt Margaret) said they called the "Crown Jewel".

After the inauguration, the Davies family and the rest of the country awaited the announcement of the president's Cabinet posts. Although my father knew Wilson was dead set against patronage and the evils of the spoils system, even to the point of refusing to make his only brother the postmaster of Nashville, Tennessee, my father's hopes ran high. But when the president announced the composition of the Cabinet, Joseph E. Davies was not on the list. The president told him that he was too young for such a major position. He offered to make my father the assistant secretary of war or the governor-general of the Philippines. My father declined. He was too proud to accept the first and the climate of the second was not healthful for children. The president then offered him the ambassadorship to European countries, including China and Russia. At that time, the U.S. government did not own their embassy residences, and the cost of accepting such a post would be more than my father could afford. He accepted the chairmanship of the first Federal Trade Commission because it would help secure his future as a lawyer in the nation's capital.

Until my parents could find a house to rent, we stayed at the old Shoreham Hotel on 15th Street. The president-elect and his family were there, waiting to move into the White House. Although I knew Margaret Wilson well enough to call her aunt, I had never met her parents or her sisters, Eleanor and Jessie. Soon after the Wilsons were in the White House, "Aunt" Margaret took me in to the president's office to meet her father and I was honored with a seat upon the presidential knee after I had made my best curtsy. I did not object to his thin knee as I had to Mr. Bryan's fat one. President Wilson played golf with my father every weekend at the Chevy Chase country club, and Daddy usually came home with a humorous limerick the president had composed. I can remember only two:

> There was an old lady named Fitch
> Who heard a loud snoring at which
> She took off her hat
> And found that her rat
> Had fallen asleep at the switch!

(Many fashionable ladies wore false hairpieces called rats under their pompadours.)

The other limerick went like this:

> For beauty I am not a star
> There are others more handsome by far
> My face I don't mind it
> Because I'm behind it
> It's the folks out in front that I jar!

Father and I often rode horseback with Margaret Wilson through Rock Creek Park to the Chevy Chase Club for tea. A groom would take the horses back, and we would ride home in a White House limousine. Once when we were riding single file along a narrow bridle path beside Rock Creek Drive, President and Mrs. Wilson drove by and waved to us. I was trotting on ahead and looked back to see my father's horse shy and rear just as the president's car slowed down to speak to us. Poor Father was thrown and saved himself by hanging around this horse's neck under its nose, in a most undignified position! The groom helped him to remount, and the only damage done was to Father's dignity! The president had a good laugh over his mishap.

Washington was a very different city from Madison, Wisconsin. I wrote a letter to a former playmate there describing the capital city as being "full of colored people" (there were none in Madison, so I had never seen one) "and white ladies who wore red paint on their lips and led little dogs around at the end of a string." Yet Washington was a small town then compared with what it is today. Most of the poor people were black and lived in shacks in Georgetown, or in the slums of Foggy Bottom where the Watergate Apartment Hotel is now, or in the northeast part of town.

Sixteenth Street was Embassy Row. At the top of the hill was the Hendersons' imposing red castle. They gave the city the large park across from it. Sixteenth Street led directly down to Lafayette Square and the White House. It crossed Massachusetts Avenue at Scott Circle, which was encircled by mansions, including the Peruvian embassy. Between Scott and Dupont Circle on Massachusetts Avenue were many handsome row houses and the Belgian and Canadian embassies. Some of the finest mansions faced Dupont Circle. Here was the Wadsworth House (now the Sulgrave Club), Cissie Patterson's house (now the Washington Club), the big Leiter mansion, the ugly red Bradley mansion with its own private theater, and the Patton house. There were three Patton sisters, and a current society joke was that the speediest means of communication in town were to telephone, telegraph, or telapatton. Handsome row houses ran up Connecticut Avenue from Pennsylvania Avenue, past Dupont Circle, and out Massachusetts to Wisconsin Avenue where the great National Cathedral was being built. At the time of the Civil War, these houses had stopped short of Dupont Circle. The streetcars did not run any farther. The British embassy had been built at N Street and Connecticut and was considered quite far out in town. Across the avenue from the British embassy and its handsome stone lions guarding the entrance was Alexander Graham Bell's big redbrick

house. More embassies had been built after the Civil War west of
Dupont Circle on Massachusetts Avenue. Here were some of Washington's finest palaces: the Walsh house, the Lars Anderson house,
the Townsend house. Anderson House is now the headquarters of
the historic Society of the Cincinnati (a hereditary order of the eldest
sons of officers in George Washington's army). The Townsend house
is now the distinguished Cosmos Club, and the Walsh house is an
embassy. Massachusetts Avenue ran up the Observatory Hill where
the U.S. Chief of Naval Operations had a big Victorian house (beginning in 1974, the official residence of the vice president).

My parents found a house on a small little tree-shaded street at
the top of the Connecticut Avenue hill called LeRoy Place, close to
the huge statue of General McClelland on his gigantic horse. I understand the general was a very small man! We were a few blocks
from the Connecticut Avenue bridge, which spans Rock Creek Park,
and the same distance down the hill to S Street, where I was entered
at a private school for girls called Holton Arms. I was a student there
from the fourth grade until I went to Vassar College in 1921. Most
of my schoolmates were from wealthy eastern Republican families
who looked down on Democrats who had recently come to town
with President Wilson's administration. The Republican Wadsworths, who owned the mansion on Dupont Circle, actually closed
it up and returned to New York, rather than associate with the uncouth Democrats!

Although there is nothing quite so snobbish as a female child, I
made friends with the nicest of my schoolmates. Among these were
Neville Johnson [grandchild of James B. Oliver (Steel Co.) in Pitts-
burgh], Gertrude Grosvenor (granddaughter of Alexander Graham
Bell and daughter of Dr. Gilbert Grosvenor of the National Geo-
graphic Society), Dorothy Warren, and Evie Wadsworth. Evie was
the daughter of Senator James J. Wadsworth of New York, not of the
Dupont Circle Wadsworths. She lived in a beautiful old house on
Sixteenth Street, which had belonged to her grandfather Hay, a
member of Lincoln's cabinet. I had only one Democratic friend and
schoolmate, Sallie McAdoo, whose father had been appointed secretary of the treasury. They were all my best friends.

There were very few automobiles in Washington. The taxi stand
on Dupont Circle was for horses and carriages. When we first arrived, the president and his cabinet officials were provided with
horses, carriages, victorias, and hansom cabs. I often rode in the
McAdoo carriages with Sallie. Her mother had died, and her father

married the president's daughter Eleanor Wilson. It wasn't long before these carriages were exchanged for automobiles. Many ladies, among them my mother, soon drove pretty little Electrics. Mother's was pale blue, with rose-brocaded upholstery and a cut glass vase for flowers. It was capable of quite a little speed after it had spent the night being charged by the "Electrifier" in the garage. As a teenager, I would race Mother's Electric down Connecticut Avenue alongside the boy next door, who was driving his mother's. However, on the way home up the Connecticut Avenue hill, the little cars frequently ran out of juice.

There was great excitement in town when the war started. It did not affect my life much as the president wouldn't let Daddy go in the Army because he had put him on many important war-related commissions. At school we were expected to do military drills with wooden guns once a week in khaki uniforms like the soldiers except for our skirts.

My friend Gertrude Grosvenor's house on Eighteenth Street backed up to the Bell mansion on Connecticut Avenue. Gertrude was the eldest of the several Grosvenor girls, and Melville was the oldest son. Mrs. Bell, who was deaf (her husband's invention of the telephone grew out of his efforts to help her hear), organized a "rhythmic dancing class" for little girls in her ballroom, and a group of us pranced about weekly, clad in floating cheesecloth. The Grosvenor children had an orchestra in which I played the violin. Mr. and Mrs. Bell were most interested in our activities and had us take swimming lessons in their indoor pool. I enjoyed my violin lessons but did not enjoy practicing exercises. I loved to play my fiddle and dance with Victrola accompaniments. When I was nine, Gertrude had a birthday party at her grandparents' house, and my piece of the cake contained a tiny wedding ring. Old Mr. Bell sat me on his knee and declared that I must marry him when I grew up. He said he would be "my long suitor." He had a fine white beard, and I liked the old gentleman. He apparently returned my affection. The Grosvenors had a farm "way out in the country" at Bethesda, and I often spent weekends with them there. All of us children slept on a big screened-in porch with a railing separating the little girls from the two boys. After we were in bed, I would regale them with stories. I was a popular guest.

At school I entertained myself and my schoolmates with a novel I was writing. I had read only one novel, by Zane Gray, but had read children's books about the West Point and Annapolis cadets. My heroine was a beautiful sixteen-year-old (which seemed a great age to me), unencumbered by parents. She lived on a splendid ranch in Texas with her guardian, a doting uncle who gave her a ball on her birthday. She wore a rose-colored gown and danced with handsome cowboys and young army officers who were fighting on the Mexican border. Not satisfied with these gentlemen, I wanted some naval officers to dance with my heroine. That was easy. I simply sailed the Navy up the Rio Grande River! The girls at Holton Arms could hardly wait to read each new installment.

Another event in my young life when I was nine was a big dance given by the Misses Breckinridge at Rauschers ballroom on Connecticut Avenue near the British Embassy. For many years, Rauschers was the scene of most of the debut balls, among them my own. The Breckinridge party was fancy dress, and the guests were aged ten to sixteen. My mother made me a lovely costume, and I went as Princess Ozma of Oz with a ballet skirt, a crown, and a wand. My best friend Neville Johnson was an adorable Bo Peep. Cabot Lodge was a dignified Julius Caesar in draped sheets, and John Lodge a dashing Mexican. I spent a wonderful evening, not dancing, but flitting around the ballroom being chased by John Lodge and other little boys who could not or would not dance! The Lodges were both handsome boys. Cabot was the elder and the more serious of the two. Several years later when I was a subdeb of sixteen, he became a beau of mine. He took me to parties, and we exchanged photographs when he went back to school. That is, I gave him mine, and he brought me a full-length picture of himself. When he left our home, I couldn't find it. Years later he confessed that he didn't think it was handsome enough so he took it home with him!

In April 1918, as World War I was ending, Senator Husting of Wisconsin died suddenly and a special election was called in the state. The leaders of the Wisconsin Democratic party urged my father to run, and he decided the time was right and went to Wisconsin. He had only two weeks in which to campaign but had no difficulty in defeating his opponent in the Democratic primary. Oddly enough, his opponent's name was McCarthy, and the main issue was loyalty! I say "oddly," because a Wisconson Senator named McCarthy and the "loyalty" issue were also paramount in the defeat of my husband, Maryland Senator Millard Tydings, thirty-two years later. The loyalty issue in 1918 had to do with the League of Nations, which was Mr. Wilson's dream for establishing peace and international law after the devastation of the war. My father, in his campaign, urged the people to be loyal to the president and support the League of Nations. A large percentage of Wisconsin voters were of German descent, however, and were cool toward President Wilson for fighting a war with Germany. They were opposed to the League of Nations and were accused during the election, by Wilson's vice president, Thomas Marshall, of being pro-German and disloyal to the president. The president, in his desire for my father to win the election, had sent Marshall to speak for my father at a large mass meeting in northern Wisconsin where a great many German Americans lived. The vice president proceeded to make a bad speech, referring to the German American voters who opposed the League as "savages." Needless to say, my father lost the election and returned to his lucrative law practice in Washington.

The World War made great changes in the manners and morals in the United States as well as in its politics. President Wilson and his League of Nations suffered political defeat by the Republicans, and Joe Davies was defeated for the Senate.

Fashions in women's clothing buried the long dust-sweeping skirts of the Victorian Era: skirts went up, necklines went down, and chaperones went out. When the daughter of a United States Cabinet minister appeared in a strapless evening gown, the women all gasped and copied her. It was the age of jazz and the flappers with their knee-length skirts, flat boyish chests, bobbed hair, and makeup. The Republicans might have won the election, but we girls embraced our Democratic liberalism with joy.

Prohibition also made a big change. The age of cocktails and crime roared over the country. When my father entertained members of the Supreme Court at a stag dinner, they all enjoyed hard liquor in our upstairs library. Both sexes happily broke the law.

Chapter 5

The Plain Duckling Becomes a Subdeb Swan with Beaux

Until I was fourteen, I thought that if a boy kissed me, I would have a baby. Mother never told me about the birds and the bees! Father didn't either, although he lectured me about never allowing a young man "to take liberties with my person."

With the end of World War I, both Prohibition and the flapper had arrived. I had barely reached my teens when my ugly-duckling self was actually turning into a swan. I discovered that I was much better looking if my straight blond hair was curled. At sixteen, I was five feet six inches tall and having dates come to call on weekends. I was already feeling attractions toward handsome young gentlemen and even occasionally thought I was in love. In those days, the physical expression of this feeling was called "necking" or "petting." Any such activity I indulged in was a real love affair to me, with marriage in mind, but I was always careful not to let it go below the neck, having been forewarned by a popular naughty verse:

> "Here's to the girl who would like to be wild
> Three things keep her from being beguiled
> Sweet thoughts of Jesus
> Contagious diseases
> And the fear of having a child!"

Mother was lavish in supplying delicious tea-party food for my friends every Sunday afternoon, and she permitted dancing to the Victrola. Hordes of boys came, and a few girls who were my close friends. No liquor was ever served, but some of the boys brought it in flasks. The house was the scene of my first dancing party on my

22

sixteenth birthday in April 1920. That morning I jumped gaily off the wall in front of school and sprained my ankle. Everyone could dance at my party except me. I enjoyed being enthroned, however, wearing orchids, being queen of the affair, having the young men dance attendance upon me! We young people sometimes sat on the garden wall separating our garden from the Hungarian embassy garden next door, watching the ambassador, Count Ladislaw Schechenyi, chase his lady guests around when the countess, the former Gladys Vanderbilt, was out of town. Mother was a friend of the countess and told me that the poor woman had not wanted to marry the count but had been forced to do so.

For a while at sixteen I thought I was engaged to marry a young man of twenty who was the son of the famous writer Mary Roberts Rinehart, but that didn't last long. Another of my beaux was Bill Sherman, a dashing Air Force Colonel, World War I hero, and aide to General William Mitchell, chief of the Army Air Force and a close friend of my father's. Colonel Sherman and I rode horseback together every week. He was brilliant and from my point of view was a very old man, at least thirty-two! Often he and his friends, other young fliers, would take me up in the old DeHaviland World War I planes. They had open cockpits with one seat behind the other. The boys would tie me in to the seat behind the pilot and loop the loop, fly upside down, and do all manner of tricks! They presented me with a pin of silver wings and a sealed, signed "diploma" stating that I was a qualified Army flier, "having looped, slipped, zoomed, and done divers sorts of flying by day and by night."

The summer of 1920 my family spent at grandfather's old camp on the Brule River. We also visited Mr. and Mrs. Edward Hines (Hines Lumber company), who were clients and friends of my father's, at their camp on the Rainy Lakes on the Canadian border. Ralph Hines was their oldest son, a Yale graduate who was completing his education at Oxford University in England. He was blond, handsome, and sophisticated, and I admired him greatly. Charles, his younger brother, was a tall, skinny, bespectacled youth who suffered from ill health. Their sister, Loretta, was a beautiful girl my age who was so devoted to the Catholic faith that her parents feared she might become a nun. We traveled by train to Duluth, Minnesota, and then by automobile to the end of the road in the northern wilderness. Here we climbed into Ford cars mounted on the lumber tracks and continued as far as the logging tracks went. There we boarded boats and finally arrived at the camp. The older people occupied comfortable cabins onshore. We young ones all slept on a houseboat moored to the dock.

Hunting and fishing was the daily program. One day we shot many more partridges than the game laws allowed. While the delicious birds were being broiled for lunch, the game wardens were spied approaching camp. Mrs. Hines ordered Charles to run to the kitchen and help hide the birds in the woods. This he did, so successfully that nobody could ever find them! One day, everyone went fishing except Ralph and myself. He took me deer shooting. I was thrilled. We went a long way by canoe and then on foot through the woods to a salt lick. We climbed two tall pines close together and straddled two boards at the top (most uncomfortable!) and settled down to wait for the deer. Ralph sat behind me, arms around my waist. It was very exciting. I had never shot a gun in my life, but Ralph insisted I have the first shot. When a pretty young deer came along, "Shoot!" commanded Ralph, and I closed my eyes and fired. Somehow I accidentally killed the poor creature, and I began to weep on Ralph's shoulder. I have never shot anything since. By the time we left the Rainy Lakes, Ralph and I were more than half in love, although our affair never went beyond the hand-holding stage. He went back to Oxford, and I was seventeen, a debutante, and starting Vassar in the fall. He turned out to be not much of a correspondent, and there were other fish in the sea!

Chapter 6

The Only Washington Debutante at College (Vassar), 1921–1935

Vassar (for young ladies only) was on a beautiful campus outside of Poughkeepsie, New York. Old Matthew Vassar had founded it for "poor but deserving young women." My four years there coincided with what might be called the F. Scott Fitzgerald years of great gaiety and prosperity in our country. It was the period of gilded youth, flappers, grand debut balls, and prom trotters. World War I was over and with it the Victorian era, and everyone wanted to celebrate, give their children a grand, gay time and have one themselves. Youth was in rebellion against Victorianism and the austerity of wartime. Young ladies wore strapless evening gowns and smoked cigarettes in long holders. In spite of Prohibition, everyone drank gin orange blossom cocktails in silver cocktail glasses and bootleggers made fortunes! Dresses grew shorter and females bobbed their hair and tried to look boyishly flat chested! My girlfriends and I didn't smoke or drink. Most Washington boys didn't drink, but it was Prohibition, and some of the more devilish ones even drank E.D. Pinaud toilet water! I was not the only pretty debutante to be wined, dined, and quite thoroughly spoiled, but I did not drink and was the only debutante who went to college in 1921. Fortunately, I had a father who was determined that I should not be totally empty-headed and sent me to Vassar. I went to be free of my parents' strict rules and restrictions. Years later the Belgian ambassador who had known me when he was a young attache at the embassy told me his impression of me as a debutante was of "red-hot rebellion"!

The rules were strict at Vassar in 1921. We had to be in our dormitories by 10 P.M. when the outside doors were locked. If our marks were good, we were allowed to go away a very few weekends a year—if we had written permission from our parents. I broke the curfew rules often by climbing in the first-floor dormitory windows of my friends' rooms, by way of a chair and a boost from my young escort. I found the classes interesting and the social life exciting with the parties and football games at West Point, Harvard, Yale, Princeton, Williams, and Cornell. I was a romantic, and thoroughly enjoyed my love affairs.

I was invited to a dance and football game at West Point soon after I arrived. A group of Vassar girls were to be chaperoned by the wife of the commandant, General Douglas MacArthur. She was the beautiful Louise Cromwell, daughter of Mrs. Edward T. Stotesbury. At West Point, I met and quickly fell in love with a senior cadet named Bill Kyle, who was tall, dark, and of course handsome. He was the regimental adjutant. I remember how deliciously painful were the big buttons of his coat when he hugged me tight and kissed me in the middle of the snow-covered parade ground, walking home from the dance. Nothing had ever been like this! Bill gave me a miniature of his West Point ring, and we wrote letters to each other almost weekly. Other boyfriends were forgotten! My parents came up to New York City for the Army-Navy game, and friends gave a dinner dance in the Crystal Room at the Ritz. My West Point cadet was my escort, and I was wearing a new gold brocade "period" ball gown, off the shoulders, with a tight bodice and huge skirt. I glanced in the mirrored elevator and thought we made a handsome couple! He looked like a young prince in his red-sashed uniform and I was part of the picture. That June I went to his graduation from the Academy and stood in the receiving line with him and General and Mrs. Mac-Arthur at the reception. My mother chaperoned me. When she found that Bill was going to leave the Army to go to work so that he could marry me, she made me tell him that I didn't want him to do so, that I couldn't marry until I graduated from Vassar. Mother knew me too well! I was having too good a time and was too young to settle down.

In December, I came home from Vassar for the Christmas holidays to make my debut. My parents gave a large reception at our Massachusetts Avenue house to formally introduce me to their friends. They also gave a ball for me and my young friends at old Rauschers catering establishment. Every day during the Christmas holidays there were luncheons, teas, dinner parties, and balls. They were all alike, now a blur in my memory. I have only mental pictures of a long, long stag line of young men who cut in on me every few

steps and of our reflections in the mirrored walls of Rauschers ballroom, the scene of many of the debutante balls. The reception at
home was only memorable because of the masses of flowers and
gifts sent to me as a debutante. Our drawing room was full of pink
roses, with yellow ones in the sun parlor and white in the dining
room. Over the drawing room mantel hung my portrait, which had
been painted in New York City that fall. I was wearing my debut
gown of palest pink and silver, which Daddy had bought for me in
Paris. Because I wore my hair piled high on my head, people said
the portrait looked much older than my seventeen years. Actually, I
was dreaming about my handsome West Pointer when I posed for
it.

One of the nicest parties that Christmas was a dinner dance given
by Mrs. Walsh at her Massachusetts Avenue mansion, in honor of
young Bertha Cantacuzene and myself. Bertha's mother was the
daughter of President Ulysses S. Grant, and her father was a Russian
prince. Old Mr. Walsh had been a miner who struck it rich in Colorado and sent his wife and daughter to Europe to be educated. His
widow was devoted to my father and would not dance with anyone
else save her dancing teacher. She had a dancing class for her
friends every Monday night in her ballroom. The Davies, including
me, were always invited. I will never forget Mrs. Walsh. She was of
average height with a good figure (tightly laced and corseted), and
her face had been lifted so many times it was frozen expressionless.
She had thirty red wigs, half of which she kept at Emile's hairdresser to be dressed, so Mr. Emile told me. Her dancing teacher
was a little mosquito of a man who looked as though he might fly
out the window at any minute. The Walsh house took up a city block
and was designed inside to look like the ocean liners of that era.
There was an enormous central hall that extended four stories up to
the roof. Each floor had a gallery running around it. Our hostess's
bedroom was painted with rosy cherubs, gods, and goddesses flying
about the gilded cornices and woodwork. During World War II,
when the house was turned over to the Red Cross, Mrs. Walsh's bedroom became my office as the chairman of the Red Cross Nurses'
Aides Corps. It took a while to get used to.

Mrs. Walsh's daughter, Evelyn Walsh McLean, lived in an enormous country estate called Friendship just beyond the National Cathedral. She was the owner of some fabulous jewels, notably the famous Hope Diamond and one called Star of the East. Both are now
in the Smithsonian Museum. The Hope diamond was said to have

brought tragedy to all of its owners. When the McLean's little son ran away from his guards and nurses out in the road beyond the gates of Friendship, he was killed by an automobile. People shook their heads and said it was the Hope diamond. The McLeans had two more sons and a daughter, a pale, slender girl whose marriage to Senator Bob Reynolds of North Carolina was arranged by her mother. The senator was more than twenty years her senior. Ned McLean had died of drink. I do not blame the diamond for any of this.

Evelyn Walsh McLean entertained constantly and lavishly until she died. All the leaders of government and society came to her parties, dinner dances, and Sunday luncheons almost every week. First-run movies were always shown for those who did not dance. Later, during World War II, she entertained a mob of enlisted boys and their girls every Saturday. She wore huge black hats and all her jewels, which she would allow the soldiers' girlfriends to try on! She would sleep all day and stay up most of the night. One of the famous features of her dinner parties was her mother's gold dinner service: plates, epergnes, candelabra, knives and forks, everything was gold! When the Prince of Wales visited Washington as a young man, I was told that the British ambassador selected Mrs. Walsh to give a dinner for him because of that gold dinner service. But when it was sold at auction after she died, I was shocked to hear that the famous gold service wasn't gold at all! It wasn't even silver!

Chapter 7

The Davieses Take Their Daughters
to Europe, 1923

In June 1923 I was in the news as one of the famous (in Ivy League circles) Vassar Daisy Chain and my parents took my sister Rahel, and myself to Europe. On the ship were quite a few American college boys, the sons of the Swiss ambassador whom I already knew, and Matilda Houghton, whose father, the Honorable Alanson B. Houghton, was our ambassador to Germany. Matilda and I were the queens of the ship! Even the captain's quarters was ours in which to play cards and have tea parties and entertain chosen members of the opposite sex. Most exciting of all, there was a young German baron on board with his grandmother. Adalbert (Adie) was a few years older than I and very good looking. He told me that his family were the rightful heirs to a throne that no longer existed. He wanted me to marry him and be queen of that country—pretty heady stuff! I rushed to the stateroom that I shared with sister Rahel (aged twelve) and asked her how she would like to be the sister of a queen. She never forgot that, and she never let me forget it either.

Adie couldn't get off the ship with us at Paris. It was too soon after World War I and the feeling in France was still too bitter against Germans. He sailed off into the sunset, waving and blowing kisses. We were to meet in Berlin where I was to visit Matilda Houghton at the embassy. Adie planned to give a party for me there in his parents' palace.

In 1922, Germany was in dire financial straits and threatened with a revolution by the Communists. Matilda Houghton and I would climb to the embassy roof at night to watch the Communist riots in the square below. One day we went to the Adlon Hotel for

29

tea (with a chaperon) and were ogled so brazenly by some Prussian officers that we never went back there again. Their uniforms and polished boots were gorgeous, but their cropped heads, monocles, and duel-scarred faces were not attractive. Adie's parents returned to Berlin from one of their chateaux in the country (he told me they had thirteen) and gave a party for us in their Berlin mansion. It was all quite splendid, but I lost interest in my German beau when I saw a full-length portrait of him in uniform, holding his German spiked helmet! The world had not yet heard of Adolf Hitler.

While in Berlin, my parents bought a German police dog for 400 million marks, equal to a few American dollars. They also gave a dinner party for the Houghtons at the Kaiserhof Hotel. There were thirty guests. It was a splendid menu with vintage wines and a regiment of waiters. Father always left princely tips, and, including these, the entire party cost him about $30 American! The Baron gave me a miniature of himself and sent me dozens of roses when we left Berlin, and I never saw him again.

I did not stay long in Germany, because my parents were worried about the political situation there and wanted to take me back to Paris. We joined the Hines family in Paris; the city was marvelous. There was tea dancing in the Bois de boulogne every afternoon with the different college boys I knew, and at night I was allowed to go dancing with Ralph Hines and his friend, Ian Campbell. Ian was a tall, slender youth with a bad complexion, but he possessed all the glamour of being heir to his uncle, the Duke of Argyle. One evening he took me out without Ralph, and we ended up sitting on the bank of the old Ile du Pont Neuf, swinging our heels over the River Seine while Ian told me ghost stories about his ancestral castle. Another evening with Ralph and Ian in top hats and tails and myself in a new Paris ball gown, we went romping through the streets after a party, the boys smashing street lamps with their canes! We were chased by police, which was very exciting, and ended up taking refuge in the home of one of Ian's aunts. My romance with Ralph had cooled off, but we remained good friends. Later Ian became the Duke of Argyle.

I returned to college and met a charming young New Yorker named Alfred de Liagre, known to his peers at Yale as "Delly" and "the Student Prince". He became my number one beau.

Chapter 8

I Meet the Confederate South and the Cheesboroughs in North Carolina

The only cloud in my sunny skies during those years was the serious illness of my much loved and loving sister Rahel. When we returned from Europe she contracted pneumonia and suffered an abscessed lung, which threatened to develop into tuberculosis. After she spent a year in a sanitarium, our parents were advised to take her to the mountains of North Carolina, and they rented a house on the golf links of the Biltmore Forest Club, a beautiful suburb of Asheville.

I went to Chicago to visit the Hineses at the beginning of the Christmas holiday for Loretta's debut ball. Her engagement to Howell Howard of Dayton, Ohio, was announced at the magnificent ball and the wedding date was set for February 1923. I was to be a bridesmaid.

Christmas day I arrived in Biltmore Forest, North Carolina. I had protested, not wanting to spend my holiday in a dreary little Southern town when I could be at all the gay parties in Chicago. I put off leaving as long as I could, but my parents and I arrived as expected. What was not expected was that I would meet the man who would become my first husband and the father of my two children.

Mother had already met many of the Biltmore Forest ladies, and she had paved the way for my arrival. The son of one of the "best families", Mr. Frank Coxe, recently graduated from Yale, arrived at our house that evening to take me to a dinner party and dance at the Biltmore Forest Country Club. The club was a handsome building of Tudor architecture overlooking a superb golf course, surrounded by mountains. There were attractive homes in the same style built around the course. Best of all, there was a most attractive group of young people my age. I found the place far from dreary or provincial!

Frank and I made a late and quite sensational arrival at the Club. The guests were already seated in the big dining room, which was at the foot of a flight of broad steps. We stood for a moment looking down at the gay scene. I was wearing one of my most dashing Paris gowns, a black velvet period affair with one bare shoulder and one tiny cap sleeve, quite risqué! With it I wore a big black Spanish shawl embroidered with red roses. All eyes below turned to us, and among those gazing up at me were the two Cheesborough brothers. These two were almost twins, being barely a year apart. Both were six feet four inches tall, blond, and extremely good looking. Jack, the elder, was studying law at Columbia University in New York. Tom was a senior at the University of North Carolina. He was a year older than I. These two did their best to fend off their cousins, the Coxe brothers, and the rest of the stag line. The Cheesboroughs were not very good dancers, walking a straight line with right-angle turns. With their heads bent down over their dancing partners, they endeavored to make up by means of their charming conversation what they lacked in terpsichorean prowess! I found them both most attractive, Tom a bit more so than Jack. Tom was a little livelier, his hair curlier, his shoulders broader than his brother's. He was an athlete, star of both football and basketball teams at North Carolina. Both boys were popular members of the DKE fraternity. They lived in a large colonial mansion overlooking the golf course.

Their parents were leaders in Asheville-Biltmore society. Their father, Doctor Thomas Patton Cheesborough, a retired tuberculosis specialist, was president of the Biltmore Forest Country Club and a member of the prestigious Society of Cincinnati. The Cheesboroughs came from Charleston, South Carolina, where the doctor's grandfather had been an official of the Bank of Charleston during the Civil War. The signature of John Cheesborough was on much of the Confederacy's paper money. Mrs. Cheesborough's grandfather, James M. Thomas Jr. of Richmond, Virginia, was one of a number of prominent men to sign the bond to get the captured Confederate president, Jefferson Davis, released from a Yankee prison at the end of the war. The doctor had inherited many acres of land around Asheville from his mother, a North Carolinian. Mrs. Cheesborough was from Richmond, Virginia, a grande dame of the old school, very stiff and haughty. She had been a great beauty and had never gotten over it. I was told that her father, John Kerr Connally, had been a young general in Robert E. Lee's army. Her grandfather, Judge Thomas, a cotton and tobacco tycoon, had wisely invested a good part of his fortune in England prior to the Civil War, thereby saving it.

After Christmas I went back to Vassar and in February returned to Chicago. There was much publicity about Loretta Hines's so-called "million dollar wedding." And no wonder! The Hineses refurbished the Chicago Cathedral with new red carpet and goodness-knows what else. The entire Chicago Symphony Orchestra played for the ceremony, and Tito Schipa, the Metropolitan Opera star, sang! There were thirty priests in the chancel and a cardinal performed the marriage. I was one of sixteen bridesmaids, counting the maid of honor and matron of honor, and an even greater number of groomsmen, all Yale classmates of Howell and Ralph. Mrs. Hines had ordered silver cloth evening gowns from Paris for all of us bridesmaids, with silver "halo hats" and silver slippers. Someone said we looked like a Ziegfeld chorus line.

The parties before the wedding were quite as splendid as those in Chicago at Christmas—and again I had a whirl. I was escorted back East on the train by a dozen of the wedding ushers, who made a great fuss over me. They regaled me with tales of the groom's bachelor dinner at the Blackstone Hotel the night before the wedding. One boy danced on the table and sprained his ankle, and another removed all his clothes and ran a hotel elevator up and down pursued by hotel police running up and down stairs trying unsuccessfully to catch him. His friends managed to grab and hide him!

Onboard the train going East, my Yale escorts made me their princess and themselves my honor guards. Some of them wrote to me. I returned to Vassar and to my Yale beau, Delly. I wore the silver bridesmaid dress to the Yale senior prom. Delly's parents were Europeans by birth and he had inherited a charming wit and dash quite different from the young men I had known. We spent most of our time together laughing, and I was soon on my way to becoming very fond of him.

Life for me was not all play during those gay, happy years. For five days a week, I studied.

My senior thesis was on the League of Nations—the political issue that had defeated both President Wilson and my father. Senator Gilbert Hitchcock sent me much material on the subject. I danced happily through those lovely years and managed to graduate. After graduation in 1925, I was offered two fascinating jobs. One was to go on the staff of a fashion magazine, and one was to teach at the American University in Peking, China. I do not recall that I ever seriously considered either, nor did my parents. Young ladies' careers were still in the field of matrimony, and I was still dreaming of living happily ever after with a prince of my choice. The only difficulty was that I wasn't sure who he was! After graduation, I went to house parties at homes on the Hudson River of my Vassar friends, and Alfred (Delly) was a guest at both of them. He and another Yale lad drove me to the parties in a large station wagon, which they had decorated with wicker lounge chairs and a bird cage! One boy drove and the other lolled in the chair. At this time I thought I might marry Delly, but I was not in any hurry. I knew there was another gay summer ahead of me in Biltmore Forest, and I had promised Mother to spend some time in Europe with her after graduation. Delly was coming to visit us (at the Biltmore Forest Club) in August.

The summer of 1925 in Biltmore Forest was a wonderful time of peace and prosperity, play and romance. There was a constant round of parties, including weekend house parties (always well chaperoned) at mountain lodges and nearby plantations. There was a great deal of singing and love making at these latter in spite of the chaperons, who cracked the whip at midnight and saw the girls safely tucked in bed away from the young men. It was when we were all going up the mountain on one of these affairs that a Miss Marian Saunders arrived on a train from New York. Her hostess, Mary Beecher, had gone ahead with Billy Coxe, so the Cheesborough boys and I were elected to meet her train. Tom drove a Model T Ford with me in the front seat. Both boys were much too big for the car and had to sit with one long leg draped over the side. Marian Saunders (Sandy) had never seen any of us before, but we knew her at once. She was the prettiest girl to get off the train! We packed her and her luggage into the backseat with Jack and took off for the mountains. By the time we reached our destination, we all felt we were lifelong friends.

On that trip up the mountain, I received a high compliment. Tom had stopped at the cabin of an old mountain woman to buy a chicken for our barbecue. She looked at us as we stood laughing, with Tom's arm draped possessively around my shoulders. Apparently she knew Tom and was interested. He was so obviously in love with me. "She's all right, laddie," she drawled in her mountain accent. "She has a good opin countenince! Better marry her if you can git her!" The chicken was delicious.

By the middle of the summer, Tom had almost completely won me over. He looked like an oversized Greek god to start with, and he was every inch a charming southern gentleman of the old school. He and his brother were duplicates of the Tarleton twins described in *Gone with the Wind*. Then my "student prince" from Yale arrived on the scene! We had planned his visit joyfully the spring before, but now I was not so sure it was a good idea. My parents put him up at the Biltmore Club next door. The week he was there ended in the great event of the summer for us young people, the Bachelors' Ball at the Biltmore Forest Club. Tom, in a magnificent gesture, had gone fishing in the mountains for one week, leaving the field clear for "the damn Yankee." He said he might not even return in time for the ball, and I drew a sigh of relief. Delly arrived and was enchanted with the Forest and Cornelia Vanderbilt's party at the magnificent Biltmore House, the Club, and, of course, with me. He was making plans for our marriage after graduation. I still didn't know which of these young men I loved the best. My family didn't make things any easier for me. They made it clear that they strongly disapproved of my "playing fast and loose" with both young men. To make things worse, they took sides between them. Mother was for Delly, Rahel for Tom, Father for neither of them!

Then suddenly, in the middle of the week, Tom returned, and I was really in trouble. Tom said that upon thinking things over in the solitude of the mountain fishing camp, he had decided that he had better return to protect his interests against that "Yankee city slicker!" The whole affair blew up the night of the Bachelors' Ball, which I attended in a state of nervous tension escorted by two very handsome, very angry young men. It was a fancy dress party, and I went as a Spanish dancer wearing a black wig (I had always wanted to be a brunette), and the boys were dressed as Spanish caballeros—not very convincing ones with their blond heads! It was a terrible evening. I was worried for fear it would end in a fight of some kind or, with Tom's Southern background, a duel! Actually, all that happened was that my Northern beau dragged me out by the swimming pool, raved and ranted and threatened to commit suicide. The club night watchman, an old Scotsman, came up just at this crucial moment and said, "Not in our pool, Leddy! Dinna upset the young laddy so!" My Yale beau retreated, packed his bags, and departed on an early-morning train. His only farewell was an envelope containing a photo of myself torn in shreds! He was very young and I was too. I wondered whether I had behaved badly!

His departure left the coast clear for Tom, whose conduct I considered exemplary compared with Delly's. This time I was sure my feeling for Tom was true love. Our parents approved and mine announced our engagement at a gala dinner party at the Biltmore Forest Club that Christmas.

Once again, my mother's wisdom later became evident. She insisted that I had promised to travel in Europe with her and Daddy after my graduation. As Tom was finishing his business course at Columbia, I agreed to sail with Mother after Christmas, returning in September for our wedding in Washington in November 1926. I know that my father was not greatly pleased over my impending marriage to Tom. The older generation considered the Cheesborough boys too wild. As Tom possessed a splendid physique, he could drink an amazing amount of liquor and not show it. His drinking, however, didn't worry me. I had never known any young men who drank much, and so I was not a very good judge. After all, we were caught up in Prohibition, and drinking was part of the culture of the young F. Scott Fitzgerald generation of the South and even of our elders. Before Prohibition, my parents had never served cocktails (my father thought his father's stroke had been caused by too much drinking), but when Prohibition came, cocktails became almost mandatory at dinner parties. When my father had a stag dinner for members of the Supreme Court during that era, he served them cocktails in the second-floor library. They drank them!

Mother and I and my sisters, Rahel, and Emlen, who was twelve years younger than I, sailed for Europe in February 1926. My sister Rahel's health had sufficiently improved so that the doctor let her go. We spent some time in Rome and a month in Florence before going to Venice and Lake Como. In these lovely places, I found young American escorts and enjoyed myself. The three American boys who followed me around Europe did not, however, compare in my opinion with my fiancé in North Carolina. I was collecting Italian furniture for the Italian house we planned to build in Biltmore Forest on land that Doctor Cheesborough had given his sons. I was also buying linens and laces. Mother was well and sister Rahel was blooming. My father met us in Paris, and after a final orgy of shopping, we sailed for home. Among the things Daddy had bought me was a beautiful sapphire ring set in diamonds. Two days before leaving Paris, he asked me if there was anything left in that city that I would like to buy! I thought for a minute and then told him there was a rhinestone pin like a bird that I would like and my indulgent father bought it for me.

Tom and I were wedding attendants at Jack and Sandy's wedding in New York in September and our wedding took place in Washington on November 11, 1926, at St. John's Church on Lafayette Square. There were continuous parties for us for a week beforehand and we received 500 wedding gifts. Father had many affluent clients! I had the regulation six bridesmaids, a maid of honor (Rahel), and matron of honor (Loretta Hines Howard). Their gowns were made in Paris of autumn shades of taffeta with hats to match, and they carried chrysanthemums. I wore a white velvet gown with a rose point lace over the velvet train, a pearl girdle and coronet, and a floating tulle veil. We spent our wedding trip at the Long Island estate of my parents' friends. My father had given us a Packard automobile. Tom was a gentle soul, good-natured, and a perfect gentleman, so marriage was not as traumatic an experience as I had expected. Neither was it quite all I had anticipated!

Chapter 9

Marriage and Children and Eleanor Goes Home

In North Carolina we had an attractive group of young married friends. We played golf and ten-cent-limit poker and entertained each other at small dinner parties. I enjoyed my work for the Junior League, driving into the mountains to bring crippled children into Asheville clinics for treatment. This took some persuading as the uneducated mountaineers were terrified of doctors and hospitals. I managed, however, to persuade a good many and ran a motor corps of Junior Leaguers to take the children up and down the mountains.

The happiest part of my married life was the birth of my son on May 4, 1928. Before he was born, I dreamed and walked and dreamed some more for the unborn child's future. I was sure it would be a boy and that he would be a U.S. senator! I ate enough for three, as was then advised by the doctors for pregnant women, and it took me two days of hard labor to introduce my son into this world. He was almost ten pounds of healthy, bald-headed baby! Mother sat beside me knitting throughout, and our relationship was much closer and warmer than it had been before. We named the baby Joseph Davies for my father.

The day Daddy's first male descendant was born was also the day he won the famous Ford tax case. This was the largest government lawsuit on record; the United States versus the men who had lent the money to old Henry Ford to start his automobile factory. Ford had bought back all their stock, and the government said those men had not paid sufficient taxes on their huge profits. Several large law firms were employed by the defendants. My father was in charge of it all. He not only won against the government but also collected big sums of money for his clients by proving that they had actually overpaid their taxes. It made him a very large legal fee.

After a couple of years, my father decided that Tom had no business future in Asheville, where he had been working for an insurance company, and arranged for him to have a job in New York. This was the start of our problems. Daddy had just put together a merger of a large radio tube company in New York (radio sets were fairly new at that time), and a job awaited Tom.

We arrived in New York in 1929, the very day of the stock market crash. We went to live in Westchester County and spent four years in Bronxville while Tom worked for a big radio company.

Across the street from us lived Captain Eddie Rickenbacker, the great World War I ace, and we became friends with him and his wife. He told me an unbelievable story one evening. He said that on a flying mission during the war, one wing of his plane had almost been shot off! He managed to land the plane behind our lines by standing on the remains of the shattered wing to balance the plane! He had a photograph snapped by a soldier to prove it.

Tom was not a success in New York, either in the National Union Radio Company or at the country club where he often played golf as a guest of Jesse Sweetser, the famous amateur golf champion. Tom expected to become a member, but his alcoholic conviviality did him no good with either the company or the club or with me. In a few years, our radio company stock dropped out of sight on the market and so did Tom's job, and he was turned down for membership at the golf club in spite of the efforts of my father's friends. My father procured a better job for him. All Tom had to do to succeed at this new job was to cultivate the president of National Dairy Products and his wife. They had no children, only a pair of lapdogs who sat at their dinner table on specially built high chairs. Unfortunately my husband, with his handsome new salary, was more interested in the bar of the Yale Club in New York City (which had merged with Tom's DKE Club) than in buttering them up. He was drinking more than ever.

We had moved from Bronxville to Greenwich, Connecticut, where friends had found us a most attractive house in a charming wooded section. After our ugly house in Bronxville, I was happier with the rock garden and dogwood trees of our Greenwich house, but I was not very happy with my husband. He was flattered when men made passes at me, which I loathed, and brought home some very uncouth characters whom I gathered he had picked up at bars or nightclubs in New York City. He loved the nightclubs there and was spending more and more nights in the city with "business engagements."

For several summers, my parents had rented a big house overlooking the ocean at Watch Hill, Rhode Island, and here a Washingtonian named Aldace Walker came courting my sister Rahel. He was a nice big ox of a young man, a Yale graduate with a job in New York. His father was a wealthy lawyer, counting among his clients Standard Oil of New Jersey. His mother had been a Washington beauty, as was his sister, Evie. The latter was a wild, daredevil girl who loved men and horses in that order. She was also possessed of a lethal wit. Her brother, Aldace, was entirely different; he resembled nothing so much as a big, friendly Newfoundland dog! My sister's ill health had kept her from any normal contacts with the opposite sex until she was finally allowed to make her debut at nineteen. So when she was growing up she had not had the complement of beaux to which her good looks entitled her. She was a tall, lovely blond, blue-eyed, and very shy. Aldace and Tom were good friends and Aldace courted her at our house in Bronxville and at Watch Hill. They were married at St. John's church in 1933 and went to live in an apartment on Park Avenue in New York City. Aldace had a job at the Guaranty Trust Company.

One summer, when my little son and I were at Watch Hill with my parents and sisters, my father told us that the daughter of a client of his and her bridegroom were coming to visit us. The client was the dictator of Santo Domingo, Rafael Trujillo. His daughter was named Flor de Oro, and her playboy diplomat husband was Porfirio Rubirosa. He later married two other fabulous heiresses, Doris Duke and Barbara Hutton. The Rubirosas spent a week with us. She was only about eighteen, and he was a small man with kinky black hair. After a few days, the bridegroom took off and disappeared. The bride had hysterics until he was found (by Daddy) in New York. He had been on a rampage, smashed up a chandelier in one of the best hotels, and was said to have killed someone! He could never return to New York save under diplomatic immunity.

In 1932 our baby girl, Little El (Eleanor) arrived, in spite of the depression. She was blonder than her four-year-old brother, and had blue eyes and dimples in both cheeks. By the time she was two years old, I had become increasingly unhappy. Tom was drinking more and more. I didn't know what he was doing the many nights he spent in New York City without me, but I began to have my suspicions. Finally one night this was confirmed in a manner that shocked me into full realization of what kind of marriage I had made. We were invited to spend a weekend at a New York hotel with old friends of Tom's from Cuba. We shared their large two-bedroom and sitting room hotel suite and after an evening of theater and dancing we returned there. The Cuban gentleman had been making passes at me constantly, and I was growing tired of parrying them. I announced my intention of going to bed and left our bedroom door unlocked for my husband, but I was no sooner in bed than the door flew open. It was not Tom, but our Cuban host. He tried to get in bed with me and I slid out of it quickly and told him to get out of the room. He laughed at me and asked, "Why should I? Your husband is in bed this minute with my wife!" I ran into the living room and sure enough, the door to the other bedroom was open and I could see Tom and the Cuban's wife in bed in each other's arms. The Cuban had followed me, but I slipped past him back into my room and locked the door. I couldn't believe what I had seen. Of course, the shock left a deep scar on our relationship. I was disillusioned and miserable. Tom was drinking whiskey straight even before breakfast. I was being pursued by an attractive New York bachelor and I was afraid of what might happen to my life.

I never thought of divorce. There had never been such a thing in our family. Besides, my darling baby girl, and little Joe were the greatest joys of my life.

I now realized the weakness I was married to. He was still living in pre-Civil War days when the men drank, inherited money, and drank some more. I saw the best and the worst of what the Old South had been. They were good men with good manners and high ideals about how their wives should behave (modeled after their mothers), but that was not enough.

After the episode with the Cubans, Tom was locked out of my bedroom. I couldn't make love with a man I didn't respect. Then on a cold gray day on April 6, 1935, Tom told me that he had lost his job and that we were out of funds. I must dismiss the maids and take the children home to Washington. I was disgusted and did so.

Part II

Chapter 10

A Senate Romance and Two Divorces

Mother listened to my story sympathetically and told me to tell my Father.

"My child," he said, "how long are you going to stand for this? Do you truly love this man? If so, I'll go on helping you as long as I am able. If not, you had better divorce him now while you are still young enough to have a happy and rewarding life. I will help you to divorce him and you and the children can come live with us. I doubt Tom will ever be any different from the weak, unstable fellow he is. Think it over, dear, and let me know your decision."

I couldn't believe my ears! It had never occurred to me that my parents would even consider divorce! I told him that I didn't love Tom.

"I can't love a man I don't respect. Tom is fond of the children in a casual way, although he doesn't want them around much. If I was sure I could have my children, I would leave him at once." I hugged him. "Oh Daddy, I am so grateful to you for everything!" He smiled and patted my shoulder.

"Take your time, my son-daughter," he said, "and stay here with the children as long as you wish. I'll do what I can in the meantime to get Tom a job." He would often call me that because I was his first born.

I felt a sensation almost of light-headedness, my relief from worry and unhappiness was so great. That night I did not sleep much but went over and over the pros and cons of a divorce. I knew that Tom was not grown-up enough to appreciate or miss the children. He never wanted to play with them. I knew that our little son did not care for his father. There was no bond between them. Joe was only five, but he was born grown-up. That spring a neighbor's child had thrown a stone that cut Joe's forehead badly. I was not home, so my little boy reported to the maid, called a taxi, and went alone to the doctor to be sewn up. I was upset but so proud of him!

The next morning I came down for breakfast with my parents and told them that I had made up my mind. I wanted a divorce from Tom. They both approved of my decision. Daddy said he was sailing for London in late May to join Mother and my youngest sister, Emlen, and he would take me with him and arrange for a divorce for me upon our return.

On April ninth, two days after my arrival in Washington, the Democratic leader of the United States Senate gave a luncheon in his committee room at the Capitol, in honor of Mrs. Edward Hines, who was visiting my parents. I was invited too, and we sat in the Senate Ladies' Gallery before lunch. I looked down upon the elderly lions on the floor below. They were almost all stout and balding and I was beginning to be sorry I had come. The only two senators I knew were the Republican leader, whose daughter had been my schoolmate, and our host, Senator Joe Robinson. I was becoming more and more bored and depressed when the door from the Democratic cloakroom flew open and so did the door into my future. A tall, slender, good-looking man strode in and up the Democratic side aisle. I had never seen a man with such magnificent carriage. His shoulders were as wide as the rest of him was slim and he carried his handsome head high.

It was not an electric shock that I experienced when I saw him, but something almost as stunning. I had never seen him before, but I recognized him! This was the man I had always hoped for. I knew his name before Mrs. Robinson answered the question in my eyes. "That is Senator Millard Tydings of Maryland," she told me and as she spoke, he looked up at me and smiled and bowed.

"I thought you didn't know him," said my hostess in surprise.

"I don't," I replied, but the words were not strictly true. Of course I knew him. Although I had never seen him before, I had heard enough about him to know that he was charming, brilliant, and fine; in short, close to my ideal. I knew that he was about forty years old and unmarried. I wondered if he had been waiting for me as I had been waiting for him! I had heard many of my Washington friends speak of him in glowing terms. I gave myself a mental shake. What silly daydreams I was having, as a married woman with two children! He could have any lovely, young lady he wanted, and I was an elderly woman of thirty. My sister Rahel's sister-in-law Evie was a popular young beauty whose parents had a handsome home in Washington and a beautiful estate on Maryland's Eastern shore and I wondered why she hadn't snared this attractive and distinguished bachelor. I found out later that it was not for lack of trying!

I had heard about his efforts to introduce a bill in the Senate to give the Philippines its independence. My father had spoken of it with interest because President Woodrow Wilson had once offered him the governor-generalship of these islands. I was fascinated. It was breathtaking to think that one senator could actually give an entire nation its freedom.

And there he was and he had spoken to me—wordlessly—as I had to him. I sighed and tried to banish such thoughts from my mind, but of course I could not know that on that April day my great adventure was about to begin. When we walked into the room where we were to be served lunch, Millard Tydings was standing there beside our host, beaming at me.

"I don't believe you know Mrs. Cheesborough," said the Democratic leader of the Senate. "She is Joe Davies's daughter from New York."

"We haven't met" was the reply, as the Marylander took my hand and held it firmly, "but in a way, I do know the lady. I have admired her portrait in her father's house and I am happy to meet the lovely original."

Still holding my hand, he whisked me over to a corner where we talked until lunch was served. He told me that he had at first declined Senator Robinson's invitation because Maryland friends were coming to lunch with him. At the last minute, they had been unable to do so and he had been able to join us. Senator Robinson had told him the guest list and he had remembered my name. I thought that he was either a very fast worker or that our meeting was actually meant to be. In any event, either way, I was enjoying it thoroughly. I smiled and listened while he told me of his recent trip to our island possessions in the Pacific, as chairman of the Senate Territories Committee. He was enthusiastic about the South Sea Isle of Bali.

"For two cents," said he, grinning, "I would walk out of here and just spend the rest of my life on that lovely island, painting pictures of it!"

"For two cents," said I, "I would too!" We laughed together. He told me he had dined at my parents' home and had admired the portrait of me, which had been painted by Halmi when I was seventeen. He had asked Father questions about me but received only

brief replies. He asked me how long I would be in town and if I
would dine or lunch with him. I said I would like to but that I would
be leaving Washington in a day or two. At that point, luncheon was
served and he was seated beside my mother. She told me later that
he talked about nothing but me all through lunch. She was amused
but assured me that, of course, she had told him nothing about my
unhappy marriage. As for me, my head was in a whirl! That night I
dreamed of Millard Tydings. Would I ever see him again?

The following evening there was a dinner party and large dance
for the young Roosevelts at the Mayflower Hotel and I went with my
aunt, hoping my Maryland friend might be there. He was not, but I
met and danced many times with two interesting men who gave me
a "rush." One was Admiral Richard Byrd, just back from the Antarc-
tic. He was most attractive and lamented the fact that he was leaving
the next day to return to Antarctica. He wanted to take me with him!
I regretted the invitation, but he kept coming back to cut in on me.
The other gentleman who kept returning to dance with me was
Major Al Williams, a handsome Air Force officer who had just broken the air speed record. He was getting a divorce and asked me to
do likewise and marry him. I thanked both men for their invitations
and regretted that I was not up for grabs. However, I invited the
major to a reception my parents were giving the following evening
for the governor of Wisconsin. Fortunately, he came, because my
husband arrived in time for the party and became very drunk. My
Aunt Rebekah Cochran (mother's sister, who had divorced an alcoholic husband) and Major Williams helped me get Tom upstairs. The
major put my husband to bed before he passed out. We locked the
door behind us. Tom had caused quite a ripple in the crowd of distinguished guests. When a man six feet four inches tall starts to sway
on his feet, people tend to shy away from him in a hurry. I was extremely upset. I sent Tom back to New York the next day, telling
him I would never forgive him for disgracing me and my parents. I
threatened not to return to Greenwich.

The next day my mother took Mrs. Hines and my Aunt Rebekah
and me to the Mayflower Hotel, which was the in place for lunch. I
spoke with two beautiful friends at a nearby table—Mrs. Frances
Rust, who had been at Vassar with me, and Evie Walker. They insisted that I stay in town for a dinner party they were giving at the
1925 F Street club. This club had formerly been the handsome home
of the socialite Mrs. Laura Curtis. When that lady lost her fortune in
the 1929 stock market crash, her friends persuaded her to remain in

the house and run it as an exclusive club for them. Evie and Fran told me the names of their dinner guests and among them was Senator Millard Tydings. I accepted at once. After some misgivings, I wrote a politely formal note to the senator, inviting him to our house for cocktails before the party. Long afterward, his secretary, Miss Corinne Barger, told me that when he received my note he jumped up and danced around his office, something she had never seen the senator do before! He arrived at 2941 Massachusetts Avenue the evening of the dinner and we almost forgot to go to it. He made me promise that I would go on to the Hi Ho Club (a popular nightspot) with him after the dinner. As we were leaving the house, my children came in to bid me good night. My enchanting two-year-old daughter came flying down the hall, golden curls dancing and dimples flashing. She threw her arms about me and then with a beaming little face she held out her arms to the senator. From that moment, he never ceased to be her devoted slave. My six-year-old son, very much a dignified little man, bowed politely and shook hands with Millard. He became a real father to both children in the years to come.

When we arrived at the F Street Club and entered the front door, something rather gratifying (to me) occurred. A tall, dark, good-looking man stood there looking at me intently for a second before grabbing both of my hands. I had never seen him before and was astounded when, gazing at me boldly, he exclaimed in loud tones, "My God, where have you been all my life? You are the girl I've been looking for!" He would have swept me into his arms had the senator not held on fast with a strong arm around me. The stranger paid no attention to him.

"You are going dancing with me tonight, lady, and I am going to marry you!"

Millard Tydings glared at him.

"She is not going to do either, my friend. She is going dancing with me tonight!" and he propelled me past the man into the drawing room. I was amused and pleased. The stranger's loud admiration couldn't have been more fortuitous. The noisy interchange was overheard by all the dinner party and gossip about the senator and me started that evening. After dinner the guests all went to the Hi Ho Club together, but the senator and I went alone and sat by ourselves. By the end of the evening, we were happily acquainted with each other and I was enchanted with him. He told me he had never been married and I told him I had been unhappily so. He told me he was going to New York to address the Southern Society at a dinner on May seventh. Would I go dancing with him after the dinner? I said I did not go out with men other than my husband, but I would with him. He drove me home in a long black convertible and I hoped he would kiss me goodnight.

I was afraid he wouldn't, but I was wrong! Our house had a drive-in porte cochere at the front entrance, well-shielded from passersby with tall shrubbery and wisteria vines. I was properly kissed and asked to lunch and dinner the next day, which I regretted. I told him that I was returning to New York to tell my husband I was leaving him. Millard Tydings kissed me again, told me I was a wonderful girl and to let him know when I was coming back to Washington. He wanted very much to see me again and would look forward to seeing me in New York on May seventh. I parted from him in a rosy haze of happiness. My life had suddenly developed a future.

Back in Greenwich, I decided not to tell Tom about my divorce plans until I knew when Daddy and I would be sailing for Europe. I just insisted that he sleep in the guest room. Millard wrote and telephoned me several times. He was eager to see me as soon as he arrived for the stag dinner on May seventh. Would I meet him for tea "under the clock" at the Biltmore at five o'clock and go dancing with him after the dinner? I would. That was the day before Mother and my sister Emlen were sailing for Europe. My birthday had been April twenty-seventh and Tom had asked me what I would like him to give me. I had replied unhesitatingly: "A night out!" He had roared with laughter.

"You go out on the town often without me on your business affairs," said I. "Now I want to go out dancing without you!"

How incredibly naive I was. I even told him, when he asked, that I was going out with a U.S. Senator. Tom thought it was all a huge joke.

The "watched pot" eventually boils and my big night out finally came to pass. Tom and I dined in New York City with my mother and sister, Emlen. Afterward, he left me at the hotel and departed. He did not tell me where he was going and I did not ask. He knew where I was going and with whom but did not seem to find it quite so amusing anymore. Millard took me to the beautiful Central Park Casino to dance to the strains of Eddie Duchin's great band. I was floating on rainbow clouds. We were enthralled with each other. I asked politely about what his speech that evening had been about and he answered, briefly, "It was just my usual talk about the need for world trade to bring prosperity and a stronger economy to our country. There won't be a return to prosperity here until there is a healthy return of world trade. The president thinks that the government spending money it doesn't have will take us out of the Depression, but it won't do it. I have been urging an International Congress to promote world trade. But this is not very interesting stuff."

"But it is!" I was enthusiastic. "I was brought up on my father's Federal Trade Laws when he was President Wilson's chairman of the Commission. I think your speech must have been very interesting." I wasn't satisfied with this information and continued to ask questions about his adventures in war and politics. I was dying to ask about his romantic ones but didn't dare to ask. From his smile and the twinkle in his eyes, I knew that he suspected it.

"Why do you want to talk about me, young lady? I once wrote some very poor and very blank verse, which I recall was something like this:"

> When people talk with their tongues, you cannot tell
> What's in the mind.
> People always talk words
> So why not listen to the Hungarians?
> It's better not to know than not to understand.

I was amused and delighted, having experimented with writing verse myself.

"That's very nice. And very wise, which doesn't surprise me, Senator, although you often do."

"Well, I suspect you of writing verse yourself, Madam, so now you owe me one." I frowned at him so fiercely that he pretended to cringe.

"Oh, all right, what do you want to know? I'd much prefer to talk about you." I said no firmly, and he sighed deeply and continued. "I surrender to superior force. If you must know, I graduated from the University, went to war, came home, and became Speaker of the Maryland House of Delegates, was elected to the House of Representatives, to the U.S. Senate twice, and in 1935 I met a beautiful person named Eleanor Davies Cheesborough. Now it's your turn."

I was afraid I had bored him with my questions.

"Oh, I haven't done anything important. I went to a private school in Washington, made my debut, graduated from Vassar, and married the wrong man in November 1926." He chuckled.

"You left out something very important that you did that I can never do. You had those two charming children." It was my turn to laugh.

"My heart bleeds for you, sir!"

He changed the subject. "Do you realize, Mrs. Cheesborough, that you married this man Cheesborough the very month that I was first elected to the Senate? If you hadn't, we would have met all those years ago. What a waste of time!" He reached to take my hand.

"That wouldn't have made any difference to you, Senator, with all the hordes of beautiful girls in Maryland and Washington after you." I drew my hand gently away from his. He shook his head vigorously.

"Frankly, I've been too busy on Capitol Hill to do much socializing. I have been learning the rules of the Senate, doing my 'homework,' informing myself about the bills under our consideration, and doing research on those that most interested me." I asked what the latter were.

"Well, I helped repeal Prohibition and wrote and passed the bill for Philippine Independence. I argued against some of the President's New Deal borrow and spend bills, although I voted for a few in the beginning to get us out of the Depression. But you can't run a government for long on hot air. When Roosevelt asked in January for an additional $4.8 billion, which we don't have in the Treasury, I voted against it. You can't continue running the country into increasing debt, without the threat of economic collapse, bankruptcy, and eventually, the end of our American Democracy." He was frowning intensely, staring at the glass in his hand. I spoke softly.

"I heard about your speeches, especially about those you made this year advocating a 'pay as you go' system for our government. It makes sense to me." He smiled.

"I'm glad you agree with me, Eleanor. At first it was all right to make work for the unemployed by borrowing and spending, but now it's time to stop. We are going to desperately need an adequate Navy and a sound economy in case we are involved in another war. The President's flood of New Deal panaceas will create an avalanche of paper money. It could easily start a fire that would be hell to put out. The way to bring prosperity back to our country lies in treaties and trade with other countries, I believe."

"Is this balance-the-budget legislation more important than your bill for Philippine independence?" I asked.

"Almost, although it pleased me greatly to help give independence to a country we had won in a war against the Spanish in Cuba. It is about the first time in history that such a thing has happened. When I came to the Senate, Old Senator Harry Hawes of Missouri had introduced such a bill and I was floor manager for it. It failed to pass. The Democrats have always advocated it, but the Republicans were always against it. I boned up on Philippine history and introduced my bill, which eventually passed."

"So now we have met and I am about to gain my freedom and I am enjoying this evening immensely. Let's dance," I said, starting to rise. But he held on to my hand.

"So am I enjoying it, and dance we will. First I want you to know that what you say is a matter of great interest to me, but I don't want anything to do with your divorcing any poor devil." He was gazing into my eyes.

"You haven't anything to do with it, Senator," I assured him. "I had decided upon my divorce before we ever met. I want to get it over with as soon as possible. Daddy is taking me to Europe in June and I will probably go to Reno or Sun Valley as soon as I return."

Some people say that there is no such thing as love at first sight, but I don't agree with them. When I first saw Millard Tydings stride onto the Senate floor, and he looked up and smiled at me, I had the sure knowledge that this was the man I wanted to spend the rest of my life with.

After that wonderful, shimmering evening dancing with him and driving around Central Park in a horse-drawn carriage, I went back to Greenwich to my children and to make preparations for a great change in my life. In any event, I would never return to live there. While I was away, my children would be safe with our reliable cook and nurse, and with sister Rahel in New York to look after them, whether Tom did or not. With a new job he would probably not be home much.

Millard telephoned me several times and I promised him to return to Washington for the last week in May. Then I would return to Greenwich for a week with the children before sailing for Europe. I flew to Washington with Tom and his new partner on May twenty-fourth in the partner's plane. They wanted to see my father about financing their new project. Tom's partner let me take the controls, which was easy and fun until I saw the Capitol dome looming in the distance. Then I turned the controls over.

Millard chuckled delightedly when I told him about it. "I seem to be constantly learning new and remarkable facets of your character. What a girl you are, Eleanor!"

Tom and his new partner left for Chicago after talking with my father. That evening Senator Tydings dined with Daddy and me on our terrace overlooking Rock Creek Park. I knew that my father was a longtime, close personal friend of President Roosevelt and that the Senator and the President were on rather cool terms. Daddy was a Progressive Wisconsin Democrat and Millard was a Conservative Southern Democrat. However, there didn't seem to me to be much difference between the political philosophy of the two men. Joseph Davies was a practical idealist, and Millard Tydings seemed to me to be an idealistic pragmatist! They were certainly good friends. I listened with great interest while they discussed the state of affairs in Europe. Adolph Hitler had taken control of the German government in 1933, "a remarkable power grab of the German government by an ex-Austrian corporal in the Great War," Millard observed, "under the rather strange circumstances surrounding the burning of the Reichstag. I don't like Mr. Hitler or his Nazi Party!"

Daddy remarked that the postwar economy of Germany was so bad that one had to feel sorry for them. The German mark was worth so little that it took a suitcase of money to pay taxi fare.

"And there were Communist riots in the square in front of the American Embassy where I was visiting Matilda Houghton!" I interrupted.

"Which is why we came to take you away from there," said my father. "One had to feel sorry for the German women selling their possessions, even their wedding rings on the street."

Apparently the Senator had been there in 1922 and didn't share our sympathy for our former enemies.

"I don't like Mr. Hitler or his Nazis," repeated Millard. "He has already denounced the Versailles Treaty and I hear he is taking possession of the Rhineland and refusing to pay war reparations to the Allies."

Daddy nodded. "But the man declares that he will never make any territorial demands or ever break the peace," he said.

"Even so," said the Senator, "I do not believe him. England and France should be on their guard, in my opinion."

"I guess they feel safe with Britain's big navy and France's great army and the Maginot Line," I remarked. "We are lucky to have our oceans for protection. Nobody I know takes Hitler too seriously. They all saw Charlie Chaplin's caricature of him in that movie, 'The Great Dictator' and it looked exactly like him." Millard smiled at me.

"Adolph Hitler is no buffoon. And our oceans couldn't keep us out of the World War. Our former allies should be thinking about stopping Hitler before he goes too far."

"Which he may do," said Daddy. "Incidentally, Senator, I am sure that you have heard that France and Russia have signed a mutual agreement to protect Czechoslovakia in case of invasion. France has agreed to send an army at once in that event."

"Yes, I understand so. Also Britain has recently signed a naval agreement with Germany. That's one reason why I oppose increased government spending on work relief. I voted for half of those bills when Roosevelt was elected to help get us out of the Depression, but I think the time has come to stop spending money that's not in the U.S. Treasury. I don't think there will be a recovery from the Great Depression until tariffs come down to reasonable levels, our currency is stabilized, and government borrowing held to a minimum. Eventually every dollar the government borrows will come out of our people's pockets."

Daddy nodded but didn't comment.

Millard continued, "Now I think it wise to 'batten down the hatches,' as they say in the Navy, and get ready for a possible 'big blow.' Since the Naval Treaty of 1922 with Britain and Japan, our Navy is practically nonexistent. We scrapped our battleships while they tore up their blueprints. Our Pacific fleet is down to nothing but a few old ships, some ancient submarines, and obsolete destroyers. We should be spending our money now on the Navy instead of on more work relief." My father nodded in agreement.

"I remember your fight for fifteen new cruisers in 1929, Senator. I think you are dead right about our need for a strong Navy. Italy has invaded Ethiopia, Japan has invaded Manchuria, and I don't like this alliance between Italy and Germany. I fear war to the east of us and war to the west of us. Do you think we could be involved in either?"

"We could be in either or both" was the reply. "I will continue to oppose more appropriations for boondoggling and continue to fight for an adequate Navy. I am receiving a lot of invitations to speak to important groups around the country and will be warning people of trouble abroad. There is real danger of Japan attacking the Philippines and Guam the minute the islands become independent and we move out. You know a group of us on the Senatorial Territories Committee went to Manila last Christmas to tell the people this and to warn them of the economic hardships they would suffer when no longer part of the United States. Unfortunately their leaders have long preached the 'pot of gold' that would come to them with independence and they believe it." He shook his head sadly. Both men looked depressed, so I spoke up cheerfully.

"I know 1934 brought lots of bad news from overseas with Mussolini on the rampage, and Hitler ranting around, and the Lindbergh
baby kidnaped over here, and Mary Pickford and Douglas Fairbanks
getting divorced! But some good things have happened too! Your
Philippine Tydings-McDuffie Bill passed, Senator, and I am going to
Europe with Daddy and get a divorce and come home to Washington to live!"

Millard gave me a wide grin. "A truly happy event for your friends
in this city, Eleanor, and far more important than the fact that both
France and Russia have pledged to protect poor little Czechoslovakia! And another happy event would be if your father accepts a cabinet post from the President. What about it, Joe? Rumor has it that
he wants you, and you would certainly be a great addition to that
bunch of second-raters he has now!"

My father laughed.

"Confidentially, my friend, I have been approached on the matter,
but I have sent the word back that I appreciate the honor but wish
to continue doing what I enjoy most—the practice of law. My law
firm is booming and I wish to continue in my legal profession. Of
course, I will always support the President and the Democratic
party. Now, I am well aware that you two have a party to go to, and
I can see my child is getting restless to leave the Old Man. She tells
me that you are a great dancer, Senator."

"She is the great dancer, my friend!" said my love. "But before we
leave, there is a piece of information being discussed in the Senate
Democratic cloakroom that might be of interest to you. Gossip has
it among my friends that the President is about to send us some
'Soak the Rich' tax bills. Some of us have been wondering whether
he might crack down on the big fortunes and the big corporations
since (Senator) Huey Long has been ranting about 'share the wealth'
and 'every man a king' programs. They say Roosevelt will steal
Huey's stuff and ask us to tax all big fortunes, big inheritances, and
large gifts. I know this information might help some of your wealthy
clients if they wish to make gifts to their children before we pass
such a law."

Daddy thanked Millard. "I have a new wealthy client in particular
and I will tell her. I am sure she will want to take advantage of this
advice and make tax-free gifts to her daughters while there is time.
I will certainly do what I can for mine in a more modest way. Again,
my thanks, my friend. I have enjoyed our talk."

I hugged him and we left, but we did not go to the F Street Club.

Instead we went to his apartment at the Anchorage. We had too much to talk about to go to a party. I arrived home later that evening in a state of bliss. I went to my father's room and knocked on his door. He was sitting up in bed reading, as usual, and I perched on the edge beside him. I joyfully confided the wonderful news that I was in love with Millard Tydings and that he had told me he was in love with me! He was going to take me to Sharpsburg the next day where he was to make a speech on the battlefields of Antietam. My parent smiled at me, half pleased and half skeptical.

"Be careful, my child. The Senator has the reputation of being a popular ladies man. He is the most sought-after bachelor in Washington and so far he has evaded matrimony. I imagine that is what you have in mind. You are naturally susceptible, darling, being on the rebound from an unhappy marriage. Most men consider a married woman fair game. Millard Tydings has been chased by experts. Don't let him add you to his conquests."

"I am not a baby, Daddy," I protested indignantly. "I care for the Senator a great deal, but I have no intention of being a conquest! I don't think he is that kind of a man, anyway."

"I hope you are right, darling," he said, smiling at my indignant tone. "He is a fine man and I would trust him a long way, but I trust no man where my daughter is concerned!" Somewhat mollified, I kissed him good night and went off to write in my diary.

"The happiest day of my life! Millard Tydings told me that he loves me!"

The next day dawned sparkling sunny and glorious. It was our fifth day together. Millard arrived in mid-morning looking handsomer than ever and almost as happy as myself. I was not going to let my father's warning put a damper on my day, but I did not intend to allow this Senator to think I was just another one of his conquests! I would try to appear sophisticated, cool but charming. As we drove through the lovely countryside northwest of Baltimore, Millard suddenly stopped the car. He pointed out a small sign at the side of the road that said we were entering Harford County. He took me in his arms.

"Now, my dear girl, we are entering my homeland of Harford County, Maryland, and this great occasion must be properly commemorated!" It was, when his lips found mine. I gently extricated myself from his embrace and gazed around at the beautiful rolling hills and fields and at the large Victorian farmhouses nestling among groves of big trees. I was still struggling to keep "cool but charming."

"What lovely country!" I exclaimed. "Do you live on any of these farms?"

"No," he replied, starting the car. "I was born and brought up in Havre de Grace, a pretty, sleepy little town at the junction of the Susquehanna River and the Chesapeake Bay. My parents' home burned down and when I came home from the war, I built my mother a pretty stone house next to the park on the bay. My mother, sadly, is very ill, with nurses, or I would take you there." I expressed my sympathy and regret. He looked so sad that I knew he must love her very much. I decided to change the subject.

"How did your county get its name and how did your hometown come to be named Havre de Grace?" His face lost its sad expression.

"General La Fayette named the town at the time of the American Revolution. Until then it was known as Lower Susquehanna Crossing. There was no bridge across the river in those days, only a ferryboat. The General said it reminded him of Le Havre, a town in France, when he crossed the river. Harford County was part of Baltimore county then. Later it named itself for Henry Harford, the bastard son of the last Lord Baltimore. Apparently he wasn't much! They say he signed away half the land of Maryland, which the King of England had granted to the first Lord Baltimore. The original grant took in all the land north to the fortieth parallel, south to the Potomac River, west to the Potomac River's head waters, and east to the Atlantic Ocean. That included all of Delaware, all of Pennsylvania as far north as Philadelphia, the southern part of New Jersey, and part of West Virginia."

"How did Harford happen to lose all that?" I asked in surprise. All that land would have made Maryland almost twice as large!

"There is a story that William Penn persuaded Harford to sign a paper with a map showing incorrect boundaries. When the last Baltimore realized what he had done, the bastard took his case to court in England and the judge ruled in favor of Penn. He said if Harford was that stupid, he didn't deserve to win it!" Millard chuckled and I laughed with him.

"There is another story," he continued," that King James II owed Penn a favor because William Penn's ancestor, Admiral Penn, had brought the king great riches from the sugar plantations of Jamaica, the island that the Admiral had taken from the Spaniards." I mused upon the strange sequence of events that could so affect the future.

"Actually," he continued, "it was probably due to the change of power in England when King Charles II died and his brother James

II became King. He arrived with the English fleet in New Amsterdam and annexed it, Delaware and Maryland property now in Pennsylvania too."

At this point I was only half listening to him. Something else was exciting my curiosity.

"Have you written the speech you are going to deliver at Antietam?"

"No," he said with an amused smile.

"Have you an outline of what you are going to say?"

"No indeed," again the impish grin. I decided to ask no more questions.

We lunched with various dignitaries in Sharpsburg, including the Governor and his wife, who was obviously consumed with curiosity about me. I sat listening to Millard make a brilliant and inspiring talk about the terrible battle when 20,000 men in the Union and Confederate armies were killed in one day. At first I twisted my handkerchief like a nervous mother attending her child's recitation. I need not have worried. Millard Tydings had won many oratorical contests, both state and national, in his college days, and was considered the finest speaker in the Senate. He had a prodigious memory for facts and figures, names and places, and never wrote a speech save for radio talks, which had to be timed exactly. His Sunday morning broadcasts, "A Report to Maryland on Events of the Week on Capitol Hill" were so popular that it was said that in warm weather you could hear Senator Tydings's voice on Sunday mornings coming from every open window in Maryland.

The more I learned about him, the more I admired him. He had lived an exciting life, fighting in France in the World War and working tirelessly in Congress for his beloved state and nation. He was a quiet, dignified man in public, but a witty, amusing person with his friends. Not for him were the trappings of success, the red carpets and motorcycle escorts, which I confess I would rather enjoy! His integrity and code of honor were such that he would lean over backward to avoid anything that might infringe upon that code. It is sad that there have been so few men in public life like him. On the way home I asked him more questions about the Philippines. I had been to Europe but never farther west than California. I also was curious about the island of Bali.

"You told me about your visit to Bali the day we met, but you didn't say you went to the Philippine Islands on that trip."

"I didn't think you'd be particularly interested in them. I thought you would rather hear about the beauties of Bali."

"I don't recall that you told me about the 'beauties.' Were there many of them or only one special beauty?"

"There were quite a few. If there had been only one, I wouldn't tell you about her, Eleanor. I don't think it would interest you."

"It doesn't. Your trip to the Philippines does."

"Well, I went because in spite of the passage of the Tydings-Mc-Duffie Act in March of 1934, I knew that the Philippine people didn't realize the economic troubles that would assail them when they cut loose from Uncle Sam's apron strings. As part of the U.S.A. they had many privileges, tariff and tax-wise and with their sugar quotas. I had managed to eventually get them a five-year transition period but couldn't do much more against heavy Republican opposition in the Congress and also from labor and agricultural organizations.

"Who went with you to the Islands?"

"Only four from my Territories Committee, although a lot of Senators wanted to go. I don't like junkets at Uncle Sam's expense. Our whole trip cost our government only about fifteen thousand dollars."

I laughed.

"Penny-pincher! The Filipinos must have given you a very warm welcome as the bearers of such glad Tydings of the Independence— red carpets and brass bands. As 'father' of their country you certainly have a large family, Senator!"

"Yes, our arrival was properly celebrated. We were royally entertained by the rich and powerful, but we managed to get about and see the abject poverty of the masses. After I had addressed their Constitutional Convention, I was not so popular. I gave them the bad news of the economic hardships the Philippine people would suffer with independence, 'with the bark on,' as old Vice President Garner would say. Their political leaders Quezon and Osmena, both presidential candidates, knew everything I told them, but had never dared to give their people the facts."

I couldn't understand this. "Why not?"

"Good question," Millard said approvingly. "That is where politics comes in. These men had been fighting each other for leadership, trying to wrest power from each other, so they had been singing about the utopia that would come with freedom for their country. In spite of my warning, the Convention voted for it, but my conscience is clear. I told them if they honestly wanted it, they would have to accept this bill's provisions. Then they should send a delegation to ask Congress to make some less difficult amendments to it. I promised to help them."

"Did they take your advice?"

"Yes, they did, but I didn't trust President Quezon, so I took out a little insurance against that wily character. I made him sign a memorandum in Manila that he would support my bill, both in the Philippines and in the U.S. Congress, or I would not help him get the softening amendments to it."

"Didn't he stick to it?"

"He tried to run out on me at the last minute, just as I had suspected he would, on the day I was to speak on the Senate floor in favor of the new bill. I had managed to persuade the Senate to soften the tariffs and taxes and to give them a ten-year transition period instead of five. Then that old bird Quezon told me he could not support the new bill. I told him that if he didn't support it I would show the memo to the press and go after him on the Senate floor. Philippine independence would be dead as Hector and so would he!"

I said cheerily, "So, of course, Mr. Quezon was terrified and the bill passed the Senate. Congratulations, Senator!"

"Yes, and I'm sorry you were not there at the time. We struck a blow for the liberty the United States had long promised the Philippine people. I made the transition as easy as I could for them in spite of the powerful interests against it in the United States."

"So the Philippines received its independence—both the bitter and the sweet. Daddy says nothing and nobody is a thousand percent, but I'm not sure I agree when there are men like you, Senator."

He stopped the car again and reached for me with a beaming smile.

"Not men like me, but women like you!" he said, his eyes suddenly sparkling happily. But this time I was not going to fall victim to the senatorial blandishments. I drew away and asked how soon we would arrive in Washington. So much for good intentions.

That evening we dined together in his apartment at the Anchorage and I stayed cool but not quite so much so! I told him of my plans for the summer. Daddy and I would sail for Europe on June eighth to join Mother and Emlen in London. Maybe I could get a divorce over there. If not, I would come home and get it in Reno. My father wanted me to go to Budapest with Mother to visit their friends, Ambassador and Mrs. John Montgomery, after a stay in Paris. I was returning to Greenwich at once to spend the rest of my time with my children.

I had been parrying the Senator's advances, determined not to be a pushover. In spite of Daddy's warnings, I was sure that Millard had found in me the person he wanted to marry as I had found in him. When he heard that I might be leaving the next day, not to return for some months, his expression changed to one of firm determination. He brushed aside my defenses and took me in his arms. He told me that he loved me and wanted to marry me as soon as I had my divorce. "And please, stay here for a few more days before you go back north, and please say you will marry me!"

That was a wonderful evening. Of course, I accepted his proposal and agreed to remain in Washington awhile longer. I knew my parents would be happy over our plans, and I was delighted that I would be able to tell future generations that the Senator had asked me to marry him the fifth time we had been together.

Those last days in May were pure joy for me. I remained in the city until the end of the month and spent every minute when Millard was free with him. When he wasn't, I sat in the Senate Gallery waiting for him to join me and listening to the debates over the President's New Deal legislation. One day when I was sitting in the Senate Ladies' Gallery waiting for him, he joined me and asked me how I thought he should vote on the Wagner Labor Act, which was being debated on the Senate floor. I told him that I knew little about it but I knew that he did and that he would vote the right way. He pointed out the rough-looking men filling the public galleries. If he voted against the bill, he said, they would try to defeat him for reelection in 1938. He had proposed an amendment to it, protecting workmen from coercion by the unions as well as by employers. It was defeated, and he voted against the bill.

Whenever he could, Millard drove me all around his beloved state, but on weekends he spent time with his mother in Havre de Grace. I didn't want to be divorced and married again in the same year, so we decided not to announce our engagement until Christmas. We would be married in the spring.

We tried to keep out of the public eye as much as possible, but this was difficult. My senator was much in the news and gossip was rife around Washington about us. The heat in the city that week was worse than usual, but I wasn't even conscious of it, and I doubt if Millard was. My dear love was evidently enjoying the same delightful euphoria that I was. He said he would come to New York to have dinner with me and say good-bye the evening before Daddy and I were to sail on the *Europa*. I was to stay with my father in his suite at the Plaza. However, there was a shadow on this happy plan. The Senate was debating some of the President's important tax legislation. Although Congress was accustomed to adjourning on June first, Roosevelt had called a special session. Millard was concerned that he might not be able to come to New York.

Of course, I had told my father the good news about Millard and our marriage plans, but my senator had said nothing to Daddy and he was still skeptical. He told me that if the senator came to New York to say good-bye to me, he would believe that his matrimonial intentions were serious. Of course, that left me in a highly nervous state.

I returned to Greenwich to spend the last week with my children before Daddy and I sailed for Europe. It would be a wrench to part with them. I had never left them before. Tom came back from Chicago, and I finally gathered up my courage and told him that I had decided to divorce him and was leaving for Europe with my father on the seventh of June. At first he laughed and refused to take it seriously. Then he grew angry, which seemed to make it easier for me to remain calm and firm. In the end, I had to agree to make no final decision until my return in a month's time.

Of course, I had no intention of changing my mind! Tom's brother and his lovely wife, Sandy, arrived unexpectedly the next day. Tom left me alone with them and the children and they were both warmly sympathetic. My sister Rahel and her husband were also there and offered to spend most of the time I was abroad with my children until my Aunt Rebekah returned from England and took them to Nississhin's lodge in northern Wisconsin. It was hard to say good-bye to my babies. A friendly neighbor drove me to New York to the Plaza Hotel. Tom had not reappeared since leaving his brother and sister-in-law with me.

I found my father quite ill upon my arrival and resting in bed. I was distressed, but he assured me it was only a slight return of his old intestinal trouble. That evening a blow fell. Millard called me late at night to say the utilities bill had failed to come to a vote in the Senate as had been expected before it had adjourned. It would carry over to the next day (my last) and he hoped it would be voted upon at noon in time for him to catch the last plane to New York to get him there in time for dinner. I was not to expect a telegram—he might not have time to wire or phone. I was utterly crushed but tried to sound brave and cheery on the telephone. I knew the Utilities Holding Company bill was very important to him and that he had proposed an amendment to it that meant a great deal to him. He had told me that the proposed tax bill would hurt both the big companies and their employees. He was optimistic however, that it would be voted upon in time for him to fly to New York.

I had nightmares that night, the few hours when I slept at all. I did not tell Daddy about Millard's call. In the morning I went across the street to Bergdorf Goodmans and bought a stunning dinner gown of purple and orchid satin, but it didn't cheer me up a bit. I couldn't eat breakfast or lunch. Then I went (of course) to the beauty parlor and the hairdresser. By the time I returned to the hotel, it was two-thirty in the afternoon and I was in despair. The Senate bill was just an excuse. Millard Tydings really didn't care a fig for me! My life was over. I was sure he wasn't coming and probably didn't want to. I was just a passing fancy and would never see him again! I would die an old maid—or worse still, an old divorcee! Almost in tears, I stopped at the hotel desk to ask the clerk, "Any message for me?" There was. It read: "By the time you receive this I will be on my way rejoicing. WAMHILY." The last word was a code between us, meaning "With All My Heart I Love You!" By this time I was ready to be either his passing or permanent fancy!

Millard arrived at the Plaza with books, flowers, and a broad smile. Daddy joined us for a cocktail, looking better, to my great relief. He soon left us to join an important client, he said. Millard and I dined alone together in my father's suite. It was a wonderful evening. My cup was running over. He left me in time to catch the midnight train back to Washington. I had forgotten to ask him how the Senate had voted on the utilities bill!

Chapter 11

Europe and Oakington, Summer 1935

Daddy and I sailed on the *Europa* at midnight, June eighteenth. Millard did not come down to the boat on account of the press. Our crossing was a gay one. Mrs. Marjorie Post Hutton was on board, beautiful as she was rich and great fun besides. In her party, besides her usual retinue of maids and secretaries, were her two attractive friends, Adelaide Hambleton Hill and her husband, Jerry. Apparently Marjorie was a client of Daddy's. She was divorcing Edward F. Hutton. I had met her before when Tom and I weekended with her daughter, Adelaide, and husband, Tim Durant, at Mrs. Hutton's Long Island estate. Marjorie Hutton had built them a charming house next to her baronial mansion.

We had a merry time on the ship. I won the waltzing contest with the young German son of the owner of the line—possibly because he was or possibly because Marjorie was the judge. I disembarked at England, but Daddy went on to Paris. Mother met me and was upset that daddy was not with me. She was staying at Claridges in London with my Aunt Rebekah and my sister Emlen. They had been traveling in Scotland together. My sister was to be presented to their Majesties at the June Court and was going to Cambridge University with cousin Jack Cochran for the "May-week" parties (in June!). Jack urged me to come too, and I did. It was interesting to compare the differences between the English boys and the American ones and their college festivities. I met a delightful titled friend of Jack's, Philip L., who was the proud owner of a gorgeous silver Rolls sports car. In this we dashed around the lovely English countryside at frightening speeds! The Cambridge parties were not nearly as much fun as those I had attended at Yale and Princeton. Here there was no stag line. The girls danced solely with their escorts or with a few partners listed on old-fashioned dance cards. At the cocktail parties (they called them "Sherry Parties"), the boys huddled together in one corner, the girls in another. I didn't blame the boys, the girls were pretty frumpy. The "Merry Widow from the U.S." did not huddle with the frumps! Nor did I dance with one man all evening. I evidently created quite a stir. The young Englishmen called me "The Duchess" or "Lady Cheesborough—Cheesborough of Cheesborough-on-the-Cheesborough!"

My friend Philip declared himself to be madly in love with me (I was six years his senior!) and persuaded Jack and me to drive back to London with him, stopping overnight at his family's ancestral home. My sister had already returned to London by train. That morning, I had a queer feeling that I must get back to the city as soon as possible, and I insisted that Philip drive us straight to London. He and Jack were disgusted, but I was adamant. Fortunately, I arrived there shortly after my father did. By the time I did, he had already informed Mother that he wanted a divorce. He was going to marry Marjorie Hutton! I was astounded. For the first time in my life, I nearly fainted. Mother was prostrated. My parents had apparently been perfectly happy for thirty years.

That awful night at Claridges I spent running between Daddy's room on one floor and Mother's on another, terrified for fear one or both of them would die before morning! Daddy told me his doctor had given him only a few years to live and he wished to spend them with the woman he loved. He said he would always be fond of Mother and would always take care of her, but Marjorie was the one great passion of his life! It was also plain to see that he was a sick man. I was equally frightened over Mother's shock and agony. She had never dreamed that such a thing could happen. Neither had I, and I'm sure neither had my father.

The following months were terrible for Mother and hard for me too. Daddy sent Mother, Emlen, and myself on a trip around Europe. Emlen was too young to cope with poor Mother's distress. I did my best to take care of her and to comfort her. It was pretty grim. The only bright moments came when I was reading Millard's beautiful letters or writing to him.

In Budapest we were guests of the United States Ambassador, "Uncle John" Montgomery, an old friend of my parents. Budapest was fascinating. The ambassador give a dinner dance in our honor on board a large yacht that had belonged to the Royal family, and we sailed down the Danube in the moonlight. I sat beside a youngish

German baron at dinner who pursued me all evening even more aggressively than my former German admirer, Baron "Adie." The next day the ambassador asked me how I had liked the baron. I said, "Not at all!" My host laughed and said that this German was reputed to be Hitler's top Gestapo agent in Hungary and was said to have organized and carried out the assassination of the late chancellor, Mr. Dolfuss! I wondered why our host had made this man my dinner partner.

After Budapest, Mother and Emlen and I motored through Germany to Berlin. I was interested in the young uniformed German boys and the pretty blond girls we saw there. They looked almost more like our young people in the U.S. than the young people I had seen in England. How different from the tall boots and duel-scarred faces of the arrogant Prussian officers I had seen in Berlin in 1923!

After a brief sojourn in Paris, we sailed home on the giant new liner *Normandy*. Mother was increasingly miserable. I was eager to get back to Millard and my children and get on with my divorce. Apparently Mother and I were going to Reno. My sister Rahel had written me regular reports of the children's welfare. She and her husband had gone out to Greenwich from New York City every week to see them. Tom was seldom home.

In mid-ocean I received a lengthy cable from Millard: "Imperative you come to Washington by Monday next." This surprised me as he knew that we were to land on Wednesday and that I would have to go to Greenwich, pack the children and their nurse off to Aunt Rebekah at the Brule River. I would have to supervise the packing of all my furniture, linen, china, glass, and silver for storage in Washington. It would be almost impossible to do all this between Thursday and Monday, I cabled the senator. A barrage of insistent cables followed from him with no explanation whatever.

Tom and Rahel and Aldace, with my little son, met our boat. I left Mother and Emlen with Rahel and returned to Greenwich. If the weeks in Europe had been difficult, that week was a nightmare. Tom departed in a rage after I had told him that I was still determined to get a divorce. I had barely shipped the children off to Wisconsin when a honk from the driveway announced the arrival of that silver Rolls bearing Cousin Jack and Philip! I was amazed to see them and far from pleased. It was not easy to get rid of them. After they left, I talked for hours on the phone with Millard. It seemed that he had an option to buy a beautiful estate south of Havre de Grace on the Chesapeake Bay, and his option expired on Wednesday. He would not buy the place if I did not wish to live there. Of course, I would have been happy in a hovel with Millard. I promised to be in Washington Monday morning.

By Sunday morning, the house was empty save for a small bed and a collection of trunks and suitcases in my room, in which I had to pack all my clothes. I was exhausted, physically and emotionally. One of my girlfriends came to help me that morning and found me sitting on the floor weeping and surrounded by a clutter of mounds of wearing apparel. She phoned her doctor and upon his advice proceeded to dose me with double bromides. There was no such thing as tranquilizer drugs in those days. Between us we finished the packing, and at five o'clock Philip arrived to drive me to New York City. (I had promised to have dinner with him in order to get rid of him.) Of course, he knew that I was engaged to marry someone after I obtained my divorce, but he had refused to accept the fact.

I took the midnight train with Mother for Washington. The bromides had worn off and I spent a sleepless night. My mother's tragedy and the empty years of my marriage with Tom were uppermost in my thoughts, in spite of the joy of a future with Millard Tydings. The strain of my days and nights nursing my mother had caught up with me, and horror of horrors, I had developed a boil on the end of my nose! The next day, however, I managed to pull myself together and plaster a cover on my poor nose. Swathed in veils, I greeted my love.

He drove me the seventy-five miles to Oakington. The temperature registered 100 degrees that day, but I didn't feel it and Millard apparently didn't see the plaster on my nose!

Oakington

While Mother and I were in Europe, my father had returned to Washington. Millard went to see him to tell him that we wished to marry after my divorce. Daddy was delighted to give his approval and his blessing and informed Millard of his own plans for divorce and re-marriage. Toasts were drunk and my father asked where Millard proposed to take his daughter to live.

"I cannot take Eleanor to the house I built in Havre de Grace because my mother lives there and she is terminally ill, I fear, with nurses. I own a house in Georgetown, which I am renting and have been keeping bachelor quarters at the Anchorage with Sam Rayburn" was Millard's reply. "However, there is a very fine estate on the Bay south of Havre de Grace that is for sale for a bargain price. It is a 550-acre working farm with a large old mansion house. It's very run-down but the whole place can be had for not much more than back taxes." When he heard the figure, my father sat up straight and exclaimed enthusiastically: "Buy it, my boy, by all means! Buy it! It sounds like a great investment!"

"You are right, Joe. I own some land in Havre de Grace, which I can sell to finance the purchase, but there is a hitch. The mansion house is in bad shape. It has at least thirty rooms and was built around 1800. The cellars are under water and there will have to be a new heating system and new wiring. The house will have to be redecorated within and the outside trim painted. All of this would cost about double the purchase price." My father assured Millard that together they could do it all. It would be the home of his beloved son-daughter, his best friend, and his grandchildren, he said. The two men drank a toast to Oakington.

"Of course," said the Senator, "the purchase must wait until Eleanor returns and wishes to live there." My father smiled. He was sure that I would be happy to live in a shack with Millard Tydings, as indeed I would!

Millard drove me north on the narrow Old Post Road through thirty-three red lights of the streets of Baltimore and some thirty-five farther toward Havre de Grace. We left the Old Post Road and turned toward the Bay, then drove through some woods and forded a stream. I murmured, "My, this *is* country, isn't it!" Millard laughed and this became a family joke about me, the city mouse. We came to tall, double redbrick gates with stone balls atop. "This is it," said Millard proudly, stopping the car under the big white pines of the lane stretching ahead of us and kissing me. The road ran for a mile past broad fields on either side. We passed two big white farmhouses before turning in at a pair of smaller gray stone gateposts that marked the approach to the mansion. Wide lawns dotted with big holly, maple, and pine trees and shrubbery stretched on either side.

Oakington House loomed before us, and I first saw the place that was to be my home for almost fifty years. I gazed happily and with an excited sense of recognition at the mansion before me. I didn't see the dead trees and shrubbery, the tall grass or the peeling paint on the entrance pillars and shutters. What I saw was the welcome of the open door and the beautiful rooms beyond. It had been waiting for me, I thought, and strangely, it seemed as though I had seen it before!

After my baby girl was born, I spent weeks near to death in the Ashville hospital while doctors argued about whether to perform a dangerous operation that would leave me an invalid if I lived at all. My father-in-law, dear old Doctor Cheesborough, refused to allow it and the high fever that had been raging in me miraculously disappeared. I had been delirious for days, but after my temperature went down I remembered only one thing. As clear as a photograph was the dream I had in my fever. I was walking toward a big house, my little boy trotting beside me, holding my hand. A tall man walked beside me carrying my baby girl. I could not see the man's face but I knew it was not Tom. It was a happy dream and I had clung to it ever since. Now I recognized the house and I knew the man. I turned to Millard with tears in my eyes.

"How did you know about my dream?" He looked puzzled.

"I didn't," he said, "but this place was always my dream from the time I was a lad, roaming the shores of Chesapeake Bay. I thought Oakington was the most beautiful place in the world. But I never imagined that Oakington and the most wonderful girl in the world might someday be mine!" Then he picked me up and carried me up the broad steps through the wide door. The house seemed to be empty, deserted save for any stray ghosts. We entered a wide paneled hall that stretched the width of the old center square of the original stone house. To our left soared a big curving stair and to the right a smaller one led up to the south wing. The long drawing room of the south wing was beyond a large archway. To our left another archway led into a big dining room. Carved marble fireplace mantels graced all three rooms as they did the two rooms east of the hall. One was a library, the other a formal parlor. The walls of the hall and dining room were paneled, but the other three rooms had worn brocade hanging in tatters from the walls. Doors led from them out onto an enormous glass-walled solarium, which looked out across a broad lawn at the vast expanse of the Chesapeake. Far across it lay the Eastern shore of Maryland and far to the southeast was Spesutie Island and the Aberdeen Proving Grounds. The latter was separated from Oakington by a little river called Swan Creek, over a mile along our shore.

I touched the heavy old velvet portieres that hung in all the doorways and clouds of moths flew out. Some outside shutters hung on single hinges or lay on the ground and the grass had grown up knee-high with weeds. The shrubbery was a tangled jungle. I giggled.

"We can't let my mother come out here until we've had extermina-tors to get rid of the moths!"

"Don't worry sweetheart, it will all be taken care of," he said, embracing me. "If you will take me and the place, I'll have the work-men in here tomorrow refurbishing everything. Just say the word." I was speechless with happiness and could only nod my head and hug him.

"Wherever you are, I wish to be, for the rest of my life," I eventu-ally managed to answer. "It is lovelier than my dreams! Are we really going to live here?"

"We certainly are if you wish to, my love. I have already talked to builders, plumbers, engineers, and electricians, and they say they can have the house ready by Christmas for my bride, if she wishes to have it and me. Will that please you, treasure?"

I tried to nod my head between his kisses.

"Enough of this lovemaking, or I'll be carrying you upstairs to the master bedroom," he grinned, "and there is much to see before I feed you the picnic lunch I have brought along." So we wandered through the house, deciding what furniture we would keep. The pur-chase price actually included everything in it.

The smaller southwest wing of the house was one of two designed by a famous New York architect named Stanford White at the turn of the century. He had been a friend of the owner, James L. Breeze. White was murdered by Harry K. Thaw, the husband of Evelyn Nes-bit. She had been one of the Ziegfeld Follies girls billed as "the most beautiful girl in the world." She had been the mistress of Stanford White before she married Thaw. When he found it out, he shot the architect. It was a celebrated murder trial. The Thaw family was enormously rich and managed to get Harry a "not guilty" verdict by virtue of his being of unsound mind. Many tales were told about the parties given at Oakington by its owner, James L. Breeze, when Stanford White and his mistress, Evelyn, and other Follies girls and their "patrons" were houseguests at Oakington. Evelyn came out of a huge pie at dinner one night, stark naked. At another dinner, some lovely naked Follies girls sat between the men at the table.

Mr. Breeze had two entrance gates and lanes that led to the man-sion. If Mrs. Breeze returned unexpectedly, the station agent would send word by telephone and the lady would be driven home in a slow hack on one lane and the Follies girls would be sent out the other entrance behind fast trotters, appropriately enough!

My children called the southwest White wing, the "Wicked Wing," partly because of these tales and partly because of the lovely plaster Adam ceilings of gods chasing goddesses in the two bedrooms. There was a large marble bathroom between them and beneath was the long drawing room sometimes called and used as the ballroom. Mighty beams held up its ceiling, but eventually the weight of the marble floor and walls of the bathroom above began to show before many years in the sagging beams below. The marble had to go. I was always worried until that was done for fear my 250 pound brother-in-law, Aldace Walker, would take a bath and land in the grand piano below.

The southwest wing was the only one of Stanford White's two wings left when the Tydings arrived. Another wealthy owner, Leonard Richards, had added a stone addition at the north end of the old center house, twice as big as that portion of the house. The dining room occupied part of it next to the entrance hall. It boasted a wall-wide window with a superb view of the Bay. A swinging door opened into a big pantry and a vast kitchen, a staff sitting room, laundry, back stairs, and outer door. Upstairs a large master bedroom occupied the space above the dining room and there were two master dressing room baths. The rest of the north addition had five smaller bedrooms and two baths. It would be the children's wing. The old part of the house had three large bedrooms and one bathroom. The third floor had five more bedrooms and two baths, but was used as an apartment for the Livingstons. All the second-floor bedrooms except the children's rooms had fireplaces. There was a secret space—almost a small room—under the floor of a closet in our bedroom and another one on the third floor. The nightclub singer Libby Holman hid here when she was evading the law after being suspected of the murder of her husband, heir to a tobacco fortune. I dare say there were ghosts at Oakington but I never saw any. They must have approved of me and left me alone. Our cook, Nadine Livingston, said she saw a Confederate soldier in the boxwood garden more than once on moonlit nights and this could have been—there had been a Confederate sympathizer who owned Oakington during the Civil War. After the war was over, he was suspected of being in on the plot with John Wilkes Boothe when he assassinated Abraham Lincoln. The Booth family owned a farm nearby in Harford County. The Oakington suspect was warned of the approach of federal officers to arrest him and was able to escape by hiding in a hollow log down on the Oakington shore. When the soldiers left, he escaped by boat and went to Canada where he lived for many years. His name was Stump. His grandfather had built the original house, which was to be home for me, my children, and my grandchildren for almost fifty years.

Beyond the kitchen end of the house was a large greenhouse, which was falling down; and beyond it, an enormous stone garage building, which contained three ten-room houses. It had been built, we were told, to house the officers of Mr. Leonard Richard's yacht! Beyond it was a small frame cottage where the widow of one of our farmers lived for many years. Like everything else on the place, except the barns, it was in a sad state of disrepair. We had to tear down the greenhouse and, after the worst of the Japanese beetles moved on, Millard made a lovely rose garden for me where it had stood.

Besides the glorious view of the Bay, what I loved the most about Oakington were the gardens. On two sides of the "Wicked Wing" lay an old boxwood garden, walled with English box more than two hundred years old. There had been a house where ours stood long before the Stumps built the present one. I asked a very old lady who had lived there long ago why the boxwood had been planted where it was, as there had been no south wing when the old house was built. She told me, in some surprise at my ignorance, of "life before plumbing" that "naturally, my dear, it was the path to the privy!"

This garden had eight beds in an "L" shape, with a big walnut tree at each end. At the far end was a grove of immense holly trees with a hedge of five-foot-high rhododendrons and laurel. When my father died, I transplanted white azaleas there from his home Tregaron in Washington. They made a marvelous white wall at that end of the garden. When I first saw it, there was nothing but weeds in it, and it took me years of expense and toil to turn it into the lovely thing it was when I left it. Behind the boxwood hedge on the south side was a long wisteria arbor, and beyond that was a vineyard and cutting garden, and a charming little white frame guest cottage. Here my daughter lived for a short time when my first grandbaby, Suzy Gillet, was born. Millard eventually built a tennis court and a swimming pool at that end of the many acres of the Bay lawn.

How Millard managed to get the mansion and farmers' houses completely decorated and repaired by the time we were married is a miracle in itself. Even the hard-surface entrance lane had to be repaved. When my mother came out to see the place with me that fall, she said, "You and Millard are stark raving mad" to even consider living there. Although the initial cost was amazingly small, the repairs were very expensive and the upkeep took all the means we could muster. She was right, but with our modest combined income and Daddy's generous help we managed, and we lived happily in our utopia for many decades.

When Mother and I returned with our divorces from Nevada the renovation was almost completed and the news media was singing the praises of the senator from Maryland, with few exceptions.

Chapter 12

My Mother and My Stepmother

My stepmother was forty-nine when she met my father. Mother was fifty-eight, he was fifty-nine. Marjorie told me she was fifty. She was known as a great beauty, but as good looking as Marjorie was, my mother had been as beautiful when she was Marjorie's age. When I was a child I remember her long, pale blond hair that looked like spun gold when sunlight reflected off of it. Her eyes were large and blue, the color of sapphire, her skin a milky translucent, and she once had a very slender figure—had been considered almost too thin. But she was eight years older than my stepmother and had done little to preserve either the lovely color of her hair or her slender figure after her third child was born. She put on weight and never took it off. Since she was not tall, she acquired the matronly look of wealthy women at the turn of the century. Mother was always lovely looking.

Marjorie Post had a very different, more modern upbringing than my mother's Victorian one. Although nineteen or twenty years older than I, she seemed to me more like my contemporary. She had kept her figure, which made her look much younger than her age. With near-perfect features, she had a fine complexion, wore her long, dark brown hair dressed high on her head, and carried herself like a queen. We often were mistaken for each other, or I was taken for her daughter, occurrences that I found complimentary and which did not displease her. We were exactly the same height and size and wore our hair alike.

Her education had stopped with finishing school, as had my mother's, and she was a naturally intelligent woman. She was trained by her father to organize her six huge homes and her 330-foot yacht with ease. She also supervised her great fortune. My mother may

75

have been born into wealthy upper-class financial circumstances, but Marjorie's father had endowed her with enormous wealth. C. W. Post made his fortune with health foods and the first coffee substitute, Postum. He and Marjorie's mother were divorced when she was a young girl. Her mother died, leaving Marjorie to be raised by her father, who married Marjorie's governess. He left the bulk of his fortune to the stepmother, but Marjorie was able to break his will when she discovered that her mother's money had originally financed his business. She paid off her stepmother and kept control of the Post fortune.

She had been devoted to her father and told me how he had made her learn to do everything for herself before she employed anyone to do it for her. When she built her splendid yacht, *Sea Cloud*, she studied marine architecture and planned every detail of the million dollar ship while it was being built at Kiel, Germany, in 1931. She had lived in Greenwich, Connecticut, with her first husband, Edward Close, a New Yorker, and they had two daughters, Adelaide and Eleanor. Her second husband was the prominent New York stockbroker, Edward F. Hutton. Her daughter from that marriage was Nedenia, who became the actress Deena Merrill. Deenie was about ten or twelve when her mother married my father. Both her older sisters were married: Adelaide to my old beau Tim Durant and Eleanor to her third husband. She was to have several more.

The Huttons maintained an elegant Fifth Avenue house; a grand estate at Roslyn, Long Island; an enormous camp in the Adirondacks; a large plantation in South Carolina; a veritable palace at Palm Beach, (Mar-a-Lago, now owned by Donald Trump); and the sumptuous yacht, *Sea Cloud*. They traveled among their homes depending on the season or demands of society. E. F. Hutton had invested Marjorie's fortune in the creation of General Foods, one of the nation's first mega-corporate establishments, and for many years Marjorie never missed the board meetings of that company. Hutton was a handsome man who was addicted to at least one extra-marital affair. At the time Marjorie met my father, she was about to divorce Hutton. She had discovered that he was often entertaining a lady friend in her absence, not only in Marjorie's South Carolina plantation, but in Marjorie's own bed. My stepmother, with her wickedly sharp sense of humor, had a wire rigged from the bed-springs to a siren on the rooftop and left her husband to entertain at his pleasure. Of course, when he was active in the bed, pandemonium would break loose on the roof!

When Marjorie divorced Ed Hutton, he took the plantation and the lady friend took him in matrimony.

Marjorie and I both loved my father deeply, and before I go any further, I would like to set the record straight about the financial settlement of my parents' divorce, the subject of some malicious gossip. The false statements were that Marjorie had bought my father's divorce from my mother for millions! This outrageous lie still infuriates me. My father was one of the wealthiest lawyers in Washington at the time of his divorce. He was a millionaire well able to take care of my mother in the manner in which they had lived and did so. He provided a generous income for her, and set up a very large trust fund and a large insurance policy that she would receive at his death. My mother continued to have four servants, a beautiful home in Washington, and another one in the north woods of Wisconsin. She traveled whenever and wherever she wished. This was all provided by my father. Marjorie wanted to give him the *Sea Cloud* and all of her vast Texas oil lands, but he refused to accept them.

My mother and stepmother were very different in personality and temperament. But they shared character traits of integrity, dignity, and independence that would allow neither of them ever to embarrass themselves or their families. Those characteristics were the qualities that made me love and admire them both.

Marjorie's sense of humor, unlike my mother's, easily embraced the ribald. One rather indecorous story she loved to relate involved an experience she had as a young woman, newly married, at a stiff and formal dinner party in one of New York City's stately mansions. The guest of honor, a distinguished foreign ambassador, sat beside her during an afterdinner concert of chamber music in the grand ballroom. Among the guests seated on small gilt chairs placed around the room opposite them was an obese dowager wearing a very short skirt, her fat knees spread wide apart on the tiny chair, exposing a vast expanse of "flesh and fur," to quote Marjorie.

"The musicians were playing 'Pilly, Willy, Wink,' " she said, "when the ambassador leaned over to me, his starched shirtfront going 'creak, creak, creak,' in competition with the music. Staring across at the dowager, he said to me in a perfectly audible stage whisper: 'Me-thinks I see the Arc de Triomphe in the distance!' He sat back in his chair, his shirt still creaking as loudly as ever, only to study the view again and creak back to me a second time. This time it seemed to me that everyone in the ballroom must hear him. 'They tell me the unknown soldier is buried there,' he said."

When Marjorie and my father were in Washington, their presence was hard for Mother. She and Marjorie never met, but my mother knew that her daughters were friendly with their stepmother. This must have been painful for her, but she kept her dignified reserve and never complained. She told us that she was pleased at Marjorie's generosity to us. Marjorie, for her part, told me firmly that if there was ever a question for me of taking sides "I must side with my mother, since Marjorie and my father had each other. Both my mother and stepmother were remarkable in that each tried hard to be considerate of the other and were genuinely sympathetic and thoughtful where my sisters and I were concerned. Marjorie told me she was certain that if my father had not fallen in love with her, he would have with some other woman. But I do not think this is so. Even today I think it was a matter of real love at first sight for both of them.

I was in a difficult position between my parents when all of us were living in Washington at the same time. Their divorce and my father's remarriage to one of the world's wealthiest women was the talk of the town. My mother was loved and widely respected, and although my father was popular, he was condemned by many for divorcing my mother and marrying Marjorie Hutton. Mother's closest women friends were the well-bred and cultured ladies of top drawer Washington society. The eminent dowagers of Washington's elite never accepted Marjorie.

My stepmother had very few friends when she arrived in Washington in 1935 as the second wife of Joe Davies—who, as a friend of both Republican and Democratic presidents and founder of a prestigious Washington law firm, was an influential and popular figure. She depended upon me to draw up the guest lists for her parties.

Official Washington and my father's friends, of course, took her to their bosoms at once. But she needed my advice and support—and the support of Millard's and my friendship to make her way through what was initially a social minefield. It would have been an impossible situation for me had it not been for Mother's loyal support. She defended me stoutly to her friends, and to my enemies. To keep a balance—to ensure my mother's feelings and social position were not hurt—whenever Millard and I gave a party for the Davies, we always hosted a duplicate affair for Mother. Inasmuch as Millard and I had limited means, this was hard on our pocketbooks. Our major yearly entertainments were the two big luncheons we gave in early May at Oakington for the senators and their wives. We would give one or two small dinners in Washington and Mother would attend one, my father and Marjorie the other.

My sisters and I alternated Christmas and other holiday visits between our parents and the Davies, whether in New York, Palm Beach, or Washington.

Both Mother and Marjorie were extraordinarily generous women. My mother denied herself during the Depression to give her children money. She was an expert needlewoman and made exquisite clothes for us when we were little, and later for her granddaughters. She started our hope chests almost as soon as we were born, and collected linens and flat silver for us over the years. She was a member of St. John's Episcopal Church on Lafayette Square and was extremely generous and thoughtful of the needs of her church and charities.

In Marjorie's employ was an elderly widow who had lost her husband and her fortune. Marjorie employed her to purchase gifts for Marjorie to give away. Each of us six daughters and daughters-in-law would be asked to make a list of our needs and desires, and those of our children, some months before Christmas and birthdays.

Marjorie herself would give us a list of not-too-expensive gifts she wanted, which she knew were within our means. Each year she also gave me and my sisters Christmas gifts of credits for clothes. Also most fortunately for me, Marjorie and I were almost exactly the same height, weight, and size. It was as if I had a genuine fairy godmother. She would lavish on me many of her magnificent silk and beaded gowns, evening cloaks of velvet or satin, ensembles, furs, items she seldom wore more than a few times, as well as new yearly clothes. I always had possessed many pretty clothes, but never had I enjoyed a wardrobe like this. I told her so frequently, both in person and in letters. My father and mother had taught us that one can never thank enough.

It was not strange that I became fond of Marjorie, and I know she returned my affection, for we enjoyed each other's company and were together often when she was in Washington. We shared a keen sense of humor, both of us liked to give and attend parties, we loved to dance, and we loved Joe Davies. After a big affair when Millard and I would stay with Marjorie and my father, she would invite us to join them before going to bed to "hash the party," as she put it. She said we could "take the guests apart and not bother to put them back together again!" We were very close friends for twenty years, but when she divorced my ill and dying father, we neither saw nor spoke to each other until Millard Tydings died.

Chapter 13

A Tale of Two Weddings, December 1935

Millard Tydings was perfection as far as I was concerned. Yet, I discovered that he was human like everyone else. He had been pursued as an attractive, eligible bachelor for many years by ladies both married and single, and he had not known me long enough to be completely sure of me. He resented any man's attention to me and was suspicious of my smiles. As he did not understand me, so I did not understand this in him. When I returned from Reno that fall, we had decided to wait until spring for our wedding. The newspaper gossip columns were a problem for us. Also, the terminal illness of Millard's mother in Havre de Grace necessitated his return there every weekend, and my friends in Washington expected me to attend their parties. There was no excuse for me not to do so unless we were formally engaged, so he agreed that I was to go to these evening affairs without him.

One evening when he was in Havre de Grace, I went to a dinner party and played cards until half after eleven. When I got home, Mother said that Millard had been telephoning me since ten o'clock and was very cross with me for staying out so late. I had been married for nine years to a man who was not at all concerned about other men's attentions to his wife. In fact, he took them as a compliment to himself. I didn't realize the great difference between Tom Cheesborough and Millard Tydings in this respect. Tom understood how naive I was where men's attentions were concerned. I did not court them. I didn't realize that my natural gaiety might be misinterpreted by the opposite sex as a come on. Millard Tydings had not

80

known me long enough to understand this or for me to understand him.

Once that fall I made the mistake of telling Millard about the verbal passes of a prominent man-about-town at a dinner party and my handling of the gentleman. I thought I was being amusing and that my behavior was exemplary. The Senator did not agree at all and was furious over this episode and very angry with me. He considered that this gentleman's suggestion that I dine with him in his apartment alone was an insult to me. Of course, I had refused to go and it was only part of a humorous, witty conversation. I finally smoothed the senatorial feathers and decided that if I loved and wanted to marry him, it had better be before any more such episodes. We announced our engagement and planned our wedding date for December 27, 1935. We wanted the ceremony to be a small, quiet affair with only our immediate families and a few close friends present. It would be at Mother's house on Massachusetts Avenue and there would be a supper party there after the ceremony. Although both Millard and I were Episcopalians, our church would not officiate because I was a divorcee, but the rector of the National Presbyterian Church, the Reverend McCartney, agreed to marry us. The Reverend and the guests were sworn to secrecy as to the date. The press were mostly friendly and complimentary. My photograph was prominently displayed with exaggerated praise, and Millard was described in glowing terms as a brilliant senator and possible presidential nominee. He "would be acquiring a wife who will become a beautiful First Lady of the Land." "Millard," said the Washington paper, "was the U.S. Senate's most eligible bachelor," and I was "the infinitely lovely Eleanor Davies Cheesborough," etc., etc. Then when my father's marriage to Marjorie Post Hutton was announced to be on December fifteenth, my relationship to Daddy brought forth a noisy outpouring from the press.

The newspapers and the radio were full of the Davies-Hutton wedding. It would be in Marjorie's apartment in New York City, which occupied three floors on top of the Fifth Avenue building. The wedding ceremony and reception took place in rooms full of masses of pink chrysanthemums. Marjorie's younger daughter, Deenie (Nedenia Hutton), and granddaughter, "Mahwee" (Marjorie Durant) were her bridal attendants. All three wore long, pink gowns. Marjorie's dress was pink velvet trimmed with much white fox fur. The wedding cake was five feet high. The publicity was awful, both before and after.

The afternoon of the Davieses' wedding there was a symphony concert at Constitution Hall and Mother had her usual box. She informed me that she was going to the concert and that Mrs. Woodrow Wilson, Mrs. William E. Borah, and I were to accompany her. I protested strenuously, but she was adamant. When Daddy heard about this, he was really angry. He had Mother in tears on the telephone that morning. I took the phone away from her and told him firmly that he was doing what he wanted to do that day, and he had no right to dictate to us what we should do. I was as mad as he was. He practically disinherited me then and there. Rahel was about to produce her baby daughter Suzanne, and the doctors were so concerned for her health that they would perform a Caesarean, so she had a good excuse to escape our father's wrath.

Millard was fond of my father and had gone to New York for the wedding, with a trainload of Daddy's Washington friends. I went to the concert with Mother, who seated me in the very front of the box. She sat in the back. It seemed to me that everyone in Washington was staring up at me and thinking about that wedding in New York. I certainly was!

To make matters worse, Rahel's sister-in-law, the beautiful Evie Walker, had telephoned me from New York early that afternoon and given me a mysterious warning about Millard. I must see and talk with her before I saw him, said she. We were not close friends, and I informed her coldly that I would not be able to do so, that I was meeting Millard when he arrived in Washington on the midnight train, and that he was going to spend the night at Mother's house. She protested but would not tell me why she must see me. So I was worried about my fiancé all that dreadful day and evening.

And well I might! When I met Millard that night, I could see at once that he was laboring under a great emotional strain and a pretty good load of alcohol. It was the first and only time I ever saw him under the influence of strong drink. He was extremely angry with me and said he would not go back to Mother's house with me but would go to a hotel. He said he never wanted to see me again. I had enough experience with handling an alcoholic and was wise enough to keep cool and tell him calmly that that was perfectly all right with me. I would be happy not to see him either. He was obviously exhausted and would be far more comfortable spending the night at Mother's house. He said nothing and we rode there in silence.

Once there, I brought him sandwiches and milk, and we sat down in the sun parlor and had it out. He raved and ranted against me. I was a light, frivolous woman who led men on, that I would not be a fit wife, etc., etc. I let him talk and finally asked him if he was finished. He was probably out of breath and certainly all blown out of steam by that time. Then I stood up and launched into my cold, angry rebuttal. If this was what he thought of me, I wouldn't marry him if he was the last man on earth.

I went to bed and cried most of the night. He doubtless passed out in the guest room. The next morning my sister Rahel, having heard my sad story, went down to breakfast and gave the Senator a tongue-lashing with his coffee.

"You wretched man, what have you done to my sister?" said she indignantly. "She is the finest person in the world and you have broken her heart!" or words to that effect.

The Senator was apparently chastened, whether because he was suffering from a hang-over or because he was ashamed of his conduct, or really regretful of both. At any rate, he requested permission to see me, and the whole matter was buried in loving embraces.

We were married twelve days later in the drawing room of my Mother's home in Washington. The city was covered with snow and the big white flakes were falling fast. The rector of the National Presbyterian Church, the Reverend Dr. Albert J. McCartney, officiated. The only people at the ceremony were the members of our families, and only close friends attended the wedding reception after it. These included:

Mr. and Mrs. Aldace Walker (sister Rahel); Mr. and Mrs. J.J. Pickett (Millard's sister); Colonel and Mrs. John Eager (Millard's sister); Senator and Mrs. George Radcliffe; The Honorable and Mrs. James Bruce; Mr. and Mrs. Demarest Lloyd; The Honorable Marvin McIntyre; Miss Margaret Woodrow Wilson and Mrs. Wilson; The Honorable Sam Rayburn; Senator and Mrs. William E. Borah; Admiral and Mrs. Cary Grayson; Colonel and Mrs. E. Brooke Lee; Mrs. Emlen Davies and Miss Emlen Davies; Mr. and Mrs. Harold Walker; Mr. and Mrs. Charles Bryan of Harford County, Maryland; Rep. and Mrs. William P. Cole Jr. of Maryland; Mrs. Gilbert Hitchcock, widow of Senator Hitchcock; Senator and Mrs. James J. Davis of Pennsylvania; Mr. and Mrs. Joseph Tumulty; Mrs. Connie Hull, later Lady Lewis; Mrs. Frances Rust; Mr. Moran McConihe; Mr. and Mrs. Donald Symington of Baltimore, Maryland.

Donald Symington was the uncle of the future Senator Stuart Symington and Millard's best man. Rahel was my only attendant. I wore a long gray velvet gown trimmed with matching fox and a big gray hat. After the reception, we drove through the ice and snow to Oakington. On the back of Millard's Packard, his office force had attached a huge "Just Married" sign. Of course, we didn't know it was there until every car on the road honked a salute at us. All Maryland knew the license number on his car.

Oakington House had been full of workmen ever since Millard signed the purchase papers in August. A new furnace had been installed, all outside trim painted, and the interior decorated throughout. Father's wedding gift was the interior decorating. Marjorie had contributed large, handsome rugs, etc. The house had been completely furnished when purchased, but many things disappeared from it while the workmen were there, and there were many things we didn't use. However, I had all the lovely furniture from my own ten-room house, and Millard had all his from his Georgetown residence. So Oakington House was very beautiful that cold night in December.

Robert Livingston and his wife, Nadine, had already installed themselves and their little boy in the apartment on the third floor, and they greeted us warmly at the door. Millard asked Bob Livingston to "bring in Mrs. Cheesborough's bags!" Bob grinned and said, "You mean Mrs. Tydings's bags, don't you, senator?", and I walked in the door. Millard had wanted to carry me across the threshold and rushed to pick me up and carry me, kicking and protesting all the way up the long stairs to our beautiful big bedroom! Here the Livingstons had set a table with sandwiches and hot chocolate, etc., in front of the fireplace, but no fire had been lit. I suggested that it be done and a minute later clouds of smoke poured forth! The damper had been closed. My bridegroom picked me up again and put me out of the room into the hall, closing the door behind me! I never ceased to tease him about throwing me out of our bedroom on our wedding night.

Incidentally, I never did find out what had made him so angry at me the night of my father's wedding day! By this time he was no longer angry with me. Nor was I any longer disinherited by Daddy! Once again I was reinstated as the "son-daughter" who was the apple of his eye. This was due in no small measure, I knew, to my stepmother's efforts at reconciliation. Also, he was so blissfully in love and happy with her that he could no longer stay mad at anybody. They telephoned us from the yacht in Florida waters the day after our wedding and sent flowers and congratulatory cables. They wanted us to join them at once for a cruise on the *Sea Cloud*, and we accepted their invitation. After an idyllic week at Oakington, we went to Florida and joined them for a Caribbean cruise.

The *Sea Cloud* was a four-masted auxiliary yacht. Inside, it was a luxurious private home with eight master bedrooms and baths; a grand piano, and wood-burning fireplace in the sitting room; a beautiful dining room; circular stair and quarters for at least sixty in crew. With her glorious sails unfurled, the yacht was a dream afloat! Two of their friends and Marjorie's little girl Deenie were on board. We all enjoyed one another and all was merry and bright until we arrived at Nassau. The British governor, Sir Bede Clifford, and his American wife came aboard for dinner and entertained us at Government House and for lunch and a swim at their beach cottage across the island. Unfortunately, the governor's good-looking young military aid was present, and although I hardly noticed him, my husband didn't like the way he looked at me, and I suffered a frigid treatment. While I was enduring Millard's chilly silence, the Governor and Lady Clifford insisted that we spend the night of the full moon at their beach cottage. I did not feel like going, but my husband accepted, and we were driven over and served a gourmet dinner there with wines. My husband was beginning to thaw out when I made the mistake of remarking how pleased I had been when the Congress passed the bill for women's suffrage, and I could vote. To my horror, my lover froze again and informed me that he had voted against it! I was speechless and horrified, and told him so! We argued until I suggested we go for a swim and cool off! We swam, but did not cool off. In silence we retired to a big bed, which was divided into two parts. My husband took the higher ground, and I was left to hang on to my side to keep from sliding off onto the floor! The top sheet boasted a magnificent thirty-inch deep border of handmade lace with the arms of Great Britain on it. I thought it would be nice if it could be exchanged for a good bedspring all in one piece. We hadn't been in bed long (still in icy silence) when I noticed that I had a growing number of insect bites. I also noticed that the occupant of the upper half of the bed was scratching too! Sand fleas!

"Is anything biting you, Millard?" I asked.

"Yes, the same thing that's biting you!" came the reply. I giggled and we laughed together. I slid off my side onto the floor and my husband picked me up and placed me on his side of the bed. We dissolved in laughter in each other's arms. A sense of humor is a real necessity in human relationships! Lady Clifford said that the Duke and Duchess of Kent had spent a night of the full moon at their beach house, and I have always thought the Duchess and I had quite a lot in common, if only that awful bed!

Millard received word after a week on the *Sea Cloud* that his mother was very ill, and we went home for a few days, and then moved in to Washington with the children to stay with my Mother for the Congressional session. Millard loved my mother, but never became as fond of my new stepmother as I did.

Ella Clarke Knight of Wilmington, Delaware, wife of John H. Knight.

Colonel John Henry Knight, Union Army, Civil War, of Dover, Delaware, and Cecil and Kent Counties, Maryland.

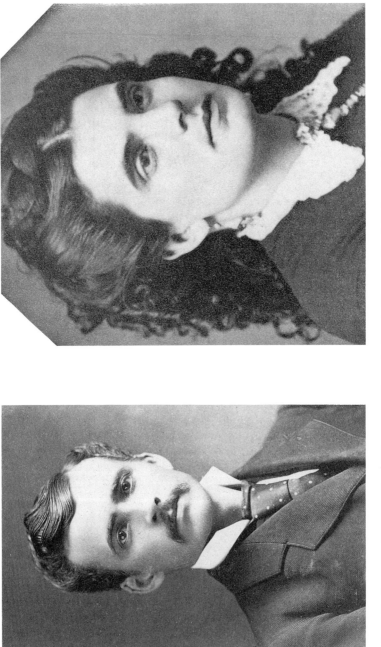

Edward Davies, covered wagon maker of Watertown, Wisconsin, born in Tregaron, North Wales, married Rahel Paynter Davies from Anglesey, North Wales.

Joseph E. Davies, born 1876, graduate of University of Wisconsin, at law school, age 24. Son of Edward and Rahel Davies. Lawyer, Ambassador, friend and advisor to Presidents Wilson, Franklin Roosevelt and Truman.

Emlen Knight Davies, born 1878, first wife of Joseph E. Davies, divorced 1935. Daughter of Colonel and Mrs. John Knight.

Eleanor Davies of Washington D.C. and Maryland. Born in Wisconsin, 1904, daughter of Joseph and Emlen Davies.

Eleanor in 1906, with Emlen K. Davies and Ella Clarke Knight, her mother and maternal grandmother.

Eleanor Davies posing in a daring bathing suit, 1919.

Eleanor carries the Daisy Chain at Vassar.

BEAUTY LEADS DAISY CHAIN at Vassar college commencement. This year the honor fell to Miss Eleanor Davies. She is the daughter of Mr. and Mrs. Joseph E. Davies of Washington, and is considered one of the most beautiful girls in the younger set at the national capital. *1922*

(Photograph copyright by Harris & Ewing.)

Eleanor Davies, Washington debutante, Christmas, 1923.

Eleanor Davies, debutante, 1921. Photograph by *Underwood & Underwood Studios,* Washington, D.C.

Eleanor's beaux taking her for a ride to a New Year's Day party. Photograph by *Underwood & Underwood Studios*, Washington, D.C.

Eleanor meets the Cheesborough brothers in Asheville, North Carolina, 1924. Left to right: Jack Cheesborough, Eleanor, and Tom Cheesborough.

The Armistice Day wedding of Eleanor and Thomas Patton Cheesborough Jr. in Washington D.C., November 11, 1926, St. Johns Church. Photograph by *Underwood & Underwood Studios,* Washington, D.C.

Eleanor Davies Cheesborough, July 2, 1926.

Eleanor divorces Tom Cheesborough and marries Senator Millard E. Tydings of Maryland, 1935.

Colonel Millard Tydings at Verdun, France, World War I, 1918.

Chapter 14

Senate Bride in Washington—My Political Education, 1936

It seemed to me that the gods on Olympus had showered all their gifts upon me then and for many years to come. My grandmother's golden spoon was really working. We enjoyed good health, a beautiful home, and two lovely children. We had the love of family and friends and, best of all, of each other. There was plenty of room for our planned-for (and prayed for) "little Tydings" at Oakington, and I longed for at least one small replica of Millard. I know he wished for it too, although he never mentioned our failure to produce a baby. It was the gift the gods withheld.

It was great fun being the "bride and beauty" of the Senate, to quote the news media! There wasn't much competition among the Senate wives at that time for either title! They were all a great deal older than I. A few years later that would not be the case.

In those days, wives of newly elected congressmen and senators were expected to pay "duty calls" upon the wives of the president, vice president, Supreme Court, the Cabinet and ambassadors. Protocol required that you call upon the wives of Senate committee chairmen also. You didn't actually go in and see them, you just left cards. Mother and I did this together in her limousine. We also received together at official "at-homes" at Mother's Massachusetts Avenue house. These teas were not absolutely necessary, but if one chose to, each weekday was designated for either the Cabinet, the Court, the diplomatic wives, the Senate or the House wives. We served tea, coffee, sandwiches, and cakes—never any alcoholic beverages! The society columns would announce that Mrs. Tydings was receiving on Thursday afternoons in January or February and ladies from Washington and nearby Maryland would come, whether they knew you or not. Sometimes unwelcome strangers appeared, so we would try to engage the services of a wise old doorman who could "tell the sheep from the goats" and who would politely turn away the undesirables. Some of these were quite famous freeloaders who carried big shopping bags in which they would stow away almost enough food to last until the next "at-home! Mother enjoyed my Thursdays and the dinner parties we gave in her big dining room. Daddy and Marjorie were on the *Sea Cloud* all winter. Their absence was a boon to Mother, and she enjoyed my position as Millard's wife, as well as our company in her home.

I soon became acquainted with Washington's strict official protocol. It wasn't long before I saw the reason for it. Senators and ambassadors, Cabinet ministers, justices, generals, or admirals, or their wives might (and sometimes did) actually refuse to sit down at a dinner party where they were not properly placed according to their rank! One had to be careful not to have the vice president and the chief justice or an ambassador at the same seated table. An ambassador ranks according to the length of time he has served in our country, a senator according to his length of service as such. The State Department ruled on all social precedence. Because of Millard's seniority (length of time in the Senate), I outranked most of the senate wives, most of whom were old enough to be my mother!

As the Senate's youngest couple, we were wined and dined and overly publicized. The press was continually writing about us and also about my father and his new wife. I enjoyed the parties but not the newspaper notoriety.

One of the first official functions we attended upon our return was an affair at the White House. President Roosevelt received the guests, standing tall and handsome with two big sons supporting him on each side. He greeted us enthusiastically, embracing me and kissing my cheek.

"Well, Millard, it's about time you brought this child to see her Uncle Frank!" he said, embracing me and clapping my husband on the back. I had admired the president in the past and I had listened to my father's description of his old friend—how he had conquered the dread infantile paralysis, had been elected governor of New York State, and then president of the United States. I found him charming that evening and looked forward to becoming as much en famille in the Roosevelt White House as I had been long ago in the Wilson's. I was to be disappointed in this, as FDR became my husband's bitter political enemy, and after that we never darkened the door of President Roosevelt's White House functions.

As the Senate bride and groom, many parties were given in our honor, both official and unofficial, in Washington. In Maryland, the parties for us were social and political. We were much in love and preferred to be alone, so we attended only the most important functions. We were photographed and talked about wherever we went, which soon ceased to be amusing. We escaped to Oakington on most weekends, taking the children with us. Millard loved them and they returned his affection. In Washington, he would try to come home early from the Capitol, and on most days I lunched there with him in the Senate dining room. Our table was the center of attention and Millard's colleagues flocked to meet his bride. I was the recipient of many courtly bows and even hand-kissing from the southern senators such as Walter George of Georgia, Carter Glass of Virginia, and Cotton Ed Smith of South Carolina. All of them sang my husband's praises to me and I was the proudest and happiest wife in the land.

I was introduced to the Senate Ladies Club as soon as we arrived back in town. It had been started in the World War, and the Senate Ladies had been meeting in the Senate Office Building every Tuesday ever since to work for the Red Cross. There was only one Senate Office Building at that time. We wore white uniforms and nurses' caps and badges for the number of hours we worked making bandages and knitting. The vice president's wife is automatically president of the Senate Ladies. When there is no vice president, as was the case when President Roosevelt died and Harry Truman became president, our chairman was the wife of the president of the Senate, Mrs. Arthur Vandenberg. I was voted acting chairman when poor Hazel Vandenberg was stricken with cancer.

In 1936, committees of ladies were in charge of providing lunch for all of us. (We met at 9:30 A.M. and worked until mid-afternoon.)

When Congress convened, the Senate Ladies gave a luncheon at the Capitol in honor of the president's wife and the Cabinet wives. These have become very fine affairs with palms, flowers, music, and speeches and, oftentimes, gifts for the First Lady. In return, the president's wife and the Cabinet wives give a luncheon party for the Senate wives at the White House—splendid affairs with the Marine Band and entertainers! We all enjoyed these functions.

I knew many First Ladies. After the two Mrs. Wilsons, I met Mrs. Warren Harding (a friend of Mother's), and then skipped Mrs. Coolidge. I do not recall Mrs. Roosevelt at our Senate Ladies Red Cross meetings. She was probably too busy with all her other good works. She did, however, entertain the Senate wives at the White House for lunch. I remember asking her how she managed to accomplish all she did, traveling and speaking all over the country. She laughed and said in that inimitable voice of hers, "Why, I guess it is because I can close my eyes and sleep anywhere I happen to be between engagements." She was a remarkable woman. I think she would have been pretty if they had put braces on her teeth when she was a child. I always thought her automobile accident helped her looks. Perhaps her own teeth were replaced.

Of course, all of us turned out in our best clothes for the White House luncheon parties. (We all wore our Red Cross uniforms at our party at the Capitol but not at the White House.) When Mamie Eisenhower was First Lady, I had purchased a very snappy, white dress for her luncheon. The young military aide who came up to escort me into the Blue Room looked at me in horror. In stricken tones he said, "Mrs. Tydings, you are wearing the same dress as the president's wife!" It sounded as though he was ordering me to leave at once.

"Well, young man, what do you want me to do, go home or take it off?" Whereupon I sailed past him to be greeted enthusiastically by Mamie Eisenhower. "How wonderful, Eleanor, now we are twins!"

I did not look at the lieutenant. I hope that he had the grace to blush!

After a few years of making things for the Red Cross, it seemed to me that we might well be learning a foreign language at our Senate Ladies Club sessions while we worked. As I could speak French, I started the Senate Ladies Spanish Class. After 1950 it became the White House Spanish Class and then petered out completely. It was great fun while it lasted, however. Bess Truman and Lady Bird Johnson were two of the Senate Ladies whom I knew and liked who became First Ladies of our Land. I remember Bess working away silently at a sewing machine in a corner at our Red Cross meetings. Little "Miss Lucy" George, Martha Taft, and I told not-too-risque stories and kept the group laughing. After Millard left the Senate in 1950, I didn't go back to the meetings. That door was closed. But I still go to the Senate Ladies' yearly luncheon for the First Lady and hers for them. Why not? After all, "Once a Senate Lady, always a Senate Lady!" I have been going to them for forty years!

Millard and I were entertained at dinners by senators, members of the Cabinet and the Supreme Court and the diplomatic corps as well as by our unofficial friends. Among our good friends, the Ambassador of the Netherlands and his wife, Nini de Withe, were notable. She was beautiful. I knew my husband admired her very much, but to my surprise he would not dance with her. One evening when he could not avoid it, I discovered the reason why. The lovely Nini was enamored of my senator! She snuggled as close as she could and nibbled his ears. The poor man blushed scarlet when he saw that I was watching with an amused smile as I danced by. I promptly invited the De Withes to Oakington for the weekend and Nini and I became good friends. She had the opportunity there to observe our devotion to each other and there was no more ear nibbling! The ambassador was definitely not the type to ever invite anything like that. He was a typical short, stout, stodgy Dutchman, not very attractive looking.

On the other hand, the British ambassador, Sir Ronald Lindsay, was a perfect example of a distinguished handsome Englishman, about six and a half feet tall. We soon discovered we had a mutual taste for E. Phillips Oppenheim's spy stories. I confessed to a great desire to come gliding in the side door of the embassy disguised in long flowing purple veils to steal the state papers. Sir Ronald said he'd be delighted to let me in and be a collaborator! Before I had met Millard, he and Lady Lindsay went to a fancy dress party in Washington; Millard dressed as an organ grinder and Lady Lindsay as the monkey. As I considered her a dignified "older person," I would have loved to have seen that!

There were other famous beauties in the diplomatic corps at that time. One was my friend "Mitzi" Sims, the lovely wife of a Canadian attache at the British Embassy. Mitzi's nationality was in some doubt, but she was said to be Danish and was a popular person in Belgium before she married Harold Sims. She was a warm, charming person, and I liked her very much.

A good friend of ours, Republican Senator Arthur Vandenberg of Michigan, apparently fell in love with her when we were all living in Wardman Park Hotel apartments during World War II. Mitzi and Arthur would walk to the Capitol every morning and lunch together in the Senate private dining room. Drew Pearson, with characteristic meanness, referred to the Senator in his column as "the Senator from Mitzigan." I liked Arthur's wife, Hazel, and felt sorry for her, but the affair fizzled out in the winds of war and Mitzi returned to Canada.

Then there was Rose Nano, the beautiful wife of a Romanian diplomat. Millard told me that once during his bachelor years, he had had occasion to escort her to a dinner party. Arriving at her home, he was directed upstairs by a maid and Rose's directions, only to find himself at the door of a large and luxurious bathroom. The lady was reclining in the tub! He told me that he had quickly "bowed himself out"! I found that hard to believe, but didn't say so.

Among other capital beauties besides the diplomatic ones were my lovely younger sister, Rahel, and her sister-in-law, Evie Walker, who had married Laurence "Chip" Wood Roberts, the assistant secretary of the Treasury. He was much older than she was. Frances Pearson Rust, a beautiful Chicago girl, who was my best friend at Vassar and a very lovely person, had married a Washington bachelor named Gwinn Rust. The marriage didn't last long, she remained very popular in Washington. Frances Rust died in 1992. Senator Gore's daughter, Nina, was at that time the wife of Hugh Auchincloss, a wealthy socialite. She was a stunningly beautiful girl, as was Evie Wadsworth Symington, daughter of Senator James J. Wadsworth of New York. Her husband, Stuart, was a nephew of our best man, Donald Symington. Evie and I had been friends and schoolmates at Holton-Arms. Evie was a wonderful person and loved by her many friends.

The Norwegian ambassador, William de Munthe de Morgensteros, and his pretty Canadian wife, Marjorie, the Chilean Ambassador, Felipo Espil, and his American wife, Courtney Letts, and the Austrian minister and Gretchen Prochnik were all good friends of ours. The Hungarian envoy, Count Szechenjy, and his wife, Gladys Vanderbilt, lived next door to my mother's house and the Sumner Welleses lived a few blocks away in her parents' beautiful mansion (now the Cosmos Club). We were all good friends except for the Sumner Welleses. They gave a formal dinner in our honor, and I sat on his right. He was such a cold, stiff stick of a man that I wished for a pin to stick in him to see if he was human!

None of these gentlemen gave my husband cause for distrust, but many younger men-about-town did. Washington was glamorous, but also dangerous for me. Millard's jealousy put unexpected obstacles in my path, which were often difficult to avoid or to overcome. If a gentleman paid much attention to or stared at me too long at a party, my husband blamed me and was angry with me. There were times when I felt like regretting all invitations to Washington parties. One of these was after a dinner we attended at the Polish embassy. Apparently a young attache stared at me during dinner too much to suit my husband. I hadn't even noticed the man. He was seated "below the salt," far down the table from where I sat on the host's right. After dinner this young gentleman came and escorted me to the drawing room where the ladies were having after-dinner coffee. He offered to bring me some, but I smiled and said I didn't drink it. Suddenly Millard appeared, seizing my arm, and glaring at the Pole. "I am quite capable of looking after my wife's needs, sir! Come, Eleanor, we are going home!" I was too amazed to do anything but murmur a few words about saying goodnight to our hosts, which my husband ignored, propelling me toward the grand staircase. The young attache apparently did not get the message and accompanied us on the other side of me. At the head of the stairs he offered me his arm, but I bade him a polite good night and slipping from Millard's grasp, I flew down to the front door. For a frightened minute I had been afraid that my husband might throw the Pole down the stairs, he looked so angry.

After that, I regretted Washington dinner invitations for some time. Eventually I learned the reasons for what I thought unreasonable behavior on my husband's part. It was probably due to the attentions and propositions he had received from married Washington women as a most eligible and desirable bachelor. As his wife, I did my best to live up to his Victorian concepts of behavior. I was more successful in Maryland. The greatest gift I brought Millard, besides my love for him, was a capacity to communicate with people from all walks of life. I liked most people and they apparently liked me. I spoke the universal language of friendliness.

My introduction to Baltimore and large numbers of Marylanders took place when we attended four Presidents' Birthday Balls in one evening! There were big crowds at all of them and our arrival must have been anticipated and was royally celebrated. Apparently all the world loves a lover! The minute we stepped into the ballroom, the orchestras would play "Here Comes the Bride," and everyone stood back to form an aisle for us to walk through to the podium. Millard spoke a few appropriate words and introduced me formally and delightfully. He looked handsome and distinguished in white tie and tails and wearing his war decorations. Everyone laughed when he said we appreciated all the well wishes, but he didn't understand "all the fuss over our marriage because, after all, people are getting married all the time!"

There were many such political banquets in Baltimore that winter when Millard was the speaker and I was often the only lady at the head table and being toasted and complimented.

Life became even busier when we moved our little family out to
Oakington in early April. Our social life in Maryland became as fast
and furious as it had been in Washington and we were still commuting to the city as Congress remained in session. The "Soak the Rich"
tax bill was debated until it finally passed in June. Millard had voted
against it. He was very pleased when the Supreme Court voted it
down as unconstitutional along with two of the bills he had voted
against—the NRA and AAA. The President was furious at the court's
actions, 1936 was election year for him. Millard's election did not
come up until 1938.

We were kept in a whirl, attending social and political affairs in
Maryland, most of which were given in our honor. Among the latter
were the Independent Retail dealers and the Retail Druggists. There
were large foreign groups in Baltimore as in all big port cities: the
Italian American Society, the Polish American, the Greek American,
German American, and Jewish societies, not to mention all the Democratic Clubs in Baltimore and the counties.

That winter we went to them all. An important group was the
United Democratic Women's Clubs of Maryland. This was composed
of women's democratic clubs from every part of the state. The
U.D.W.C. gave a big dinner and ball in my honor at the Lord Baltimore Hotel in Baltimore. They asked what color gown I would wear,
and when I told them blue, they composed and sang a song to the
"Beautiful Lady in Blue" when we arrived. I loved it and them. In
later years, some of them wanted me to be president of their organization and also asked me to be Democratic National Committeewoman from Maryland, but I declined the honors. I felt one member
of a family in public life was enough and I knew Millard would prefer it so. Also, I knew that if I ever accepted such an important office,
I would make some enemies and that would hurt his candidacy.

What might have been one of my life's most embarrassing moments came at Governor Ritchie's funeral. There would be great
crowds of people at the church, so we borrowed Mother's car and
chauffeur to take us to Baltimore. The church was packed and we
had difficulty squeezing our way into a reserved pew. We were no
sooner pushing into our seats than I felt my underwear sliding
downward. It was embroidered pink satin with handmade lace, part
of a trousseau of exquisite lingerie that my stepmother had ordered
made for me in Paris. This quite spectacular garment would have
created quite a sensation if aired in public that day on the church
steps. I could see the headlines: "Senator's Bride Loses Pink Panties
at Governor's Funeral!"

I whispered frantically to Millard, "My panties are coming off. Is there someplace I can go and hide to remove them?"

My husband grinned at me. "Of course not! You can't even get out of this pew. Can't you just hold them on?"

"They're too far gone! I can't!" I whispered back.

"Well, you'll just have to try!" was the unhelpful reply.

Fortunately I was wearing a black, fur-trimmed suit with a matching hat and a long military cape. I clutched the offending garment through my skirt, hands hidden by the cape as we walked out. I prayed, and we made it, out onto the wide steps where the newsmen and their cameras were waiting for us. I made it down the steps and into our car. As we stepped in, the wretched pants dropped 'round my ankles, blessedly unseen by the public. The chauffeur drove off and nobody saw my lovely lingerie, except my husband, who had seen them before. He smiled at me and suggested that I should check such items of apparel in the future so that they might not leave me at the wrong moment in public. I took his advice and they never did. I will never forget Governor Ritchie's funeral.

I enjoyed the political affairs in Maryland. My husband's popularity and my friendliness seemed to be a passport everywhere, and we began to hear good reports of my popularity. When my husband made speeches, I listened enthralled and learned a lot about our government and economy.

At a luncheon in Baltimore, I sat beside the Most Reverend Archbishop Curley of Maryland. The state had always had many Catholics, and their church was much opposed to divorce. Millard had endangered his career when he married me, a divorcee.

The Archbishop was a kindly man and soon had me telling him all about myself and my divorce. After that, we heard that His Reverence had passed the word along to the priests and members of his diocese that Mrs. Tydings was a good woman, and her divorce was a proper one, according to the tenets of her Protestant Church. This fine man's friendship was of great political value to my husband and helped him to be reelected twice more by the people of Maryland.

When we moved the children, the nurse, and ourselves to Oakington, the daffodils bloomed everywhere and the pink tulip magnolias were in their full glory. Millard was relieved to be close to his mother, who was obviously failing fast. He tried to be with her as much as possible. I grieved with him, especially because I had never known her. She must have been a wonderful person to have been so beloved by her son.

April marked the beginning of the height of the Maryland "social season." The great Maryland Hunt Cup steeplechase race was the signal for many beautiful luncheons, cocktail parties, dinners, and the final event, the Hunt Ball. Of course, we were guests of honor at many of them, guests of the great names of the state: the McIntoshes, Bruces, Brewsters, Fenwicks, Jenkens, and Symingtons, to name a few. It was all new to me and great fun. The race cross-country over its high hurdles was very exciting. Of course, I had a marvelous time at the ball, dancing with new and old friends. Among the latter was my old beau, Tim Durant, who was being divorced by Marjorie's daughter, Adelaide. "At last we're related, Eleanor," he said with a grin. "Oh, no!" I retorted, "you are being divorced from our family!" I was having too good a time to notice that my husband was not. The next day was my birthday and, according to my diary, it "began badly, but ended happily!" No wonder. Millard's mother died May 1. He must have been very sad and apprehensive while I was having such a gay time. I did my best to make it up to him.

Life had to go on and it was necessary for us to appear at Maryland's second great event, the Preakness race at Pimlico on May 16. Again we cheered the winner and went to the parties. One of my favorite Baltimoreans was old Mrs. Spalding Lowe Jenkins, who gave a big dinner party for us and entertained us at lunch in the Pimlico Club House and in her box every year at the famous Preakness. There are five great occasions for Maryland society. Five are not the only ones, but it seemed to me they overshadowed all the rest. There was the Maryland Hunt Ball, the Bachelors' Ball for the debutantes, the Preakness (flat race), the International Race at Laurel, and the Maryland Hunt Cup (steeplechase). Many parties were given before and after all of these, and I enjoyed them all. I remember Mrs. Jenkins's dinners. She always had a darling little boy to open the front door, dressed in the satin costume of an Indian raja with a plumed turban with paradise feathers!

In May, Oakington was gorgeous with masses of peonies and azaleas, tulips, etc. We had our first big luncheon there for the senators and their wives. The guests had their choice of two Sundays, and we usually had about forty or fifty at each. They were seated at tables on the lawn overlooking the bay, and Baltimore caterers handled everything. My mother and sisters and Millard's sisters were always invited.

Mother and Great-Aunt Elizabeth Kettle Clark visited us that May. Aunt Bess was ninety years old and as bright and perky as a plump little robin. "To think, my dear, that you have returned to the land of your ancestors," she said many times. She was delighted over my marriage to a senator from Maryland and still more pleased with Millard's charm and the beauty of Oakington. "It is nice that he is so handsome too!" said she.

That first spring of 1936, I discovered that there was no Women's Democratic Club in our home county of Harford, and it seemed to me a good time, in a presidential election year, to organize one. This I did with the help of Millard's lifelong friend and law partner, Colonel Robert Archer of Bel Air. He provided a list of names and phone numbers, and I sat at the telephone for hours on end, inviting the Harford County ladies for tea and to organize a Women's Democratic Club. These conversations went something like this:

Me: Hello! Mrs. Jones? This is Eleanor Tydings, Millard's wife. I want to invite—
She: Who did you say?
Me: I am Millard Tydings's wife. I want to invite you—
She: Oh, are you? What do you want?
Me: I want to invite you to Oakington.
She: Where did you say?
Me: Oakington Farm, near Havre de Grace.
She: Oh, yes, you are Millard's new wife!
Me: Can you come to tea on June 30 at our house? I thought we might organize a little democratic club.
She: What did you say? When is it?
Me: (Desperately) June 30th at three o'clock. I hope you can come.
She: Well, I don't know. I'll have to see.
Me: I hope you can come!

All the conversations went like that, but it was worth it. More than 100 ladies showed up, mostly out of curiosity, I think, and the Harford County Women's Democratic Club was born. It became the largest in the state. I never accepted any office in it, except that of assistant chairman of the Program Committee. My husband selected the speakers they heard.

I next made bold to suggest to my husband that we give a huge Democratic rally at Oakington and invite all the lady Democrats in the state. This was ostensibly to help President Roosevelt's campaign for reelection in November, but actually to get further support for Millard's reelection to the Senate in 1938. My husband approved this idea, and the invitations went out through the state Democratic

Clubs. As it turned out, we were going to need every supporter we could acquire in 1938. We set the date for the rally at Oakington for September 5.

The next thing of importance to me politically was an invitation to address the annual Rural Women's Short Course at the University of Maryland that year. I was about to turn it down when, to my great surprise, my husband told me to accept it!

Me: But, darling, I have never made a speech in my life. I can't do it!
MT: Nonsense. Of course you can! Do you want to write it yourself, or do you want me to?
Me: Yes—No—Look, I'm the girl who couldn't even stand up to recite in school!
MT: You told me you had the lead in that play at Vassar. Now, go ahead and write your speech and memorize it.
Me: Lordy, Millard, I couldn't do that!
MT: You can. Now go ahead and do it!

I did. I wrote a nice speech all about peace and the League of Nations (my thesis at Vassar) and practiced reciting it in front of mirrors for weeks. Robert Livingston caught me orating in front of the drawing room mirror and quickly withdrew. After that, I practiced in my room behind locked doors. The great day came, and to my horror, Millard announced that he was accompanying me. He had found out that the university had invited Miss Jeanette Rankin, a member of the House of Representatives, to speak also. I guess they weren't sure I would be able to make it. Old Miss Rankin was an out-and-out pacifist and had voted in Congress against our participation in World War One.

She spoke first and advised the women to write to their congressmen and senators, and tell their Maryland friends not to vote for any member of Congress who voted for military appropriations for our armed forces. She said we didn't need an army or navy, that the Boy Scouts could defend our shores! I was furious. My shyness vanished.

"Let me answer her," I said to Millard.

"No, stick to your speech, and then I'll take care of her," he said.

I managed mine without reading it, but I'm afraid I got the last part in the middle, and the middle part last, but I did not stumble once! Then Millard marched forward to the platform.

"You do not have to waste your time writing to me, ladies" he said. "I fought in the last World War, and so long as I have a vote in

Congress I will vote to keep our armed services prepared to defend us in the next war! All of you who agree with me, raise your hands!"

They all did.

After my speech at the University of Maryland, I was deluged with invitations to speak at all kinds of women's clubs throughout the State. Millard approved, so I went dashing about, wearing beautiful hats (for which I became famous) and telling them about being a Senate wife in Washington. I gave them lots of juicy bits of gossip about the inhabitants of that fair city, having lived there most of my life. But more important, I managed to tell them a great deal about their senator, Millard E. Tydings, and his achievements! I entertained many of these women's clubs at Oakington over the years. Every May we opened Oakington to the public for the Garden Club's House and Garden tours. All of this did no harm at election time, but I was never allowed to do any active campaigning for my husband at election time until the ill-fated campaign of 1950.

Two of the things I talked about to the Maryland ladies were the Senate Ladies' Red Cross and the great Wallis-Windsor romance with the King of England. They seemed to enjoy my talks and my hats!

At Oakington we were well served for twenty-five years by our friends, Robert and Nadine Livingston. He was born in Scotland and his wife in South Carolina. They both had worked at Pierre's, a popular restaurant of the Anchorage Apartments where Millard had shared an apartment with Speaker of the House Sam Rayburn. The Livingstons had a little boy, Johnny, who was younger than my little girl, and they wanted to live in the country. When they heard we had a country home, they asked to come with us. Nadine was a superb cook and dietitian and dear Bob was good at everything. I called him the Mayor of Oakington for he held the big house together, as Millard said, "with a prayer and a piece of string!" Nadine's sister, a sweet pretty girl, and Mrs. Cain, one of the farmer's wives, were housemaids. Local women came to do the laundry. Our budget for the house help and almost everything was about $1,000 a month!

Two couples in Harford County were Millard's closest friends. They were Sue and Charlie Bryan and Donald and Elsie Symington. I loved them all. The Symingtons both died in the 1940s. Sue died in 1952, and Charlie, the oldest, lived to be more than ninety. We saw a great deal of these four people, and they became as dear to me as they were to Millard.

Part III

Chapter 15

Democratic Presidential Campaign of 1936

In the midst of all the social and Congressional activities, the political pot had begun to boil. The year 1936 was election year and everyone knew that Roosevelt would run for reelection. What they didn't know was whether the conservative Democrats in Millard's Southern group would refuse to support him and bolt their party as Al Smith had done in January. The former governor of New York State and Democratic presidential candidate had announced that he had only two alternatives: "to be a d—n hypocrite or to take a walk!" He preferred to do the latter.

It seemed that not only the press but every voter in Maryland wanted to know whether Senator Tydings would support the president. He had opposed so much of Roosevelt's New Deal legislation, which the president had showered on Capitol Hill. The newspapers were full of the rebellion of Tydings and his conservative Democratic friends in the Senate against Roosevelt's unconstitutional measures and against the soaring national debt. They were not all Southerners. They were Peter Goelet Gerry of Rhode Island, Fred Van Nuys of Indiana, Dietrich of Illinois, Gore of Oklahoma, and Guy Gillette of Iowa, as well as Walter George of Georgia, Cotton Ed Smith of South Carolina, and Carter Glass and Harry Byrd of Virginia. They all believed in a balanced budget, a small federal government, states' rights, and the Constitution. However, all except Millard had come out for the president's reelection. Pressure was mounting upon my husband from advocates of both sides. There was a lot of Tydings-for-President talk from the conservatives and the business community, and threats and sneers from the New Dealers.

103

The Democratic National Committee named six Senators to the Resolutions Committee at the Democratic Convention—Millard and five of his "Irreconcilables." They all refused categorically. Millard decided that he should go to see the president and set matters straight. I knew that he told Mr. Roosevelt that he would support the Democratic ticket and all the Democratic nominees, but that he reserved the right to vote on all bills as his conscience dictated. Needless to say, the meeting was not a love fest! But the newspapers chose to make it so, most unfairly.

A *Baltimore Sun* columnist, Frank Kent, wrote a particularly scurrilous article saying that Tydings had knuckled under like a coward to the president and toadied to him, promising to vote for him and any and all bills he would send to the Senate. This appeared in the Sunday edition of Maryland's most powerful and prestigious paper. The Hearst *News Post* followed suit in an only slightly less virulent vein. We were lunching at Oakington when Millard read the Kent article. His face turned scarlet. I had never seen such controlled fury. He rose from the table and went to the telephone. I could hear his voice, cold as Arctic ice, giving Mr. Kent the tongue-lashing of his life for writing vicious lies based on nothing but mean, unsupported supposition.

"You, sir, are the liar and the coward, not the Senator from Maryland!" he told the columnist. "I faced enemy bullets on the battlefield for my country, which I never heard that you did! Furthermore, I went to face the president of the United States out of courtesy. I did not promise to support him, but only to campaign for the Democratic ticket. I also informed him that I would not vote for his legislation unless my conscience approved, which it has not always done in the past! This was not the act of a coward, Mr. Kent, but your words are those of a cowardly newspaperman who would rather lie about an honorable man than ascertain the facts. I expect you to print a full retraction in your column, sir, and if you do not, I shall certainly pay you a visit, which would not be a pleasant one for you!"

The Senator hung up the receiver and returned to his lunch. I complimented him upon his choice of words. I have never forgotten them.

"Do you think he'll print an apology?" I asked.

My husband laughed. "I rather think he will. He's not the kind of man whom you'll ever find out in front of the trenches looking for a fight!"

Millard was right. The newsman did.

Shortly after that, Millard addressed the Young Democrats of Maryland at a banquet in Baltimore and made a roaring speech, praising the Democratic party and urging all Maryland members to join him in doing all possible to support the Democratic candidates. Again there was no mention of the president but the senator received a standing ovation. So did I when he introduced me! I was the only lady at the speakers' table. It was an indication of the changing times that a woman would be seated there at all. Millard's speech was about the need to modify some of the recent emergency economic measures voted upon in Congress and the importance of paying more attention to local problems.

Still the pressure was upon my husband—stronger than ever. The Democratic Committee wanted him to deliver the seconding speech for Roosevelt's nomination at the Democratic Convention in Philadelphia at the end of June. Millard flatly refused at first, but after many meetings with such powerful leaders and friends as Jim Farley and Mr. Jesse Jones of Texas, he consented, provided, he said, "it would be only two minutes in duration and would be no eulogy!"

It was a sizzling hot summer in Maryland, but Oakington with its tall trees, green fields, and broad expanse of the Chesapeake along its shores was never unpleasant. We enjoyed swimming in the bay at the end of a long stone pier. There was a diving raft at the end and deep water, which was clear and clean in those days. Here we swam with the children and two large shaggy Chesapeake retrievers. These dogs had webbed feet and waterproof undercoats. They were great swimmers and were said to have rescued drowning children. Millard bought a thirty-foot Hacker speedboat and we acquired three riding horses. Marjorie gave my children a pony and a delightful "basket pony cart." Once Congress adjourned in July, we were able to enjoy our lovely home.

The Senate passed the "Soak the Rich" tax bill early in July with Millard voting against it and myself in the gallery listening to the debate. Millard was able to spend some time then at Oakington between political speeches. He thoroughly enjoyed running the big farm, and I became an enthusiastic, if ignorant, gardener and joined the Harford County Garden Club. There was nothing much in the boxwood garden except weeds when I first saw it. In time, it became very beautiful, with brick paths dividing the eight flower beds each twenty feet square. It took me forty-five years with only an occasional real gardener to help, but each bed became full of flowers and edged with low English boxwoods and the giant box that walled it.

The ruins of the old greenhouse became a wonderful rose garden with Millard's help. We had only one outdoor man, Jim Donnelly, who was no gardener! He drove the triple gang mower behind the big Percheron horses to cut the many acres of lawns around the house. Jim preferred to build the duck blinds offshore and go ducking with the "Senter"—otherwise he was supposed to help me with the gardening. He was sole supporter of a blind mother and his father, who had been coachman in the old days. Jim had gone to work to support them after a few grades at school and had gone to France in the World War. The Donnellys had always lived in a tenant house on the place.

Millard enjoyed running the farm with the help of a head farmer and a few farmhands. Mr. Morris Schapiro, a friend whose son would one day become my son-in-law, gave us some Ayrshire milk cows that supplied the farm with milk, cream, and butter. We had a great many white leghorn chickens, which enabled us to sell eggs to the Senate Restaurant and some of the large embassies. Unfortunately, the miserable hens went on a sit-down strike and turned cannibalistic toward their young! That was enough for me to insist that we get rid of the chickens. Millard then went on to the Belted Hampshire Hog business upon the advice of a neighbor, Mr. Donaldson Brown, chairman of the board of General Motors and husband of a Du Pont. They had a big farm across the Susquehanna River high on the cliffs. They sold us our royal hog ladies and my husband bought the Hampshire grand champion Glory Bound. The resulting piglets were adorable little black satin animals with pale pink belts around their middles. Their living quarters were immaculately clean and one could not enter save with disinfected boots. That was great fun until we found that Maryland farmers were not as used to the high prices of the hog royalty as mid-Westerners were. So we parted with Glory Bound and his harem and progeny and Millard bought a herd of white-faced Hereford cattle and a couple of young bulls from old Mr. Willie Du Pont. This necessitated fewer farmhands and was much less expensive farming.

In the month of May, I wrote in my diary: "Millard and I drove to Sharpsburg to deliver the Memorial Day speech on the Antietam battlefields. He accepted because we went there together one year ago when our romance was just beginning. We drove home and visited the barns to see a new Percheron baby colt, which was born last night. At home we discovered Nadine's cat and a litter of its babies comfortably ensconced under the pillows of our bed. We removed them!"

Technology came to Oakington that June and I wrote in my diary: "Millard and I had watched the farmhands cutting and tying sheaves of barley themselves. Now all was done by one machine drawn by our new tractor. The poor Percherons are going to have a rest and be retired, given to the sisters of a Baltimore convent."

As I read my diary, I am impressed with the constant family houseguests whom we entertained under Oakington's spreading roof. My mother and sisters and Millard's sisters came often to visit us. I marvel at his generous hospitality for he was not a gregarious man and wished only for the company of myself and my mother. He loved her devotedly and my children too, and they were well-behaved youngsters, a delight to have around. He was a wonderful father to them always.

I had never been to a National Democratic Convention so it was a new adventure to attend the one in Philadelphia at the end of June. My father and Marjorie had rented a large and luxurious penthouse atop the Barclay Hotel, where we were to stay, and a large box at the Convention Hall for our use. They did not arrive until the last day, and the rest of my family enjoyed the box and the penthouse with us. The Davieses did not stay to hear Millard's seconding speech, but we entertained many of their friends in our box—Jerry and Adelaide Hill and the Duchess of Reading, among others. The duchess was the wife of the late viceroy of India and was very nice. She was much interested in my husband's political career and advised me to keep an index file of the names of every Maryland constituent I met. Of course, I never did. It wasn't necessary because Millard Tydings's memory was my file. He always kept me informed as to the people it was important for me to greet wherever we went and always spoke their names clearly when we did. We gave two nice parties for Maryland leaders in the penthouse and went to quite a few given by friends. One was given by Mr. and Mrs. Stotesbury at their palatial home White Hall. Her son, Jimmy Cromwell, was there with his wife, the tobacco heiress, Doris Duke. He was tall and rather attractive, but I thought her a thin stick of a girl, very spoiled. Our hostess's daughter was the beautiful wife of General Douglas MacArthur, who had been superintendent of the West Point Military Academy when I went to Bill Kyles's graduation in 1922. She asked us to set a date when she and the general could give a dinner party in our honor at their country estate Rainbow Hall in Baltimore county.

I enjoyed some, but not all, of the convention proceedings. Senator Barkley's keynote speech lasted a good two and a half hours, and the orations nominating FDR for president took all day. Millard's seconding speech didn't come until 5:30 P.M. It was certainly unique in the annals of political conventions, lasting only about two minutes and consisting of only 169 (?) words. He said that the Republicans could never blame the Great Depression upon our Democratic president, but he never mentioned Franklin Roosevelt by name. He pledged that he and all Maryland Democrats would support the Democratic ticket and would work hard for all the candidates. Then he left the podium and we left the muggy hall.

I wondered what my father thought of that speech and whether Jim Farley and Jesse Jones were satisfied. I was sure that the president was not. The New Dealers pushed the Roosevelt ticket through the Convention with little, if any, opposition. There was a row between the northern and southern delegates over seating black delegates, and some of the white delegates from the deep south walked out. Otherwise the proceedings were cut-and-dried and boring.

It was hot even at Oakington that summer in spite of swimming in the bay and dashing around in Millard's speedboat. But I was overjoyed when my stepmother invited us to take the children on the *Sea Cloud* for a cruise up the northeast coast. I joyfully packed them up, and the nurse, Millard, and myself, boarded the yacht at Oyster Bay. It was heavenly cool out on the water, and the children and I were blissfully happy. Our pleasure didn't last long. The second day out, Millard informed me he had received a wire from Washington calling him back. We packed up and went home to the 100 degree heat. Long after, my husband told me that he simply couldn't stand the thought of the enormous cost of operating the yacht and the thought of his own modest bank balance, so he had his secretary call him to return at once on official business! However, he eventually became accustomed to cruising on the *Sea Cloud*—as most of us do to luxury. Even some of the Davieses's very rich friends found the yacht hard to take. Once when the president of the American Express Company and his wife were onboard, we found them on the aft deck, the gentleman pacing up and down furiously, face flushed, apoplectic. "What is the matter with Bobby?" I asked his wife. "Oh, he's just figured out how much it costs to run this ship every time he draws a breath," she replied. Millard said he knew exactly how our friend felt!

The *Sea Cloud* had sailed around the world once and would cross the Atlantic several times while my father was our ambassador in Europe.

Back home at Oakington, in 1936, Millard was in demand to speak for the Democrats all around the state and further afield. I usually accompanied him. We had missed so much of our lives apart from each other that we didn't want to lose a minute of each other's company. His speeches stressed the Democratic party—its principles and achievements. He also stressed the need for economy in government, increasing our world trade as a means to prosperity and spoke of the need to strengthen our Navy and our Armed Forces, which had been largely disbanded after the World War. With his phenomenal memory, he had facts and figures at his fingertips and received enthusiastic ovations wherever he spoke. He asked support for the Democratic candidates and their leader, the Democratic president. That was all he said about the latter, but I doubt if most of his audiences noticed that. He had been in the Senate long enough to achieve seniority, which meant power in the Senate, and he was a person of importance both in his own state and others.

It was remarkable that the friendship between my father and the president was strong enough to survive the rift between my husband and Mr. Roosevelt. As far as I know, it was never mentioned by any of them. Joseph Davies, as vice chairman of the Democratic National Committee, made many speeches for Franklin Roosevelt that summer and raised a great deal of money for his campaign fund. I have wondered whether Daddy had anything to do with persuading my husband to make the seconding speech for FDR at the Convention. I decided not. Millard Tydings made up his own mind on most things.

We went on another cruise that summer, thanks to Marjorie Davies's thoughtfulness, this time with her and Daddy. It gave my husband a chance to get away from political demands upon him and relax. We sailed up the New England coast and it was a great thrill to round Cape Cod in a stiff breeze under great billowing sails, our lovely ship keeled over, her deck awash. We were all good sailors and if anyone wasn't, Marjorie prescribed a great remedy—a tall glass of champagne on cracked ice with thin red pepper sandwiches!

We returned from this short holiday by train from New York to Aberdeen (the Pennsylvania Railroad would always stop to let the senator disembark at the Oakington crossing). We couldn't believe the marvelously air-cooled Pullman car. It was our first experience of such luxury outside of a movie theater.

We were invited to bring the children to spend August with the Davieses at Marjorie's Camp Topridge. Millard came and went and

I went campaigning with him, leaving the children at Camp. They had an excellent nursery-governess and were very well behaved. Both Daddy and Marjorie enjoyed having them around.

Camp Topridge was beautifully situated on upper St. Regis Lake in the Adirondacks on a ridge between St. Regis and two smaller lakes called Upper and Lower Spectacle. The term camp was a total misnomer!

There was a magnificent, huge main lodge, charming separate cottages for family and guests and a little Russian house, or dacha, which was my father's sanctum. No roads led to Topridge. One came by motorboat, and there were many boats and a staff of around seventy men and maids to service this huge establishment. The guest accommodations were luxurious suites on top of and on the sides of the ridge and each had its own fireplace, maid, and valet. It would accommodate at least twenty guests. An outdoor elevator wafted you up from the boathouse to the main lodge atop the ridge where there was a tremendous great room at least fifty feet long with two huge fireplaces and giant picture windows, and a dining room almost as large. The staff lived in large hotel-like accommodations a short distance away.

The main lounge was furnished with a magnificent collection of Indian rugs and artifacts, among them Sitting Bull's war bonnet and a deck of playing cards made from human skin. There was a little private golf course at the far end of Lower Spectacle Lake that Marjorie called the Goat Course. There was also a tennis court, putting green, and a bathing beach. She would take her guests on wonderful picnics in Canadian canoes called bateaux through the chain of St. Regis lakes. The guides would paddle these and carry them over the land between lakes. The picnic food was a banquet cooked by the guides. Marjorie liked to dance, so there were generally two couples of Arthur Murray's dancers among the guests to teach us all the new steps. She was a very good dancer but Millard told me I was better. One night a week was movie night at Topridge, and all the friends in the neighboring camps were invited. They were also included at dinner parties, which my stepmother gave frequently.

When we arrived, the Davieses and the Tydingses settled by the roaring fire after dinner for some good conversation without the usual houseguests who would arrive in a few days. I wanted to hear talk about the European situation as a welcome change from politics, national and state. However, it began with Franklin Roosevelt.

"Confidentially," my father said, "the president has asked me to go as our ambassador to Germany, as soon as he is reelected this fall. He thinks that Hitler might be persuaded to join an International Disarmament pact, down to the arms a man can carry, and that I am the man to do it. It's rather far-fetched but an interesting challenge and I agreed to go."

"Congratulations, Joe!" said Millard, clapping Father on the back. "You will make a great representative of our country, and if anyone can calm Hitler down, you can. With your experiences as a mediator both in the Federal Trade Commission and in corporate and international law, you are the best man for the job and the president knows it. There's no question that he will be reelected by a landslide, in spite of Al Smith and a few Southern senators. As you probably know, Jim Farley and some of our Democratic leaders practically bamboozled me into making the seconding speech for the president's convention. Al Smith said he had only two options, to be a hypocrite or take a walk, but I considered that I had *three*, and I chose to take the third. I could not walk out on the party that had honored me so many times. I don't think either the president or the New Dealers liked my speech very much. It was by all odds the shortest on record!"

Daddy chuckled. "Our Eleanor gave me a copy of it and I had a good laugh. I was sorry that we couldn't have been there to hear it, but I think you will agree that under the circumstances it was better that we not be in your cheering section! Marjorie and I had a good laugh over the only sentence that mentioned the Boss when you said that at least the Republicans couldn't blame the Depression on the president. He should have smiled at that."

"I doubt it," said my husband. "I said I would do all I could to support and reelect the Democratic candidates but I never mentioned Roosevelt by name. I'm afraid he may come after me in 1938."

"Not if I can help it," said my parent. "And I think I have a little influence at the White House."

I spoke up emphatically. "Let us fight our own battles, Mr. Ambassador. My husband can take care of any president any day! Everyone in Maryland admires and loves Millard Tydings."

"Here, here, my love, methinks you protest too much! There are certainly more than a few who don't love me." Millard laughed and put his finger on my lips and then replaced it with his kiss. I returned it and then hugged Dad.

"That's the first time I ever hugged an ambassador," I told him. He patted my shoulder and turned to Millard.

"What do you think about what is going on in Europe, Senator? This bird Hitler is becoming more and more of a threat to peace there."

Millard frowned. "I agree with you. Britain and France should call his bluff right away before he can build up his war machine any further or there may be another bloody war over there."

Marjorie spoke. "Our European friends in Washington don't seem to be the least bit worried about Germany. The French Ambassador assured me that their Maginot Line defenses are impregnable and their army is the best and the biggest in Europe. The ambassador said Hitler is only bluffing and if necessary Mr. Daladier and Mr. Chamberlain will step on him."

Daddy and I smiled at her, but Millard looked deadly serious.

"Our World War allies should make a treaty with Russia to preserve peace against *any* German aggression," said my father.

"You are talking about the old balance of power in Europe, Joe. I don't like Communist Russia. I voted against the U.S. recognizing the Soviet Union." I nodded agreement with my husband. Daddy was fiddling with the radio set.

"The commentator says the riots against the Jews in Germany are growing worse. Hitler is talking about the return of all the German-speaking lands that were taken from Germany after the Great War. He has been talking about taking back the Sudetenland, which has been part of Czechoslovakia since the World War."

"Surely Hitler wouldn't start hostilities over that," protested my stepmother.

"I certainly hope not," said Millard. "Poor Czechoslovakia is a polyglot mess of different nationalities. There are about 7 million czechs, about 3 million Sudeten Germans, and at least a million Poles and Hungarians!"

My father sighed, "We'll just have to wait and see, I guess, and pray for peace."

Millard stood up and pulled me to my feet. "I think it is our bedtime and we should all go up and start praying. We must say goodnight, Treasure, for your Daddy and I must leave for Washington tomorrow morning."

Goodnight kisses were exchanged, and we went happily off to bed in our luxurious cabin with its comfortable little fire burning on the hearth.

Before I slept, I lay in bed wondering whether the Germans would march to the east to take Czechoslovakia or to the west as they had done in the last war. If they went west they would surely go through the Low Countries of Holland and Belgium and the Ardennes Mountains in Belgium as they had done before. Mother and I had driven that way the summer before and had seen Frenchmen working on the Maginot Line and Germans on the Siegfried Line opposite it. Nobody had been allowed near them. I had not brought the subject up. After all, the French ambassador apparently wasn't worried and he should know. The men in my family were obviously concerned. They departed the next morning, and the children and I stayed with Marjorie at Camp.

My father returned after a few days. He had spent some time with the president in Washington discussing the European situation. Millard could not come home with him, to my great disappointment. Debate was still going on in the Senate. The president had called a special session for more talk about the Neutrality bill. My husband telephoned me every night to report on it and to tell me how much he was missing me.

He was opposed to giving any more power to Roosevelt and was being attacked as an isolationist. People were bitterly divided on the subject of becoming involved in another European war. In the end, Millard voted for the least undesirable neutrality measure. He was making speeches in Maryland and everywhere for economic and military preparedness as the best way to stay out of the mess in Europe.

I stayed at Topridge until my father returned and told us about his conversation with the president. Mr. Roosevelt had told Daddy that he wanted him to go first as ambassador to Russia for a year and then to Germany. The ambassador to Berlin would not leave until the Inauguration was over. The president wanted to wait to see what Hitler would do before paying him the compliment of sending him one of Roosevelt's closest friends. FDR felt that even Joe Davies's famous powers of mediation, both in his government posts and in his law practice, could not persuade Adolph Hitler to agree to anything. He told Daddy he had another very good reason to send him to Russia. He thought it was most important to make friends with the Russian leaders of government, to prevent them from joining forces with the Axis powers of German and Italy.

Neither my father nor stepmother seemed at all disappointed at the change of embassy posts for them. On the contrary, they seemed interested and excited over the prospect of going to Russia. Marjorie immediately sent for her "tame" interior decorator to plan her trip to Moscow to refurbish Spasso House, the residence of the United States ambassador. My stepmother pronounced the mansion to be "quite beautiful" from its photographs. It was to be completely rejuvenated and partly refurnished with many of her beautiful things and much of her handsome furniture. She also sent for Cappy, skipper of the *Sea Cloud*. It was to be sailed over to Europe in the spring.

Millard and I left Topridge and, according to the usual arrangement of dividing time between my parents, we went to stay a short time with Mother in New Hampshire. September was going to be a busy time for Millard with the election in early November. We took Mother home with us. When I did not go campaigning with my husband in and around Maryland, I was entertaining family and friends at Oakington. However, I did not like to be separated from Millard and often accompanied him. The weather was still uncomfortably hot and our new speedboat was a blessing. We explored the bay and the Elk River across it from us, where my great-grandmother was the fifth generation to be born on her ancestral acres of Bohemian Manor. We had tea with former Senator Bayard from Delaware and saw the mansion that he had built, a copy of the original Bohemian Manor built in the mid-seventeenth century by our mutual ancestor.

The big excitement for me came on September fifth with our Democratic Womens' Rally at Oakington. The wild ducks arrived on the bay in front of our house early that morning by the thousands and by early afternoon, the ladies. So did most of their husbands! They came in buses, trucks, and automobiles, and our farmhands directed parking in a large pasture field halfway between the big house and a nearby grove of trees on the bay shore. The grove (ever after known as Democratic Grove) sheltered a wooden platform and rows of chairs supplied by all the undertakers in the county. Our speakers were Mrs. Nellie Taylor Ross, director of the Mint, and Mrs. Emma Guffey Miller, sister of Senator Joe Guffey of Pennsylvania. Mrs. Miller was Democratic National Committeewoman from that state and a real battle-ax! Millard was the third (and last) speaker. I was a blushing, shy introducer. After the speeches, some two thousand ladies strolled back to the bay lawn in front of our house and partook of soft drinks, sandwiches, and cakes. The empty guest cottage provided W.C. facilities and a powder room, and the big house was locked up tight. The women did everything to get inside it and used every imaginable excuse to do so, but Livingston was on guard. The affair was a howling success and was talked about for years. It came at the right time.

President Roosevelt came up the bay to celebrate the opening of a

new bridge in southern Maryland and brought a company of dignitaries with him on the White House yacht. I do not know whether
Millard suspected what might happen. He did not want me to go
with him. As the senior senator of the state, he was responsible for
the construction of the much-needed bridge. He never told me what
happened. The president dropped anchor and sent aides ashore to
escort the governor, the mayor, judges, and the junior senator on
board, but left Senator Tydings standing on the shore. The press
called it a "royal snub" but I don't think FDR's bad manners hurt
my senator much with the independent, well-mannered Marylanders. Wherever Millard spoke in Baltimore and the counties, he received large, enthusiastic ovations.

Toward the end of September, a great hurricane roared down the
bay, sweeping most of the water out of its upper portion and leaving
the wildlife stranded on the mudflats in front of Oakington's shores.
It swept away that summer of 1936 also.

October came and still no Tydings baby was in the offing. I decided to do something about it and checked into a Washington hospital for surgery to be sure all my innards were correctly located and
behaving normally. It cost me only a few days of discomfort, but it
cost Millard more pain than I experienced. He was bitterly opposed
to it and never left my side. Nothing was wrong, just as he had always declared, said my gynecologist. Millard said he had me and my
children, whom he always referred to as *his* children. He said he
saw no need for any more.

In between political meetings of the state's leading Democrats at
Oakington, Millard was being sent to speak in other states. We went
to Philadelphia and Pittsburgh, Boston and Concord, New Hampshire, and Vermont. Then we went to Illinois, Ohio, and Indiana.
Sometimes he even spoke to Republican groups on Long Island.
Once, changing trains in a small Midwest town, the stationmaster
rushed out to greet Millard enthusiastically. He had been one of Millard's machine gunners in France in the World War. Everywhere,
veterans of the war greeted him enthusiastically.

From Chicago, we drove three hours to LaSalle, Illinois, where
we spent the night in a small bed in the Kaskyan Hotel and were
driven to and from Chicago by the mayor and the chief of police. In
Maplewood, Indiana (or was it Ohio?), the town druggist had insisted that Senator Tydings address a large gathering, which turned
out to be a small crowd. The entire population was Republican. Millard gave them a fine patriotic talk, and I'm sure from the applause
they gave him that they would have elected him mayor of the town.

Home to more big rallies of Maryland Democrats and the opening night of the Baltimore Opera with Rosa Ponselle singing *Carmen*. One of Baltimore's great doctors, Hugh Young, gave a supper party afterward. Mayor Howard Jackson and his son, a young bachelor, were guests. The diva and the bachelor took one look at each other and I told Millard I knew "that look." They were married soon after.

Then suddenly it was Election Day, 1936. My husband spent the day "working" at the Harford County polls, but he would not let me accompany him. Of course, the president (and most of the Democratic candidates) were reelected everywhere by large majorities. The big day came in February 1937 when my father was sworn in as the United States ambassador to Russia, the Soviet Union, by the secretary of state, Mr. Cordell Hull, at the State Department. The family was all there except, of course, my mother, which made me sad, as I always was in spite of my friendship with Marjorie. There was a party afterward with many important friends of Daddy's. Among these were Secretary Roper, Judge Walton Moore, Judge Richard Whaley, Attorney General Homer Cummings, Senators Pat Harrison, Duffy and Pittman and Tydings, Marvin McIntyre, Steve Early, and Robert Allen.

The Davies were to leave after Christmas and we invited them to come and spend our first Thanksgiving (1936) at Oakington with us. When the Davieses came to Oakington, it was quite a production for our household. As our man Bob Livingston said, something vital at Oakington was sure to go wrong or break down. Still, it was always fixed up in time, and we all enjoyed their visits. They rarely stayed more than two nights. So far as I can remember, nothing happened this time to mar the visit of the ambassador, his wife, his valet, Marjorie's little girl Deenie, the child's governess, two bodyguards, whom Marjorie called the "pinks" (Pinkertons), and assorted chauffeurs! No wonder our small staff of household help, consisting of the Livingstons and her sister, had nervous jitters! But Oakington House had a suite of two bedrooms and a bath for Marjorie and her maid, and the same for Daddy and his valet; and there were rooms for Deenie and her governess in the children's wing. Fortunately, the chauffeurs disappeared when not needed and the "pinks" stayed out of sight. I could sympathize with Marjorie's fears of having her child kidnapped after the tragedy of the Lindbergh's baby.

Our young Joe was very pleased and excited over Deenie's coming. We lunched with the three children when they had their Thanksgiving dinner and entertained at a small dinner party that evening.

Our friends, Donald and Elsie Symington and Charlie and Sue Bryan, were the only other guests. I wrote the menu of our party in my diary. We dined on oysters, terrapin, corn muffins, wild ducks, wild rice, green vegetable, salad, and apple pie, chocolate pie, and pumpkin pie—all 100 percent Maryland food—plus wines!

The Symingtons were not such near neighbors as the Bryans, so we were all invited to dine with Sue and Charlie the following evening. We dined at Mt. Pleasant, their beautiful home on the heights, above Havre de Grace. Actually, it was directly above Oakington, but our house was invisible in the trees. Charlie was a horticulturist with more than one thousand acres of apple and peach trees and lovely terraced gardens leading down to the clouds of pink apple blossoms in the spring and the blue Chesapeake in the distance. It was said that it had once been a residence of Governor Paca, and Charlie had designed a handsome house of that Colonial period. He was a small man, at least twenty years older than Millard, and his wife was about ten years older. Charlie was a highly intelligent, highly conservative Republican. Sue, was a lovely, equally intelligent and charming woman, and a liberal Democrat. She became my closest friend in our county. I suspect she always loved Millard, maybe was even in love with him. She was careful never to show it. She had been a widow with a son slightly older than mine when she married Charlie. It certainly was no love-match, but a meeting of two fine minds.

After dinner we settled down to a discourse of politics at home and abroad, as usual. Charlie congratulated Millard on the Supreme Court's decision that Roosevelt's NRA and AAA laws had been unconstitutional.

Naturally, Russia was the number one topic of conversation that first evening. My father was guarded about comments and did not refer to the president's instructions. I realized that it was a great mark of his trust and confidence in Millard and myself that he had told us about them. Sue Bryan, always the optimist, expressed her hope that the U.S.S.R. would eventually evolve into a more democratic form of government. My father agreed with her that it could happen sometime in the distant future. Charlie and Millard were not so hopeful. My husband remarked: "The one thing in life we can be sure of is change itself. The pendulum will always swing back, but it sometimes takes a very long time." Daddy said he thought there was hope for Russia.

"Nothing—either good or bad—is a thousand percent," he said.

Chapter 16

The Ambassador, 1937

Joseph Edward Davies was a popular man among the distinguished citizens of Washington, D.C. This was undoubtedly partly due to his good looks, charm, and brains, but also to his friendly warmth and generosity. He made and held friends in both public and private life with thoughtful gifts to them. He was a very successful lawyer. Never a so-called womanizer, he was a devoted husband and father for thirty years. Then he met the beautiful Marjorie Post Hutton.

One of the farewell parties given in honor of the newly appointed ambassador to Russia and his bride, Marjorie, was a dinner given by Mr. and Mrs. Edward Stotesbury at their palatial home, White Hall, in Philadelphia. "Aunt Eva," as my stepmother called our hostess, was a regal beauty in her late fifties, and charming. We became friends at once and she urged me to call her Aunt Eva. Millard and I and the Davieses were houseguests for the occasion. We were installed in separate suites of rooms, each suite with its bedroom, bathroom, and sitting room with fireplace, all most luxurious, gold fixtures in the bathroom, etc.

What impressed me the most, however, were the engraved cards spread over a large French desk—invitations to the dinner and ball and to parties the next day. That was not all. There were also engraved cards, each telling us the names of a chauffeur, valet, and personal maid who were assigned to us, and the ring to summon them. All were engraved, not printed! Daddy and Marjorie had given me a most beautiful emerald and diamond necklace as a wedding gift, which had nearly rocked me off my feet! I wore it that evening for the first time with a plain white brocade evening gown, empire style, with tiny puffed sleeves. Millard said I looked as a princess should look. I sat beside the governor of Pennsylvania at dinner.

118

He was quite inebriated and evidently paid me too much amorous attention. In any event, Millard and I stayed home from the Widener Ball. I admit to being a little disappointed.

Many farewell dinner parties were given in Washington for the Davieses before they left for Russia. The largest and most lavish was a dinner at the Mayflower Hotel given by a committee of some of the most outstanding members of the government: One was Chief Justice Richard Whaley of the Court of Claims (who had been best man at the Hutton-Davies wedding), Senator Pat Harrison of Mississippi, Attorney General Homer Cummings, General William Mitchell of the Air Force, and, of course, Senator Millard Tydings of Maryland, who was a member of the committee. As I look at the huge photograph of that big assemblage of the most important men in Washington and their wives, I see both the Democratic and Republican leaders of the Senate, the Speaker of the House, the Russian ambassador (Troyanovsky). The future vice president, Senator Alben Barkley, was there, as well as Vice President Henry Wallace. The president sent word that he would have come had he been physically able to attend parties.

Some of the guests at the farewell dinner for Ambassador Davies were:

> Attorney General and Mrs. Homer Cummings; U.S.S.R. Ambassador and Madam Troyanovsky; Vice President and Mrs. Henry Wallace; Speaker of the House of Representatives, Sam Rayburn (TX); Secretary of State and Mrs. Cordell Hull (TN); U.S. Ambassador to Egypt and Mrs. Hampson Gary (DC); Chief Justice of the Court of Claims, Richard Whaley (SC); Admiral and Mrs. Cary Grayson (President Wilson's doctor); General and Mrs. William Mitchell, First Chief Army Air; Democratic Leader of the Senate and Mrs. Joe Robinson (AK); Republican Leader of the Senate and Mrs. McNary (OR); Senator and Mrs. Millard Tydings (MD); Senator and Mrs. Alben Barkley (KY); Senator and Mrs. George Radcliffe (MD); Senator and Mrs. Duffy (WI); Senator and Mrs. Bennett Clarke (MO); Senator and Mrs. Wallace White (ME); Senator and Mrs. Guy Gillette (Iowa); Senator and Mrs. William G. McAdoo (CA); Senator and Mrs. James Byrnes (SC); Senator and Mrs. Tom Connally (TX); Senator and Mrs. James J. Davis (PA); Senator Arthur Capper (KS); Senator Pat Harrison (MS); Senator Henry M. Ashurst (AZ); Mr. Martin McIntyre (Secretary to Roosevelt); Mr. and Mrs. Steve Early (Press Secretary to Roosevelt); Honorable and Mrs. Jesse Jones (TX); Mr. Sidney Weinberg, Goldman, Sachs (NY); Mr. Alfons Land, JED Law Firm (DC); Mr. and Mrs. Ray Beebe, JED Law Firm (DC); Honorable and Mrs. Richberg, JED Law Firm (DC).

Russia—1937 to 1938

En route to Russia, my father stopped in Berlin on the first of many such missions he undertook as the president's special envoy during the years he served him. He would establish personal friendships with the leaders of every country in Europe, not only the government heads but also with the captains of industry and the banking world. He wrote me in January 1937:

> I have had a talk with Doctor Schact, the Secretary of the Treasury, but I did not see Mr. Hitler as he was ill at Berchtesgaden.
>
> We both speak of you so often and with such pride! It would do you both good to hear us get going on the subject. You are wise in knowing what a priceless possession you have. It makes me particularly happy, for Millard is all I would hope a son of mine could ever be. And, Eleanor, my firstborn, you know how much you mean to me.

Unfortunately, my father's popularity did not extend to the officers of our diplomatic corps in Moscow or the career men in the State Department. His achievements as ambassador were not due to much help from the State Department in Washington or the Foreign Service aides at his embassy in Russia. He did not deserve the many difficulties that they threw in his path or the virulent criticism of him, which they spread in Washington.

The basic underlying cause of this bitterness was unquestionably the natural resentment of our Foreign Service system. It was only natural that men who had worked hard to reach the top of their professional career saw wealthy friends of the president appointed to the important ambassadorial posts. In Daddy's case these feelings were exacerbated by the flamboyant news stories about the Davieses divorce and his marriage to the enormously wealthy Marjorie Post Close Hutton. The stories were made worse by the simultaneous divorce of Joe Davies's daughter Mrs. Eleanor Cheesborough and her marriage to a distinguished senator.

Never before or since has an entire U.S. embassy staff actually planned to walk out on their jobs when the new ambassador arrived. When we heard about this, we learned that Loy Henderson, the number one assistant to the ambassador in Moscow, had prevented it. He was a fine man and a friend of Joe Davies.

The second reason for my father's difficulties with his Moscow aides was that the president's instructions to him to fraternize and make friends with the Russian government leaders were kept secret and were in direct conflict with the opinions and policy of the Department of State, the foreign service officers, and the Secretary of State himself. They were strongly opposed to any kind of friendly relations with the Soviet government. The president's instructions to my father were exactly the opposite. The two men thought (as Millard did) that Europe was on the verge of war. The president had first asked Joseph Davies to be his ambassador to Germany. An old and trusted friend then asked him to take the Russian post for a year first. Roosevelt could be confident of Davies's capacity to make friends with the Russians to forestall any possibility of their joining Hitler in a war. At first the president had hoped that his friend Joe Davies might be able to persuade Hitler to join an international conference on disarmament. When it appeared that would not be possible, the president asked him to go to make friends with Russia. The president did not take the Secretary of State into his confidence. When my father discovered that his reports to the State Department from Russia were not being given to the president, Mr. Roosevelt arranged to have them delivered to him directly. My father did his best to win over the men at the embassy but with little, if any, success. The Press Corps in Moscow, however, and in most of the European countries that he visited at President Roosevelt's instructions, became his friends.

The Davieses arrived in Moscow in February 1937 on the eve of the infamous "purge" trials, which ended in the execution of so many Russian leaders of the Soviet government, press, and armed forces. My father sat through them all with an interpreter beside him. As a former trial lawyer, he believed that many of the accused were guilty as charged of plans to overthrow Stalin, and that some of the military also had been plotting with the German army to do so. Thousands of these government officials and Red Army officers were convicted of treason and executed. My father deplored these horrors. I will not describe what he has written in *Mission to Moscow*.

He was the only Western ambassador to meet and talk with Stalin and to travel beyond the Ural Mountains and all over the U.S.S.R. under the auspices of the Russian government.

Upon his arrival in the Soviet Union, Ambassador Davies proceeded to cultivate the leaders of the Russian government. This was something none of his predecessors or the ambassadors from the other western countries had done. They had presented their credentials and then retired behind their embassy walls, never deigning to have anything to do with the Russian officials socially. The single exception had been a party given at our embassy for them by Ambassador William Bullitt, who preceded my father. Madame Litvinov, whose husband was the Soviet foreign minister and later Russian ambassador to the U.S., told me this story. She said the Bullitt party was supposed to be a "fancy dress ball" and the Russian leaders were all invited. The ball turned out to be an "animal party." The great rooms of our embassy were filled with animals in cages and the stench was terrible! The Russians were furious. They took it as a personal insult and walked out.

The Davieses parties were very different. They entertained the Russian officials at beautifully but simply appointed dinners followed by a concert or a motion picture. Marjorie gave a luncheon for the wives of these officials, and, in return, Madame Molotov, whose husband was a member of Stalin's cabinet, gave a luncheon in Marjorie's honor at the Molotov dacha (country house). I quote a letter from Marjorie to me:

> All the Russian ladies there were wives of important men. Molotov is called Russia's prime minister. The Molotov dacha in the country is as luxurious, new, and large as you could find anywhere. Madame Molotov's bathroom is as big as my bedroom at home. She is an attractive, well-dressed, small woman about forty with tremendous energy. She runs a large perfume factory. Luncheon was delicious and beautifully served. The conversation might easily have been at a party of ladies in Washington, D.C.—about women's rights, cosmetics, equality of women, and children.
>
> You have no idea what a joy your letters are to your Daddy and me. Your way of putting things and your keen observations give us the greatest delight. We look forward to your letters. We have such fun over them.

Mrs. Davies amazed the British ambassador afterward by describing the Molotov luncheon.

The ambassador: "My dear lady, I didn't even know the Molotovs had such a country home!"

Marjorie: "Oh, yes, all the Russian officials have beautiful dachas on that country road. It is closed to the public and is surrounded by armed guards. The Molotov house has all the conveniences and plumbing we have at home."

One of the Davieses dinners was for the Red Army. It was certainly unique. The banquet cloth was red satin. The table garniture, as at all her dinner parties, was simple, American china and crystal. Marjorie used artificial flowers brought from the U.S.A. She wore only modest gowns and jewelry.

The Russians entertained the Davieses in return. Marjorie had brought a supply of frozen foods from the U.S., and she and my father noticed that the Russians sampled our cooking with hesitation and did not eat much of it at first. She and Daddy laughed because they also ate their meal at home before going to a Russian dinner!

When my father expressed interest in their industrial achievements, the Russians sent him in a private government railroad car all over the U.S.S.R. on inspection trips. This was something no other westerner had been allowed to do. Father wrote me, "There are great cities as big as Pittsburgh beyond the Ural mountains, which we didn't even know existed!"

Marjorie and Joe Davies took long walks around Moscow and Leningrad and discovered the Russian "Commission Shops," state owned like everything else. Here, under piles of worthless junk, they sometimes uncovered Czarist treasures (at that time there was no restriction on taking things out of Russia).

A letter from my father of March 23 reads in part:

> These Commission Stores resemble our antique shops. They sell all manner of things brought in by the owners, from pictures to bedroom sets and from jewels to china. We are having fun shopping.

My father became interested in Russian paintings, and his pictures and icons were the beginning of the Davies-Post Collection. The Davieses brought these treasures back to Washington that year to adorn the beautiful home he had bought in Washington, which he named Tregaron after his father's birthplace in Wales. They presented the Russian government with a magnificent table service of American china (Lenox) and glass (Steuben) when they departed. Since then, the Russians have clamped down on their exports. The famous "Hammer Collection" has long been completely sold out and there are very few prerevolutionary Russian treasures to be found save in private ownership and Russian museums.

Most of the Russian paintings and icons were given by my father to the University of Wisconsin, and he gave the church chalices and artifacts to the Washington National Cathedral. He made many gifts to that cathedral, including the great baptistery window in honor of his parents. His ashes are interred there, and the cathedral honored him with an inscription carved in the stone of the transept next to Woodrow Wilson's tomb as the "servant of his country, friend of presidents."

The "Davies Collection" at Tregaron was divided between Joe and Marjorie Davies when they separated years later. My two sisters and I inherited his half. Marjorie's part can be seen in her Washington home, Hillwood, now a museum. At both Tregaron and at Camp Topridge in the Adirondacks are two charming dachas which Marjorie had copied from the little country houses of Russia, for Daddy's private sanctums.

In those days there were no sophisticated listening devices like those recently put in the walls of our new embassy office building in Moscow. The walls then did not have ears, but the telephones did. Once when Marjorie was trying to get a long-distance call through to the captain of the *Sea Cloud* in the Baltic, she was having great difficulty and became highly indignant.

Marjorie: "Hello, Gay pay oo! (KGB or Russian Secret Police). I know you're on the line. Now listen to me! I am trying to get the captain of our yacht, *Sea Cloud*, to order him to meet us at Yalta next week. Will you give him the message or shall I?" The Russians obliged!

In the summer of 1937, the Davieses went to London where they attended the coronation of King George V and his queen, Elizabeth. They visited all the Baltic countries on the *Sea Cloud* and all those adjacent to Russia as the president's ambassador-at-large. This they did, sailing on the *Sea Cloud* to Latvia, Lithuania, Estonia, Denmark, Norway, Finland, and Danzig. They then traveled by train to France and the other European countries. They had entertained the leaders of both government and finance of fourteen countries in all on the yacht and had been entertained by them. Daddy had written voluminous reports home to the president. He told us that all of the countries visited wanted peace at almost any price in Europe. They all cherished their independence and did not want to be taken over by either Germany or Russia. Of the two, my father said they were more afraid of Russia. He wrote Millard that these trips were not a holiday and that he had never worked harder in his life, making a record of all the conversations. There were no tape recorders then. After returning to Leningrad, he wrote us:

We took a six-day trip into the Ukraine. I am satisfied that no one in our diplomatic service will turn in a more comprehensive report on the conditions in any country to which they are accredited than I.

In the meantime, the well-meaning junior diplomats in Moscow and the U.S. State Department were doing their best to undermine Ambassador Davies with the president and his administration. They had the able assistance of the columnist Drew Pearson and a few others in the news media. My husband knew what was going on but had little, if any, influence at the White House. He did not tell me about it.

The Davieses had been in Moscow for some time when it was found that Russian secret agents had been living in the attic of the embassy, eavesdropping! Our young diplomats there were furious and became even more angry when the ambassador told them: "So what difference does it make? All they will hear will be the good things I say about them. Any criticisms will be sent to the president and the State Department in a sealed diplomatic pouch."

The autumn of 1937, the Davieses returned from Russia. The cold weather there had begun and had aggravated Marjorie's arthritis and Daddy's diverticulitis and they returned home at Christmas to receive their expected change of diplomatic posts and get ready to go to Germany. They hoped the planned exchange would be less taxing to their health, but it was not to be. The president said he wanted my father to return to Russia. It was more important than ever to keep the U.S.S.R. out of the Axis camp, Roosevelt told him, and my father agreed to do another tour of duty. The president told my father that the Russian post was now more important than Germany, and that it was too late to accomplish any disarmament deal with Adolph Hitler. The fuhrer was definitely about to try to take over Germany's former possessions in East Europe. He had already sent several divisions to the Czechoslovakian frontier. There were rumors that some of the top German generals were going to resign if Hitler moved toward war. That situation made it so important, the president said, to keep Russia from joining the German-Italian Axis. Besides, Roosevelt did not wish to honor Hitler by sending him one of his close friends, and so he was sending Hugh Gibson, a career diplomat.

November 29 was my father's birthday, and my sisters and Charlie and Sue Bryan came to the birthday celebration at Oakington. Poems were read, songs were sung, and toasts drunk. Sometime that evening Marjorie said she had heard that our big Democratic rally for the Democratic Women of Maryland had been a great success.

"How many do you think actually came?" she asked.

Millard said he guessed there were more than a thousand, and I said I thought there were at least twice that many.

"Our farmers built the speakers' stand and the county undertakers loaned us the chairs," Millard said. "The guest cottage, halfway between there and our house, was a ladies' room and W.C. Of course, the plumbing eventually gave up the ghost and the shrubbery had to take over. We served sandwiches and cold drinks on the bay lawn at the big house. It was a great success. Eleanor was a great hostess and made a good introductory speech." I beamed and so did my daddy.

My father wanted to hear about the political picture and Millard wanted to discuss the Japanese invasion of Mongolia and the German arms buildup. Occasionally, the dinner party conversations would touch upon the Civil War in Spain, but that was not a pleasant subject and usually became a condemnation of the Communists and support of the Fascist leader, Franco, in Spain.

After a brief discussion of Mussolini's cruel terror bombing of the primitive Ethiopians and Hitler's growing power, Sue Bryan mentioned a letter she had received from a schoolmate who had married a Spaniard and was living in Spain. This friend had written of her worries over the political situation there. Apparently the Communists and the liberal Democrats were bitterly fighting the power of the Crown, the Church, and the Nobles. A group of Fascists was also involved with a leader called Franco. The government was about to have an election, which might be the last. Sue's friend wanted to come home to the U.S. but didn't wish to leave her husband. I thought what a mess things were in Europe and how lucky we were in America.

Daddy's doctors gave him the okay, and they returned to Moscow soon after Christmas. Marjorie sent her "tame" decorator to Europe once more to refurbish the Palais D'Asque, which our government had rented for their new embassy residence in Brussels.

The time came for the Davieses to bid good-bye to Russia in June 1938 when my father paid his farewell call upon Prime Minister Molotov and Foreign Minister Litvinov.

Chapter 17

The Tydingses Visit Hawaii on Statehood, 1937

After the Senate adjourned for the summer of 1937 (having complained that the Congress ought to have air-conditioning, like the movie theaters), Millard turned his attention to the question of our Pacific territories. He was concerned about the growing threat of war in that region. That summer, the Senate and House Territories Committee's Subcommittees on Statehood visited Hawaii to decide whether it should be made the forty-ninth state. As chairman of the Senate Committee, Millard was the leader of the delegation. Besides ourselves, there were six senators and four congressmen and their wives. Millard and I were honored guests of his friend Princess Kawananakoa, the widow of the late Prince Kalakawa, heir to the throne of Hawaii.

Millard first met the princess in Hawaii when he went to the Philippines about his independence bill in December 1934. Ever since then, the princess had wanted him to come back to Hawaii as her guest. Considering her feelings for Millard, she was very nice to me. What a hostess this lady turned out to be! I quote from a letter to my mother:

> We are guests of the Princess Kawananakoa, widow of the heir to the Crown of Hawaii. Millard and she are great friends, in spite of the fact that she's the Republican national committeewoman! When we landed in Honolulu, she sent twelve noble Hawaiian ladies who are her ladies-in-waiting to the ship bearing flower leis (flower wreaths) for each of us. She also sent two fine-looking, white-haired Hawaiian gentlemen (one the former mayor of Honolulu, the other probably would have been her prime minister) to greet us. The Royal Hawaiian band

127

was on the dock and played "Maryland, My Maryland!" Her own special movie photographer, Jimmy Williams, photographed our arrival and our every move during our visit there.

The princess is a tall woman and quite stout. She has been partly lame since childhood. She has a wealth of beautiful dark hair with very little gray in it, coiled about like a crown; and large dark, dancing eyes. She is only half Hawaiian. Her father was a Scot who left her a fortune, which made her one of the richest women in the islands. From her husband she inherited the Crown lands, including Waikiki Beach.

Millard told me that before we were married, the princess had wanted to adopt him as her son, to be heir to the Hawaiian throne! There would have been a great ceremony involved with no men present, she told him, only herself and the most beautiful hula dancers on the islands. So it seems I saved him from this extraordinary fate! It is difficult to tell where humor stops and reality begins with her. She even told Millard that his father was really his archenemy, President Franklin Roosevelt, and that she was his mother! She said Millard had been conceived under a gardenia hedge! Considering that she couldn't have been more than ten years his senior, it would have been a remarkable conception.

We disembarked with the Royal Hawaiian band playing for us, each of us with a hundred and sixty double flower leis hung around our necks. It was hot as blazes, but most exciting! We were receiving a real royal welcome!

A few days later, after all the official business, the princess chartered a plane and flew us all around the islands. We spent a few days on the big island of Hawaii, visiting the princess's pet project, homesteads for poor Hawaiians, and we spent the night on top of the volcano at Volcano House. We explored the lava flows and listened to stories about the Hawaiian Goddess of the Volcano, Madame Pele. We threw flower leis and champagne into the crater in tribute to the goddess. Many people said they had met her walking on the barren lava flows and even talked to her, only to have her disappear suddenly! The park superintendent even told us that Madame Pele once had thumbed a ride with him and after leaving his car she simply vanished. He was perfectly serious about it!

The princess said that the last eruption of the big volcano some years before had threatened to engulf the city, and the U.S. Navy had sent planes to deflect the lava flow with bombs. Hawaiians protested in vain against this, saying the goddess wouldn't like it. Sure enough, the young fliers involved met violent and terrible deaths soon after. Two of the planes collided inexplicably, crashed into a huge oil tank and burst into flames. As the fliers floated to earth in their parachutes, a gust of wind blew them straight into the conflagration! The last living flier disappeared from an ocean liner going home to the States. The princess said that every Hawaiian knew that it was a death warrant for Amelia Earhart to have a monument erected to her when she was in Hawaii on the first leg of her flight across the Pacific. Her plane disappeared and Amelia Earhart was gone forever.

During the more serious moments of our visit, the princess spoke about the imminence of war with Japan. She was bitterly opposed to statehood for Hawaii because of the great influx of Japanese into the islands. She told us there were only about forty thousand genuine Hawaiians left, and that many of the Japanese, including the small Japanese fishing boats buzzing about our fleet in Pearl Harbor, were on spying missions for their country. She was quite sure that the owner of a Japanese newspaper in Honolulu was the head of that spy ring.

Millard told her that he, too, was worried about Japanese military power, almost more than he was about Adolph Hitler's growing armed forces. Millard thought the United States could stay out of another European war, but he feared Japan might try to take our Pacific islands, Hawaii, and the Philippines by force, and he knew we were not prepared to fight a naval war in the Pacific.

"Japan has recently invaded China," the princess said, "so maybe her warlords are planning to take all of Asia first!"

At that time racial tensions between Hawaiians and Americans (white) had been heightened by the notorious Fortescue murder that took place just before we arrived. The case stirred up much animosity between Hawaiians and Americans in the islands, almost to the point of riots. The princess was especially concerned because the young Hawaiian who was accused of raping Mrs. Fortescue's daughter, Thalia Massie (wife of a Navy lieutenant stationed in Hawaii), was a lad whose mother had worked for the princess all her life, and she had known the boy as a good young man. Mrs. Fortescue was the daughter of Charles Bell of Washington, D.C., the brother of Alexander Graham Bell. Her daughter Thalia was a wild young person who drank a lot and had been having an affair with another naval officer in her husband's absence. Thalia had been with a gay group at a nightclub some distance out of town and had left the party to walk home alone. She claimed that on the way she was accosted and raped by several Hawaiian boys. She identified the son of the princess's maid as one of them.

The princess hired the best lawyers and Pinkerton detectives from New York, who proved that the Hawaiian boy had been at a party on the other side of the island on the night in question. But when he was released from prison, he was promptly picked up by Mrs. Fortescue and Thalia's husband. They took him to Mrs. Fortescue's house and tried to castrate him. The boy was bleeding to death when they put him into their car and headed for the nearest volcanic blow-hole to get rid of his body. Nothing ever appeared again once dropped in one of these holes. Foolishly, the murderers were speeding and were stopped by a policeman, who saw the boy's body and arrested them. The case created violent feelings between Americans and Hawaiians, but was smoothed over and dropped.

A few years later, Thalia and her husband were divorced. We met two people (respected Americans) who had picked up Thalia on the road after her alleged rape. They told us she had been wearing a dress covered with beaded fringe, and not a fringe was broken or a bead missing.

The princess told us that our U.S. governor of the Hawaiian islands was a solitary drinker and most unpopular. FDR had appointed him governor, but he was not the choice of anyone in the islands. The princess did not ask him to the spectacular luau she gave in our honor.

The luau was the social event of the season, given at her royal home. She said it was "in the manner of the King's smaller parties!"—with calabashes of poi and all the delicacies of Hawaiian cuisine; pig cooked underground, and fish steamed in ti leaves. There were masses of yellow and red roses and anthuriums everywhere. There were 150 guests, including the congressional delegation, seated at a long dinner table on the lanai (veranda). All the leaders of Honolulu were invited, except for the governor. The princess received her guests with two elderly Hawaiian gentlemen wearing black satin knee breeches. One of them wore the rare royal yellow feather cape and announced the guests as they arrived, chanting a description of each one in Hawaiian. He introduced Millard as "the great young king of the East," and myself as "Princess Lyolani, beautiful queen of the skies." Behind our hostess stood two beautiful ladies-in-waiting wearing white satin holokus and holding tall standards topped with big red paradise feather fans. The princess herself was queenly in a trailing black lace holoku, a magnificent diamond tiara, and a jeweled Royal Order on her bosom.

There was an army of Hawaiian waiters in black, wearing the

royal yellow feather capes with black and red crescents. We were entertained by more than 100 entertainers in an amphitheater after dinner. Millard and I were given huge leis, his was of jasmine and the royal rare yellow ilima, the golden yellow flower of the Kalakaua dynasty. My lei was made of double strands of jasmine (pikaki) tied with huge orchids.

Toward the end of the entertainment there was a "presentation of a souvenir to Senator and Mrs. Tydings." The princess's beautiful daughter, Kapiolani, in white satin holoku, came out on the stage, and I stepped forward to receive a long package and the most beautiful basket of orchids that I had ever seen. In the bundle was a large woven grass mat, one of the very finest, like tapestry, which used to be made only for kings. It belonged to King Kamehameha the Great, who first conquered and unified the Islands. The head of the Bishop Museum in Honolulu told us he had been trying to get the princess to give it to the museum for years. They are not made anymore, and she had the few left in existence. Many years later, I returned to Hawaii and gave it to the museum.

The presentation was a most dramatic business. Floodlights were on, Hawaiian music played, and movie cameras filmed it all. I turned, basket in arms, to show it to the other guests and made a deep curtsy to the princess, which made a hit with her and with the guests too. I wore my new gown, a white tulle, hoop-skirted, off-the-shoulder Gone With the Wind affair. With the pikaki leis, it was spectacular!

Later, when leaving the party, we met the princess's son Prince Kalakawa, or "Koke." I had heard of his many drunken peccadilloes, including the most recent and serious one. He had played football at the University of California, then had married the daughter of an admiral of the U.S. Naval fleet. After a late party where they both got drunk, their car went over the Pali (a high cliff on a mountain on Oahu island) and the bride was killed. The prince was found guilty of manslaughter and was out of jail on probation at the time of our visit.

After all the guests had left, there was a loud commotion from the kitchen. Out burst a tall, naked young giant, drunk as a lord and bellowing a welcome to my husband. It was Prince Koke.

"Senator," he shouted, "I want you to know you can have any or all of the dancing girls you saw tonight! Together or singly! They would be honored. . . ."

It was not his mother's sharp rebuke, "Koke, go back to the

kitchen!" that stopped him. He suddenly saw me, sobered instantly, and with a low bow to me, which would have done credit to a lord at Buckingham Palace, he said contritely, "But, of course, you are Mrs. Tydings! No man would ever look at another woman who had you!" With which pretty speech he bent over and kissed my hand. I was tongue-tied! The princess waved us into the automobile and that was the only time I ever met Prince Kalakawa. He was one of the handsomest men I ever saw.

Our final evening in Honolulu was spent at the princess's home with only a few of her closest friends and the best Hawaiian singers and musicians in the islands. I had been given a lovely hula costume and several hula lessons at the princess's insistence. She had asked me to dance for her guests. I was reluctant to do so but had to comply with her request. I danced and was applauded and photographed in movies by her photographer, Jimmy Williams. We sailed for home the next evening and had not been at sea long when we received a cable that Prince Koke had been arrested for the murder of his Hawaiian mistress! It happened, of course, at a drunken party, and the prince, in a rage, had flung a plate of poi at the girl, which cut her jugular vein. This time he went to jail for several years (in California) before being let out on parole for good behavior.

Although the princess had promised to visit us at Oakington and we had promised to return to Hawaii to see her, the promises were not fulfilled. We never met again. When Millard went to Manila in 1945, the war was still on, and in 1946, when he went back after the war to celebrate Philippine independence, Princess Kawananakoa was dead. Millard visited the royal tomb and left flowers with our love for a truly royal lady.

Christmas at Mar-a-Lago

The Davieses invited us to spend the Christmas holidays with them at Marjorie's palatial estate, Mar-a-Lago, in Palm Beach. We had entertained Mother and my sister, Rahel, at Oakington the previous Christmas and so this year was my father's turnabout-is-fair-play year! I was excited and pleased to be visiting the famous Florida resort. I had been there only once with both of my parents and we had stayed at the Breakers hotel.

It was an unforgettable Christmas. We took the children and their nurse, and Rahel and her husband brought their little girl. Marjorie's daughters, Adelaide Riggs and children,. Eleanor Hutton Rand,

and Nedenia Hutton completed the group. I have an enormous group photograph of us all that Marjorie insisted upon. There were children's parties and grown-ups' parties and a fantastic, enormous Christmas tree in the huge drawing room with stacks of hundreds of gifts heaped around it. We had always had beautiful Christmas celebrations with our parents, but this was almost too much! I think that was the year I received a gorgeous (wide) diamond bracelet, among other things.

She had employed Josef Urban, the famed artist and designer of elaborate stage sets, to design her house—Mar-a-Lago. The property encompassed a very large nine-hole golf course, the mansion, a building that housed a staff of sixty or seventy servants, an enormous slat house or greenhouse, and a cottage for her personal secretary. She had another secretary to keep accounts and pay bills, and her first husband's brother (known as "Unkie" to his nieces) looked after her investments, most of which were in General Foods at that time. The property originally included the land that she gave for the Bath and Tennis Club. The main road ran between the house and the sea, so the former was built on land high enough to screen out the road! There was a tunnel under it so that one could reach her private beach and cabanas. The golf course was on the lake side of the property, which ran from the Atlantic Ocean to Lake Worth, the whole enclosed by a high stone wall and landscaping.

The mansion contained, both inside and out, a famous collection of ancient Spanish tiles that Marjorie told me was the largest in the world, now that the Spanish Civil War had destroyed the largest. There was an enormous dining room and drawing room, replicas of two in Rome and Venice, and besides three master suites (for her and Daddy and Dennie), there were four guest room suites. The house boasted a tower, which had several bedroom-baths, each on a different floor, where the children loved to stay. On the lake side of it was the most beautiful, and certainly the biggest, semicircular patio with a carved Italian stone loggia embracing it on the house side. On the lake side, circular stairs descended to the golf course with tiers of fountains from patio to lawn in between the stone stairs.

I have described it as briefly as possible, for I have never seen anything comparable to Mar-a-Lago. Millard and I spent many happy times there, although it was closed up during World War II.

We were royally entertained at the most splendid Palm Beach mansions by charming friends of my father's and Marjorie's: the Reases, Stotesburys, Donahues (she was a Woolworth of ten-cent store fortune). Marjorie gave several formal and informal parties.

Senator and Mrs. Tydings at the Preakness Race in 1936.

Ambassador Joseph Davies and Senator Tydings on the yacht, *Sea Cloud,* 1936.

Oakington Farms, Eleanor Davies Tydings' new home, on the Chesapeake Bay, Maryland. Photograph by PHYFE, New York.

The Gold Parlor with portrait of Ambassador Joseph Davies in robes of the University of North Wales.

Eleanor Tydings at Oakington, Spring, 1937.

Eleanor and Millard Tydings in Honolulu, 1937.

Senator Tydings wins re-election in Maryland in spite of FDR's effort to defeat him, 1938.

Emlen Davies married Robert Leon Grosjean at Oakington in 1939. Photo by
PHYFE, New York.

Eleanor Tydings (right) and sister Rahel Walker at the Grosjean wedding.

Eleanor Tydings at the wedding of Emlen Davies and Robert Grosjean at Oakington, with daughter Eleanor II and son Joseph, 1939.

Millard and Eleanor at home at Oakington.

Ambassador Joseph E. Davies on the *Sea Cloud*.

Eleanor and Millard at the Brussels Embassy, with Ambassador Joseph Davies and Marjorie Davies, 1938.

The U.S. Ambassador and Marjorie Post Davies in Moscow, 1937.

Marjorie Davies and Eleanor Davies Tydings, Brussels Embassy, 1938.

Ambassador Joseph Davies is the first member of diplomatic corps in Russia to meet Joseph Stalin, 1938.

Ambassador Davies, Joe Davies Tydings, Eleanor, and Millard Tydings, Maryland's favorite son for President, at Democratic Convention in Chicago, 1940.

SOVIET ENVOY GREETS SENATOR'S WIFE AT RECEPTION *10 - 1944*

Mrs. Millard S. Tydings (right), wife of the Senator from Maryland, being received yesterday at the Soviet Embassy by the Ambassador, Andrei A. Gromyko, and Mrs. Gromyko, as she arrived for the reception which celebrated the twenty-seventh anniversary of the Russian revolution.

October, 1944.

PRESIDENT ROOSEVELT ACCEPTS INAUGURAL MEDAL.
Sculptor Jo Davidson presents Franklin Delano Roosevelt with the First Medal commemorating the President's Fourth Inauguration, January 18, 1945. Above, left to right, are members of the Medals Committee, Joseph E. Davies, Chairman; Melvin D. Hildreth and Alfons Landa.

President Roosevelt accepts inaugural medal, January 18, 1945. Ambassador Davies, far left.

Ambassador Joseph Davies, the Special Advisor to President Truman, and Winston Churchill, on Davies' way to join the President at the Potsdam Peace Conference, 1945.

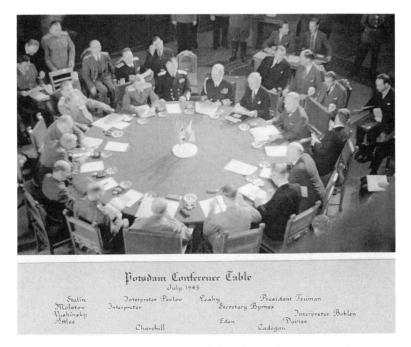

Potsdam Conference Table
July 1945

Stalin	Interpreter Povlov	Leahy	President Truman
Molotov	Interpreter		Secretary Byrnes
Vyshinsky			Interpreter Bohlen
Attlee		Eden	Davies
	Churchill		Cadogan

Joseph Davies sits on Harry Truman's left at the Potsdam Peace Conference.

Mrs. Tydings Calls D.C. Women
Slackers in Plea for Nurses' Aides

1946

Agreed—More Nurses' Aides Needed!

Mrs. Carl Pforzheimer jr., who has 3,000 hours as a nurse's

Hospitals' Need for Workers Is Stressed

By SPENCE DRUMMOND

Mrs. Millard Tydings yesterday criticized eligible Washington women who, "apparently believing VJ-day solved all the Capital's hospital problems," have allowed the Volunteer Red Cross Nurses' Aide Corps to dwindle to less than half its wartime strength.

In effect, she said they are slackers, "for the war is not over."

"If the ranks are thinning because of exodus from the city of a number of zealous wartime residents, as it seems according to the records, then it is indicated that it's time Washingtonians came to their own aid," declared the Maryland Senator's wife, who heads the District corps.

Pointing out that the corps is "a peacetime as well as a wartime necessity," Mrs. Tydings announced that a two-week recruiting campaign will be opened tomorrow.

200 Recruits Needed

In one year, she said, the number of aides on active duty has dropped from 2,000 to 950. Of the 950 remaining, only 345 actually worked last month.

At least 200 recruits for day duty are needed for classes beginning January 21, requests to the corps offices show. Women from 18 through 55 years of age, who have completed high school, are eligible. One hundred and 50 hours of service yearly will be required, after completing 80 hours training in a seven-and-a-half-week course.

Eleanor Tydings, Chairman of Nurses Aid Corps during World War II.

Eleanor Tydings II voted sweetheart of Joe Tydings' regiment in Germany 1947. Photographed by Mershon Studio, Baltimore.

T/5 Joe Tydings, Horse Platoon, 6th Constabulary Regiment, Army of Occupation, Germany, 1946.

Millard and Eleanor Tydings at the Democratic Convention, Philadelphia, 1948.
Photograph by *Jules Schick Photography,* Philadelphia.

The Tydings' and the Davies' at a party in Versailles, 1948.

T/5 Joe Tydings comes home from the Army Occupation in Germany during World War II. With Eleanor at Palm Beach, 1948.

Senator Millard Tydings gives away the bride, Eleanor II, at her wedding to Francis Warrington Gillet Jr., at Oakington, 1953.

Emlen Knight Davies watches the senator kiss the mother of the bride at the wedding of Eleanor II at Oakington, 1953.

Senator Tydings kisses the bride. Photo by *Vernon M. Price,* Baltimore.

Senator and Mrs. Tydings at the Preakness Race, 1956, after his primary nomination victory in Maryland. He was forced to resign the nomination because of illness.

Eleanor Tydings II greets her grandmother at wedding in 1953.

Eleanor Tydings meets Governor Adlai Stevenson, in the rain at Baltimore, when managing his Maryland campaign for the presidency.

Eleanor Tydings and Millard Tydings II, June 2, 1958.

A CANDIDATE FOR 30 HOURS

When Fame Came To Mrs. Tydings

MRS. MILLARD E. TYDINGS

Fame came in a big way for 30 hours to Mrs. Millard E. Tydings, who hit the spotlight in every State in the Union, on Aug. 26, 1956, when she announced her candidacy for the U. S. Senate, a position held by her husband for 24 continuous years.

Mrs. Tydings sought to run in place of her husband who had won the Democratic nomination in the primary but was forced to resign because of ill health.

She was urged by not only women and the United Democratic Women's Clubs of Maryland but by numerous men leaders. A candidate for just 30 hours, she lost by a narrow margin at the State convention.

"Brought up in politics" is the way Mrs. Tydings describes her life in Washington from the age of 8. She continued in politics after marrying Sen. Tydings in 1935 and making "Oakington," Harford county, her home.

SHE WAS born in Watertown, Wis., daughter of the late Joseph E. and Emlen Knight Davies. Mr. Davies came to Washington in 1912 and held executive positions under President Woodrow Wilson. Later he was Ambassador to Russia, Belgium and Luxembourg and a member of Truman Potsdam Delegation.

A graduate of Holton Arms School, Washington, in 1921,

and of Vassar College in 1925, Mrs. Tydings has made politics—local, state, national and international — and hospitals her major interests. She organized the Harford County Women's Democratic Club in 1936 and, in 1956, before the primary, organized the Women's Committee for Tydings-For-U. S. Senate.

She has taken an active part in the United Democratic Women's Clubs of Maryland and the National Democratic Women's Club in Washington.

Son Joseph is following in his parents' footsteps in politics, having been re-nominated to serve a second term in House of Delegates in the recent primary.

During World War II Mrs. Tydings was dissatisfied with conditions in Washington hospitals. So with 2 outstanding civic minded women, she worked to make a "dream come true"—the Hospital Center. Her husband sponsored legislation in the Senate for this work. Mrs. Tydings is an honorary member of the hospital board.

CHAIRMAN of the District of Columbia Red Cross Nurses Aides from 1944 to 1946, Mrs. Tydings worked in the Senate Ladies Club Red Cross Unit from 1935 to 1950; in D. C. hospitals as a Red Cross Nurses Aide from 1941 to 1945, in Junior League of Asheville, N. C. from 1926 to 1928.

She is now a member of the Women's Auxiliary, Johns

Hopkins Hospital and Harford Memorial Hospital; on the board of governors of St. John's College, Annapolis; member of the board of UN of Maryland; member of President Eisenhower's Conference on Foreign Aspects of U. S. National Security; member of the John Eager Howard Chapter, Daughters of the American Revolution, and of the Sulgrave Club, Washington.

Her avocations are gardening, golf, the theater and music. At one time she played the violin.   M. K. G.

Candidate for the U.S. Senate for thirty hours, 1956.

Part IV

Chapter 18

The Supreme Court Packing Bill Fight and FDR's Purge Campaign, 1938

On February 5 I had come to the Capitol to have lunch with my husband and was sitting in the gallery, waiting for him to come on the Senate floor and signal to me to join him in the Senators' lunchroom. It was a lovely day, and I had hoped that he might be able to join me for a golf game. I should have known better, as he was planning to introduce "Pay As You Go" legislation for the Congress once again. However, there were only a few senators on the floor, chatting quietly, or sitting at their desks reading. Nobody expected anything to happen, but something certainly did that day. A messenger from the White House marched up the aisle to the rostrum and read a message.

The president wanted legislation, which became famous as the "Supreme Court Packing Bill." The bill would give the president the power to appoint a new justice to the Court for every one who did not retire at the age of seventy. The president would be allowed to appoint six new justices! He would control the Supreme Court and our tripartite system of government with its checks and balances of the executive, legislative, and judiciary branches would be on the way to presidential dictatorship.

"So this is the way FDR is going to control the court!" I exclaimed to two Marylanders beside me. I hurried to Millard's office to give him the news. His jaw set and his eyes were icy.

That evening he was host at a stag dinner at our house. The guests were a group of conservative Democratic senators concerned with curbing the president's reckless increase in the Federal debt. They had all supported the pledge for economy in government in the

137

Democratic platform when Roosevelt was first elected president. Instead of discussing means of curbing his reckless spending, Millard's dinner became a council of war on how to defeat Roosevelt's Supreme Court bill. It was decided that Tydings would be the general behind the scenes, in charge of attack strategy. The group needed an outstanding liberal to be their front man and they decided upon Senator Burton K. Wheeler. Millard had telephoned that gentleman already and ascertained his opposition to the bill. He came to join them that evening.

Senator Wheeler agreed to be the front leader of the opposition in the Senate. His one proviso was that if and when it became conclusive that they could not get enough votes to defeat the bill in the Senate they would accept Senator Wheeler's decision and try for a compromise. It was agreed, and they began to canvass the Senate Democrats for votes against the bill. Republican Senators would be against it anyway, and the Tydings's group persuaded their important leaders, Senator Charles McNary, Arthur Vandenberg, and Bob Taft, to let the Democrats take the lead in the fight. Millard's steering committee of eighteen included southern Senators Walter George of Georgia, Harry Byrd of Virginia, Joseph Bailey of North Carolina, Cotton Ed Smith of South Carolina, Bennett "Champ" Clark of Missouri, Peter Goelet Gerry of Rhode Island, and Tom Connally of Texas, among others. The president's men for the bill were Senator Joe Robinson of Arkansas, Alben Barkley of Kentucky, Jimmy Byrnes of North Carolina, Bob LaFollette of Wisconsin, Hugo Black, etc.

I spent the evening hanging over the stair rail and listening at the pantry door, trying to hear the senators' conversation. I had a good idea that it was going to prove pretty important. I was right.

The president's enormous power of patronage, granting funds to most of the states to get the economy moving (called "priming the pump") would make it a tough fight. He practically controlled the House of Representatives, and to a lesser degree, the Senate. Any president could be a virtual dictator if the bill was passed. He would control the Supreme Court.

The Democratic leader in the Senate, Joseph Robinson (who had introduced Millard and I to each other), was a man of limited means. There was no government retirement provision in those days, and a senator's salary was modest. Senator Robinson had served many years in the Senate. His ambition was to become a member of the Supreme Court with its handsome salary and pension. The president had promised to appoint him whenever a seat on the Court became available. Roosevelt knew that the appointment of the mildly liberal Robinson would be a popular one. One of the justices might even resign to give him a seat. But the president needed Senator Robinson in the Senate to lead any fights for his legislative bills.

At this time, the Supreme Court consisted of four conservatives, Justices Butler, VanDervanter, McReynolds, and Sutherland. These gentlemen represented the sanctity of property rights, contracts, and the status quo. They believed that the best government would keep law and order and represent business. The three liberals on the Court were Brandeis, Cardozo, and Stone. They believed in leaving constitutional theory and law to the other two branches of the government and that the Supreme Court should only impose the judicial veto when necessary. The Chief Justice was Charles Evans Hughes, whom Woodrow Wilson had defeated for the presidency. He and Justice Roberts were considered to be the two moderates on the court.

Justice and Mrs. Harlan Fiske Stone lived on Wyoming Avenue, not far from my mother's house. The justice took a daily walk past our house and became interested in April of 1935 when he saw the car belonging to the young Senator from Maryland parked in front of 2941 Massachusetts Avenue every evening. He remarked upon this to Mrs. Stone, who replied that there were three pretty Davies daughters, and maybe Senator Tydings was finally going courting! These two dear people took a great interest in our marriage and entertained at a dinner in our honor soon after. Mrs. Stone always served the soup course from a large tureen in front of her at the table.

In 1936, the Supreme Court had invalidated Roosevelt's first big piece of New Deal legislation, the National Industrial Recovery Act, or N.R.A., which Millard had fought against. Two old maids in Havre de Grace who ran a tiny notions shop (pins, needles, etc.) had come to him in tears. They had received notice from the Federal government that they must take on two paid assistants. This was impossible. They barely earned enough in the shop to support themselves and their aged parents upstairs. Millard told them to pay no attention to the Federal order. He would represent them in court at no charge, if necessary.

This had happened before Roosevelt was reelected president by 27 million votes in 1936. Now the battle was on between the president and the liberals versus the conservative constitutionalists in the Senate.

The president's Supreme Court bill came up first before the Senate Judiciary Committee. Senator Henry M. Ashurst was the chairman. He was a charming, courtly old boy who was said to have been a cowboy of little or no education from his western state. He was an avid reader however, and one of the most intelligent men in the Senate, serving his fifth term in that body. He didn't like the bill and at first had made a speech attacking it, but he was a loyal "party man" and was persuaded to go along with the president. So he made another speech supporting it the next day. I was in the Senate Ladies' Gallery when Millard inquired: "How can the distinguished Senator speak on both sides of the question?"

Senator Ashurst: "When my dear young friend from Maryland has been in the Senate as long as I have, he will find himself voting on all three sides of every question! Inconsistency is one of the greatest virtues!"

As chairman of the Judiciary Committee, however, Senator Ashurst was not expected to expedite the hearings on the bill, and he let it drag on for two months.

Another senator as adept as Ashurst at staying on the high side of controversial issues was Senator James Hamilton Lewis of Illinois. He was another courtly old gentleman whose curling whiskers were faintly pink, although his hair was white. He always wore a cutaway coat and carried (not always clean) white gloves.

Once when Millard asked him how he could vote for a New Deal bill when he had recently denounced it, he replied, twirling his mustache and combing his fingers through his beard, "My dear and distinguished young friend, if you would wring from my reluctant lips an answer to your interrogatory, I must tell you, Senator, that in these mighty United States, in the sovereign state of Illinois, in the great city of Chicago, I have the honor, sir, to represent a lot of G-D thieves!"

On July 9, Senator Burton K. Wheeler opened the debate against the Supreme Court bill on the Senate floor with a violent denunciation of it. Millard waited for weeks until thirty-two of his group had spoken against it. Then he delivered the thirty-third speech attacking it in the Senate. This was important because thirty-three votes could defeat a vote against cloture (a vote to cut off debate).

Millard and his senatorial group met secretly and almost daily to report progress and discuss strategy. They worked tirelessly to line up Senate votes against the bill during the months that the committee hearings dragged on. They also tried to persuade one of the Supreme Court Justices to testify against it but did not succeed. Many distinguished lawyers spoke against the bill before the committee and Chairman Ashurst let the hearings drag on. All the senators called "Millard's Irreconcilables" spoke against it, including my husband.

Then something wonderful happened. Senator Wheeler's daughter was in the hospital with her newborn baby, and Justice Brandeis's wife came to see her, bringing flowers and a gift for the baby. As she was leaving, Mrs. Brandeis said, "Tell your father that I think he is right about the Court Packing bill!" Of course, his daughter told Senator Wheeler this, and he promptly called upon his friend the justice. That gentleman in turn went to see the Chief Justice, Charles Evans Hughes. The result was that Mr. Hughes himself wrote a fine letter to the Senate Judiciary committee, which legally condemned the bill! The Committee voted against it and so reported to the Senate for debate by that body. I sent Senator Wheeler's grandbaby a beautiful bonnet.

Almost sixty years later, I heard a charming story about Senator Wheeler's courtship of his wife, as told by an old friend. The Senator was just a poor young man without a job, and he told his future wife that he "had nothing to give her except a pat on the fanny." Whereupon the lady replied demurely, "Well, that *would* be nice!"

In the meantime, the nation's press had informed the general public of the dangers of the bill, and it became increasingly unpopular.

We heard that some of the president's close friends were urging him to withdraw it, or at lease to modify its present form, but Roosevelt was obdurate. The Supreme Court had invalidated several of his unconstitutional pieces of legislation and he had not been able to replace any of the justices with men of his own persuasion. The president was still determined to control the Court.

In May, the Supreme Court upheld the Social Security bill. Millard had voted "present" on it because he thought it failed to adequately protect the Social Security funds from the general Treasury money. He felt it should be used only for Social Security payments.

Then, on May 21, Justices VanDervanter and Brandeis announced they would retire. These events were major reasons why the president should have accepted one of the alternative compromise bills. It was a blow to Senator Robinson that no word came to him from the White House giving him one of the two newly vacant seats on the Court. Finally, the president did send for him, and once again promised him the appointment to the Court, if he would continue to lead the fight for the Supreme Court Bill. Senator Robinson was sixty-five years old and had served as Democratic leader of the Senate for more than fourteen years. Although he was tired and did not like the bill, he remained loyal to the president. He had great influence and popularity in the Senate and had lined up many votes for it.

The senators all knew of Roosevelt's shabby treatment of Senator Robinson. The news media had daily discussed the merits and demerits of the Supreme Court bill and the public had become concerned. Old Vice President Garner was so disgusted with it that he went home to Texas. Before he left, he shouted in the Democratic cloakroom that Tydings was "a real patriot"! He was very fond of Millard and would often invite him to his office (which he called the "Bureau of Education"), for a shot of bourbon, "to strike a blow for liberty!"

Early in April, the Davieses had come home from Russia. My father was coming back as planned to report to the president and prepare for his new ambassadorial post. Marjorie had been ill in Moscow and was going into a hospital in New York. I lunched there with them both and Marjorie told me enthusiastically about the collection of Russian historical objets d'art and paintings they had purchased in Moscow and Leningrad. My father had brought the great collection of paintings home as a gift to his alma mater, the University of Wisconsin. The president had asked Daddy to bring the pictures to show him, so they were being hung in the East Room (the ballroom) at the White House. We heard later that when my father asked FDR to show him which pictures he liked best, the president selected two splendid paintings of the Caucasus Mountains with glaciers running down to the Black Sea. These had already been given to Millard and me, he told the president! They were a beautiful addition to the big glass-walled room at Oakington, which looked out on the Chesapeake Bay. I often wondered about the artist's surprise if he could have seen where his pictures ended up. They hung there for forty years. I teased Millard that this gift to us must have been the cause of FDR's bitter enmity toward my husband!

I rode to Washington in a private compartment on the train from New York with Daddy and fought the battle of the Court Packing bill most of the way. He used all the arguments of the liberal New Dealers, and I repeated all of Millard's constitutional arguments and principles, which had become my own.

Finally I said, "All right, Daddy! You know the law better than I do, you are more eloquent than I am, and you have a far better vocabulary than I have! But you must admit that all my principles and theories of government you have taught me!"

My father tossed back his head and gave his deep, hearty laugh. "You win, my darling!" he said, and that was the end of the argument.

Our friends among the most powerful Republicans in the Senate had agreed to let Millard's group of Democrats take the lead in the debate. The Republican leader, Senator Charles McNary, and Senator Arthur Vandenberg sat silent. The president had not consulted with the Democratic leaders of Labor or Agriculture or the labor unions before introducing the bill. All through April and May, stories of the pressure brought to bear on Democratic senators by the president's administration were rife around town. Judgeships, diplomatic posts, and Works Progress projects were handed out in return for Senate votes. One Senator was told if he "didn't go along" the WPA would stop all operations in his state. Senator Bert Wheeler had been working hard to get a $17 million dollar dam for Montana. The dam was built, but the president gave the credit for it to Senator Wheeler's colleague, Senator Murray. Millard said, "Pap, patronage and projects were the order of the day."

The great debate raged on the Senate floor. Senator Robinson roared his support of the bill for two hours, his face flushed crimson, perspiration dripping from his brow. Senator Royal Copeland, a medical doctor from New York who was fond of Joe Robinson, interrupted his speech begging him to stop, but he would not. It finally became clear that there were not enough Senate votes to defeat the bill. The president's power and Robinson's popularity made it impossible. Senator Wheeler reminded my husband of his pledge to abide by Wheeler's decision when the fight was lost. Millard finally reluctantly agreed to telephone Tommy Corcoran, the president's close aid. He asked Corcoran to inform Mr. Roosevelt that the opposition to the president's Senate bill would accept it, with the exception of the present Court, and would give him two additional court appointments of justices who would retire. The president's man lightheartedly turned Senator Tydings's proposal down cold. "The Boss won't accept it unless you give him the Chief Justice too," said he. "Over my dead body!" said my husband. He told Corcoran that "this offer is 'showdown,' not poker!" The senator would wait at Oakington to hear the president's decision.

It was a beautiful weekend on the upper Chesapeake. No phone call came from the White House. We became resigned to a long hot summer's filibuster in the Senate, with small chance of success. In Washington, Senator Robinson was worrying about his reluctant leadership of the president's faction in the Senate, about his own health, and his family's economic future.

Early Tuesday morning, July 14, Senator Joseph Robinson dropped dead of a heart attack and our phones started to ring. One was from Corcoran.

"The Boss will accept your version of the bill, Senator," said he.

"Nothing doing!" said my husband.

The president's Supreme Court bill died with Robinson. His death had released enough unhappy senators' votes to kill it.

And that is the story of a president's attempt to control one of the three branches of our government. Mr. Roosevelt was not content with his executive prerogatives and his great "power of the purse" over Congress. Many years later a Republican president who was after illegal powers would be forced to resign his high office in disgrace. His name was Richard Nixon. In 1937 nobody had ever heard of Richard Nixon. I felt then, and still firmly believe, that God is looking after our country. In 1937, two justices had retired and the president was able to appoint their successors, but our dear friend, Joseph Robinson was dead. His widow told me of the promises the president had repeatedly made to her husband, how FDR had constantly postponed acting upon them, and how shabbily he had treated his great Senate leader. She begged me to prevent Millard from working too hard as Joe Robinson had. As Senator Robinson had little, if any, savings, the Democratic party gave Mrs. Robinson a position as postmistress in a small town in Arkansas.

The tragedy of Senator Robinson's death was followed by another near tragedy involving a high official in the Roosevelt administration. This gentleman, handsome and dignified when sober, became a homosexual when drinking. Apparently he was drunk on the Robinson funeral train and attacked a porter. The train was full of government dignitaries going to the funeral and the scandal went like wildfire.

Everyone on the Robinson funeral train knew that the president's bill was defeated. All that was necessary was to give it a decent burial. Vice President Garner went to the White House upon his return from the funeral. He told Millard that he gave the president the bad news "with the bark on it!" The vice president said that if a

Texan wanted the naked truth and did not want to be let down easy, they asked for it "with the bark on." The vice president told Senators Tydings and Wheeler to "write their own ticket," about the bill. They did.

On July 21, the full Senate voted to recommit Bill No. 1392 to the Judiciary Committee, and there it died an ignominious death on the Senate floor as Senator Hiram Johnson (one of my favorite Republicans) shouted, "Is the Supreme Court out of the way?"

"Yes, the Court is out of the way," some senator replied.

"Then glory be to God!" roared Senator Johnson.

I had been in the Senate Gallery at the birth of the bill and I was there that afternoon at its burial. I was wearing my best hat. Maybe God had nothing to do with the birth of a baby or the death of a senator, but I prefer to believe He did!

Millard had introduced his "Pay As You Go" bill for balancing the Federal budget soon after the Senate convened in early February that year. Right afterward, the president had introduced his Budget bill and the Supreme Court Packing bill. After the latter was "out of the way," Millard managed to pass his "Fair Trade Enabling" act by putting it on a budget bill as an amendment. Small business and small independent retailers had long suffered and often were put out of business by the big chain stores who could sell products under their cost. It was called "loss leader selling." The president signed the Tydings Bill into law in August.

It was a very hot summer. The country was beginning to worry over Germany's bellicose dictator, Mussolini's war in Ethiopia, and the civil war in Spain. Americans were bitterly divided between isolationism and interventionism. Neutrality bills came up in the Senate, and Millard voted against one that he thought gave too much power to the president and took away the constitutional prerogatives of Congress. When another bill came up that did not do so, he voted for it. Nationwide polls showed that our people did not want to become involved in another European war. Millard told me we were totally unprepared to fight Hitler's war machine. He was working to pass new amendments to the Philippine Independence bill to make the transition from a part of the United States to independence easier for the Filipinos. Once that was achieved, my husband did not bring it up for the Senate to vote upon. He simply sat silently and waited. The president wanted it passed and out of the way. He wanted the Senate to repeal the Arms Embargo bill. Millard knew this and did nothing to introduce his new Philippine bill. Of course no other senator would or could. The president finally sent for my senator to come to the White House.

"Well, Millard, what about that Philippine bill of yours? Are we going to pass it in the Senate this session?"

I could imagine my husband's smile. It wouldn't be reflected in his blue eyes. He would be relishing his old enemy's invitation.

"If you wish, Mr. President. I think I can get it passed."

Roosevelt snapped his mouth shut and the ever-present cigarette holder tilted up belligerently. "You must bring Eleanor to see us," he said.

"Thank you, Mr. President." Millard bowed and left. We had not been invited to the White House since the evening party in January 1935, and certainly would not have gone if we had been, although many considered an invitation to the Executive Mansion the same as a command to attend. I had gone to the Senate Ladies' yearly luncheons there given by Mrs. Roosevelt, but that was different.

Millard had been criticized as an isolationist when he didn't vote for the original Arms Embargo bill. Later, when it didn't give too much power to the president, he voted for it. His great achievement that session was the passage of the largest peace-time appropriation in history for the Navy. He played the major role in the Senate in getting more than a million dollars for two battleships, two Navy cruisers, eight destroyers, eight submarines, and five hundred airplanes. After Pearl Harbor's terrible destruction of so much of our fleet, the ships in that bill were about all the Navy we had left.

There was a hot debate in August over another of the president's bills. This one was for $700 million dollars for Slum Clearance and Housing. Millard succeeded in getting an amendment to it that would limit every state to one-twentieth of the total amount. Again, he was protecting states' rights, he told me. The Senate remained in session most of the summer and complained bitterly about the sizzling heat.

When I wrote to my stepmother, I tried to tell her the most amusing and gossipy stories about Capital City Socialites. When I wrote to Daddy, my letters were mostly about political life there and in Maryland. Some of my tales involved people whom Marjorie knew, and several were about the Polish embassy before Poland was conquered in 1939. A new ambassador and his wife had arrived, and Millard and I were invited to a dinner party at the embassy. The ambassador, Count Jerczy Potocki, was quite young and good looking. I was seated beside him and our conversation turned to the pleasure of country living. I proudly described our farm, Oakington, and he was most interested.

"I have one too," he said. "How many acres have you at Oakington?"

I told him with some boastfulness, "Five hundred and fifty. How many acres have you?"

"Twenty thousand or so" was his nonchalant reply.

I felt small indeed! I learned afterward that the Potockis were the largest landowners in Poland. They owned many castles, each with a house staff of sixty or seventy servants.

Now Adolph Hitler was making threatening noises about taking over Danzig and the Polish Corridor, as well as Czechoslovakia's Sudetenland. When we had moved back to Washington after our trip to Hawaii, I found myself once more in conversation with Count Jerczy. I asked him whether he wasn't concerned about his property in Poland.

"No indeed," said he. "My mother, Countess Betska, is German, you know."

"What about Russia?" I queried.

"There is no danger" was his reply.

"I would like to make you a bet," said I. "I'll wager my Oakington acres against yours that you are wrong!"

He was wrong. He lost the bet, and so I should be the owner of all those thousands of Potocki acres!

Another story involving the Polish embassy happened the evening when I made my bet with the ambassador. A senator and his wife who were dear friends of ours were also guests. They were not people of any great wealth and the senator's wife owned one small "fur piece", which could hardly be dignified by the word scarf. She was extremely proud of it and always draped it around her neck at formal occasions. She was wearing it at the Polish embassy dinner. It was a warm evening and during dinner it slipped from around her shoulders. At the end of the repast she saw that her fur was gone and exclaimed in distress. The butler dived under the table and to the accompaniment of shrill yaps and barks, the man brought up a snapping, struggling poodle with a furry, bedraggled thing in his teeth, which had been the lady guest's prize possession. She moaned in distress as the hostess picked up her erring pet and crooned over it, "My poor baby! He was hungry! He always sits at the dinner table and eats his dinner with us!" The ambassadress apparently didn't even notice the limp object in her guest's hand, which had once been a "fur piece."

Fortunately for the count, his wife was a very rich South American. After the war, the count was on the ship I was on going to Paris. His traveling companion was a pretty, young married lady I knew. One day when I was having a fitting at one of the Paris dressmaking establishments, the vendeuse told me that Countess Potocki was lying down in the next room (she suffered from ill health) and would like to see me. I went in and she greeted me languidly.

"I understand you came over on the *United States* last week. My husband and little Mrs. B_____ were on board. I do feel sorry for that poor woman. She is just the most recent of Jerczy's little friends. Of course, this affair won't last long, because, you see, I have the money!"

Because of Millard's opposition to the president on so many issues, FDR spent all of 1938 working for my husband's defeat in the election. As we had only been married a little more than two years, this election was to be my first experience with the lies and mudslinging of political contests. Millard himself had never been through a very bad experience in his past elections. This time it would be very different!

When Roosevelt's opposition to Tydings's reelection first became clear after the Court Packing fight, my husband began dividing his time between Washington and Maryland, trying to maintain the support of his constituents so he could stay in the Senate. He drove hundreds of miles a week, attending meetings of state and local organizations, and then drove back to Washington to be there when the Senate was in session. The president tried to persuade Congressman Davey Lewis from western Maryland to run against Millard in the primary, but Mr. Lewis was almost seventy and didn't want to run. Then Secretary Ickes and Drew Pearson began scouring the state to find an adequate candidate.

Toward the end of the spring session, President Roosevelt went on the attack in earnest. On June 1, he spoke nationwide on the radio, saying it was his duty to tell the voters which members of Congress were anti-New Deal, so they could vote against them. Then Secretary of the Interior Harold Ickes fired a man Millard had appointed to a high federal position in our state. Next Roosevelt vetoed Millard's bill for the construction of a huge bridge over the Chesapeake Bay, and Ickes killed Tydings's plans for two other bridges, one across the Susquehanna at Havre de Grace and one at Morgantown in southern Maryland. All these bridges were important for commerce in Maryland. Millard began making speeches all over the state. He told the voters he was running on his record both on the battlefields of France in World War I and in his years in the House and Senate. He said he didn't want to be a senator if he couldn't vote his honest convictions. He told the people that he had supported the Democratic platform of economy in government and the New Deal had not. He said he would not be a rubber stamp for any man. His oath of office as a senator was to the Constitution, not to the president.

Roosevelt then gave another nationwide radio talk against Millard on August 16, and Millard responded with a statewide radio address on August 21. His speech was on a Sunday evening, just before Edgar Bergen's popular *Charlie McCarthy* show. Millard said he was no Charlie McCarthy and told Marylanders about their constitutional rights. They should not be bribed or intimidated into voting for other than a man of their own choice by anyone from outside their state. By this time, everyone expected the president to come into the state to campaign against Millard. So it was no surprise when he came on Labor Day weekend, after a trip across country, boosting his New Deal program and lambasting the conservative Democrats who had opposed it, especially Millard.

The president of the University of Maryland (supposedly an old friend of Millard's) formally invited FDR to come to Maryland to inspect sites for bridges. Roosevelt and his entourage campaigned through Maryland by car and by boat on the bay and made a major speech at Denton on the Eastern shore. We were told that few Marylanders turned out to see him. Those who did gave him polite applause but cheered when Millard's name was mentioned. The president criticized Millard for voting against the New Deal legislation, and urged Marylanders to vote for Davey Lewis, who had decided to run. He even told the Marylanders that they would probably get their bridges if Lewis were elected! But the strategy backfired. The newspapers called it the "Invasion of Maryland" and the "Bridge Bribe." They had a field day with Roosevelt's efforts to defeat a leader of his own political party.

Meanwhile, Millard continued to speak all around Maryland. His speeches were based on the themes of the "Great Free State of Maryland" and our sacred individual freedoms. He said that if a president of the United States told the people whom they should vote for, he would be taking away their constitutional right to vote for the man of their choice. From there Millard would relate historical events when the people had lost their rights and their freedom. It followed naturally, he said, that we never really appreciate our blessings—our eyesight, our hearing, our health, or our loved ones—until we have lost them. He would begin speaking very quietly and factually and work up gradually to an eloquent climax that would produce an ovation.

Just before primary day, the columnist Drew Pearson wrote a despicable pamphlet about Millard and circulated it all over Maryland. It was nothing but lies, with a horrible cartoon of "Milord" Tydings on the cover. There were photographs of Oakington and the entrance gate to our lane, saying Millard had paid for both the estate and the lane with government money! It said we owned a mansion in Washington—we didn't, it was Mother's—and listed columns of blue-chip stocks, which we were supposed to own but didn't. Millard had only what he earned and I had my small income, which took care of the children's expenses. Pearson also went after me in his brochure, calling me a snob and a social climber. Millard was furious, but there was no time before the election to go on the air in rebuttal.

The primary election was on September 12, Defenders' Day in Maryland, commemorating the date that the British forces failed to take Fort McHenry in Baltimore in the War of 1812. That little reminder of foreign attackers certainly helped Millard's cause. The newspapers had been more and more critical of the president and more pro-Tydings. A nationwide poll showed 61 percent against Roosevelt's "Invasion of Maryland." John Owen, editor of the *Baltimore Sun*, ran front-page editorials for Millard almost every day, and marvelous cartoons. Millard won the primary by a huge majority, and then won the general election easily two months later. The publicity about the Maryland campaign had made Millard such a popular figure nationwide that he returned to the Senate the acknowledged leader of the conservative Democrats.

While Millard was fighting for his political life, Washington had finally become concerned about German intentions, and the impending war in Europe became the topic of numerous dinner-party conversations.

"We have little time to attend social functions here these days," I had written my mother (who was in Florida) before the primary, "but you will be interested to hear that we went to one next door at the Sczychenyi house, which is rented to the new German ambassador, Dieckoff. He and his wife are stout, middle-aged Germans, and quite pleasant people. The first secretary, Hans Thomsen, and his wife are our age and not unattractive. I have heard that he is a member of the German secret police, but she never misses an opportunity to rail against Hitler. I asked her once whether it was not dangerous for both her and her husband to criticize their fuhrer. She just shrugged and told me that her family and her husband were too important for anything she said to hurt them! Since then I have heard that both of them are members of the German Gestapo."

On March 12, 1938, Hitler invaded Austria, and Washington went into an uproar. That Saturday night, I sat beside the ambassador from Switzerland at dinner, and I never saw such sadness on a man's face. He said, "Would to God that I had not lived to see the day which I fear I shall see." His utter hopelessness was terrifying.

Millard and I talked for hours about U.S. policy. I argued for United States economic intervention immediately and declaration of our intent to apply sanctions against the Germans. But Millard said the country would never stand for that. His office was being deluged with isolationist letters.

The events in Germany made Millard even more determined to oppose Roosevelt's efforts to get more powers for the executive branch. During the debate on the Executive Reorganization bill, he pointed to the recent fall of the German Republic of Weimar to prove his point that the executive should not become too powerful! Many senators and members of the House came on the floor to hear him. Millard said he also opposed any neutrality law that would delegate congressional powers to the executive. He wanted Congress to remain in session all summer to deal with any more crises in Europe as they came along. After all, he said, that is Congress's job! About this time, an item appeared in Oleg Cassini's gossip column that I was pregnant and annoyed about it because I didn't want to be bothered! Of course it was politically motivated. Sadly, it was not true.

While this fight was going on, my father was working to set up a meeting between Roosevelt and Stalin. Marjorie's letter to me about their last few weeks in Russia before going to Belgium were full of gossip and descriptions of their farewell party. On June 5, 1938, my father wrote that he had gone to pay his last official call on President Kalinen and Premier Molotov.

He was amazed that he had no sooner made his farewells when the door opened and Josef Stalin himself walked in! This was an unheard of occurrence in the diplomatic community, no members of which had ever met the dictator. My father wrote me that he was surprised that Stalin was not a tall man, that he was quite pleasant, and that they had a complimentary exchange of polite conversation. They then discussed the trade relations between their two countries, trade concessions from the United States, and repayment to us of their World War I debt. Stalin asked my father to request that our president expedite the Russians' request for a war ship, which the United States had contracted to build for them. It was a friendly meeting, but apparently nothing very constructive came of it—except the first friendly relationships between the two great powers, which later was to prove invaluable in 1943.

Marjorie's letter described the "final tribute to your Daddy and me in appreciation for our friendly attitude. The Molotovs and Litvinovs hosted a magnificent farewell party in our honor in the Kremlin—a dinner, reception, and ball. The diplomatic corps was invited only to the latter two but not to the dinner. The affair created a sensation in Moscow second only to your father's meeting with Stalin."

She described the banquet, with the czars' plates and porcelain, and the menu. "We were impressed by the splendor of the setting, the Oriental rugs on the terrace (as it was a warm evening), and much pleased by the complimentary toasts to both of us," she wrote. "Molotov said: 'We like you, Mr. Davies, because the best you have said about us you have said behind our backs and the worst you have said about us has been to our faces."

There was Russian music at the party, of course, and a dance band from Paris. Daddy wrote: "Litvinov opened the ball by dancing with Marjorie. She looked beautiful and was the belle of the ball. Marshal Stalin was not present as he was not well, but everyone understood that he was the real host. There would have been no party had he not authorized it!"

My father was decorated with a high order of the Soviet government. Marjorie was presented with a pair of large, beautiful vases from one of the czar's palaces by Madame Molotov, and my father with an autographed photograph of Stalin in a handsome silver frame decorated with a red jeweled star. The Davieses gave a small farewell party at the embassy residence for his embassy aides and their wives, and gave them a cordial invitation to visit them in the States, "as you are all our children," said my warmhearted father.

They returned to Washington for a short while, where my father was praised and decorated by the secretary of state for his distinguished service to his country. Marjorie and I and my sisters and Millard were present at the ceremony and at the party afterward at the State Department. Then the Davieses left for their next ambassadorial post in Belgium, to keep a close watch on Adolph Hitler. He had accomplished the president's orders.

While my father settled into his new ambassadorship, I was busy being the wife of a senator who was fighting my father's friend for reelection to the Senate. In spite of his friendship with Roosevelt, my father was upset at his treatment of Millard. He cabled me that he would come home at once to get the "Boss to call off his dogs!" I cabled back: "You stay there and do your job! We can take care of ours over here!" Daddy also wrote me from Belgium that summer: "I have just received a bunch of newspaper clippings, among them a particularly scurrilous article about Millard. It made me boiling mad. Marjorie and I are concerned about the possible effect upon you and your Millard. Always bear in mind, Eleanor dearest, that life rocks along under the inevitable law of compensation. You and Millard have so much between yourselves which these birds never could have. Envy breeds shafts of this kind, and acts of malice are boomerangs! I wish I could say more! You know how important you and Millard are to me. He is like a son to me."

Although my father did not directly protect Millard from Roosevelt, some of his old friends did. Millard came home one evening with a broad grin on his face.

"Sometimes old friendships and past favors bring home the bacon!" he said. "One of my close political allies tells me that a friend of FDR's had been calling him every night to report the enemy's plans to do us in!"

The friend wanted Millard and my father to receive that information. I was not surprised, because I knew how generous my father had been to that man.

Chapter 19

The Tydingses Visit Brussels

November 1938 was only yesterday! It is clear and sharp in my memory, all in Technicolor! Perhaps this is because it was one of the happiest times of my life, which has had more than its share of Alpine highs and abysmal lows. I have been told that I have a photographic memory for events long ago. I am glad that this is so. Certainly the passage of time is one of the strangest phenomena of life on this planet. Dr. Einstein said that time and space are the same. If this is so, then one should be able to look ahead as well as look back, if one could climb high enough or travel fast enough to see both ways! I think that perhaps it is a blessing that, not being an angel or an Einstein, I can look only backward to the happy times. I am sure that most people have their ups and downs in life, but I doubt if many have had the celestial highs and painful lows that I have experienced. I am thankful that many of the latter are behind me and that I can have only the former in my heart and mind.

So I will recount one of these joyful times for my husband and for me.

In November 1938, my husband had just won a battle for reelection to the U.S. Senate in our state, in spite of all that our powerful fellow Democrat, President Franklin Delano Roosevelt, could do to prevent it. We celebrated Millard's victory by visiting the Davieses at their new embassy in Brussels. Both of us were in high spirits, having survived an unusually nasty campaign.

A crowd of friends (political, personal, and from the press) had given us a big send-off at the railway station in Baltimore with flowers, banners, and a brass band. I loved it, but Millard didn't care for it much. When we sailed from New York on the giant liner, *Normandy*, there was another (not so large but more social) crowd to see us off with more flowers and champagne, but no donkey! My husband heaved a sigh of relief when the captain ordered all guests ashore and our friends departed. He locked the door behind them and took me in his arms. "And now, Mrs. Tydings, may we please settle down to our own little party together!"

He had won the toughest political fight of his life. The national press was eulogizing him, and some of the leading Republicans, as well as the conservative Democrats, were urging him to run for president in 1940. This he steadfastly refused to consider. He said he never wanted to hold any government post save his seat in the Senate, and he meant it. Our trip across the Atlantic was a celebration and a honeymoon.We spent most of it in our suite, avoiding friends and well-wishers. My husband made up small poems in praise of his wife and sang a new one to me every morning at breakfast! True love! We were both on top of our world. The sun was shining and the birds were singing!

In Paris, we were welcomed by my father and stepmother and spent a gay week with them at the Ritz, dining and dancing at fancy restaurants and going on jolly shopping sprees. I have never seen anyone spend so much money with such joy and good taste as my stepmother. Born heiress to a great fortune, she considered it her duty to "spread the wealth," and I thoroughly enjoyed helping her do it! We dragged our indulgent husbands through the fascinating shops and couturiers of Paris and hilariously tried hats and coats on the two of them, to the huge amusement of ourselves and the salesladies.

After a week of this, we went on to Belgium. The U.S. Embassy residence was a beautiful palace rented from the owner, the Marquis d'Asque. It had once been the home of young King Leopold who had been born there. One parlor contained a magnificent malachite mantelpiece given to his father, the late king, by the Czar of Russia. The Davies malachite collection was placed in that room.

"Now, dear," said my stepmother briskly when she took me to our rooms, "I think you may succeed in becoming pregnant here! This is the royal suite and the bed on which the king was born. After a time here with us, maybe you will be able to have a small Tydings! My Christian Science practitioner is working on it. Please let me know as soon as you are sure. Your daddy and I will be so delighted and I know how happy you and Millard will be!"

She knew that it had been a great disappointment to me that in the nearly three years of our marriage no baby had arrived. Millard's doctor had assured my doctor that "it certainly isn't *our* fault. We could knock up the whole city of Washington!" Millard repeated this to me. I had never heard that crude expression before but repeated an expurgated version to my gynecologist. He at once telephoned Millard's doctor and informed him haughtily that "it certainly isn't *our* fault! We have already proven *ourselves* with two healthy youngsters!" These doctors sometimes identify themselves pretty closely with their patients!

My stepmother was an ardent Christian Scientist. I tried to read Mary Baker Eddy and talked to her practitioner, "Miss Jane," and even attended the Christian Science church with Marjorie, but it didn't take. I remained a good conservative-liberal Episcopalian and tragically no Tydings baby arrived in spite of Miss Jane's promise.

Our first evening in Brussels was great fun. There were no guests at dinner and no party to attend. Marjorie and I had dressed up for our husbands in our best ball gowns. She even wore my father's latest gift—a magnificent diamond tiara, which had belonged to a Hapsburg Grand Duchess. It was composed entirely of diamond roses. My younger sister, Emlen, was out on a date that evening with a dashing young Belgian named Robert Grosjean. Their engagement would be announced later that winter at a ball at the embassy, which I was sorry to miss.

After dinner, we were drinking coffee in the malachite room and my father was standing, leaning against the mantel. The three of us were seated, facing him. I looked at his reflection in the great mirror and admired my handsome parent.

"We are eager to hear about what has been going on over here, Joe," Millard said.

"Before we go into any discussion of affairs over here Millard," Daddy said, "we want to hear more about your Maryland campaign. You know, Millard, I cabled Eleanor when it became apparent that the president was going after you boys who had opposed his bills in the Senate. I would have come home and gone to bat for you with the Boss. I might have at least persuaded him to call off his dogs, even if I couldn't have handled Drew Pearson and the rest of them myself. I was all set to come when I received that cable from your wife ordering me to tend to my own job in Russia. She informed me that you two could take care of yours in Maryland! What a girl she is! I can't tell you how proud of you both I am, my boy. I hear that my daughter is becoming quite an effective politician in her own right."

"You don't hear the half of it, Joe," replied Millard, laughing. "She is by far the most popular woman in Maryland and becoming a first-rate speaker! I'll have to watch my step. If she ever decides to run for the Senate, my goose is cooked!"

"Unless you have already been elected president," said my father, chuckling.

"No way!" said my senator forcefully. "I wouldn't have that job if you gave it to me! It's a real killer nowadays, Joe. I am happy in my Senate job. After twelve years there, my seniority makes me more effective. I have a hunch that the next few years are going to be pretty crucial for our country and the world, and I want to have a hand in protecting the U.S.A. I fought for it in the world war and I have been trying to get our country into a strong position, militarily and economically, so that we won't be caught off guard in another big war. My attempt to restrain the president's domestic spending and hold down the national debt is one of the reasons he tried to get me defeated. It was all right to borrow and spend, to 'prime the pump' during the worst years of the Depression, but now we should get ready for any future storm. One appears to be darkening the horizon over here. Do you realize that our national debt is up to several billion dollars now? Of course my opposition to the president's Supreme Court bill was the last straw where our friendly relationship was concerned. I was pretty sure that he would try to get rid of me."

I spoke up. "And he certainly did! No wonder, after you had led the fight against his Supreme Court bill and won it! And now you have won the 'purge' fight too!"

"It's nice to know that some kind souls like yourself want me," Millard said. "My office staff tells me that my mail is flooded with enthusiastic letters from would-be supporters and the press is most complimentary. Nothing succeeds like success! I had a chap from the editorial staff of the *New York Herald-Tribune* working in my campaign who wants to stay on as my public relations man. He claims he can get me elected president. I told him that I appreciated the compliment but no thank you!"

Daddy smiled. "I think you should have a go at it, Senator. If not against FDR in '40, then maybe the next time. I'll pick up the tab to pay your man!"

My husband shook his head. "I truly appreciate your offer, Joe, but you and Marjorie have already done too much, contributing so generously to my campaign. It was a tremendous help."

My father patted him on the back. "You know we would have done a lot more if the law allowed. And we have the satisfaction of knowing that we have helped a little to keep a great public servant in the United States Senate!"

Millard's face flushed with pleasure. "I can't tell you how much I appreciate your words, Joe, and your campaign help. I told the New York writer that I honestly would never be a candidate for president. You and Marjorie have heard and read more than enough about our recent activities. The president's interference in my election campaign didn't change things much except to make it a little hotter than usual!"

And a darned sight meaner, I thought.

The Davieses protested that they had not heard or read much about our recent political battle, but my husband was not to be drawn into further discussion of it. I realized that he didn't want to voice any criticism of my father's old friend, the president. He thanked them again for their financial campaign help.

"It came in right handy as the boys on the Eastern 'sho' would say."

My husband did not want any political battles with my father's old friend. But he did say, "I was telephoning our county leaders around the state to see how the voting went and when I asked this old friend down in southern Maryland how they voted in his precinct he told me in disgusted tones, 'It was twenty-nine votes for Tydings, Chief, and one for Davey Lewis, and we got a posse out now, lookin' for the son of a bitch!'

"I want you to know, Joe, that in the entire primary campaign, I never mentioned the president's name or criticized him personally in any way. Some of his New Deal policies and executive power were the only objects of my attack. I sent word to all my friends when Roosevelt was traveling through Maryland, speaking for my Democratic opponent, that there were to be *no* demonstrations or any posters in my behalf! Only proper respect was to be shown to the president of the United States."

My father put his arm around Millard's wide shoulders. "You didn't need to tell me that, my son! I never thought you would do otherwise."

I couldn't resist putting in my two cents worth, so I spoke up. "The Marylanders were polite when the president drove by, but there wasn't much applause for him. In spite of Millard's orders, there were Tydings's posters on the telephone poles along the way and a huge one behind the stand where Roosevelt spoke. Very few of the license plates on parked cars had Maryland tags!

"I guess the Eastern Sho' fellows all went fishing" Millard said, laughing. "You talk too much sometimes, Precious."

Marjorie had whispered an invitation in my ear to come to breakfast in her room the next morning before our husbands awoke. "They will be sleeping late, unless I am much mistaken," she said, "and then they are going to have a golf game with the king at Laaken so we can have a nice long talk. I want to hear more about the Maryland primary fight, and I know you two don't want to upset your daddy with the gory details!"

So the next morning I left my husband sleeping peacefully. In a negligee, I crept from our room to the Davies' quarters. I knew they sometimes used separate bedrooms, and I was not surprised to find Marjorie alone on her big French bed, balancing a tray on her knees. I was surprised to recognize the magnificent bed. After a warm greeting, I said, "I thought you had taken your bed to Moscow when you refurbished Spasso House (the U.S. Embassy residence)." She smiled. "Oh, I did, dear, I have quite a few beds, one of which usually goes with me wherever I go—even shipboard—after all, one's bed is pretty important! One spends quite a lot of time there, you know. Your father is getting spoiled because I bring one of his along too! It is great fun to pamper the dear man! I hope you left yours sleeping, as I did. Your Millard looks tired and thin."

"He is both. He lost more than ten pounds during the primary campaign. The general election was much easier. The primary was a battle against the president and all his power and patronage. But Millard won and a big victory is big medicine! I think Daddy is looking lots better than he did when he came home to resign his post last winter. We thought you were going to take over the embassy in Germany when you left Russia until you told us Daddy had been appointed ambassador to Belgium."

"So did we. But the president asked your father to take Belgium, the 'listening post' of Europe. He calls your daddy his 'eyes and ears' over here."

"You don't think FDR failed to give him a more important post because of us?" I asked anxiously.

"No, dear, I don't, although the same cabal that disliked and was jealous of your father and Millard were certainly not helping either of them. The president trusts your father. Your daddy and I don't want to stay over here much longer. The Russian winters didn't help our health any! We want to go home and enjoy the rest of our lives together, with you and Millard and all our children. Now, I want to hear the lowdown about FDR and the Maryland purge primary. I know you and Millard don't want to discuss it with your father, and I won't repeat anything you say, so talk!"

"Well, the press called the men who were trying to defeat Millard the president's 'Elimination Committee!'—Secretary Ickes, Harry Hopkins, Tommy Corcoran, and, of course, Drew Pearson. They wanted to defeat the Democratic conservatives in the Senate who were running for reelection this year. The newspapers called the other conservative Democrat candidates the 'Intrepid Six'—Walter George of Georgia, Cotton Ed Smith of South Carolina, Fred Van Nuys of Indiana, Alva Adams of Colorado, Champ Clarke of Missouri, Guy Gillette of Iowa."

"The suspense of waiting to hear what the president was going to do must have been agonizing!"

"It certainly was for me, but Millard said he thought he could win the election against any Democrat in Maryland."

"Did you make speeches during the campaign?"

"No, we thought it better for me to just go with him, glad-hand the voters, and lead the cheering. Men may adore us, but that doesn't mean they want competition from us! There were some places where he wouldn't take me, and I would pull weeds viciously in the garden at Oakington. Every weed was a hair out of Roosevelt's head! Once, our old Irish gardener was watching me and said, 'Don't you worry none, Miz Tydin's. Folks in Maryland don't want no dern dictatorship!' " We laughed together.

Marjorie shook her head. "You must both be worn out!"

At that point I changed the subject and asked her what had happened when my father had returned to Washington the previous spring to tender his resignation from the Russian post to the president.

"The president told your father that he would have appointed him ambassador to Great Britain had it not been for the rule against divorced people being received at the Court of St. James in London. The opposition of the career men on his Moscow staff and at the State Department didn't help your father. Bohlen, Kinnan, and Durbrow hated the Russians, whereas your father was following his instructions from the president, being tolerant of their form of government. It has always been easy for him to make friends, as you know, and this he did with the Russian leaders, especially Litvinov and

Molotov. He thought that the U.S.S.R. might have a possible peace role in the balance of power in Europe. His staff aides ignored that idea. They underestimated the strength of the Russian people and their armed forces, which your daddy learned about in his inspection trips all over the U.S.S.R."

I told her that Sumner Welles had been appointed Assistant Secretary of State and he also hated the Soviet Union. He had married the divorced wife of Peter Goelet Gerry of Rhode Island. People said it was because she thought Welles could be elected to the United States Senate and Welles undoubtedly was encouraged to run against Millard by the president. In the meantime, Matilde Welles's divorced husband, Peter Gerry, had been elected to the Senate and had married George Vanderbilt's widow, Edith. She and her daughter, Cornelia, had been friends of mine in Biltmore Forest.

"We knew about the cabal working against Joe in the State Department with Drew Pearson and company," said Marjorie. "There wasn't much we could do in Moscow to keep our fences mended at the White House, as you politicians say. So two career boys have been appointed, Hugh Gibson to be Ambassador to Germany and Bill Bullit to France. Your daddy's talk with Stalin and the magnificent banquet and ball given in our honor in the Kremlin caused a great sensation in the diplomatic corps in Moscow, I can tell you. The diplomats there gave farewell parties for us also, and came to the railroad station with gifts to say good-bye. Quite a change in their attitude toward your father!"

"I'm sure it set the 'nasties' like Drew Pearson and old Ickes back on their heels too!" I chuckled.

I asked my step mother whether there had been much gossip about the great romance of the Baltimore woman, Wallis Warfield, and the Prince of Wales, now the Duke and Duchess of Windsor. There had been so much talk in Washington and Baltimore.

"Well, you can imagine how it was," said Marjorie dryly. "Only, those people took violent sides according to their politics! Those who were Prime Minister Chamberlain's "appeasers" were quite pro-German-Italian Axis and violently anti-Communist-anti-war, like the Prince of Wales and Wallis. Those who were anti-Fascist like Churchill were 'agin' the Windsors and against Wallis in any event. Most British loved their Prince of Wales and blamed Wallis for costing them their King Edward VIII. Did Millard know the duchess?"

"He says he thinks he may have met her but doesn't remember. She was a little younger than he and about ten years my senior, so I didn't know her," I replied. "I feel sorry for them both—theirs was certainly one of the great romances of all time! Did you meet anyone in London who knew her?"

"Yes, I met a few and heard many hair-raising tales about her. Of course, we only met those in official circles who were more or less close to the royal family and they were bitter against her. Queen Mary was particularly bitter against her because her son was King Edward VIII and he gave up his throne to his brother in order to marry Wallis. His brother, the Duke of Kent, had to become king, and he is, as you know, a shy, retiring man with a speech impediment. The prime minister's wife, Mrs. Stanley Baldwin, disliked Wallis. Apparently King Edward had given her precedence over Mrs. B. at his formal dinners!"

"I heard that in Washington," I said. "Also that she had many lovers besides her two husbands, especially in China where her first husband was stationed by the Navy."

"There was a lot about that in London too," said my stepmother. "The British Intelligence Service was said to have made an investigation of her past."

I interrupted. "Did they dig up anything about a Chinese warlord who was her lover who taught her a lot of sexy tricks?"

"Of course," laughed my stepmother, "and I don't doubt a lot of it was true, or close to the truth."

"Then after they were married in June 1936, they went to Germany and even went to visit Adolph Hitler after he had broken the Versailles Treaty of World War I and remilitarized the Rhineland. What does Daddy think of that?"

"He thinks it was *most* ill-advised," said my stepmother.

There was a knock at the door and a maid announced that the senator was eating his breakfast and would like his wife to join him when she was free to do so.

Marjorie laughed. "Morning, noon, and night—like mine. Better hurry down to him, my dear."

Soon after that, I found myself alone with my parent and he asked me to tell him about my husband's speeches.

"You know, darlin', I love the man like a son and I have some little reputation as a speaker myself, so I'm interested in hearing about them. It won't hurt my friendship with either Franklin Roosevelt or your husband. I am fond of both and I understand what makes them tick!"

I breathed a sigh of relief and I told him that Millard had talked about the people's constitutional rights, about the freedoms we enjoy, for which men had fought and died for thousands of years; why Maryland is called the Free State; and why no one from out of the state, especially from the federal government, had any right to tell them how to vote.

"The primary fight was not his, but theirs. They must keep the Free State free!"

My father nodded his approval. "His speeches had great subject matter. They must have been real orations! What a guy that husband of yours is, my child. No wonder he won!"

I was relieved to hear his words. Millard need not have worried about Daddy's reaction to the fight between his son-in-law and his old friend. I hugged him and told him so. I also told him that I thought my husband's political stand was absolutely right!

The next time we four were free to dine alone at the embassy we met early, for cocktails, in the malachite room. Millard grinned at his host and told Daddy we were still waiting to be briefed on the events that had been taking place in Europe during the past two years. My father paced back and forth for a few minutes in front of the czar's mantelpiece. Then he seated himself and his face brightened with a smile.

"That's a long story, my friend, and before I start on it I have a couple of questions I want to ask you that Marvin McIntyre and Jim Farley didn't answer. Did Frank Roosevelt go after your other 'purgee' boys as strongly as he attacked you?"

"No, Joe, he didn't. Most of the southern Democrats who had opposed his New Deal measures were not up for reelection this year, and those who were received only a light tap on the wrist."

My father asked whether anyone knew if the president would run for a third term in 1940. Millard replied that Postmaster General Farley had told him "Missy leHand (FDR's private secretary) doesn't know, Mrs. Roosevelt doesn't know, and I don't know. But I can tell you this: Every time any of us discusses the leading Democratic candidates for the presidency in 1940, the president vetoes them all and then says: 'Of course, in the event of war, all bets are off'!"

"My friend in the White House is a wise old bird," said daddy with a chuckle.

"Not as wise as the senior senator from Maryland," I said.

"That's enough about me and my small triumph," said Millard, laughing. "My wife is a little prejudiced, Joe. You are the man who has scored the points with your sensational meeting with Stalin and the great send-off you and Marjorie received from his top officials in the Kremlin. It's a shame you didn't go to Germany as planned. You might have been able to calm Hitler down a bit."

"No chance. He has gone too far and nothing can stop him now, in my opinion. The poor old League of Nations, which might have held him down, is dead as Hector. There was a time when Britain, France, and the U.S.S.R. could have created a powerful balance of power, but the English and French let Hitler take over Austria and Hungary, and now Czechoslovakia, and the Sudetenland, without firing a shot."

"We know that the president sent you all over Europe as his 'roving ambassador' to find out what the leaders were planning, if anything, to stop Hitler. I have followed his rise to power from the time Hitler got control of the German Reichstag, when the building burned down, and President Von Hindenberg appointed him chancellor. The old man was apparently senile at the time. Your Baltic trip was only a year ago. Are the people there and in Britain and France all oblivious to what Hitler is up to?"

"They are. We visited all the Baltic countries, and Paris and London, as well as those adjacent to Germany, at Roosevelt's request. Before we went back to Moscow I was to report back on their economic and military strength and their attitudes toward Germany and Russia. I have never worked harder in my life, interviewing all the leaders and sending written reports directly to the president."

"Your father nearly killed himself, Eleanor! I was actually glad to get him back to Russia. But no sooner were we there than he was off on another inspection trip, which took him all over the U.S.S.R., courtesy of the Russian officials. He even traveled beyond the Ural Mountains. I am having a hard time holding him down."

He patted her shoulder. "You don't hold me down, dearest, you keep me going. You should have seen her take the press boys into camp! They had been panning us after the *Sea Cloud* arrived at Southampton. Marjorie invited them all aboard to inspect the ship and have a drink, and they fell for my wife and her yacht and her lunch!"

My husband smiled at them and continued his questioning. "What was the consensus of opinion you found in your travels, Joe?" My husband was listening intently. So was I. And of course, Marjorie.

"Their heads were in the sand!" my father exclaimed angrily. "Those chiefs of state and of industry would do almost anything to avoid another great war like the last. The universal sentiment was 'peace at any price'!"

"I can't blame them too much," said Millard, "except for the 'peace at any price' part, if it means sacrificing a neighbor."

"They all indulged in wishful thinking. They firmly believed Hitler would not precipitate a general war. They thought he was bluffing and that the power of England and France would hold him down. France and Russia had signed a treaty with Czechoslovakia in 1935 to protect the little country if Hitler got too greedy and attempted to take their Sudetenland back."

Millard nodded. "I know Czechoslovakia is a polyglot of many nationalities: Polish, German, Hungarian, Czech, and Slovak, all put together after the war at Versailles. I believe there are more than twice as many other nationalities as there are German-speaking Sudetens. Unfortunately, many of the great industrial plants and most of the Czechs' strongest fortifications are in the Sudetenland. Tell us about the leaders in the countries you visited, Joe."

"Because I was the president's personal emissary, they talked quite freely to me. In London, I talked with members of the House of Commons, Winston Churchill, the press magnates, old David Lloyd George, the senior statesman, and our ambassador, Bob Bingham. Churchill is by far the ablest and most brilliant man there. He is an old friend and we have kept in touch. He has been warning about Hitler's intentions to conquer Europe for some time. He sponsored a bill proposing an alliance with France and Russia to stop Hitler's continuing buildup of the German armed forces. My friend, Maxim Litvinov, the foreign commissar of the U.S.S.R., has been urging this too, in the League of Nations, Paris, and London. He told me Russia would have joined France and Britain to stop Hitler's putsch into Austria last March and the German invasion of Czechoslovakia this September, but the French and British wouldn't agree. 'It would rock the boat,' they said. We saw Charles Lindbergh in London. He was talking about the remarkable buildup of planes and tanks he had recently seen in Germany. Marjorie can tell you an amusing tale he told her about his recent visit to Germany."

Marjorie laughed. "The great flier said that he had been taken around all the factories building planes and bombers by General Hermann Goring, himself, who invited him to dinner at Karin Hall, his country estate. There he was received at the door by an honor color guard with flags. Lindbergh was ushered into an immense room, handsomely furnished, where he was to await the entrance of his host. He said that he was horrified to see, stretched out full length on a large sofa at the far end of the room, a huge, live lioness.

As he looked, mesmerized, the great beast rose, and slowly stalked toward him. Lindbergh said he was completely terrified, when the door opened and a smiling Goring entered the room, clad in a magnificent baby-blue uniform covered with gold braid and medals. He smiled and clucked to the lioness, which went to him, purring. The animal stood up on its hind legs, put its big paws on the general's shoulders, and licked his face. The smile on Goring's face suddenly vanished and turned to rage as he slapped the beast away and rushed out of the room. The front of the baby-blue uniform was dripping wet. The lioness docilely followed him out, to Lindbergh's great relief. A few minutes later the general reappeared, resplendent in a pure white uniform also covered with decorations, and smelling strongly of eau de cologne!"

My father joined in our laughter and beamed at his wife. "Well told, darling!"

Millard remarked that Lindbergh had been criticized in the United States because he described the German planes and industrial plants in such glowing terms.

"Hermann Goring has apparently risen in Hitler's esteem and has accomplished the big buildup in Germany's armaments. But now, Joe, please give us a blow-by-blow account of what has happened over here the past two years."

My father shook his head. "I came home expecting to be sent to Germany, as you know, and the president asked me to return to Russia with two secret proposals to sound out with Litvinov. In view of our common concern over Japan's invasion of Mongolia, Roosevelt suggested that a joint U.S.S.R.-U.S.A. mission be created of military-naval men to report on events in Asia. It was to be kept strictly secret. Our naval attache in Moscow, Colonel Faymonville, was on friendly terms with the Russians. The president suggested that he be our representative."

"Did the Russians agree?" Millard asked.

"No. Litvinov said that they could keep it secret but that our people couldn't! There would surely be leaks in Washington! FDR's other instruction was that I sound out the Russians on the subject of a possible meeting of the president and Stalin at some place like Alaska. However, I had no sooner arrived in Moscow than I received word from FDR canceling that last."

"No wonder, with visions of a third term in his head! The Communists are unpopular in our country, Joe. When the president made a speech mentioning more friendly relations with the U.S.S.R., there was an unfavorable political reaction."

"The President is well aware of that and of the anti-Russian fervor of the secretary of state and the foreign service boys. The Russian purge trials have made the Russians even more unpopular. I attended a lot of them and they were terrible. The poor devils didn't have a chance. They had none of the protections that the accused have in our country. They all pleaded guilty of plotting against the state—I guessed a lot of them were. Diplomatic gossip in Moscow said that some of the Russians, specifically the military men, had been holding hands with their German counterparts—maybe Hitler himself. Probably most of them have been executed."

Marjorie interrupted her husband. "A high-ranking Russian general was sitting in our box at the ballet one evening when he received a message and left. He was never seen again, so far as we know."

"Until the German Anschluss last March, Millard," continued Daddy, "I had hoped that the League of Nations could bring about peace in the world. Now I believe that only the old balance of power in Europe with a British-French-Russian alliance can hold Hitler and Mussolini in check."

Millard nodded agreement and asked what had been going on in Moscow when he returned there.

"There was furor in the diplomatic world about the Russian mistreatment of foreign nations. I talked with Litvinov and managed to squeeze out a few concessions and soften things up a little. Then there was the Amur Island incident, when Russia and Japan were in collision. I knew the Japanese ambassador fairly well and so I practiced a little personal diplomacy and went to see him unofficially, with apparent success, but I received a sharp reprimand from Secretary Hull. I tell you, Millard, I am tired of this job and would like to retire!"

Marjorie shook her head indignantly. "That was inexcusable of old Cordell Hull! When your father was only practicing brilliant diplomacy!"

Daddy beamed at her fondly and continued his story. "The Russians have always been suspicious that the British and French may gangup against them and that the U.S. might join them. I got this from Commissar Litvinov himself. If they thought this was about to happen, they would undoubtedly embrace Hitler and the German-Italian Axis."

My stepmother interrupted again. "Litvinov told Joe that the Russians actually had a recording of the English and French officials planning to foster a war in which they hoped Germany and Russia would fight and destroy each other!"

"Not a bad idea!" laughed Millard. "It would remove a lot of our worries! Hitler was evidently encouraged by his takeover of Austria."

"We were down on the Black Sea on the *Sea Cloud* last May on one of my inspection trips when the fueher started ranting about the Germans in the Sudetenland again and sent several military divisions to the Czech border. The Czechs were no pushover! They mobilized a sizable army behind their western fortifications and appealed to Britain and France for help. The French said they would fight to defend Czechoslovakia. The British said they would go along, and Hitler backed down! They had called his bluff and Europe had won peace for a while."

"You two will be amused to hear a story about what else happened on our ship when we were on the Black Sea," said Marjorie, smiling. "My maid and Joe's valet had been having quite a love affair. So we were delighted to hear that the valet had won the great Irish sweepstakes lottery. Of course, we gave a party in their honor on the boat and invited the entire ship's crew to drink to their health with us! The champagne flowed. Then they left and were married!"

"And lived happily ever after," I said.

"Presumably! Now, we must go to dinner," said our hostess.

The next free evening at home we were eager to hear more about the Czechoslovak crisis. Daddy leaned back on the sofa, one arm around his wife.

"Roosevelt wanted me to report on the Russian industries, oil refineries, and military installations in the Ukraine and Caucasus and we were on the yacht early in September when we heard on the ship's radio that Hitler had made a particularly bellicose speech at Nuremberg. The European governments were shaking in their shoes for fear France and England would declare war on Germany if Hitler tried to take Czechoslovakia. The U.S.S.R. had previously advocated that the League of Nations take action in the threat of war. Now the Russians proposed a conference to implement the Russian-French Pact. Churchill spoke in the House of Commons, urging mobilization of the fleet, conscription in England, and a conference of the U.S.A., France, and Britain, along the lines of our discussions in April! Prime Minister Chamberlain vetoed this and sent a note to Berlin asking for a meeting with Hitler. A cordial invitation came back, inviting the prime minister to Hitler's retreat at Berchtesgaden. That was the first of three meetings."

"After our return to Moscow from Washington last February, Eleanor, your father was confronted with a diplomatic crisis in Moscow," Marjorie said to me, "which he handled wonderfully!"

"You prejudiced women!" Daddy laughed. "I didn't do much. The British ambassador was trying to persuade the entire diplomatic corps to file a harsh protest against the Russian government for their ill treatment of foreign nationals in their country. I felt it was no time to start a fight over this and was able to persuade Litvinov to ease up on their actions, so the protest was not filed."

"Your father was wonderful!" interrupted his wife.

"Enough of that, darling!" Daddy patted her shoulder. "The senator wants to hear about what happened next over here. We came to Brussels in July after my brief trip to Washington to report to the president on my talk with Stalin. The shadow of future war hung over Europe. Our intelligence boys told us that Hitler had given orders to his generals to march into Czechoslovakia on October first and the British and French were kowtowing to the German dictator. Prime Minister Chamberlain had secured the approval of the British and French of Hitler's demands for Sudeten representation and freedom in their country and everyone was happy. Chamberlain said he was confident that Hitler was a man of his word and could be trusted!"

"Poor, stupid man!" said Marjorie.

"Not entirely," said my father. "He was only reflecting the fears of his countrymen and of the French people."

"They had lost almost an entire generation of their young men," Millard sighed. "God knows we lost too many of ours."

"When Chamberlain and the French Prime Minister, Daladier, returned to report to Hitler that the British and French would accede to his demands, they were in for a big surprise. The German stomped and roared and said he had changed his mind. He was tired of the Czech's mistreatment of the Sudetens, he declared, and demanded nothing less than the return of all the Sudetenland to Germany—all of Czechoslovakia's richest industrial section and its western mountain fortifications. Hitler gave them only a few days to win the approval of their government. 'If they wanted war, they could have it,' he said. The two prime ministers went home. They had been told to return to Munich with an answer September 28, or the Germans would seize the Sudetenland. Chamberlain told Daladier that if the French would live up to their treaty with the Czechs, Britain would join them. Russia had offered to come to the aid of Czechoslovakia and Norway, if they were attacked, but those two countries wouldn't give the Russians permission to cross their frontiers. Churchill said it is the riddle of the sphinx whether they feared Germany or Russia the most!"

Marjorie spoke up. "Then Mr. Benes, the head of the Czech government, asked the French if they would fight, and the French said they would have nothing to do with it! We heard that the Londoners were so frightened for fear of German bomber raids that they were actually digging trenches in the streets to hide in!"

My father said that General Goring was building hundreds of bombers a month and had sent twenty or more divisions to the Czech border.

"I can understand the terror of the French and British at the thought of another war only twenty years after the last," said my husband. "They would do anything to avoid it apparently."

"The Italian duce, Mussolini, promptly offered his services as mediator," said Daddy, "undoubtedly assuring Hitler of his support! So Italy, not Czechoslovakia, was the fourth power present when Chamberlain and Daladier signed Hitler's demand, giving Germany the entire Sudetenland. The Czech government was not even represented! I understand the signing took place at one in the morning, the last day of September."

"Will there be another Great War in Europe, Daddy?" I asked.

"Maybe, my child. Only God knows what will happen next. I have kept the president informed and tried to make friends as his ambassador-at-large around Europe, as well as in Russia. I don't think there is much more that I can do. I hope our government will let this old man go home soon!"

Millard chuckled. "You are no 'old man,' my friend! However, I hope for the sake of family and friends you can do so. You and Marjorie have done a fine job of making friends with the Russians and keeping them out of the German-Italian Axis. I don't think there is another man I know who could have achieved what you have in Russia, Joe. I honestly believe that you could have tamed Adolph Hitler, had FDR sent you to Germany! How stupid the French were not to build up their defenses when they saw Hitler building his war machine. You know, Joe, many Americans like myself hate Communism."

"I know, Senator," Daddy replied, "but one must live in the real world and play the game of reale politique, with an international balance of power. I suspect, from what Litvinov told me, that Hitler may have agreed when the nonaggression pact was signed, to give

Russia the Baltic states and possibly the cordon sanitaire portion of Poland, which Stalin unquestionably wants. We will have to wait and see, but it looks like 'the hog's eyes are sot', as the Wisconsin farmers say. My thanks for your praise, Senator! You give me far more than my due."

"Not at all!" Marjorie spoke up. "You opened the door for future dealings with Stalin about trade and their war debt. It is too bad that the president has not followed through! I am so proud of you, Joe! I will never forget your farewell talk to the embassy staff in Moscow. You said that if diplomacy means anything, it means the art of getting matters in difference settled with the least irritation consistent with the ideals of our government, and never yielding one's self-respect!"

"Bravo!" said my husband. "You have laid the foundations of future peaceful relations between the U.S. and the U.S.S.R., Joe. Someday your efforts may pay off in a remarkable way. We can't look into the future, but it is possible that the Russian government may sometime evolve into one more like our own."

We sat silent for a few moments. Then Millard continued. "If Hitler sent twenty divisions to the Czech border, he couldn't have had enough left to defend his western front against France and Britain for two weeks!"

"War was too high a price for them to pay, Millard. The prime ministers of those countries were thankful that there would be no war. Chamberlain went home to joyfully proclaim, 'Peace for Our Time,' to the welcome of cheering Londoners."

"Hitler took Austria and has gained control of most of southeastern Europe without a shot fired," said my husband, frowning. "And he will doubtless take the rest of Czechoslovakia next spring. His avowed intention to conquer Europe will have begun. Then it may be our turn."

"So far has Britain fallen to buy peace without honor," said the ambassador sadly. "Hitler played the French and British for saps! Now he has jumping-off points to take the Romanian oil fields and the Ukraine! Our former allies called his bluff in May. Now he has outsmarted them and has protected much of his eastern border."

Millard asked again whether the Russian armed forces, which Daddy had seen, could stand up against Hitler's mechanized divisions. My father said that he thought they might, given a few more years to get ready.

Before leaving Brussels, Millard wanted to visit the battlefields where he had fought in the World War. So my father sent us off in an embassy limousine with chauffeur. It was cold and raining when Millard, my sister, Rahel, and I drove through the Ardennes Mountains to Verdun and explored the broken woods and underbrush to Etrayes Ridge. Here young Millard Tydings had used his machine gunners to push the Germans back off the ridge, a last western point of their line. Here he had crawled up a ravine under enemy fire, from shell hole to shell hole twenty years before. How long ago that seemed to me then, but not to him. We scrambled through brush and shell-broken trees of the Ridge and Millard found his way straight to a spot where he said the kitchens and their horse-drawn carts had been a direct hit. He picked up a rusty kettle and some bits of horse bridle to show us. We visited the war cemeteries of the American boys who had been killed in that terrible war. Millard took photos of the graves of his friends and I shed tears over them.

It was typical winter weather, cold and wet, and we were delighted when the sun broke through the clouds as we were driving through the mountains on our way back to Brussels. We stopped at a charming little castle-chateau surrounded by a lovely valley where we were served a delicious lunch. We drank absinthe cocktails and ate trout freshly caught in a mountain stream.

A highlight of our short visit in Brussels was the night a young Belgian, Robert Grosjean, came to dinner to meet my sister Emlen's family. She told me that she and Bob Grosjean had fallen in love and were going to be married. I dressed hurriedly and was first on hand to meet the young man. He was handsome, of average height, and had curly dark hair. He looked like a young prince should look! His father was a member of an old Brussels banking family and his mother was a Kentuckian. We all found Bob charming and plans for the engagement announcement went forward.

Before leaving Brussels, I talked to Daddy about my one great concern. It was worry for my children in case anything happened to cause my death. The judge in Reno had told me that in that event the children's father could lawfully claim them. I knew that with his alcoholic weakness and irresponsible behavior, they might lose whatever property I left them. My father suggested that Millard might adopt them, but I objected to that. They were not his children, and I hoped we would have our own. He should not have the burden of another man's children. Daddy said he would be happy to adopt them himself if Millard would approve. I thought he would and had felt vastly relieved.

There was to be a marvelous ball given at the embassy in January for Emlen and Bob, but Millard and I could not be there. It was more important for us to be at home for Christmas with the children. So ten days beforehand, we bade fond farewells to the Davieses and returned home on a big ocean liner full of both frightened Jews and Gentiles escaping from European countries that they feared would soon fall victim to the horrors of Hitler's regime. All these people could tell terrible stories of the persecution of the Jews and all who were opposed to Hitler's government and the horrors of their mistreatment by the Nazi thugs. The refugees on our ship considered themselves lucky to be squeezed onboard ship, no matter how uncomfortable their accommodations.

It was wonderful to be home. Christmas at Oakington was always special, and this year Mother and my sisters and Millard's were all there. Charlie and Sue Bryan celebrated with us at Christmas Eve dinner and other friends who had no children to make the occasion joyful in their homes. The house was festooned with holly and greens and we decorated a huge Christmas tree in the entrance hall.

Little Joe was ten and I was thankful he was no older in case of another big war, which might involve us. Little El was six and growing more enchanting every day. She played carols remarkably well on the piano and I accompanied her on my violin. We all sang the familiar old songs and I was thankful to be home.

Marjorie wrote me in January 1939 that Emlen's engagement to Bob Grosjean was announced at a beautiful dinner and ball at the embassy. The young Belgian men were all in uniform, called on Army alert, waiting for Hitler's divisions to invade Holland and their own country en route to take Paris once again. She said that everyone remarked that it was like the ball in Brussels the night before the battle of Waterloo. They heard afterward that young King Leopold was very disappointed that he could not come to the party because it was not in his honor but in honor of the engaged couple! The poor young man had lost his wife, the beautiful Norwegian Princess Astrid, in an automobile accident some time before.

Chapter 20

The Windsor Story

Wallis Warfield Spencer was a Baltimore girl who belonged to a distinguished Maryland family. Her grandfather was Governor Warfield of Maryland and great-grandfather of Francis Warrington Gillet, the man my daughter married. Warfield had been a handsome man. He rode a white horse in President Woodrow Wilson's inaugural parade, and they say the crowds cheered him more than they did the president. Wallis's father died young and left his widow in straightened circumstances. A wealthy Warfield uncle sent Wallis to private schools and financed her debut in Baltimore's polite society. Meantime, her mother had married a politician who was considered a rough diamond. Wallis married a young Naval officer named Spencer, and went to California and to China with him. Gossip had it that she became the girlfriend of a Chinese warlord who continued her education where the finishing school and the lieutenant left off! She and the lieutenant were divorced, and she then married a respectable Englishman named Simpson, whom some of my friends at the Embassy classified as "middle-drawer, my dear, definitely *not* top-drawer!" Wallis went to London.

Since we knew them well, especially the prince, I will tell some of their story as we knew it. We both were fond of the prince. He was a nice man as well as a charming, modest person. Not so the lady, in my opinion!

The first time I met the Prince of Wales (who was later to become the Duke of Windsor) was on the occasion of his first visit to the United States and Washington, D.C. I was only ten or eleven and he was about twenty-one. My parents decided that I should attend with them a big reception given for the prince at the Capitol. All the Washington VIP's were invited. Of course, they couldn't be prevented from bringing their families, and it was a terrible crush. The poor little prince looked dazed and bleary-eyed by the time we were presented to him. He was not much taller than I was and looked as tired and as bored as I was. I felt sorry for him. He brightened up sufficiently to smile back at me. Every mother in Washington with a daughter, eligible or not, was moving heaven and earth to throw that daughter in his path. I thought the prince resembled a slightly pink-nosed and beleaguered bunny!

From here on, the story was told to me by my friend, Consuelo Morgan Thaw Landa. Her third husband was Alfons Landa, a member of my father's law firm. Connie's sisters were the famous Morgan twins—Thelma, Lady Furness, and Gloria Morgan Vanderbilt, widow of Reginald Vanderbilt. Connie was married to Ben Thaw of Philadelphia, a young U.S. foreign service officer, when he was stationed in Rio de Janeiro at the time the Prince of Wales was on his world tour. There the prince met the young Thaws, and they became his close friends. When Ben Thaw was sent to our embassy in London, they were included in all of the prince's parties, large and small. Connie met the Baltimore girl, Wallis Simpson, and thought her bright and amusing. She introduced Wallis to the prince and took her along to the prince's weekend house parties at Fort Belvedere. The prince apparently did not much admire Wallis at first. Connie said he told her so and warned her not to drag Wallis along to his parties, or he would stop inviting the Thaws! At that time, he (the prince of Wales) was having a hot affair with Connie's sister, Lady Furness, who had also become a friend of Wallis. Reggie Vanderbilt had died on the Titanic and left Gloria a widow with one little girl. The child's great-aunt, Mrs. Cornelius V. Whitney, highly disapproved of Gloria's gay life abroad and brought suit in New York to take Gloria's child away from her. Mrs. Whitney said Gloria was unfit to be a mother. Lady Furness sailed for New York with her twin sister to combat this suit. According to Connie, Thelma Furness's parting words to her friend Wallis were an admonition to her to "take care of David (the prince) while I am gone!" Wallis did, and the rest is history.

Millard did not know Wallis well, but he had met her, and he was much concerned over the adverse publicity that the Maryland woman had incurred as a result of her affair with the prince. The senator even considered making a speech in her defense (upholding the honor of Maryland womanhood!) on the Senate floor. I was not enthusiastic, and he did not make the speech. One day, at the height of the excitement, Millard lunched with Wallis's uncle, old General Warfield, at the Maryland Club in Baltimore. The general said, "Millard, what do you think of my niece Wallis? I received a letter from her asking me to send her a copy of our family tree. I wrote back and told her to start acting like a lady, and she wouldn't need to prove it." Wallis's Aunt Bessie Marryman, who went to be with her niece at the time of the wedding to the prince, was a friend of my mother's. She was a bright old lady, and the prince was very fond of her. He gave her a limousine and chauffeur, and I'm not sure what else, but Wallis neglected her Aunt Bessie in the last years of the old lady's life. She lived to be over 100.

When the Duke and Wallis first came to Baltimore after their marriage, friends of ours gave a large party for them at their estate in Baltimore County. Millard and I forgot the seasonal daylight saving time change and arrived late, but the host and the prince were both waiting on the front steps to greet us. The prince escorted me to the seat beside him at lunch, and we had a delightful time together. There was none of the old British snobbery about him. He was a simple, friendly man. We laughed together over that awful long-ago reception at the Capitol when I met him. I told him the world would be singing songs about him and Wallis long after it had forgotten the names of Franklin D. Roosevelt and the British prime minister!

As for Wallis, I never found her personally very attractive. She was extremely slender, had straight dark hair, small eyes, a long nose, and thin lips. Both Connie and Marjorie liked her and found her witty and amusing. Perhaps I would have if Millard and I had gone on a Caribbean cruise on the *Sea Cloud* with the Davieses and the Windsors. Wallis and I might have become friends, but Millard's Senate duties had prevented it. Marjorie said they had great fun, and the duke and duchess laughed together constantly. She and Daddy would hear them laughing in their cabin. A sure sign of happiness.

The Windsors visited Maryland and Washington, D.C., frequently during and after what she referred to as their "Exile at St. Helena" (Nassau) when he was governor-general there during World War II. After the exciting life she had led in the United States, China, Paris, and London, the little island must have been boring for her. We saw them whenever they came north, and Millard and the prince played golf together. The duke asked Millard's advice about when to publish the book he was writing about his marriage and abdication. He wanted his side to be known. He asked Millard whether perhaps he should wait until his mother, Queen Mary, had passed on. Millard agreed this might be best, but the duke of Windsor didn't wait.

When I saw them in Paris after they were married, I was rather disgusted with Wallis's behavior. Marjorie's daughter, Eleanor de Bekessy, gave a big party for the Davieses and Tydings at her home, and the Windsors came. Wallis was wearing a ball gown with a huge skirt of tiers and tiers of lace ruffles, and she was covered with jewels. She was playing the part of duchess with all the airs and graces she must have thought a queen should have! As I have personally met three queens of England, I can testify that she was completely wrong. She flourished about waving her fan and holding up her hand to be kissed! The silly French women made elaborate curtsies to her—I didn't. I sat in a corner with Windsor and talked about U.S. politics and about his friend and golfing partner, Millard, whom he called "my senator". He made you feel you had known him all your life. We were invited to a party at the Windsor's country place outside of Paris, but unfortunately, we had to return home and missed it.

Stories were rife about the duchess's shopping expeditions in Paris. Apparently she ran up enormous bills at the great dressmaking and jewelry shops and seldom paid for anything. The duke was a wealthy man, having inherited from his grandparents, and was well able to pay her bills.

Once when we were on the *Sea Cloud* with the Davieses, a British nobleman and his wife were onboard. She told us an unbelievable story about Wallis and our ambassador to France.

Lady Williams-Taylor was a member of the British secret service. She said that Wallis was having an affair with the U.S. ambassador in Paris! The duke would escort his wife to one of the dress designers for fittings and return for her after an hour or two. Wallis would slip out the back door for a rendezvous with the ambassador. As the British secret service was guarding both Windsors, this affair was reported to their government. The British were afraid that the prince might find out, and there would be a great scandal again. So the secret service was protecting Wallises transgressions from the duke! Lady Williams-Taylor told me this story, and Marjorie corroborated it. The duchesses' future behavior in New York City in later years after the war makes it seem plausible. She had a whirl with the leading man in the Broadway show *Call Me Madam*, and it was the talk of the town. The next man she went about with was Jimmy Donohue, a homosexual, whose mother had been Jessie Woolworth Donahue. Wallis actually deserted the duke's table at a large party in New York and spent the evening at Jimmy's table, fawning over him. The Duke quietly left the party and went home, leaving her there. I did not know the actor personally but considered him much too attractive for his part in the play. As for Jimmy, he was at least twenty years younger than Wallis and had an unsavory reputation. Jessie Donahue was an old friend of Marjorie's and I knew her and her two sons, Jimmy and "Woolie," in Palm Beach.

The last time I saw the Windsors was at a large dinner dance the Morris Cafritzes gave for them in Washington in the early 1950s. I was told Wallis had her face lifted, and he had had the bags under his eyes removed! Neither operation was much of a success in my opinion. The duke had lost his boyish charm and looked old and sad. I felt very sorry for him. He died soon after. How tragic to have been king of a great empire and to have given it up, along with his home, family and friends, for such a woman. I hope he thought she was worth it, at least for their first years together! Since this was written she has died.

Part V

Chapter 21

Hitler Marches Across Europe

Hitler persecutes the Jews, takes Czechoslovakia, and demands Danzig and the Polish Corridor. Davies talks with Churchill in England. Davies resigns and becomes assistant secretary of state for war problems. Franco wins Spanish Civil War. Tydings urges big U.S. Navy appropriations. Filibusters. FDR's borrowing billions.

If I had thought 1939 would be a nice quiet year after the political battles of the last two years, I was much mistaken! I was happy in the anticipation of a pleasant, peaceful New Year with Millard. If Hitler stirred up a war in Europe, Millard and the Congress would surely keep us out of it. I had no worries!

The year started off beautifully with the excitement of seeing my husband sworn in for his third term as Senator from Maryland. Of course, there was a big party afterward in his Territory Committee rooms for family and friends.

The other wonderful thing that happened then was a priceless gift from Millard. He told me that my father had discussed the adoption of my children with him, and the senator had told him that if anyone was going to adopt them, he was going to do so! He seemed indignant when he told me this, with a stern expression. I was about to burst into tears—of pure joy! He looked at me anxiously.

"Is that all right with you, Treasure? I love those kids like my own, but if it displeases you?!" I dissolved into the senatorial arms. "I was so worried, Millard, about what would happen to them if anything should happen to me and their father could legally claim them!"

"You should have told me, sweetheart, about your worries about them. Your father told me that he was going to adopt them. I told

181

him they were my children and no man was going to adopt them
except myself!"

Apparently my father's law firm handled the whole business very
smoothly with Tom. He had married again and was living in Florida.

"Oh, darling, nothing could have made me so happy!"

We told the children and they looked puzzled. "But the senator *is*
our Daddy!" they said. We explained that nothing would change except their last name. As mine had become Tydings, so would theirs,
and they looked vastly relieved.

My happiness was complete and it seemed that Millard's was also.
The children already loved him and he loved them. He was a wonderful father to them for the rest of his life. That was the greatest
birthday gift I could have received from him. However, another
birthday gift arranged by my husband came the day before my birthday when I christened the first Pan American clipper to fly the Atlantic Ocean. It was a historic occasion. I have a news photo of myself
hanging on to my big hat with one hand and swinging a bottle of
champagne in the other. It was a very windy day but fortunately not
a rainy one.

Our social, family, and political life kept us busy. We had a big
apartment at the Wardman Park Hotel in Washington, with four
master bedrooms and baths and a beautiful view of Rock Creek
Park. It would prove to be a godsend in future war years when it
would be impossible to run Oakington House. Enough Senators
lived there to almost constitute a quorum vote, Millard said.

Soon after we moved into town, we gave a small dinner party for
the senators whom the president had tried to defeat in 1938—a
"purge party." It was great fun, although not all of them were in
town. The "purgees" were our old friends in the Senate—Senators
George, Gillette, Van Nuys, and Cotton Ed Smith and their wives.
As each senator arrived, I decorated him with a large imitation jeweled cross to pin on the chest. Instead of place cards, I had silly
limericks at each man's place at dinner, which I blush to quote:

For Senator George:

Georgie Porgie wouldn't lie.
Killed the Court, made Frankie cry:
Frankie fought with might and main
But Georgie Porgie's back again.

For Senator Cotton Ed Smith:

The Smith a mighty man is he
He's South Carolina's apogee.

The president yelled from the back of the train
But Cotton Ed won out again!

I can remember only one of the limericks for the wives. They are even worse than the above!
For Rose Gillette:

Rose is red but not a bit blue
Guy won the election—
She helped him to!

For Millard I sang:

Maryland's bridges falling down, falling down, etc.,
Maryland's bridges broken down, broken down, etc.,
My sad Tydings!
Maryland will get her bridges, get her bridges, etc.,
Maryland will get her bridges because of
My Glad Tydings!

I certainly am no poetess or a singer! When the guests read them aloud I cringed, but they all laughed and many toasts were drunk and stories told by each senator of how he won his election. There is no excitement like winning one!

There were a number of other celebration parties. We gave a big one for the chief campaign workers and contributors at Oakington; and the Democratic party leaders gave one in Baltimore where Millard spoke and everyone stood on their chairs and cheered him.

Most Washingtonians were interested but not too concerned about Hitler's actions in Europe. Stories were beginning to circulate about the German Nazi's cruel treatment of the Jews. We Americans felt safe and secure behind our oceans and not many saw the menace as the president and my father and my husband did. This was exemplified at a big dinner given by the Robert Woods Blisses at their Georgetown mansion, Dumbarton Oaks, soon after New Year. It was a large gathering of the city's most important and powerful people, those whom my father called the movers and the shakers. Among them was our friend, Senator William E. Borah, the chairman of the Foreign Affairs Committee. I considered him a typical nineteenth-century man, very pompous and stuffy. His wife, affectionately known as "Little Borah," was a dear friend of my mother's, a charming and witty little lady. In my opinion, she was a lot smarter than her husband.

At the Bliss party many guests crowded around Millard and my-self, asking us about what we had seen and heard about Hitler and the Nazis in Europe. Would there be a war over there, they wanted to know.

We told them that the Belgians were in a state of war alert and that the Grosjean brothers' regiment had been called up. Marjorie wrote us that everyone at the engagement party for my sister Emlen and Bob Grosjean said it was like the ball before the Battle of Water-loo! I also told friends that our ship coming back here from Europe was jammed full of Jewish people escaping from Germany. While I was telling an interested group of the preparations of Holland and Belgium for a German invasion, which they expected at any time, Senator Borah interrupted me:

"You are all wrong, Eleanor! I have it from impeccable private sources that Hitler will never attack the Low Countries or France!"

Even though the senator was the chairman of the Foreign Affairs Committee he had never been outside of the United States!

When Congress convened, the president asked the Senate to re-peal the Arms Embargo clause in the Neutrality Bill, which had been passed by the Senate. Millard had been opposed to the original bill, as giving too much power to the chief executive at the expense of the prerogatives of the Congress. Eventually he had voted for a much weaker form of the bill. Now the president wanted to help the Brit-ish build up their armaments and Millard feared it might involve the United States in another World War. He was chairman of the Senate committee dealing with the Arms Embargo repeal and a leader in the debate, which went on all summer. The fight was not limited to the halls of Congress.

The great majority of Americans before Pearl Harbor were either interventionists or isolationists. The more affluent citizens tended to be the former, in favor of our going to war against Germany to save Great Britain. The isolationists were opposed to this. I might have been an interventionist had it not been for Millard Tydings's prag-matic arguments against it. After all, he had fought in France in the first World War and had described it to me graphically. He said that there would always be wars in the "Old World" (of Europe and Asia), and we were not prepared to fight a war against the powerful German war machine. Millard had been trying to build up our armed forces ever since he was first elected to Congress, but the Great Depression intervened. Congress would not spend the money to build up our army or our navy, much less our air force. In spite of the interest of some Washingtonians in Europe, the major topic of conversation in political circles was whether the president would run for a third term in office in 1940. Although there was no law against it, no president had done so and there was much opposition to it. Not only Republicans and conservative Democrats were against it, a few of the president's supporters were too. Even Postmaster General Farley and Secretary Harold Ickes and Vice President Wallace were said to be opposed to a third term. A group of Millard's Senate friends met to plan to stop a draft of FDR at the Democratic Convention on the first round of voting.

Many wanted Millard to head the Democratic ticket. His stock was soaring after his triumph at the polls. Marylanders admired and boasted of his achievements in the World War and in the state legislature and the United States Congress. The people and the press were prophesying the presidency for him either in 1940 or in 1944. There was even talk of a third party movement to nominate an East-West ticket of Garner and Tydings. Virginia Senators Glass and Byrd were leading the parade for Millard. Major newspapers in the country, such as the *New York Times*, the *New York Herald Tribune*, and the *Baltimore Sun*, were praising my husband as one of the most powerful leaders in the Senate and its finest speaker. One article was entitled "The Tide is Running for Tydings." When a reporter asked him about it, Millard's reply was, "They didn't say whether it was running in or running out, did they?" He laughed at all this and at my transparent pleasure over it.

I knew that he truly did not want to give up his Senate seat, even for the presidency, but I was enjoying the idea enormously. I was so much in love with him and so proud of him. I was younger than my husband and not nearly so wise.

The president asked for another Work Relief Bill of $3.5 billion and Millard led the opposition to this recent "Borrow and Spend" plan.

March came in with a blast of bad news from Europe. Hitler's army had taken the rest of Czechoslovakia and he demanded the return of Danzig and the Polish corridor. The world was dismayed and held its breath waiting to see what the fuhrer would do next.

My father wrote us of a visit he made to London in the spring when he saw Winston Churchill at his country home at Chartwell. Daddy described Churchill working in his garden in old clothes and muddy boots. The two men discussed the fall of Czechoslovakia and my father brought up the necessity of a balance of power, with Britain, France, and Russia together, holding back the German-Italian Axis threat. Davies suggested a meeting of the World War allies with the United States. Churchill was agreeable, but he was not enthusiastic. Like the other European leaders, he underestimated the power of the Red Army. He didn't think it would be much help against the Axis. The Russians undoubtedly wanted Poland and so did Germany. Maybe they would fight each other!

There was another meeting soon after in Moscow. British, French, and Russian leaders met to discuss means of containing Hitler's warlike tendencies. The meeting accomplished nothing of the sort. My father sent word to the president that he would go to Moscow and try to see Stalin, officially or unofficially, if Roosevelt wanted him to. Roosevelt didn't. Daddy had suggested that it might be wise to try to split the Axis, since there wasn't enough room in Europe for two Caesars, and the president did see the Italian ambassador.

After his talk with Churchill, my father came home to report to the president and to request that FDR accept his resignation. Daddy's health was failing and he felt that there was not much effective service he could render in Brussels. He must have realized that the cabal against him had finally influenced Roosevelt in his absence, although he didn't discuss it in my presence. The president asked him to stay on at the listening post of Belgium for two months longer to see which way the "cat was going to jump" and my father agreed to do so. The cat in this case, of course, was Hitler. We didn't have long to wait. That spring, Germany had gobbled up the rest of Czechoslovakia. FDR wanted daddy to accept the post of assistant secretary of state for war problems and policies when he came home in August, and he did.

My father had reported to the president that the European leaders still had their heads in the sand. They were convinced that Hitler would be satisfied with Czechoslovakia, and they didn't trust the Russians. Our ambassador to London, Joseph Kennedy, agreed with them in this and in disparaging the Red Army. The president was enthusiastic about a book that Daddy was writing about Russia and the Russians, which might help to soften American opinion toward them. The book's title was to be *Mission to Moscow*.

Millard and I dined with the Davieses before they left for Belgium, and my father told us about his conversations with Churchill, the president, and his friend, Maxim Litvinov, who had been recalled as ambassador to the U.S.A. and was now the Russian ambassador in London. Molotov was to replace him in Washington, another indication of Stalin's suspicion and distrust of the British, my father said. Daddy was discouraged over the international picture. Litvinov had told him that he had been urging our government to ask the League of Nations to move against Hitler. He told my father that the U.S.S.R. was still suspicious that the Western powers were ganging up against them. My father was afraid the Russians would decide to join the Fascist Axis powers.

"I deeply regret that the president didn't follow up on Stalin's requests last year, or upon my suggestion of a conference with Russia, Britain, and France, to contain the German forces, or to let me go to Moscow this spring. I think I could have met with Stalin. Litvinov says he trusts the president. It may have been a great opportunity lost," Daddy said.

"I know he trusts you, Joe, more than anyone," said Marjorie.

My husband smiled at her and nodded agreement with Daddy.

"That reluctance on the part of the president was probably due to the fact that 1940 is election year and I'm sure that he wants a third term in office. Any moves toward deals with Russia might rock the boat for his plans. The American people detest the Communists. Incidentally, Joe, I understand that Molotov is coming to be ambassador here."

My father sighed. "I know, and I fear it is another indication that Stalin has lost his trust in us. Another strong signal is that the recent meeting of our friends with the Russians in Moscow came to nothing. Stalin was sending a message to Hitler that he was no longer angry over not being included in the Munich conference of last year."

"Is the president going to get his repeal of the Arms Embargo clause of the Neutrality bill passed, Millard?" Marjorie asked.

"Not in this session of the Senate, I think. We are about to adjourn for the Easter recess and it is a pretty hot potato to handle. I opened the debate against it. Our country is overwhelmingly opposed to war. The Arms Embargo repeal would be a challenge to our enemies to attack us," he said. "We are totally unprepared to fight the German war machine. I have been urging for a buildup of our armed forces for a long time, and at last people are beginning to listen to me! Fortunately, the president is finally with me this time for a buildup of our national defenses."

"That is good news," said my stepmother. "Let's talk about a pleasanter subject." "Tell them about the new home you have bought for us, Joe." She was as enthusiastic as I was when Daddy told us he had bought the Parmelee estate, twenty-two acres on the edge of Rock Creek Park, which we had long admired. Daddy and I had often ridden our horses past it and galloped up the dirt road past the imposing gate.

"We are going to call the place Tregaron after the town in Wales where the Davieses came from."

Marjorie was beaming. "So I'll be coming home before your father does to start fixing the place up. Eleanor, I hope you will help me."

The Davieses went back to Brussels and the Congress continued to debate the president's bills until it adjourned without voting on any of them.

The Davies-Grosjean Wedding—May 1939

May was always a busy month for me, this year especially so. There were our two large luncheons for the senators and their wives at Oakington and many political meetings there in preparation for the Democratic Convention of 1940. Also the Maryland Garden Tour visited our gardens and we were hosting a big wedding at Oakington that month for my younger sister, Emlen, and Robert Grosjean. Marjorie, with characteristic consideration, had persuaded my father that Mother must be present at the wedding and they should be absent. The affair was high on the social calendar. Millard arranged for trains from Washington, Philadelphia, and New York to make special stops at Aberdeen where buses would pick up the wedding guests. We had a large marquee on the bay lawn, and some 500 guests attended the wedding itself and the reception and bridal dinner afterward. The guest cottage and the big house took care of our family and Marjorie's daughter, Deenie, who was a bridesmaid. The rest of the bridesmaids stayed at the inn in Havre de Grace or with friends in the county. The bridegroom, his brother, parents, and ushers all stayed in Baltimore at the Belvedere Hotel. The night before the wedding, the families and the wedding party (numbering sixty) were all entertained at a seated dinner dance at Oakington House. There were thirty at the table in the dining room, and thirty in the Rose Parlor. Our servants did all the catering for this dinner. Nadine Livingston (cook) almost had nervous prostration and broke out with a bad case of hives. Dinner had been scheduled for 8 P.M. on the invitations, but the Belgian contingent didn't arrive until after 9:30 P.M.!

I was looking forward to the bridal dinner dance. I was wearing a new white satin ball gown and the emerald necklace. There would be lots of young men in the wedding party to dance with and we had hired a good dance orchestra from Washington for both evenings. I was planning to dance as long as anyone would ask me to. I loved to dance with my husband, but it was fun to dance with other men too, if they were good dancers. The senator, however, had other ideas. I was dancing happily with a Belgian groomsman when, to my dismay, the music changed to "Good Night Ladies." I ran to tell the orchestra to keep on playing and they told me it was the senator's order to play the Belgian national anthem and our "Star Spangled Banner" next and that was the end. I argued with my husband to no avail. I was angry and disappointed, but my anger didn't last long. I never could fight with him. I couldn't and he wouldn't. I would have loved the man no matter what, I think.

There were a few hitches in the two days of wedding festivities. The first occurred the afternoon before it, when our houseguests were arriving. Every bedroom in the great house and the guest cottage was to be occupied with our immediate family and relatives. It was a very warm day, and the arriving guests would want to bathe when they arrived. Robert Livingston came to me with a stricken face to announce, "There is no water, Mrs. T.!"

"You must be wrong," I said firmly. "Our wells have never run dry and we have had plenty of rain. If something is wrong with our well, just go and hook it up with the farm wells."

"I tried, Mrs. T. The connection is broken. You remember I spoke to the senator about it sometime ago."

"Well, please go speak to him again," I said. I had great faith in my husband, although he was anything but a handyman around the house. This time, however, he quite literally rose to the occasion. Livingston returned and whispered to me as I was receiving my guests: "Mrs. T., the senator has climbed to the top of the water tower behind the guest cottage and is now climbing down inside the tank!"

I gulped. "My lord, Robert, he'll kill himself!" I ran to the rescue, but he had not. He triumphantly informed me from the heights of the tower that he had fixed it and the water was flowing.

Another hitch in the carefully laid wedding plans involved a professional wedding coordinator from New York whom the bride wanted to employ so that everything would go smoothly. The woman was an expensive disaster from the first. She drove everyone crazy, got drunk, and stayed that way until Millard ordered Livingston to lock her up in an attic bedroom with a bottle of Scotch, where she went happily to sleep. The next near tragedy was the nonarrival of all the bouquets for the bride, the bridesmaids, flower girls, and mothers of the bridal couple on the wedding day. Again, the bride had wished to order it all from an expensive New York florist. I wanted to have a Maryland florist, but it was my sister's wedding and we were not paying for it. Daddy was.

About a half an hour before the ceremony, the truck with the flowers still had not arrived. Phone calls to New York elicited the information that the truck had departed at daybreak and must be lost somewhere in the wilds of New Jersey. Again Millard came to the rescue and telephoned the governor of that state. The truck driver was located in a local Jersey jail. The governor bailed him out and sent him on his way to Oakington with a police escort! So much for political pull. I thought it would be remarkable if our Maryland florists ever voted for Tydings again.

Praise be, it did not rain that day. The guests sat on the bay lawn and the wedding party came out of the solarium, down the steps, across the terrace and the lawn to the altar, against the ancient English boxwood. Millard looked very handsome when he escorted the little bride (who looked like an exquisite Dresden china figurine). All the bridesmaids looked lovely in pink organdy. Rahel and I were matrons of honor, my little girl and Rahel's were adorable flower girls, and little Joe was a dignified ring bearer.

The morning of the wedding the bride did not feel well and a slight rash had broken out on her face and neck. Our family doctor from Havre de Grace came to see her and agreed with her that it was just nerves. As the wedding ceremony and reception were to be outside and the weather prediction was for rain, I was having nervous jitters myself. One of my gifts to the bride was a garden full of flowers (in and out of season) and a bank of Easter lilies edging the terrace on the bay lawn where the bridal party marched to the altar.

The bride and bridegroom departed after the wedding reception and dinner were over and the houseguests left the next morning. Not long after they waved good-bye, the bridegroom phoned from Baltimore. He was terribly upset and reported that the bride's face was all swelled up and she had locked him out of their hotel room! Millard phoned Johns Hopkins Hospital where she had been taken by ambulance and where they formally diagnosed her case as measles. The bridegroom returned to Oakington to spend the first week of his honeymoon with us. I asked our family doctor whether he knew the morning of the wedding that Emlen had the measles and, if so, why he hadn't told us. He replied that he had known it but that nothing could have stopped that big a wedding! The 500 guests had all kissed the bride, but apparrently none of them caught her measles. Millard and I turned Oakington over to the newlyweds and spent the next two weeks in a Washington hotel.

The bridal couple went to Belgium and shortly thereafter returned to Washington, D.C. Bob Grosjean had been appointed aide to Monsieur Teunis, former prime minister of Belgium, who came over to the United States on a mission to buy war planes for his country. The storm of war was creeping closer to Europe. Adolph Hitler apparently was not satisfied with gobbling up all of Czechoslovakia and was roaring demands for Danzig and the Polish Corridor.

The next excitement on the Washington social scene, was the arrival of King George VI and Queen Elizabeth to visit the Roosevelts at the White House. There were state dinners for them, both at the White House and at the British Embassy. My little girl was a friend of Harry Hopkins's daughter and told me a nice story about the queen and the Hopkins's child. Harry Hopkins's wife had died and he was such a close friend of the Roosevelts that they invited him and his little girl to live with them at the White House. The child was introduced to the queen. Her Majesty heard later that she was disappointed because the Queen wasn't wearing a crown. Queen Elizabeth arranged to have the little girl brought in to see her when she was dressed for the White House dinner and wearing her tiara and all her jewels.

Social Washington was agog over the royal visit. When it was announced that there was to be a big garden party at the British embassy in their honor, the excitement verged on hysteria. Not all members of Congress and their wives were invited. The wives of the House members were so enraged that the Speaker of the House had to go to the vice president about the matter.He went to the president and they were all finally invited. Rain had been predicted, and I hesitated to buy a new hat for the affair. Instead, I bought a spray of white butterfly orchids at the florist and pinned them on a large old hat. Even the queen was sufficiently interested to ask me whether they were real. She looked lovely in a real British garden party costume of white lace, with hat and parasol to match. She had a flawless complexion and bright blue eyes and I found her much more attractive than the King. I thought George V shy and rather insignificant looking. He talked some time with my husband.

Another royal couple who came to Washington was the Crown Prince and Princess of Norway. We met them at a dinner given at the Norwegian embassy. The princess remained in Washington throughout the war and became a good friend of the president. She was beautiful and there was some gossip about them. FDR liked to take his small motorboat out on the water in warm weather without any guards or attendants. The princess was often his companion. People all queried: "Could he —?" and "if so, would he in a boat?"

While I was busy with my sister's wedding and the social life of the Capitol City, important matters were affecting the peace of the world. Stalin, Hitler, and Churchill were building up their armed forces, tanks, planes, and guns. The senator from Maryland was speaking both on and off the Senate floor on the immediate necessity of building up our Navy to be second to none as the best guarantee of peace and avoiding war. France was sitting smugly behind her supposedly impregnable Maginot line and the Germans behind their Siegfried line, both of which stopped short of Belgium's Ardennes Mountains.

Millard's friend, General Douglas MacArthur, was now the military advisor of the Philippine armed forces. Congress adjourned without voting on the Permanent Neutrality bill or repealing the Arms Embargo clause in the existing bill.

As I read my diary for June 1939, I see that the Civil War in Spain had finally come to an end with the Fascist dictator Franco the victor. Millard was doubly concerned because it meant that a large part of Hitler's German troops, which had been fighting in Spain for Franco, would be returning home. My husband was bitterly opposed to the President's Arms Embargo repeal. He warned again that it would challenge an enemy to attack us. We were totally unprepared to fight a war against an army like Germany's.

My father invited our young Joe to visit him in Brussels, and the boy sailed for Europe on the *Sea Cloud* with some of Daddy's friends, his law partner, Ray Beebe, Judge Richard Whaley, and his doctor, William A. Morgan. The Davieses always took a doctor with them on long cruises, often Doctor Morgan. My father wrote us that his friends had all sung the little boy's praises. They admitted to teasing him about his dad's reelection to the Senate and that our son had behaved like a polite young gentleman. The ambassador's guests went home after a week or so. My father had sent official word to the Secretary of State that he wished to resign his post.

Millard was filibustering against the president's Monetary bill until the last night of June when Congress adjourned, to my great delight, but my husband was recalled for another special session in July. Meantime, he was able to spend some leisure time with the children and myself at Oakington. It was a much needed rest for him from long days of work in Washington on both the Appropriations and Naval Committees in the Senate. He had been working to build up our Armed Forces and was chairman of the committee dealing with repeal of the arms embargo. The country was buzzing with isolationist sentiment and interventionist feeling and my husband was trying to steer clear of rocks ahead. He was being criticized, unjustly and bitterly, by both sides. At first I had been an interventionist—all for sending mountains of supplies to England and for applying economic sanctions on Germany and Italy—but Millard changed my mind. He explained that repeal of the arms embargo would tie our hands and encourage enemy attack. He said we were completely unprepared for war against the powerful German war machine. A majority of the American people did not want war or sanctions. For once, the president was on his side for a buildup of our armed forces.

Millard spent a hot, exhausting month of July fighting against the arms embargo repeal and urging his big Navy appropriation. He opened the Senate debate on the embargo repeal. Russia had invaded Finland, and Millard voted for aid for the little country and became head of Finnish war relief. He urged the fortification of Guam, expansion of the Panama Canal, selective service, increased appropriations for the Army and the biggest Navy in peacetime history. I was his cheerleader in the Senate gallery most of the session.

Marjorie came home the first week in July, bringing with her two Belgian friends, the Count and Countess de la Faille. We were invited to her New York home at Two East Ninety-Second Street to meet them and, following a suggestion of my stepmother, took them home to Oakington to spend a weekend. The De La Failles were an attractive couple and became interested in our small daughter's riding ability. They owned a large stud farm in Belgium where they bred Arab horses and they insisted upon giving one to my child. When they returned home, they sent her a beautiful little silver gray mare named Challa. Of course, Millard paid the freight for the small horse on a luxury liner, and he maintained that Challa's accommodations cost more than the royal suite.

My stepmother invited us to bring our children and spend August at Camp Topridge with her and my father. She also suggested that we leave the heat of Washington and take the *Sea Cloud* for a short cruise. In July, when Congress adjourned we happily took two friends and the children and sailed up the East Coast for a few days. The President called a special session of the Senate to continue debate on the arms embargo in September.

My father returned with his grandson and a Belgian guest, the Duke D'Asque, at the end of July. Millard and I joined the Davieses and the duke on the *Sea Cloud* for another delightful cruise up the New England coast. This time we were royally entertained at Southampton, Newport, Nantucket, etc. The Davieses, in turn, gave parties on board. The weather was perfect and I was careful to give the duke a wide berth and only a few cool smiles and Millard showed no displeasure. The Davieses and the Tydings went back to Marjorie's camp on Upper St. Regis Lake and the duke went back to Belgium. Our children had already gone to Camp Topridge with young Deenie, her governess, and the "Pinks." Millard and I were guests at Camp Topridge each summer for many years.

On the evening of August 23, we four were alone at Topridge and Daddy was playing with the radio controls. Suddenly bad news came over the air that left us all silent and subdued. Germany and Russia had signed a nonaggression pact! Herr Von Ribbentrop had gone to Moscow to sign it with Molotov, the foreign commissar. We sat quietly for a few minutes. This was the blow to the free world that my father had warned us about.

"There goes the ball game," he said, shaking his head sadly. "Now Hitler has protected his eastern border against possible hostility and has a free hand to gobble up Poland and the Romanian oil fields. He and Mussolini have been partners since Italy took Ethiopia, and Germany has no potential enemies save England and France."

"The air bombing of Ethiopian civilians was horrible," said Millard, "like shooting ducks in a pond. Haile Selassi's ancient kingdom fell in only a week or so. Did you read his appeal to the League of Nations at Geneva, Joe? He said, 'It is us today and it will be you tomorrow!' "

My father nodded. "The only hope for peace was a pact between Britain, France, and Russia," he said.

"France alone could have stopped Hitler at any time with all its trained divisions—still could," observed my husband.

"I'm afraid they are still gambling that Hitler will be satisfied now that they have let him have all of Czechoslovakia," said Daddy.

"Does this mean there will be war in Europe?" Marjorie asked.

"It depends upon what Hitler does now that his Russian back door is secure. It means that Stalin decided there was no hope of the western nations joining him to stop Hitler. Russia has tried to ally itself with France and England and our country ever since Litvinov warned the League of Nations at Geneva about Germany's military ambition. The European governments have been too busy playing politics to bother about what Hitler was up to."

"And our president has been too preoccupied fighting the 'purgees' and getting ready to run for a third term. I have feared a second world war as you know, Joe. We have both seen it coming. I have been trying to build up our military defenses and put us in a strong position so that we can escape the conflagration. God help the Europeans!"

"Did Stalin think this pact with Germany would help Russia?" I asked.

"It gives him one great advantage, my child. Time! Time to build up his defenses and get ready for Germany after Hitler's forces have rolled over the rest of Europe."

"If Hitler sends his panzers to blitzkrieg Poland, it will mean war with England and France." Millard looked grim.

Marjorie and I spoke in unison. "Thank God you are both too old to go if we get involved!"

"Many Americans like myself hate Communism and would have been loath to ally ourselves with Russia," my husband said.

Millard asked again whether the Russian armed forces, which Daddy had seen, could stand up against Hitler's mechanized divisions. My father said that he thought they might, given a few more years to get ready. We all went to bed to spend a sleepless night.

On September 1, Hitler's divisions overran Poland with terrible bloodshed, mowing down the brave Poles on their cavalry horses with the big German tanks. On September 3, France and Britain lived up to their treaties with Poland and declared war on Germany. The president called another special session of Congress. The German "cat" had jumped! The German army settled down in their Siegfried line fortificatons.

We were fortunate to be able to enjoy another lovely cruise on the *Sea Cloud* before the Senate convened. Marjorie had suggested that we take the yacht again for the second week in September and invite some friends to go up the New England coast again. Millard was especially grateful that he could express his gratitude to friends who had been among his chief supporters in the 1938 election. The guests on our "political cruise" were state Senator and Mrs. Edward Colgan of Baltimore (she was the Democratic National Committeewoman), Mr. and Mrs. Jim Bruce of Baltimore, Mr. and Mrs. William Labrot of Holly Beach Farm (a splendid estate on the Chesapeake Bay near Annapolis), and Mr. Vincent Jamison of Western Maryland. Mrs. Eleanor Labrot was the sister of the man who had been my best beau before I decided to marry Tom Cheesborough instead. Eleanor was a beautiful, witty person, and I enjoyed her company more than the others, although I liked them all. We were sad to hear that she was divorcing Bill and tried to dissuade her, in vain.

Our party was royally entertained at Bar Harbor by the writer, Mrs. Mary Roberts Rinehart, whose son and I had briefly contemplated matrimony when I was sixteen. We entertained all our Bar Harbor hosts on the yacht and sailed happily homeward. Our guests had been an interesting combination of politicians (the Colgans), socialites (the Bruces and Labrots), and a tough old businessman (Vincent Jamison). Tragically, the Colgans died shortly after our cruise. Certainly everyone got along splendidly onboard ship and (we thought) went home happy.

One evening with Daddy and Marjorie, I recall the conversation between my father and my husband. They were discussing the brilliant successes of Hitler.

"Speaking of generals," Millard said, "there was a story I heard from a man high up in our secret service last spring. He told me that a group of German generals headed by the chief of the German general staff was planning to rebel against Hitler if he began to move toward starting a big war. They had even contacted London to see if England and France would back them up if they seized Hitler and their government buildings."

"That must have been when General Beck retired and Hitler replaced him with General Halder," said my father thoughtfully. "There were rumors about it, but it was all blotted out by Hitler's move into Czechoslovakia. I never heard that the German generals contacted the British."

"I was told that the British refused to cooperate. If Hitler found out about it, I imagine most of the poor devils in the plot are dead." My husband shook his head "Hitler, like Stalin, has little regard for human life." How little, we didn't know at that moment.

On October 1, when the maple trees were scarlet and gold and the holly trees loaded with red berries, a prestigious club in Baltimore came out for Tydings for President. Now the situation had greatly changed and on October 27 my husband and the Senate voted for repeal of the arms embargo. Russia invaded Finland, Daddy was sworn in as assistant secretary of state, Millard was chairman of Finnish war relief, and my children's adoption papers were signed. We moved into our apartment at the Wardman Park Hotel and spent our weekends with family guests at Oakington.

There was great excitement at Oakington when the little Arabian horse arrived with her little shoes hung around her neck. When she was first turned loose in the pasture field, she took off instantly, at a wild gallop, her long mane and tail flying and her nose to the ground, sniffing the strange land. Challa and "Little El" fell in love at once and I truly believe they talked to each other. The child told us quite seriously what Challa said to her and to the farm horses. She usually rode the mare bareback and I have a picture of them swimming together in the bay, my child wearing a little red bathing suit. We bred Challa to a fine gray stallion, but she lost her foal and we didn't breed her again. The vet had given us the wrong date for the birth and the children were heartbroken. The Arab mare lived with us for many years and when she became quite elderly, we gave her to friends with children on a nearby farm where she spent a pleasant and pampered old age. My daughter *still* insists that Challa talked to her.

The Davieses did not come often for Christmas at Oakington, and I recently found a beautiful letter from Marjorie after spending it with us one year that greatly pleased both Millard and myself. I will quote it here. It bears no date, but I value it highly as an expression of our warm feelings for each other.

Dearest Eleanor:

We had such a lovely Christmas with you. Just the joy of being with you two and your darlings would be enough to make Christmas for us. But added to that were the lovely presents and all the beautifully arranged Oakington House decorations and the Christmas ceremonies. It was just perfect, dear. You have no idea what a joy and pride both Daddy and I have in you, your family circle, your home, your beauty of being and spirit, your intelligence, and ability. You see, we not only love but admire our Eleanor! Lots of love dear to the two of you—Millard and the dear young ones.

Devotedly,
Marjorie

Chapter 22

The 1940s

Tydings urges preparedness, economic and military. The German blitzkrieg takes Netherlands, Belgium, and Luxenbourg, and defeats the French. The British escape across the Channel. Tydings put in nomination for U.S. President. FDR nominated and elected for third term. Davies unofficial liaison officer for FDR with Russian Ambassador. German army invades Russia. Stalin requests Britain and U.S. to open a second front in France. The Japanese attack the U.S. Navy at Pearl Harbor.

The Forties—the fascinating, fabulous, ferocious forties of my life! In the middle of the forties I became forty years old—a bit wiser maybe, and fortunately not much changed in appearance. I knew that the compliments I received were mainly because of my brilliant, powerful, and good-looking husband. For me personally, they were happy, exciting years, although increasingly terrible worldwide. Millard's political star was shining even brighter and he was as happy with me as I was with him.

When Congress convened in 1940, President Roosevelt quickly declared a state of neutrality and national emergency and asked Congress for more help for our former ally, Great Britain. The British were desperate for us to give them fifty of our old destroyers to help them convoy merchant marine ships bearing supplies to them.

Most Americans, like ourselves, sympathized with the English, but few wanted to be pulled into another European war. Millard was bitterly opposed to giving any part of our small navy to Britain. He continued to speak on and off the Senate floor for the need to build up our armed services (especially the Navy) and to urge the government to economize. The Senate debate over these issues continued through 1940 and into 1941. Millard insisted that the best way to stay out of war was to build up our military and naval defenses. I

198

was in the gallery when he told the Senate that he would rather be all the way in the war than halfway in, "like a Roman rider, with one foot on the neutrality horse and one foot on a war horse!"

Life in Washington went on as usual, but with more charity benefits for war relief for France, Finland, and England. I succumbed to the usual wave of cold and flu and was sent to the Davieses in Palm Beach, where I quickly recuperated. Social life there was in full swing and I enjoyed the parties at Mar-a-Lago and many other magnificent homes—the Stotesburys, the Rays, Jessie Woolworth, etc. Millard came down for a week and took me home. He was busy with the Maryland election, helping George Radcliffe to be reelected to the Senate. This involved many political affairs a week in Maryland, which we attended. By this time I recognized many constituents and remembered their names, which pleased Millard.

He kept on speaking of our need for preparedness, economic as well as military. His speeches against the rising national debt and government spending were prophetic. I quote a newspaper account: "The senator said we must elect one of three paths. We (government) can continue to spend more than we take in and borrow the difference with which to pay our bills, or we can decrease appropriations so that our income and outgo will balance, or we can increase taxes. We have to do one of these three things. If we cannot balance our budget now, when we have prosperity to a reasonable degree, what are we going to do in case of war or the depression predicted by the Chairman of the Federal Reserve Board and by economists worldwide? The burden of national debt would be inherited by future generations if the Federal budget is not balanced!"

Millard's speeches earned him the support of Ogden Reid, the powerful publisher of the *New York Herald Tribune*. As my father had told him one day on the golf course, "Seriously, my boy, I think you have a good chance to be elected president either this year or in 1944. Ogden Reid's wife tells me that their paper would back you. Their man who worked for you in 1938 has been urging us to employ him to work for your election. He is sure he can do it! Also, your *Baltimore Sun* paper and the Washington papers are for you, I understand. People are tired of the New Deal and like your speeches on 'pay as you go' preparedness. You would make a great president, Senator."

My husband simply smiled and shook his head. He studied his approach shot to the green. "There really isn't a chance to defeat Roosevelt while the war goes on, Joe, and I don't want the job. I want to stay in the Senate." The news media had written articles about "Tydings for President" ever since his last election. Being in the national spotlight this way was very exciting for any young wife, especially one who idolized her husband. Although my father had long been a close friend and adviser of the president's, he was devoted to Millard. I knew he was pleased over the publicity his son-in-law had been receiving.

The so-called Phony War between Germany and our old allies of the First World War came to a tragic end that spring. Their armies had been crouched safely all winter behind their "impregnable" fortifications of the French Maginot and the Siegfried (German) lines. Then, in April, under the command of the German General Erwin Rommel, Hitler's mighty army of Panzer divisions crashed through Denmark and invaded not only Norway but Holland, Belgium, and Luxembourg, in a blitzkrieg, bypassing the Maginot line. It was the same route the Germans had taken in 1914, but under different circumstances. They had been bogged down that time in bloody trench warfare. In our capital city, we Senate ladies were working hard on hospital supplies for the Red Cross, and I was working in the city's hospitals. There were horror stories about atrocities committed by the German troops. One tale was that the Germans were using human pilots attached to their big bombs.

On May 10, the Germans had reached Belgium, and my sister Emlen and her Belgian husband planned to sail to France on the first available ship. My brother-in-law had been in Washington as an aide to Monsieur Teunis, a former prime minister of Belgium who had come to buy war planes. Now Bob was going back to rejoin his regiment, and Emlen was going to work as a Red Cross nurse in the hospitals behind the lines, as people did in the World War. We were all horrified, remembering the bloody trench warfare of World War I. In mid May, the Grosjeans stopped at Oakington on the way to board their ship in New York. With them were two young men from the Belgian embassy in Washington, Pierre de Muelemeister and Henri Greban, who were also going home to fight for their country.

The gardens were in full bloom that beautiful day at Oakington. We all drank cocktails and toasted the young Belgians at a gay and festive luncheon, and the boys clowned in the garden. All of us were trying to pretend that they would soon come home safely when the war ended. The following weekend, the Norwegian ambassador, Wilhelm de Munthe de Morgensternes, and his wife, Marjorie, were our houseguests. It was another sad occasion. The Norwegian people were fighting a bloody, losing battle with the German invaders. The four of us spent most of the weekend sitting on the floor with maps of Norway spread out around us listening to the sad news of the fall of that country on the radio. I wept with the Morgensternes and Millard looked grim and I knew he was wondering whether we would have to fight Germany again. General Rommel had reached the French coast on the channel and entrapped both the French and English armies. The bad news reports said they had taken thousands of French soldiers prisoners. The good news was that Chamberlain had been defeated and Churchill was prime minister of England.

Then occurred the dramatic epic escape of the British army across the channel under the overwhelming attack of Hitler's mechanized divisions. Outnumbered, outgunned, and out-tanked, the British soldiers stood in the waters of their channel while fleets of boats, great and small, steamed and rowed out from England to rescue them. They came in yachts and warships, tugboats and rowboats, in anything that floated, and saved a great many of their soldiers. We listened, glued to our radios. The terrible bombings of the German V2s were smashing British cities, and a triumphant Hitler marched into Paris on June 22 to receive the French surrender in the old railroad car in which the Germans had surrendered at the end of the first World War. Our family all worried about what had happened to the Grosjeans.

Hitler planned to cross the channel and take the British Isles, which were suffering from his cruel bombing. Many of the ships carrying supplies for the British were being sunk by German submarines. General de Gaulle had escaped to England and then to Africa to lead the "Free French" escapees. Old Marshal Petain headed the so-called Vichy government of southern France. The British were now fighting the Germans in Africa, Crete, and Greece, and were being forced to retreat in those places. In our country, the internationalists and isolationists were arguing with each other.

To my indignation, both sides were criticizing my husband because he would not support either one. He was in favor of aid for Britain, but opposed to giving them anything like a ship, which would take a long time to replace. Of primary importance to him was the need to build up our own armed forces. I sat in the Senate gallery many times in June listening to him speak on the subject. "We must prepare, prepare, prepare!" he told the Senate. He would rather "have a strong Army and Navy and not need it than need it and not have it!" The Congress agreed. He succeeded in passing bills for $753 million for our armed services, and increasing our Navy by 25 percent! He also introduced an amendment to an emergency tax bill to pay for it, which would slash federal expenditures by 4 percent. "Our first line of defense is not in Europe or our ocean, but it is in the marble walls of our treasury!" he said, and he was "going to be a realist as long as he lived in a realistic world!"

The Davieses, my sister Rahel, and my mother sat in the Senate gallery with me sometimes and joined in the enthusiastic applause from the crowded galleries. I never thought that we would be drawn into the war in Europe. I was confident that Millard wouldn't let it happen. Everyone knew that Roosevelt was very friendly with Churchill (as well as with the princess of Norway) but he was too much of a politician to go against the majority of public opinion. Of course, as my husband said, if FDR was to be reelected, it could happen. Millard thought he probably would be, but worked against it nevertheless. When Senator Radcliffe won the Maryland primary which was tantamount to winning the general election, Tydings was free to plan the opposition to Roosevelt's third term.

Senator Richard Russell of Georgia, representing a large group of southern senators, urged Millard to run against Roosevelt for president, and the Maryland Democratic State Convention unanimously voted him the state's favorite son for the office. My husband thanked the senators and his supporters and replied graciously, as usual, "I want to stay in the Senate and that is *all* I want!"

I knew that it would be very good for the United States if he were president, but I knew that the burdens of that office would be far heavier than those of the Senate and that I would see even less of the man I loved. So I agreed with his decision, but I was happy that so many fine Americans wanted his leadership. Would we stay neutral and would the president run for a third term were the two hot questions in our capital city. I had faith that Millard and his friends would not let a third term or the war come to pass. Unfortunately, I was mistaken on both counts.

At the Democratic Convention of 1940, it became apparent that the war in Europe made Americans loathe to "change horses in the middle of the stream." We left for the convention in Chicago on a "Tydings for President" train bedecked with banners and loaded with Marylanders, singing and shouting "Tydings for President." Important members of the Maryland delegation were Ed Colgan, a Baltimorian whom Millard had named as Maryland's Democratic National Committeeman, and my friend May Cronin, of Aberdeen, as the Committeewoman. May had helped me form the Harford County Women's Democratic Club, and I had lobbied the statewide club to have her elected president of it. Her husband had been state senator in the Maryland legislature and owned the Aberdeen paper. They were with us when my father met us in Chicago at the Blackstone Hotel. With him was my son, Little Joe, who was wearing an enormous "Tydings for President" button almost as big as my hat.

At first I enjoyed the gaiety and excitement of the convention. We were guests of the Ohio delegation the first evening, which had invited Millard to address them at a banquet. There I met Governor and Mrs. Paul McNutt. They were both charming and extremely good looking and we became firm friends. Old friends like Ralph Hines gave dinner parties for us. Daddy arranged for me to give a party for the ladies in our delegation. But the convention itself was a travesty of the democratic process. I was angered and disgusted. The night before it started, Millard had called a meeting of the Maryland delegation and told them they were released from their pledge to him, it became evident that the president would be drafted on the first ballot. Most of them stayed loyal to Millard, and he sat at the head of the Marylanders, holding the state flag when the New Dealers for FDR started parading around the convention hall. I was seated in a box not far above the floor with Mrs. Cordell Hull, whose husband, the secretary of state, was the favorite son of Virginia. Once, when I tried to go down on the convention floor to ask Millard for a ticket for an old Vassar friend, the police would not let me do so, although they knew well who I was. When the parade of delegates shouting, "We want Roosevelt" marched around the hall, I saw these same policemen pushing many men through the doors from outside to join the marchers. They looked like tramps and thugs.

Mrs. Hull and I were shocked. We watched as the ragtag and riffraff of the city was herded in by the policemen to swell the parade of shouting Roosevelt delegates. The New Dealers persisted in marching 'round and 'round the hall, waving FDR banners and screaming, "We want Roosevelt!"

Most of our Maryland delegation stood firm and dignified and refused to join the marchers. Then, all of a sudden, the "voice from the sewers" (to quote the subsequent news stories) raised the shouts of the marchers to an earsplitting cacophony! We were deafened. Afterward we learned that the roaring had come from an engineer in the basement under the hall! He had discovered that by shouting through a pipe, which was in some way connected to the loud speaker system, his voice was magnified a thousandfold. No one knew that at the time. A huge red-headed man from Massachusetts kept trying to get me to join with the FDR delegates parade. "Come on, little Tydings; come join us!" he shouted each time he came by. Our box was only a few feet above the convention floor, which put me about on a level with this tall man. Finally, he made a grab for my waist and tried to drag me down to march with him.

That was the last straw. I was so furious that I let him have it and slapped his face with all my strength. He looked more astounded than angry and moved on. He did not come back. I was thankful that the newspaper photographers who had been taking pictures of Mrs. Hull and myself did not record my unladylike behavior. Millard was the last of the presidential candidates to concede to the draft for FDR on the first ballot. When Ed Colgan put Tydings's name in nomination, there was a great deal of applause. Vice President Garner had left early to go home and "go fishing" and Senator Wheeler had also withdrawn his name. Old Senator Glass withdrew Secretary Hull's name with a speech against a third term, which conceded Roosevelt's nomination.

Then Millard spoke with his characteristic dignified simplicity. "Some of us in Maryland have stood out for a great principle of democracy," he said. "It was a fair fight and we lost. It is overwhelmingly evident that this convention wishes the renomination of President Roosevelt. We bow to your wishes and cast the sixteen votes of Maryland for President Roosevelt." He had told me all along that FDR would probably be reelected.

"It is better to have one good man with you than a mob of bums like those that were pulled in off the street to shout for Roosevelt!" I told my husband.

The newsmen pestered him with questions. His answer was always the same. "I am a Democrat. I have always been a Democrat and will work for the Democratic ticket," which he did, but never mentioned Roosevelt's name.

Daddy had stayed in Chicago only overnight and returned to Camp Topridge. Millard left at once after the president's nomination, and Little Joe and I took the train to Mother's lodge on the Brule River in the north woods of Wisconsin. It had been my Grandfather Knight's fishing camp, built of oiled logs and much modernized and decorated by Mother. I was physically ill over the travesty of politics that I had seen in Chicago, especially after Millard told me of a conversation he had with Postmaster General Jim Farley, about the Chicago convention. Farley was angry at the hypocrisy and sham of the whole business. He said the president had told all his best friends that he would not run for a third term and then he had organized the "spontaneous demonstration" for himself at the convention, which was a sham. He had engineered his own nomination to look like a real draft. It seems to me the candidates have been doing it ever since.

My sister Rahel had brought her little girl and my small Eleanor to Mother's lodge with her. I breathed the sweet air of the pine woods and paddled and poled a canoe on the Brule's cold, rushing water while my mother fished for the trout hidden in its depths. I went home all refreshed and eager to rejoin my husband.

Millard and the children went to Topridge the first of August, but Congress was still in session and so Millard spent most of the month in Washington. The Paul McNutts and the royal family of Luxembourg and their children were also guests at Topridge. Prince Felix (consort) and the Grand Duchess were pleasant people of middle age who had escaped from their palace only minutes before the German army arrived. The duchess said she had barely had time to stuff her jewels and a few valuables into a pillowcase and run.

In mid-August I went to Ocean City, Maryland to be chief speaker at the annual meeting of the United Women's Democratic Club. This was an honor usually reserved for elected officials. As usual, I simply told them about what Senator Tydings had done and was trying to do for them. Millard was still voting his conservative convictions in the Senate on domestic issues but was supporting aid to Britain and Finland.

In September, my sister and all the Grosjeans landed in New York and Millard and the Davieses and I went to meet their boat. They had managed to escape from France through Spain into Portugal by motor and obtained passage to America on a boat. It was a harrowing tale and could not have been accomplished had it not been for Daddy's help. As assistant secretary of state, he was able to pull strings and get money to them. They came with Mother to visit us at Oakington and there was a great celebration. Bob Grosjean was going to enlist in the U.S. Army. Afterward Emlen Grosjean wrote the story of their adventures trying to find the Belgian Army in France and afterward trying to get to Lisbon.

Bob Grosjean had obtained American citizenship, and since he was equally fluent in French, German, and English, he was given an officer's commission in the U.S. Army and was sent to London as aide to Tony (Anthony Drexel) Biddle, who was serving there as U.S. ambassador to the occupied countries of Middle Europe. I suspected that Bob did a great deal of underground work between Europe and England. One of his Belgian friends, who was a flier in the Royal Air Force, was extremely bitter against the German Gestapo, which had executed members of his family. He told Bob that he knew exactly where the Brussels headquarters of these Germans was located and at the first opportunity he planned to leave his squadron and bomb it. Bob tried in vain to dissuade him, but the Belgian flier bombed the German HQ in Brussels. The tragedy that ensued caused the young flier to deliberately take his own life when he found what he had done. The head of the Belgian underground had been posing as a German officer and was one of those killed in the bombing. The Germans found material on his body that enabled them to round up and execute most of his friends in the Belgian underground. When the poor young Belgian flier heard what had happened, he flew out to sea after his next bombing mission and did not return.

As late as November 1940, FDR was still saying on the radio: "I have said it before and I say it again and again. Our boys are not going to be sent into foreign wars!" He was reelected to a third term, but only by a small majority.

When the Tydings family moved back from Oakington into our Washington apartment in January 1941, we had no premonition of the terrible events of the coming year. We thought that the only battles in our country would be the political ones carried over from the past Congressional session.

My father had resigned from the State Department because of his health, and the president appointed him chairman of both the committee on war relief and of his inaugural committee. Little Joe, who was almost as tall as his grandfather, was to be his official aide. The boy was thrilled. He would wear his cadet uniform from Maryland's great military school, McDonogh, and would sit on the podium with his grandfather when the president took his oath of office in January. He would also sit in the president's box to review the inaugural parade and have lunch with my father in the White House. As if all this were not enough, my son confided to me wistfully that it would be fun to ride in the parade. I passed the word to Daddy, who, of course arranged for it, and his grandson was as pleased and happy as the president himself that day!

I wrote to Mother in Florida, describing the inauguration and some of the social affairs going on that winter of 1941. "This is FDR's third and last inauguration, I hope. Last night was the inaugural concert at Constitution Hall. Rahel, Emlen, Millard, and I sat in a box, we girls all gussied up in our best gowns with large orchid corsages. Several senators and generals told us between acts that they had never seen three such beautiful sisters. Of course, they probably complimented all ladies! The entertainers on that occasion included a new woman opera star and Nelson Eddy, Irving Berlin, Ethel Barrymore, and Mickey Rooney. They were all grand.

"We had seats directly in front of the president's stand at the inaugural ceremony at the Capitol," my letter continued. "It was a gorgeous day but very cold. As always, it was an impressive ceremony. Fred Essary of the *Baltimore Sun* said that he was disappointed that there was so little enthusiasm manifested by the crowd for FDR. There was hardly any for his speech. I was pleased, it was nothing like the convention in Chicago. Maybe there were a lot of 'Tydings Democrats' in the crowd!

"It might interest you to hear that a member of the House of Representatives died a couple of days ago, so the flags on the House office building right behind the president were flying at half-mast. You might like to hear also about some of the parties we attended. First (but not important!) was a dinner given by Mrs. W. and her daughter Mrs. R. in honor of Louise Cromwell MacArthur Atwill, who is fatter than ever. You remember she was divorced from General Douglas MacArthur. She is now married to the actor, Lionel Atwill. Mrs. S. was a shade snooty to me when we arrived (but of course all over Millard like a tent). I was amused when the two ministers (Sweden and Ireland) on either side of me, and Congressman Hamilton Fish across the table, would talk to nobody except to me! They were all for all-out aid for Britain, short of war. Their arguments were good.

"The next night we went to a big dinner in Washington at Mr. and Mrs. George Maurice Morris's historic old house in honor of His Imperial Highness, Archduke Otto of Austria. I intended to wear my emerald necklace with my black velvet ball gown with the long train, but when we got back from Baltimore the bank was closed so I couldn't take out the necklace. Millard ordered a lot of enormous gardenias and pinned them all around the neck of my gown, with no jewelry, the effect was good, better than emeralds, he said. There were forty people at this dinner and I never had so many compliments. The archduke is not much taller than I am, with dark hair, brown eyes, nicely chiseled nose and mouth, soft round chin, and a bristly little mustache. He looked sad and morose, but I worked hard and actually won several good laughs from him. He cheered up and seemed to be enjoying himself.

"Our host informed me later that he had seated me next to Otto especially to give him a good time because according to protocol he usually had to sit beside dull old ladies at dinner parties. George Morris said he thought I might 'provide some comedy relief!' That crack took me down a peg."

I wrote to mother again:

"The president has proposed 'lend leasing' fifty overage U.S. destroyers to Britain, and of course Millard has been fighting it. I have been sitting in the Senate gallery every day not wanting to miss anything. Millard says it takes too long to build a destroyer in case we need it ourselves. He supports an amendment to the bill limiting lend leasing any part of our Navy to six months replacement time.

"Awful stories are circulating about the German's treatment of the Jews. I pray they are wrong, or at least exaggerated. I miss you. Love, Eleanor."

All was not fun and games in our capital city. The war news about the fighting in Europe increasingly worse. We worried over what would happen to us if Hitler crossed the English Channel and Great Britain went down before the German tanks, planes, and submarines. German U-boats were swarming in packs in the Atlantic, attacking merchant ships bearing desperately needed supplies to Britain. British forces in Africa, Crete, and Greece were being driven into the sea. German bombs were continuing to smash British cities, and the great battleship *Hood*, the pride of the English fleet, had been sunk, as well as half of the British destroyers. Roosevelt was still pushing for a repeal of the arms embargo so he could "lend or lease" supplies to England. My husband was all for giving the British any of our guns, tanks, or planes, but no Navy ships. It would take years to replace a battleship and, if Britain was defeated, we were sadly unprepared to take on Hitler's might. So he assembled the senators who had held the fort with him against Roosevelt's Supreme Court bill at a stag dinner to discuss strategy.

There was not much going on socially in Washington or Maryland in 1941. There were not many embassy parties. We went to a few small informal dinners given by our friends, both in the Senate and otherwise, and to only one or two political affairs a week in Maryland. I was happy because I saw more of my family and friends, and best of all my husband. He let his friends in the Senate carry on the debate over neutrality, and we went to New York with my mother to see the play *Life with Father*, and with the Davieses to the Metropolitan Opera. In Washington we dined with a few senators from both political parties. In April I spent two weeks with the Davieses in Palm Beach. Senator and Mrs. Alben Barkley and the Paul McNutts were guests at Mar-a-Lago too, but left soon after Millard arrived to celebrate his birthday on Easter Sunday. We all enjoyed each other, but were all worried.

After the guests left, my father told us that he had been acting as unofficial liaison officer for the president with the Russian ambassador, Mr. Oumanski, who had replaced Litvinov. Oumanski was a cold, austere man whom nobody in the State Department could get along with, but Daddy had known him in Moscow and they were friends. My father also told us that the Russians were more suspicious than ever of the British. They thought the English were turning the United States against them. The president thought that Daddy's book, *Mission to Moscow*, might help to promote friendly relations.

I was happy to get back to Oakington and have the children with us for their spring holidays. A few friends came to enjoy it with us on weekends. My mother came to visit and celebrate her birthday the last of May, and the Davieses came to spend a few days in June. After they left, I spent some peaceful days painting the guest cottage and planning a small buffet supper party with dancing to our new Magnavox.

That party was unexpectedly a most memorable occasion. The husband of Millard's older sister, James Pickett, a fine man, sadly, crippled from multiple sclerosis, was fiddling with the radio in the library and a half-dozen couples were dancing in the "gold parlor" after supper. I was dancing with my cousin Jack Cochran when "Pick" shouted suddenly for our attention. We crowded around the radio. Hitler's army had invaded Russia! I remember crying out, "Thank god! Now Germany will be defeated and the world will be saved!"

Millard smiled and put his arm around me. "Don't be too sure, darling. Anything can happen!"

Cousin Jack, who was a junior foreign service officer, said that if Britain fell, we might still have to take on Hitler and his Nazis.

There was no more dancing at Oakington that night. We all clustered around the radio until there was no further news. It was June 22, 1941.

My father had been delivering a speech that day in Madison Wisconsin, and he was besieged by reporters. His words were reported in every major newspaper in our country. "The extent of the resistance of the Red Army will amaze and surprise the world!" he said. He was the only man who had been or was then a part of our government to make such a prophecy. The officials in both state and military departments were all pessimistic about the survival of the Russian army. The newspapers said that 164 mechanized German divisions had rolled into Russia in a three-pronged attack from the Baltic to the Black Sea with strong air support. The Russians had only 119 divisions, a much smaller air force, and very little modern equipment. My father conferred at once with Oumanski and the president. One German army marched on Leningrad in the north, and one on Moscow in mid Russia and the third army went southeast to lay seige on Stalingrad. Russia was asking the president to send more supplies to the U.S.S.R. and pleading for the U.S. and Britain to open a second front on the English Channel.

The next evening we dined with the Davieses. Daddy told us that Oumanski thought the Red Army could hold out until winter, when they would try to establish a permanent front with the aid of the United States. The Russian also said that the German attack was not a complete surprise to them. They had suspected that it might come that summer. Oumanski had passed the word along to my father and the president, whose advisers thought the Russians would not be able to withstand the German onslaught. My father's encouraging words relieved FDR's fears somewhat. The president agreed that the U.S.S.R. was fighting the greatest danger to the United States and deserved all the aid we could give them. Stalin had already requested that we help Britain open a second front across the English Channel, but neither England nor the U.S. had the men or armaments to do so. Roosevelt had already sent our World War I army rifles (150,000) to Churchill to defend their shores in case Hitler crossed the English Channel. More than thirty years later, I learned that an American officer, who had graduated from West Point and later ran a large rubber company, had been sent to England to create a rubber army of dummy soldiers and fake buildings along British shores to fool the Germans and deter their possible landing. They never crossed the channel.

My father said the president wanted to know when *Mission to Moscow* would be in bookstores. Daddy said it was promised before Christmas and the movie moguls were after him to make a film of it.

The president laughed and asked whether Daddy would play the role of himself. My parent had said no, he didn't have enough hair on top. Marjorie was indignant when she heard that. She stated emphatically that Daddy had enough hair and that he was handsomer without it on the front of his head than the president was with a thatch all over his!

The Davieses put the *Sea Cloud* in a Florida port, afraid to use the ship with German submarines prowling the seas, and spent most of the summer in Washington. The Tydingses commuted between the city and Oakington, Millard commuted by train unless we drove in together. Hitler's "Operation Barbarossa" had changed many people's plans. The neutrality fight was still going on in the Senate, but Roosevelt announced all-out aid to Russia and gave the orders to the State Department. He told Congress the Neutrality Act did not apply to the U.S.S.R. and asked my father to go back to Russia as ambassador. When Marjorie put her foot down, FDR sent Harry Hopkins to Moscow.

In August, the Davieses gave a cocktail party at Tregaron for three young Russian army fliers. They must have helped their country's image, for they looked not unlike American boys. Everyone came who had been invited, and a few who had not been. After that, I took the children to visit Mother on the Brule River and hurried home to Millard after a few days. We didn't know it, but he was about to engage in his last bitter battle with Franklin Roosevelt.

The president and Prime Minister Churchill had met on their ships that month at Newfoundland and signed the Atlantic Charter, a declaration of joint principles. They also discussed how to send maximum aid to Russia and England and composed a note to Japan about a planned embargo on that country. Germany had taken much of middle Europe, and Japan was invading China and threatening Singapore and the Philippines, as Millard had feared. In the Senate, he was supporting an emergency tax bill to pay for our defense buildup. It was defeated.

From August to December, the contest to revise the Neutrality Act continued in the Senate. On September 3, the president came up with a bright idea and announced that he had completed a "deal" with Great Britain: our fifty old destroyers for some of their military bases. He had sidestepped the Congress and they could do nothing about it. Millard didn't like it, but he admitted to me that the British bases in the Pacific would help us to protect the Philippines from the Japanese.

On September 11, the president went on the radio asking for a bill to arm our merchant ships to carry goods into war zones and belligerent ports. The president wanted them to "shoot on sight" in case of a German attack. My husband was angry. If one of our ships fired first, it would be an act of war and we were not ready for it. He was more than ever suspicious of the president's intentions. FDR had cited cases of three of our destroyers and a merchant ship that he said had been attacked with no provocation by German U-boats. My husband called for an investigation of the president's charges by the Naval Affairs Committee. He listened to testimony by the ships' officers and Admiral Harold Stark, the chief of naval operations. What he heard made my husband furious.

He waited to address the Senate until that body had debated the subject. It had been a hot, tiring summer, and he joined the Davieses and me for ten days' restful holiday at the Homestead Hotel in the mountains of Virginia. When we came home, he was, as they say down there, "loaded for bear!"

On November 7, Millard Tydings addressed the Senate and went on the air to deliver a scathing and dramatic speech answering Roosevelt's "shoot on sight" broadcast. The U.S. ships cited by the president had deliberately provoked the Germans' attacks by acts of war, supporting British ships and planes. In the case of the ship *Robin Moore*, the Germans thought it was part of a British convoy and sank it, but there was no loss of life. The Germans rescued the survivors. The U.S. destroyer *Kearney* was dropping depth charges over a pack of German submarines when attacked. In the cases of the two destroyers, the *Greer* and the *Reuben James*, one was cooperating with British planes, giving them the position of German U-boats. The other U.S. ship fired first, helping a British convoy. Admiral Stark had proof that the U.S. ships were the aggressors and had provoked German attacks in the cases that Roosevelt cited.

Speaking on the Senate floor, Millard went after the president's statements as completely untrue. He accused Roosevelt of deception, withholding information, and lack of candor with the American people. It was a scathing indictment of the chief executive, supported by facts. I think it did Millard good to score points against his old enemy. It certainly pleased me as I listened in the Senate gallery, with inordinate pride, as usual. However, the bill to arm our merchant ships passed the Senate, and my husband's amendment preventing their access to enemy waters and belligerent ports did not. The president was the commander in chief.

Exciting events of 1941 continued to come along, happy as well as unhappy ones for us. In November, there was a happy one for our family. My father's book, *Mission to Moscow*, was finally published, and proceeded to break all the best-seller records for nonfiction that year. We had been dining with Daddy the evening in July when Mr. Harry Warner was his guest. He was the senior of the Warner Brothers moving picture producer and wanted to film *Mission to Moscow*. He and my father agreed on a contract that evening, and Mr. Warner invited the Davieses and the Tydingses to come out to see the filming in Hollywood. Millard replied that he would be too busy on Capitol Hill, but that I should go, by all means.

An unpleasant event of that month was a message from Japan to the president rejecting the terms of the note sent them by the U.S. and Britain at the time of their Atlantic charter meeting. The news leaked out in our capital city with the arrival of two emissaries from Japan to protest the harsh terms of the note. It had stipulated that Japan must withdraw all its military, air, and police forces from China. The Japanese government must not support any Chinese government save that of Chiang Kai-shek's National Government of the Republic of China. Nobody knew the above details, but my father knew what was going on.

One of the envoys from Japan turned out to be Daddy's friend, Sabur Kurusu, who had been the dean of the diplomatic corps in Belgium. The other was an Admiral Nomura. My father invited Mr. Kurusu for lunch, and the two men discussed the gravity of the situation between their countries. Daddy told us about this conversation when we were together at his birthday at the end of November. He had asked Kurusu if anything could be done to prevent hostilities between their two countries from breaking out. Kurusu said there was only one thing that might: if the president of the United States would immediately send a personal message to the emperor of Japan urging a peaceful solution. My father at once informed the president, and he apparently took Ambassador Kurusu's advice. We heard later that the Emperor never received it. I also heard that Admiral Nomura tried to commit hari-kari in the Shoreham Hotel but never heard it confirmed.

Neither Daddy nor Millard suspected that the Japanese would attack Pearl Harbor, the headquarters of our Pacific fleet. My husband thought that the Japanese might attack us, so long as Germany seemed to be winning the war with England, but he thought they would hit Guam or the Philippines. In April the Japanese had struck both Hawaii and the Philippines. Millard had voted to fortify both places and the Philippines had been warned.

There were other warnings prior to the Pearl Harbor attack. One came to Senator Guy Gillette, who passed it on to the secretary of state. It came from a Korean whom the senator had befriended when our Territories Committee visited Hawaii in 1937. This man had become a member of the Korean secret service and had obtained a copy of Japanese war plans against the United States from the admiral commanding the Japanese navy. These plans described the attack planned on Pearl Harbor and even gave two dates for it. One was December 7 of 1941.

Chapter 23

December 7, 1941, Japanese Destroy U.S. Fleet at Pearl Harbor

Tydings supports war measures and works to protect U.S. economy and security as chairman of committee to convert federal government to wartime. Senator Harry Truman is chairman of committee to keep down war profiteers. British Admiral Wavell is supreme commander allied forces South Pacific. General Douglas MacArthur commander of Eastern Pacific, including Australia and the Philippines. I become a Red Cross nurses' aid in D.C. hospitals.

Did President Roosevelt and Winston Churchill deliberately push Japan into attacking our navy at Pearl Harbor that December? Certainly his actions had forced the Japanese into a difficult position. They had been able to wage war successfully against China with the help of oil and scrap iron from the United States. Then the president suddenly threatened to cut off these supplies unless they stopped fighting in China. Modern armies run on oil and iron the way an army of the past "ran on its stomach!" I do not think the president thought the Japanese would attack Pearl Harbor. He knew that most of our citizens were opposed to war and he did not declare war against Japan until they had attacked us. Nor did he declare war against Germany until they declared war against us, a few days after Pearl Harbor.

Sunday, December 7, was Bob Grosjean's birthday, and Millard and I were at a midday family dinner to celebrate it at Tregaron. We took an early-afternoon train home to Oakington, and Bob Livingston met us with the car. He looked unusually pale and excited. "Senator, did you hear that the Japs have attacked Pearl Harbor?" The man was stammering.

215

Millard gave him a stern look. "Wherever did you hear that?" but Bob had already turned the car radio to a higher volume, and we sat stunned and listened to the unbelievable news. The Japanese had indeed attacked the naval base of our Pacific fleet early that morning at Pearl Harbor. The extent of the damage was not known exactly as yet, but it was reported to be high. The president would address Congress the next day.

"We are at war with Japan and its friends the Axis powers," said my husband grimly. Later he telephoned Admiral Stark, who vouchsafed no information save that he would be at the meeting of the Senate Naval Affairs Committee after the president's speech the next day. "It will probably last into tomorrow evening," Millard told me. "I was to have addressed the Maryland legislature and the governor tomorrow night. You must take my place, darling"

"Oh, Millard, what on earth can I say?" I gasped. To address the governor and the entire state legislature was a far cry from making informal talks to the women's groups. And on such an occasion! It was the first time I had seen a smile on his face since we had heard the news.

"That'll be no problem! Just follow the president's example and declare war on Japan! I don't need to tell you what to say, Mrs. T., you'll do all right."

I lay awake all night worrying about it. The next morning I drove to Washington with him and listened to the president address a joint session of the Senate and the House of Representatives. He declared December 7, "a date which will live in infamy! . . . The United States was suddenly and deliberately attacked by the naval and air forces of Japan." He asked for a declaration of war against Japan, and Congress obliged. He had a wonderful voice and it was a fine speech.

My husband responded to questions from the press at once. He had no word of criticism for it, he said. "The president said exactly what needed to be said." Millard Tydings urged support for the chief executive. "It is time to forget past political strife and gird for war!"

That evening I made my speech to the high moguls of Maryland while my husband remained in Washington to attend long sessions of the Naval Affairs Committee. I had made no notes and do not remember what I said. I think I "pulled out all the stops" and made quite an oration. FDR had declared war and so had I! At least it was brief and my "terminal facilities" were adequate. The newsmen said it was okay, the governor and the legislature apparently approved, and Millard was pleased. So was I!

Millard came home the evening of December 9. The Naval Affairs Committee had been in session all night and the next day after the Senate had declared war on Japan. I thought I had never seen him look so stricken, except for one evening when he had returned home to find that a newly acquired prize Hereford bull had caught its tail in a wire fence and pulled the tuft off the end of it. I immediately rejected this unworthy thought when he started to tell me the full terrible story of our loss of lives and ships at the Pearl Harbor Naval Base in Honolulu. My first thought then was again of thankfulness that my son was too young and my husband too old to go to war.

Millard told me that the Japanese fleet, which attacked us early on December 7, consisted of six aircraft carriers, battleships, and cruisers, and 360 aircraft. They hit 94 of our Navy ships, sinking three cruisers and three destroyers. On December 8, they sank two of Great Britain's capital ships in Malaysia, the *Prince of Wales* and the *Republic*. This meant that Japan now controlled the Pacific and nothing prevented their invasion of our western coast! We had no defenses out there worthy of the name. The one small bit of good news for us was that the fifteen destroyers Millard had fought to have built in 1929 had not been harmed.

"Of course, wartime security has clamped the lid on the extent of the damage," Millard confided. "I shouldn't have told you this much. It is dynamite information. Top secret! I know you will keep it so, Treasure." I promised and kept my word.

Hitler declared war on us, a few days later, to no one's surprise, and Congress declared war on Germany. Litvinov arrived to take Oumanski's place as ambassador. Stalin claimed the Baltic States and Poland east of the Curzon Line. Nobody knew yet the extent of the damage the Japanese had inflicted on our fleet, and it was a long time before the American people heard the full tragic story of the death and destruction of our navy at Pearl Harbor.

Ten days later, on December 18, my sister Rahel and I joined Daddy and Marjorie on the train for Montreal, where Daddy was to make an address for Russian war relief at a big rally. My sister had been divorced for years from Aldace Walker and had a new admirer named Major Burdette Fitch of the U.S. Army. He was divorced also and was tall and good looking. She was considering marrying him the following June. We had barely arrived in our hotel in Montreal when a telegram came for her from the major. He was "ordered out of the country" immediately and wanted to marry her before he left. This probably meant that he was going out to the Pacific to join General MacArthur in Australia. Rahel and I heard Father make his speech and took the night train back to Washington. We telephoned Millard to help expedite a marriage license for Rahel and also phoned Mother to get ready for an immediate wedding at her home at 2941 Massachusetts Avenue.

The evening of that same day, Mother, Millard, and I escorted the bridal couple to the courthouse in Alexandria, Virginia. The clerk was delighted to see Millard, his commander in the World War in France! He happily produced the marriage license. This helpful man suggested we go to the nearby home of an Episcopal minister, a friend of his. The bride and groom could be married there by a minister, instead of the clerk in his office. This we did and it was very cozy and nice.

The bride looked lovely in a blue and silver gown and my husband gave her away. We returned to Mother's house, where our wonderful parent had arranged a beautiful wedding reception complete with a large wedding cake and an assemblage of close friends to eat the delicious menu and toast the bride and groom. All this Mother had accomplished with little more than twenty-four hours' notice. The bride and groom left the next day for San Francisco, where they spent a week before he left to join General Douglas MacArthur in Australia. It would be several years before he returned for a short furlough before once again crossing the Pacific to join the General as his adjutant general in Tokyo.

Prime Minister Churchill arrived in Washington and made a speech to crowds from the balcony of the White House on Christmas Eve. He spoke to Congress on December 26, but the Tydings family was with the Davieses in New York City for Christmas and didn't hear him say that this war could have been prevented five years before by stopping German rearmament. "In the future," Churchill said, "the British and American people will walk together in majesty and in justice, and in peace." A story went around that a Canadian had prophesied at the start of the German-British hostilities that in three weeks England's neck would be wrung like a chicken! Winston Churchill's rejoinder had been: "Some chicken, some neck!"

Admiral Wavell of Great Britain was named supreme commander of all Allied Forces in the South Pacific, and the American General MacArthur was given command of the Eastern Pacific, including Australia and the Philippines. Millard told me we were sending four army divisions to Ireland for training. Prime Minister Churchill went home in mid-January.

My husband supported the president's war measures wholeheartedly, but he continued to work for his determination to protect his country's economic security as well. Senator Harry Truman of Missouri became chairman of a watchdog committee to keep war profiteers in line. The senior senator from Maryland chose to be chairman of an equally important committee to transfer or convert the federal government to wartime and to streamline its ballooning bureaucracy. He asked the Brookings Institute to aid him in his endeavor. This brilliant assemblage of scholars devised a questionnaire for all government offices to avoid waste and inefficiency and eliminate wastefulness. When we heard that a government agency for promoting physical fitness was paying a stripped-down fan dancer named Sally Rand and Walt Disney films, Millard exploded. "Millions for defense but not one buck for Donald Duck!" he roared on the Senate floor to the delight of his wife and the onlookers in the galleries. How I loved that man!

When our country entered the Second World War, Millard tried to get back in the Army, but the Army refused to let him; he was too valuable where he was. My old friend Cabot Lodge gave up his Senate seat to join the army and told me he was almost captured by the Germans in Africa. When he returned at the end of the war, he was defeated for the Senate by John F. Kennedy. The combination of the Kennedy millions, the Irish Catholic vote in Massachusetts, and Jack Kennedy's brains and charm were hard to beat, although I thought Cabot was much handsomer and from a far more distinguished family.

Bob Livingston went into the Navy and it became impossible to get household help out in the country. I was thankful that we had moved to the Wardman Park Hotel in D.C. We took Nadine Livingston to cook for us and Little El's governess, Eulalie Beauloc. I stood at our windows high over Rock Creek Park and the Connecticut Avenue bridge and watched the lights go off in the wartime blackout of all night-lights in the country. It would be almost four years before they would go on again. Except for that, and the rationing of sugar and gasoline, we never suffered the agonies of war such as invasion or the bombing of our mainland.

Millard was trying to hold down the federal budget and was angry when the Senate voted to borrow the money to pay for the war. He denounced the vote, saying there should be a big appropriation to import squirrels to consume some of the nuts running around in Washington. The Senate galleries roared with laughter.

My husband was also campaigning busily in Maryland and I tried to curtail our social obligations. Daddy and Marjorie were spending the winter in town and entertaining a lot. They always wanted us present!

I was debating what more I could do besides working for the Senate Ladies Red Cross, teaching first aid, and doing chauffeur work for the American Women's Volunteer Services (AWVS) (modeled after the BWVS) in England. I wanted to go to work for the war and discussed the various jobs I could apply for with my husband and my friend Elysabeth Barbour, wife of the Republican senator from New Jersey, Warren Barbour. She had taken a course to become a Red Cross Nurses' Aid and wanted me to do the same. I was already working for the Red Cross two days a week and was teaching first aid in Washington and Havre de Grace, but there was still time in my life to do more. In our city apartment I had no domestic chores and a fine governess for Little El. So I gave up working for all the society benefits for British, Norwegian, Finnish, and Greek war relief, which had kept me busy the past two years, and joined Elysabeth in the Red Cross Nurses Aid Corps. I persuaded another Senate wife, Elizabeth Maybank, to join as well.

Elizabeth Maybank was the shy, retiring wife of Senator Burnett Maybank, a democrat from South Carolina. When she learned that the Red Cross Aids would be required to nurse anyone of any sex or color in the Washington civilian hospitals, she quailed and told me she couldn't do it. Inwardly, I quailed too at the idea of giving bed baths to men—black, yellow, or white—but I persuaded myself and Elizabeth that it was our patriotic duty. Many registered nurses had joined the Army and the hospitals were desperate for help.

After some weeks of study and training we were issued our uniforms and were ready to go to work at whatever hospital we were assigned to. I will never forget the first day we went to old Garfield Hospital. It was a cold, gloomy morning and we had to report at 7 A.M. We were given our first assignments, and sure enough, it was the black men's ward. Poor Elizabeth Maybank turned pale. I grabbed her arm and we marched into battle. As it happened, we were both extremely lucky. We each had a single patient in a private room. Mine was a dear, gentle, old white-haired man who smiled at me and said, "Jest tak yo time, honey, an don' yo' fret. Old Jim ain't goin' nowhere. We got all the time in the world!" I changed his bed linen and gave him a bed bath and a good rub of the poor skinny back, and we had a perfectly delightful time. He remembered me from the times when he drove old Dr. Bowen to our house. We laughed and chattered so that Elizabeth Maybank asked me afterward what on earth I had been talking and giggling about.

Elizabeth's patient was a seriously ill young black man who only spoke a few words to her in deep southern accents. I later realized that this nice man knew from her accent and demeanor that she was a southern lady and scared to death. I found out that he was a professor of languages at Howard University and he was speaking "Gullah" (the dialect of black people in southern coastal areas) to put her at ease!

My father had bought me a pretty little automobile called a Bantam, so I was able to breeze around the city hospitals from early morning until late afternoon. With gas rationing, it was the answer to a prayer. My new car's tank held only three gallons and I didn't fill it more than once a month! Of course, I never took it out of the city. Millard, being a senator, could get gasoline for his car to drive us back and forth to Oakington, but we did most of our commuting by train.

After Pearl Harbor I became more and more involved with the hospitals in the District of Columbia. I became a member of the Women's Auxiliary of Emergency Hospital, one of the largest and best in D.C. The ladies of our auxiliary started a tiny shop in one corner of the entrance hall of Emergency where we sold cigarettes, papers, and magazines. It was a surprising success. We raised quite a lot of money for the hospital.

In March of 1942 bronchitis sent me down to Palm Beach. Millard joined me at Mar-a-Lago a week later. The romance of another war love affair came with the arrival of Marjorie's beautiful daughter, Eleanor Rand, and a young Hungarian hero of the battle preceding the fall of France. Janos Bekessey had escaped the Germans and written a novel about his wartime experiences, *A Thousand Shall Fall*. He had come to Washington to raise money for French war relief. Eleanor Rand was an active member of that group in Washington and she had met his train upon his arrival. She was a lovely girl, tall and slender with long blond hair and a fine singing voice. We all knew soon that they planned to marry. I don't think her mother or my father were exactly enthusiastic about it. Eleanor had been married and divorced twice. However, they left Palm Beach, were married, and went to live in a house in Washington. I didn't think he was good enough for her, and it turned out that I was right.

When Millard arrived in Palm Beach, there were more long talks between him and my father about the situation with our allies, Britain and Russia. My father was still the president's top adviser on the U.S.S.R. The two men saw eye to eye on the necessity of keeping Russia friendly, more so now that the U.S.S.R. was fighting our enemy, Hitler. The Russians distrusted England more than ever, however, as Litvinov had told my father upon his arrival in Washington. One reason was that the English had fought against them (the Communists) in the Russian Revolution.

Stalin continued to demand that the British and the United States mount a second front in Europe immediately. Daddy told us that Churchill said it would be impossible to mount an invasion across the English Channel until our two countries had a million trained men for the armed forces and forty armored divisions. Churchill had talked with Litvinov in London and they had had a real fight. The Russian told my father that the prime minister had actually been insulting. Litvinov thought the British wanted Russia to fight their German enemy until the Russians were bled white, then Britain would ditch them. They weren't too far wrong, Millard said. It seemed that my father thought so too. He said he thought Churchill's attitude toward the U.S.S.R. was a case of the tail trying to wag the dog!

While we were at Mar-a-Lago, Lord Beverbrook came to lunch to see Daddy as an emissary of the prime minister's. He obviously wanted to discuss Stalin's demands with my father. The Russian wanted Britain and the U.S. to recognize his claims to Finland, the Baltic States, and the eastern part of Poland, as defined by the Curzon Line. The latter had been agreed to at the end of the First World War, as defined by Lord Curzon. Churchill had agreed to this, but Roosevelt would not. He had told Daddy that this argument should not "muddy the waters" now that there was still a war to win. It should be discussed later when the war was over. Churchill and Stalin signed a treaty agreeing to Stalin's territorial claims, but Roosevelt would not do so.

"Churchill will never agree to fighting the Germans close to his country," my father said. "He wants us to help him win in Africa this year and then attack the Germans through Sicily, 'the soft underbelly of Europe,' as he has said. There are the Romanian oil fields to consider also. Churchill is willing to hand them over with the Baltic States and half of Poland in order to keep the Germans at arm's length from his country."

"Friends in the U.S. military tell me they must have a conference of the Big Three leaders soon," Millard said.

"The president agrees," said Daddy. "Confidentially, he has sent an invitation to Stalin and it has been rejected. Now that I have had this talk with Beaverbrook, I will be going to see the president in Washington." Then Daddy asked Millard about his efforts to make the government balance its wartime budget. "Do you really think you can do that, Senator?" Daddy asked.

"Between us, Joe, I doubt it" Millard replied, "but the president has sent up a $109 billion dollar war budget, and my committee has the Brookings boys doing a great job. They have made up a book of questions to be answered by all federal bureaus. Over fifty pages! It should show up the waste and inefficiency that exists in a lot of them." "But what about your book, *Mission to Moscow*, Joe? I hear it has broken all records and is being published in almost every language on this planet."

Daddy laughed, "Not quite, Senator, but enough to be highly encouraging to your old father-in-law."

"Are you going to Hollywood to see them make a movie of it, Daddy?" I inquired, and was delighted when he nodded a smiling confirmation.

"If your husband agrees, will you come with us?" Millard grinned and nodded. The three of us went back to Washington on the train together—Millard to Capitol Hill, myself to the hospitals, and my father to continue working with Ambassador Litvinov and the president to keep Russia fighting Hitler.

A few days after our return from Palm Beach I went to hear Millard speak, urging "pay as you go" tax legislation to balance the huge war expenditures. He said again that the president's policy of borrowing the money would put a great burden on future administrations. He was doing his best to do away with unnecessary New Deal bureaus.

My father met with the president on April 6 and with Molotov and Litvinov the day before. Marjorie told me that FDR and Harry Hopkins had urged him to go back to Moscow as ambassador or special envoy to try to smooth Stalin's ruffled feathers. The Russian was angrier than ever that we hadn't opened a European front and that the president would not agree to his territorial claims to parts of the Baltic states and Poland.

My father told FDR that his doctors would never permit him to take the strenuous trip to Russia. It involved more than four weeks' travel round-trip by ship and train. Daddy had suggested that Hopkins would be a fine special ambassador. Harry knew the president's mind better than anyone. My father thought that he himself could serve better in Washington as an unofficial liaison among the president, Ambassador Litvinov, and Lord Halifax, the British ambassador.

Russia's foreign commissar, Molotov, had come from London to see the president the first week in April. The treaty recognizing Russia's claims to Poland had been signed by Churchill but he had refused to agree to a second front in western Europe that year. We knew Molotov was probably in Washington to persuade Roosevelt to recognize Russia's territorial claims as well as to set a date for a second front in Europe. The president announced that the second front could be in 1942, but he did not agree to discuss the Baltics or the Polish Curzon line until the war was won. He sent General George Marshall and Harry Hopkins to Moscow to persuade Stalin to attend a tripartite meeting on the conduct and strategy of the war. Daddy told Millard that before Molotov left Washington he appeared to be pleased over his last talk with the president.

Roosevelt was doing all in his power to expedite shipment of supplies to Russia. As spring was turning in to summer and no agreement had been reached to open a second front in France, the tensions between the big three (Stalin, Churchill and Roosevelt) stretched tighter and became more dangerous. When Churchill persuaded the president to send our armed forces into Africa to help the British fight the Germans, it became worse. People were worried for fear of a separate peace between Germany and Russia because of the initial German victories in Russia.

In June 1942, the Davieses gave a big cocktail party for three Russian air force heroes. The Russian pilots were nice-looking young men who looked not unlike our American boys. The guests at Tregaron were all favorably impressed, although only one pilot spoke much English. Ambassador Litvinov was glowering when he told me that the United States and Britain were sitting at home making all the decisions on the war while the Russians were doing all the fighting and dying. However, by the time he and his wife, Ivy, came to Camp Topridge later that summer, all was cheery and bright! The Germans had not taken Leningrad, Moscow and Stalingrad. We spent the rest of the summer at Oakington with the children, Nadine, and Eulalie.

Young Joe had been made captain of the middle school and a member of the cavalry team at McDonogh Military School and worked on the farm all summer. He and his little sister won ribbons in the Maryland pony shows. Marjorie had commissioned a lady portrait painter named Vicaji to come to Oakington to paint my portrait. The artist was an Englishwoman, half Iranian, half British, and a fine painter. Sadly, she died suddenly soon after the work was completed.

Millard was invited to the famous Bohemian Grove Club in California for a week of much needed rest after his unsuccessful fight to do away with unnecessary New Deal bureaus. While he was away, I went to visit a charming Washington friend, Katherine Lloyd, at Potomska, her beautiful estate in New Hampshire on the Atlantic Ocean. Our children were enjoying summer camps run by friends near Oakington. Katherine's young son was home to say goodye before going out to fight in the Pacific. He was a pilot on an aircraft carrier. There were rumors of German submarines being right near the coast, so I amused the Lloyds and their houseguests with a romantic story about a U-boat wrecked off the shore of Potomska and the rescue of its handsome young German-American captain by Katherine's pretty teenage daughter, Angelica. It kept them all amused and prevented any frightened fears of ugly possibilities, but tragically, her son never returned. Actually there were German U-boats near Potomska shores.

In November the Davieses took me to Hollywood for the filming of *Mission to Moscow*. Walter Houston was to take the role of Ambassador Davies and Ann Harding that of Marjorie Davies. We were driven straight to the Warner Brothers' lot upon our arrival, just in time for lunch. The Warners' lot was enormous, and several movies were being made there all at the same time. We were seated at luncheon on the movie set with about thirty people. A long buffet table was loaded with every delicacy imaginable, from caviar to lobster, ham and turkey. Daddy sat at one end of a long table and Marjorie and I sat on either side of Mr. Jack Warner. In front of him was a battery of telephones, which he would answer whenever they rang every few minutes.

J.W. (shouting): "Hello, hello! Yes, this is Warner! Where are you? In London? (or Paris or Africa or Alaska!) I told you what to do, man, now go ahead and do it!" And bang! would go the telephone receiver. I could hardly suppress a giggle at the constant repetition of all this and I didn't dare look at Marjorie. Whether it was an act on his part or not, and I strongly suspected it was, I was highly entertained. My father missed the show. He was seated at the far end of the table on the senior Warner brother's right. Our hosts said that

I must be photographed by their best man, which Daddy agreed to. So I was coifed, painted, false-eyelashed, and so on, so that I hardly recognized myself. It took all day! However, the photographs were marvelous. I don't know how they did it, but in each different pose I bore a strong resemblance to a different movie star! I like the Claudette Colbert pose the best, although I actually look nothing like her.

That evening (still in my movie star makeup), we went to a big dinner party given for us by Jack Warner in his *Gone With the Wind*-type mansion. Set in the midst of many acres of the most expensive real estate in California, the place was most impressive. We entered a marble hall and were escorted downstairs where there was a theater and an enormous circular rec room with a semicircular bar around half of it. Many of moviedom's great were leaning on it. Among them was Hollywood's newest "baby" starlet, wearing a bright red evening gown slit up to the hip, and with one bare shoulder. Dangling over her single covered shoulder and over one ear were large bunches of imitation red geraniums! Her long blond hair completely obliterated half her face. I think she was the originator of the style.

I was wearing my most chic black Bergdorf dinner gown. In less than five minutes the crowd of men surrounding the starlet had moved to my end of the bar! They were plying me with questions about Washington and my husband and our business—politics! Daddy and Marjorie were amused. At dinner I sat between the host and a world-famous comedian who was the most profane man I ever met—Jack Benny. I don't mind a few d-s and h-s, but I don't like it when every other cussword is J.C.! Besides which, the man's wife at the other end of the table was apparently jealous of him. Every time she thought he was paying too much attention to me (which he did all through dinner), she would scream some question at him the length of the table. After dinner, we saw a preview of a movie of the fall of Norway in the private theater and Mr. Benny's cussing went on, louder than ever.

My father had his troubles with the filming of *Mission*. It seemed that before we came to Hollywood, old Mrs. Ivy Litvinov had been out there giving orders about the picture and changing things from the book. One of the things she did was to insist that they make the scene of the reception for the Davieses a grand ball in the Kremlin with herself as hostess. Of course, such a thing never happened as Ivy herself was not even present. She was in Stalin's black book when the Davieses were in Moscow and had been banished to the Ural Mountains to teach basic English.

We had a good time in Los Angeles. Before leaving for home, we went to a party given for us by my old friend Florence Hamburger Bryan, who still lived up to our 1930 nickname for her, "The Blond Bombshell." Marjorie's niece by marriage, Barbara Hutton Grant, and her current husband, Cary, also entertained us. Poor Barbara ("Bobbie") Hutton had broken her health by too violent dieting in her late teens and had never been well since. She was a sweet, rather pathetic person, very beautiful.

In November 1942, the first American armed forces finally joined the British against the Germans in North Africa, in Operation Torch, three months after Churchill had come to see the president about doing so. The British were having a tough time there against Germany's famous General Rommel. Stalin was still furious in spite of FDR's latest promise to make our European landing in 1943. The Russians' final message to Roosevelt was that the United States must open a front in Europe in the spring of 1943 or there would be no reason for any tripartite meeting of the U.S., Britain, and Russia. The meaning was clear. The battle of Stalingrad started in August and continued in bloody fighting in the city until November. New Russian forces joined General Zhukov to defeat Field Marshal von Paulis and took thousands of German prisoners.

My father, Marjorie and I were driving with Barbara and Cary Grant in California when we heard the news of the great victory at Stalingrad.

"Let us hope that this will be the turning point of the war in Russia," daddy said, "and that the strength of the Red army has surpassed the Germans."

"Will it make Stalin agree to a separate piece with Germany like everyone has been so afraid of?" asked my stepmother.

"Let us hope not. I think Stalin is a wily bird and won't set on a hot stove twice," daddy said.

My service as a nurses' aide had made me acutely aware of the truly dreadful condition of our hospitals. They were all old and inadequate. By the end of 1942, Elysabeth Barbour and I were increasingly concerned, and conferred frequently with the chairman of the Women's Board of Emergency Hospitals, Mrs. Reginald Huidecoper (Bessie). She was considerably older than we were and one of our city's truly great ladies. We decided to call a meeting in December of the heads of all the leading hospitals and some of the business leaders at the Huidecoper's handsome home. This we did. Since 1930, the city's population had nearly doubled. The hospitals were a thousand beds short and few of them were fire resistant. The president of Emergency Hospital, my old friend George Garrett, and Sam Kauffman of the *Washington Star* came to the meeting. Also attending were William R. Castle; Thomas Dunlop, of Garfield Hospital; and Clarence Aspinwal, Episcopal's president; Henry Blair, Children's president; Charles Drayton of Children's Hospital; George Washington Hospital's president, Dr. Cloyd M. Marvin; and Reverend David V. McCawley of Georgetown Hospital, all among the cities most distinguished men. All decided something must be done about the problem.

I had been made chairman of the Red Cross Nurses' Aid corps, and we had invited an expert from a large New England medical center to advise us. He urged the wisdom and economy of consolidating the old hospitals into a new hospital center, saying that it would be a mistake to pour money down a rat hole to try to improve the existing hospitals; a new hospital center would effect great economies. Next, we invited another expert to advise us on raising the funds necessary to build a new hospital center. He told us that it would be impossible to do in our city, as Washington did not have the rich manufacturers or businesses to help do so. It was obvious that the only place to go for the necessary millions would be to the U.S. government. I went to my husband. He had already heard my graphic descriptions of the run-down old D.C. hospitals and agreed to introduce a Hospital Center bill (number 648) in the Senate. Charles Drayton of Children's Hospital, a lawyer, drafted the bill. After Mr. Drayton's bill had passed both houses of congress and been signed by the president, his hospital refused to join Garfield, Emergency and Episcopal hospitals to form a hospital center. The Children's Hospital Board chose to remain in their old building. We heard that one of the most important old ladies on their board had once said, "Do those two little girls, Elysabeth Barbour and Eleanor Tydings, think they can succeed in doing something we can't do?" We did!

Elysabeth and I and important doctors and civic leaders testified before the Senate committee, which reported the bill favorably to the Senate. My husband, as the leading advocate of economy in government, had no difficulty in getting the bill through the Senate. The Tydings bill provided that the Federal government would give an adequate piece of land (150 acres of the Old Soldiers Home land), and build and equip a one thousand-bed hospital center at a cost of $40 million. In return, the participating hospitals would turn over to the U.S. government their existing hospital properties, but not their private endowments. These, along with their separate identities, they would keep. Bessie Huidecoper was our "anchorman." I told the story of the unsanitary conditions and the big rat I had seen in broad daylight in the corridor of Garfield Hospital. Elizabeth said the rat had grown to the size of a baby elephant before I stopped telling about it! The Tydings bill finally passed the Senate, almost unanimously. Our (supposedly) good friend, Senator Bob Taft, was one of the few who voted against it—in spite of all those boring dinner parties at our house or his when I had to sit beside him. I liked his wife Martha, but found him a most unattractive man.

During the war there were very few large parties and only a few small ones. We could seat only eight or ten in the dining room of our apartment at the Wardman Park Hotel, so our dinners were limited to a few of Millard's colleagues and close friends. One of these parties, in February 1943, we gave in honor of Clare Boothe Luce, who had been elected to the House of Representatives and rented an apartment in our wing of the Wardman. As she had entertained us in New York, we decided to have a small dinner to welcome her to Washington. I wrote a note asking her to set a time when she and her husband could come. Her secretary phoned and gave me a date two months ahead of time. We had invited Senator and Mrs. Homer Ferguson of Michigan, Senator and Mrs. Walter George of Georgia, Secretary of the Navy Forrestal, and Vice President and Mrs. Wallace.

The day before the dinner, I received a telegram from Henry Luce saying he found himself on a train going in the wrong direction and wouldn't be with us! I phoned his wife. Her secretary said she would come or not, as I wished. I told the secretary I would expect Mrs. Luce at eight o'clock. Fortunately, an attractive young colonel who had just written and produced a hit Broadway play came to town unexpectedly and accepted my invitation. Of course, Madame Clare was late. All the rest of us ladies wore our usual modest wartime dinner dresses. Not so Mrs. Luce! She was wearing a great-skirted, bare-shouldered satin ball gown and much jewelry! She walked in and threw her arms around Millard's neck with an enthusiastic greeting. I stood and waited until she deigned to notice me and extend a limp paw.

She: "Oh, hello. I could have gotten you an extra man, you know."
Me, smiling sweetly: "Oh, I never have any trouble getting men!"
It was not a very pleasant evening for the ladies. Mrs. Luce held

the floor, talking nonstop so that even the high-ranking gentlemen couldn't get in a word edgewise. The next morning dear Myrtle Ferguson phoned me, laughing about it. It seems she had asked Homer what he thought of Mrs. Luce's gown, slit high above the knees and displaying red stockings and slippers. She said Homer was most upset.

"Now Myrtle," he said, "you know you should always make me wear my bifocals!"

Lots of people remarked upon Clare Luce's resemblance to me, including the desk clerk at our apartment building. He called me Mrs. Luce just once and, after a second look, apologized profusely. "Oh, no, you are Mrs. Tydings! Mrs. Luce doesn't really look a bit like you!" From the way he spoke, I thought the comparison was in my favor.

Another of our dinner parties in April 1943 was quite different. Marjorie had planned it at Tregaron in honor of Barbara and Cary Grant, who were to spend the weekend. They were coming to visit the Davieses, but Marjorie and Daddy would not be in town, so Millard and I were asked to act as host and hostess at Tregaron and invite twenty-six high-ranking guests for a dinner party for them, which we did. Barbara and Cary seemed to be very much in love with each other. She told me she wanted very much to have a baby. This much, at least, we had in common! After divorcing Cary, she married Count von Reventlow, a Dane, and had her only son by him. (Years later, the boy was killed in an accident.) The Grants apparently enjoyed their visit with us.

We gave a lunch party for them also, in Millard's committee rooms at the Capitol. They were so pleased they sent me an aquamarine bracelet and earrings! (Not even flowers had come from Mrs. Luce, needless to say!)

During the war years we would often play Millard's conversation game after dinner at our small parties. He would pose a question relating to the war's duration or cessation, or concerning an important legislative debate or military plan. Each one of our six or eight guests would have three minutes to answer it and what they knew about the subject. Much inside information was reported off the record in this way, but so far as I know, none of the answers ever leaked out. I regret that I never put any of them in my diary.

These small dinners in our apartment came close to my childish desire for a salon of the city's intelligentsia. Our dinners became quite famous, as did Mrs. J. Borden Harriman's big Sunday night suppers (seated) in her handsome house. At one of hers, Alice Roosevelt Longworth (daughter of President Theodore Roosevelt and wife of Nicholas Longworth) boasted that she could tuck both her legs under her cross-legged, tailor fashion without rising from her chair, and she did. She was quite a show-off!

Chapter 24

Ambassador Davies's Second Mission to Moscow, 1943

U.S. Navy fighting in Pacific, Army in Africa and Sicily. Tydings wants Pay As You Go instead of borrowing billions for war budget, votes for international peacekeeping after the war. Russian winter and army defeat the Germans at Kursk. U.S. Ambassador Standly insults Russians, and FDR sends Davies on second mission to Moscow.

Nineteen forty-three, the third year of the war, was a crucial one for the world and a most important one for the Tydings-Davies family. Our navy was fighting in the Pacific and our army in Africa and Sicily. Millard Tydings was fighting his own battles on Capitol Hill to stop the administration's policy of borrowing billions (the war budget FDR sent to Congress was more than $100 billion). He voted for everything the president wanted for our armed forces and voted to put the U.S. on record for an international peacekeeping authority when the war was over.

At the same time, he was campaigning in Maryland for his reelection to the Senate in 1944. The president was also up for reelection that year, if he chose to run for a fourth term. He looked ill, but there wasn't much doubt he would win if he ran. Of course, Millard was among the group of Democrats opposed to his running. He feared the president would further expand the power of the executive branch of the government at the expense of Congress and the states. The Tydings's watchdog committee was demanding a close accounting of all wartime expenditures. The Senate passed two weak tax measures to hold down borrowing, but the president vetoed them.

Nineteen forty-three also brought more serious concerns than the Washington hospitals or my husband's efforts to contain the coun-

232

try's war expenditures. The business of winning the war was all important, and my father's second and third missions had a great deal to do with it.

Marjorie told me he was often conferring with the president and was advising him. She said that Stalin was so mad that he had turned down more than one invitation from FDR to meet with him and Churchill for the important conference of the Big Three. My stepmother also said the president was pressing my father to return to Moscow as ambassador.

Old General Winter had helped Russia with ice and snow, enabling the Red Army and the citizens of Leningrad, Moscow and Stalingrad to survive the Germans' siege. A Russian victory at Kursk and Stalingrad lessened Stalin's desperate need for U.S. aid and the promised Allied second front. "Stalin must be feeling pretty cocky," my father said, "and he will probably keep both Hitler and the Western Allies dangling while he waits to see the best way to jump!"

Then a completely unforseen event made the situation even more worrisome. The United States ambassador to Russia, a former navy admiral named Standley, called an international press conference at our embassy in Moscow on March 8, 1943. He proceeded to drop what amounted to a diplomatic bombshell, which reverberated throughout the U.S.S.R. and the world. It almost destroyed the friendly relations between our country and Russia, which my father had tried so hard to build. Ambassador Standley announced that the Soviet government had concealed from the Russian people the origin of the huge amount of supplies, military and civilian, that the United States had been pouring across the ocean to help them ever since Germany had invaded Russia.

Two days after Ambassador Standley's press conference, the *London Times* printed an article suggesting that the situation was so bad that the British government should intervene between the U.S.A. and the U.S.S.R.! Two days later, Anthony Eden, the British foreign minister, arrived to formally offer his services as mediator. Now it was Roosevelt's turn to be angry! We were the ones who had been the mediator. When we went to Tregaron on April 26 to see a preview of the *Mission to Moscow* movie, Daddy told us that the *London Times* article and Eden's visit had greatly irritated the president. Washington was full of rumors about a peace treaty between Hitler and Stalin. Ambassador Litvinov told Daddy that if this happened the armies of Germany and Japan would gobble up the world! My step-mother said it was too bad the president didn't let my father go back to see Stalin when he offered to do so in 1939.

"The president thought it unwise at the time," replied Daddy. We did not know then that he and his old friend FDR had long been discussing the advisability of a meeting between the president and Stalin without the British prime minister.

Mr. Roosevelt thought that if he could talk with the Russian alone he could establish a friendly, cooperative relationship. My father agreed and the president asked him to go to Moscow once more to deliver an invitation for the meeting and to smooth Marshal Stalin's ruffled feathers.

Daddy went to Boston for a checkup with his doctors at the Lahey Clinic. They gave their okay for a flying trip to the U.S.S.R. and Daddy departed on his second mission to Moscow in early May. The president announced that Mr. Davies was going as his special emissary to deliver a letter to Stalin, and that was all the press was told. The newspapermen assumed that the letter pertained to the tripartite meeting of the Big Three, which had been much discussed. The president had already sent several invitations for that, which had been coldly turned down on the grounds that it was impossible for Marshal Stalin to leave the front.

There was a photograph in *Life* magazine of the official plane that carried my father to Russia with "Second Mission to Moscow" painted on its fuselage. He said that the president had coined the title. Poor Daddy was ill and miserable when he arrived at Leningrad and laid a wreath on the Tomb of the Unknown Soldier. The cold welcome he received from a surly Ambassador Standley, I'm sure didn't help. He spent two days in bed. Mr. Standley was angry over being superseded in rank by Special Ambassador Davies. My father refused to either let him read or tell him the contents of the president's letter. Ambassador Standley had already been informed by the secretary of state that the letter was "eyes only for Stalin" and the marshal wished to see the president's envoy alone, as the president had stipulated. The ambassador was so furious that he actually tried to force himself into Stalin's presence when my father was ushered in to see him. Molotov (who had returned from Washington) told me that he had to bar the way!

My father later said Stalin was stiff and cold at the beginning of their meeting, but became warmer as my father read Stalin the president's letter inviting him to meet that summer at anyplace the marshal chose, without the British. My father told Stalin of Roosevelt's friendly feeling toward the Russian leader, and said the president was confident that if the two of them could meet alone, man to man, without a third party, they would understand each other's problems and see eye to eye on the important issues. My father said that the United States, as a democracy, had a very different foreign policy from that of the British Empire. The marshal mellowed visibly after that remark, and even more after Daddy told him that although Roosevelt could not agree to Russia's territorial claims with the presidential election approaching, he was sympathetic to them and would discuss them when the war was over. Daddy left Russia with Stalin's agreement to meet with Roosevelt in Fairbanks, Alaska, but the date would depend upon the outcome of the Russian war with Germany. The marshal had to be constantly at the front. Stalin also agreed to reform the Comintern. Daddy heard later that Stalin had watched a screening of *Mission to Moscow* and was pleased with the film.

His mission accomplished, Ambassador Davies arrived home on June 3 and went at once to report to the president, who thanked his old friend gratefully. FDR did not tell my father that soon after he had left for Moscow, Winston Churchill had come to Washington and persuaded him to invade Italy instead of keeping his promise to Stalin, via Ambassador Davies, to open a second front in France! That invasion was again postponed until May 1944. Daddy's health had deteriorated during his trip to Russia, and he felt betrayed when he heard about Roosevelt's deal with Churchill. It only corroborated Millard's opinion of FDR!

Joseph Davies sent several messages to Stalin that summer, but Stalin always sent word that the war made it impossible for him to leave the Russian front. Daddy then sent a message through Molotov assuring Stalin that he could rely upon what he had said in Moscow about Roosevelt supporting Stalin's claims to Poland for "security reasons." No answer came to that, so the president sent Daddy to Mexico City where Umanski was the Russian ambassador. That mission brought the usual reply that Stalin would not meet with the Allied leaders on account of his war duties.

Partly because of all my father's efforts, the Russian made no deal with Hitler for a separate peace and finally came to the Big Three meeting in Teheran in 1943. When Secretary of State Hull went to Teheran, we all knew that he was going to try to keep Stalin fighting on our side against the Japanese. Everyone was anxious about this. When the secretary of state returned from Teheran, I met him at the entrance of the Wardman Park Hotel where we both lived. I was waiting for a taxi to take me to my hospital job when his car drove up.

Secretary Hull: "Well Eleanor, my child, can I take you anywhere on my way?"

E.T.: "Thank you, Mr. Secretary, I am going to Emergency Hospital which is very near your office and I would appreciate a ride."

Secretary Hull: "Climb in, my dear. How is your father? And how is the Senator?"

E.T.: "Both are well, thank you, Mr. Secretary. I know I shouldn't ask you about this, but we are so concerned about the results of your conference at Teheran. Is it good news or bad?"

Secretary Hull: "Good news, Eleanor, good news!"

I knew this meant that Russia would help us fight the Japanese. One didn't have to love the Russians to appreciate what having them fighting Hitler and Japan meant to us. The necessities of our very survival, fighting the great war machines of Germany and Japan, were obvious. The first all-important one was to keep the Russians fighting the Germans. The second was to keep them on our side fighting Japan. I have listened to so much criticism of President Roosevelt and Secretary of State Hull at Yalta and Teheran, "toadying to Stalin!" What did these critics want us to do, drive Stalin into making a separate peace with Hitler? In 1943 we were still unprepared to fight Hitler or Hirohito. We had to have time to build up a war machine. England and Russia bought that time for us. We didn't have to get in bed with an ally who was killing off half of our enemies in order to appreciate the sacrifice. Unfortunately, a few years later, a Republican Senator named Richard Nixon was able to use this "sympathy toward Stalin" to start a witchhunt of Communists in the U.S. State Department.

When we were in Washington, I was thankful to be able to eat dinner in the hotel dining room when I was too tired to cope with the kitchen. Nadine and her child were at Oakington. When we were at Oakington, our station wagon was drafted as a Red Cross emergency ambulance. I was the Red Cross nurse, and Nadine was the driver. We were on call at any hour of the day or night. Sometimes, during training exercises, we would be summoned in the middle of the night to come to remote corners of the county after a "bombing raid" to find "casualties" laid out on the ground awaiting my good offices. Once there were even "dead bodies" (storefront dummies) covered with sheets. These nightly forays greatly annoyed my husband, who said it was ridiculous to expect enemy raids in Harford County, Maryland! I continued to do my nurses' aid work in the D.C. hospitals and to teach first aid classes at the Havre de Grace Hospital, which had been built recently with federal funds from Millard's bill.

It was 1944 and election year again, and still no second front across the English Channel. My husband was running for a fourth term and so was the president. Both were expected to have easy victories and did. Millard, Little El, and I closed up Oakington after Christmas and moved back to our Washington apartment. Joe went back to McDonogh School. He told us that when he was eighteen he was going to enlist in the Army. This worried me, but Millard said war in Europe might be over by that time. He was working harder than ever on Capitol Hill by day, and in Maryland, mending political fences, by night.

Most of Millard's campaign speeches in 1944 ended with a slogan, "we must win the war, win the peace, and bring our soldiers home quickly!" It never failed to bring a roar of applause.

In May, Millard's full Senate committee held hearings on the Hospital Center bill. Elysabeth and Bessie and I were busy testifying to the imperative need for it and holding meetings and bringing doctors and city leaders to testify. The committee reported the bill favorably to the Senate, which passed it. Elysabeth, Bessie and I were jubilant.

That spring, I was assigned as a nurses' aid to a private room in Garfield Hospital where one of the top C.I.O. labor union leaders was a heart patient. He was a grumpy old Scot who spoke with a broad brogue. I was interested because his union was opposed to my husband's election. I went briskly about my nursing tasks—pulse, temperature, sheet change, bedpan, bed bath, etc. I gave him an extra backrub, which achieved his appreciative attention. There are more ways than one of getting the attention of a man in bed! He asked me if I was married and where my husband worked. I replied demurely that I was, and that my husband worked on Capitol Hill. He was interested and finally drew the information from me of just who my husband was.

"Well, now," he said, "I never did approve our union's attempt to try to defeat your man! Sure and he's a good man and I intend to tell Phil (head of the C.I.O.) that when he comes to see me! And I wish you could be a wee mousie in the wall to hear what I'll have to say to that fella!"

I told him not to worry, and to tell his chief that Tydings was going to win anyhow. When a group of tough-looking union men arrived, I departed with dignity after telling them severely not to upset my patient in any way! They seemed sufficiently impressed.

The Davieses entertained a great deal and we were expected to go to most of their parties and to dine with senators of both parties, mostly members of Millard's committees, as well as with other friends. I was speaking often at women's clubs around Maryland, telling the gals about all that Senator Tydings was doing for them. I managed to include some juicy gossip and the ladies loved it.

Meantime, my friend, Elysabeth Barbour, was divorced and had a devoted new admirer, a British war hero who had commanded the forces that fought the German army under General Rommel in North Africa. Air Marshal Sir William Welsh had arrived in Washington as the head of the British Air Mission. We went to their dinner parties and they weekended with us at Oakington. It was a very happy marriage, unlike the one of the Hungarian veteran of the fall of France, Janos Bekessey, who had eloped with Marjorie's daughter Eleanor.

The Bekesseys had rented a pretty house on Kalorama Circle and had a baby boy, Marjorie's first grandson. The marriage didn't last long afterward. On March 3, the baby's christening was quite a production. For some reason Marjorie was not able to be present, but my sisters and Deenie and I were there. We waited with Eleanor de Bekessey, the Hungarian priest (who spoke not a word of English), the baby, and the nurse for the arrival of the baby's godmother. The child's father had carried on a correspondence with Mrs. Roosevelt after the success of his book. She had accepted his invitation to officiate at his baby's christening.

It seemed hours that our little group waited for her arrival. Finally, we heard sirens blowing and the roar of her motorcycle escort, and the president's wife came rushing in. She glanced around, apparently looking for a familiar face, before bursting into hurried apologies for her late arrival and explanations that she would have to make a quick departure, and so sorry she couldn't stay for the luncheon party. I imagine that my face was faintly familiar to her from the Senate Ladies luncheons at the White House. She descended upon me with a cordial embrace. I don't think she had any idea that I was the wife of the president's most detested enemy! Or if she did, I don't think it would have made a bit of difference to that remarkable woman.

"So nice to see you, my dear! And where is the young mother and the darling baby?" Eleanor de Bekessey tried to introduce the priest to her, but the First Lady ignored him and took the baby in her arms. "Well, now, let us start!" said Eleanor Roosevelt. The poor little priest started to stammer a few words in Hungarian, the baby woke up and began to cry lustily. Mrs. Roosevelt jiggled him desperately for a few minutes, said a few proper God-parent words, and then handed him firmly to his mother. "So sorry, dear, so sorry. I really must go! Such a lovely baby! Good-bye, good-bye!" And she departed, as suddenly as she had arrived. We heard the roar of the motorcycles and the sound of their sirens disappearing in the distance. The whole visit hadn't taken more than five minutes, if that! The priest stood gaping, the baby stopped yelling, and Eleanor handed him over to his nurse. "Let us go into the dining room and have lunch," she said. Of course, I drew the priest to sit next to!

That spring the German armies were retreating on the Russian front and my father's prediction that the Red Armies would amaze the world had come true. In April, he told us of his recent involvement in the Kravchenko affair. He was still acting as the president's chief adviser on Russia and as unofficial liaison with the U.S.S.R. Kravchenko had come from Moscow to the United States as a civilian member of a Purchasing Commission from Moscow and had defected, explaining why with a terrible denunciation of the U.S.S.R. in a letter to the *New York Times*. The Russian government had promptly demanded that we send him home for trial as a military deserter.

Millard and I dined with Daddy shortly after he had been to see Ambassador Gromyko about the Russian's request. Legally, it was up to Secretary of State Cordell Hull to deport Kravchenko, and the secretary was disposed to do so. The president wanted to push the whole matter under the rug and forget about it, if possible. Daddy was eventually able to mediate the matter with the Russians with the excuse of the importance of the U.S. Polish vote to the president's reelection! The whole affair could be settled at the peace conference after the war. Gromyko passed the message to Stalin that FDR agreed with him in legal principle, although there was much argument that Kravchenko had been a member of a civilian commission and was not here as a military man. Daddy told Gromyko that there was a lot of anti-Communist feeling in the United States that the president did not wish to stir up. "Your Dad is a wonderful mediator," Millard said.

On another occasion, after Roosevelt had been nominated for a fourth term at the Democratic Convention in May, Daddy sent a personal message to Stalin through Ambassador Gromyko, warning that if the Russian press went after his Republican opponent, Governor Dewey, in an attempt to help Roosevelt, it might well have the opposite effect on American public opinion. Daddy asked that Stalin prevent the Russian press from expressing any preference in the presidential election. My stepmother told me that Stalin had carried out the request.

I sat beside Assistant Secretary of State Sumner Welles at a dinner party, and he told me that all diplomatic relations between our country and the USSR were practically nonexistent until my father became ambassador. He said that a way for the two countries to communicate had to be found and my father had found it. Joseph Davies had kept the Allied relationship from falling apart until the war was over.

On June 6, 1944, the huge Allied armada finally sailed across the English Channel and invaded France. On June 7, D Day, our soldiers were storming the Normandy beaches. It was my daughter's twelfth birthday and it was a beautiful morning in Harford country, Maryland. I was doing errands in Havre de Grace when I heard the news coming over a little radio in a store: our allied armies were fighting the Germans on the French coast! I ran to the nearest church and fell to my knees to pray for our boys and for all mothers' sons who would be killed and wounded that day. Millard told me later that our Blue and Gray, Maryland's 29th Division (Millard's old World War I division), went ashore that day at Omaha Beach, the very place where the Germans were concentrated practicing war games. I thanked God that neither my husband nor my son was on that beach. Millard told me that as a member of the former Naval Affairs Committee and the newly created Armed Services Unification Committee, he had been informed of the approximate date of the invasion at the same time as the commanding generals, on May 28. It took the Americans only six weeks to defeat the German army in France. Millard said he believed over half of Hitlers forces were in Russia.

Young Joe had a job at the McDonogh summer camp and Little El was having a wonderful time at Happy Valley Camp on the heights above the Susquehanna River, where horses and riding were a specialty, so I went to Camp Topridge without them and it proved to be an exciting visit. There were several guests there when I arrived, including the ambassador from Yugoslavia, Mr. Fotich, and his wife. At lunch one day, my father announced that General and Mrs. George C. Marshall were arriving the next day to spend a week! My father said the general was tired and was coming up to Camp Topridge for a rest. He asked us all to refrain from discussing either the war or politics while he was there. Later that day, Ambassador Fotich and I were swimming in Upper Spectacle Lake. The rotund little ambassador was floating on his back, looking exactly like the ads for the Kelly tire, when he demanded indignantly: "If ve can't talk about de var or de politics, Eleanor, vat de h—- are ve going to talk about?" I wondered myself.

The general and his lady and some military aides arrived the next day as we were all finishing lunch. They came in and sat down with us and the general jovially related amusing stories of his experiences in England. After that, there was obviously no restriction on our conversation.

He told us about his first trip to England to meet with Churchill after the U.S. entered the war. He arrived at night in a thick fog and a total blackout and was driven to the manor house of some titled personage. He walked into a large, extremely cold, damp mansion where his lordship and family were crouched around a small fire. The general said the room looked as though a great flood had washed everything up against the walls, broken furniture, old toys, etc. The host looked as surprised as the general was. Yes, said he, he was Lord so-and-so, and to what did he owe the pleasure of the general's visit? The general explained that he was to meet the prime minister there. His Lordship looked even more surprised. It turned out that there were two lords of the same name and this was the wrong one.

Another story the general told was funnier. He had arrived to visit Mr. Churchill at 10 Downing Street in London. An aide escorted him to a guest room and informed him when dinner would be served. The prime minister's valet then appeared and asked if the general would like a bath before dinner. The general said he would. "The general will have to wait," replied the valet haughtily. "There is only one bath and the prime minister is in it!" The general waited and was finally escorted to the bath. As he was luxuriating in an immense tub, the valet returned. With his nose in the air, he informed the general that there were no clean underpants in his luggage. Would he like a pair of the prime minister's? The general blushed and accepted a pair of Mr. Churchill's. I could imagine they would be much too large around his slim midriff!

Marjorie had arranged a canoe-carry picnic for the Marshalls. Guides were provided for most of the big Adirondack bateaux, and the trip led through a series of lakes and portages to an island picnic ground. General Marshall wanted to paddle his own canoe and I was fortunate to be his passenger. I was much impressed by him, he was a big, unassuming, good-looking man with a great sense of humor. I can see him now, swinging the big bateau up onto the wooden yoke across his shoulders, striding through the woods. We became great friends. We were usually the only late-afternoon swimmers at Topridge and had many long talks. He told me that as a young lieutenant he had served under General Pershing in the Philippines and that General Pershing had later given him a great boost in Army rank. He felt that he had Pershing to thank for his present position as commander in chief of all the Allied Forces. Marshall said that Dwight Eisenhower had served under him in the Philippines as a young lieutenant and that he had been able to jump Ike over many higher-ranking officers in the Army to his present command of the European theater! The vagaries and coincidences of fate, I thought!

He told me that he had very much wanted the European command himself, but that he and Churchill had fallen out over the priority of opening a front in Europe. The prime minister had insisted upon invading Greece and Sicily and Italy before doing so and General Marshall thought we should have opened a second front in France instead. Eisenhower had been able to get along well with General MacArthur, so George Marshall felt that he would be able to do so with the British.

The general chuckled about Omar Bradley's appearance when Marshall arrived in France in June after the Allied landing. General Bradley, who was commanding the invasion, had an enormous boil on the end of his nose and was totally unaware of it! Marshall said there was no question in his mind that Omar Bradley was the greatest general of the war.

I was amazed when the general told me that at the end of every working day at the Pentagon he went to his home across the Potomac in Virginia and there were strict orders that he was not to be called, under any circumstances, until morning.

"Even if we lost the war?" I gasped.

He smiled, "Then it would be too late for me to do anything much, wouldn't it?" He said that he would not have been physically able to carry the burden of the two wars any other way.

High-ranking officers would fly in to Washington from all fronts daily, desperate for more supplies, more help. He had a way of handling them. Every morning he would attend a meeting of his top aides in the map room. One entire wall was a map of the world with pins indicating every battleground, east and west. He would receive a briefing on the conditions at all these points. They all needed a lot more of something. The officers who had flown in from every part of the world were invited to attend the map room sessions. Afterward, they seldom asked for much! We had a taste of generals flying in from all the war fronts while our general was at Topridge. One even flew in from Russia!

General Marshall told me about Field Marshal Sir John Dill of Great Britain when he spent a weekend with the Marshalls in Virginia. Sir John wore his uniform with the chest full of decorations and hat covered with military "scrambled eggs" everywhere he went, even to the small country church. George Marshall never wore his uniform when at home in Virginia, although he always wore it in Washington. So when he escorted the field marshal to church, the general wore his country clothes. The field marshal was magnificent in full military regalia. When General Marshall introduced him to the minister after the service, the poor cleric was overwhelmed and stammered: "What a great honor to have you here, Sir John, field marshal sir! A great honor to me and to my church and to the State of Virginia, my lord!" Then, turning to the general who commanded all the armies of the Allied western world, he asked politely: "And who might you be, sir?" The general smiled, "My name is Marshall," he said.

He told me that the allied armada which sailed from England to France June 6 was the greatest assemblage of war ships that had ever sailed the seas. He said the English Channel was completely filled with ships. Then he grinned and asked me if I knew the allies code word for the armada. I said I did not and he told me that I knew it well, that I had lived near it all my life. I was consumed with curiosity and asked what it was. "The code word we used was Dupont Circle!" he said.

My friend was surprised to hear that I had never been in the huge Pentagon of the U.S. military in Virginia. He invited me repeatedly to come and lunch with him there, but I never did. I never saw George Marshall again save at large parties. Millard admired him greatly and said that George Marshall was the only man he ever knew who was like George Washington. The general told me that he was a great admirer of my husband and I told Millard.

He told me that we had over a million men in France and that the Germans were retreating into Germany and were being defeated in Russia.

Late one afternoon when we were sitting on the little beach after a swim, a man servant came to ask us if we would like some refreshments. We said no and the general asked the man what time it was. "Six o'clock, sir," he said. We watched him walk away and the general smiled at me. "Well, I guess I can tell you now Eleanor! Our troops just landed on the south coast of France!"

A big excitement in my life came on August 20 when I left Topridge and christened the U.S. Navy's newest and biggest aircraft carrier, the *"Antietam,"* in Philadelphia. I had wanted to christen a battleship ever since the war started but Millard wouldn't let me. The wives of many congressmen, naval officers, and those of important officials had done so and all had received handsome pieces of jewelry from the ship's builders. My husband felt that these gifts were paid for by the United States government, a scandal which would surely come up later for congressional investigation. I said I didn't care about receiving diamonds, I had all I wanted. I just wanted to "push a rowboat" into the water before the war was over! I had forgotten all about this conversation when Millard telephoned from the Capitol one day to tell me that he had a rowboat for me. The "rowboat" was the aircraft carrier *"Antietam,"* the largest Navy ship that had ever been launched!

The "christening" was great fun. Millard and "Little El" and I rode in a parade to the Navy yard in Philadelphia. I swung the champagne bottle at the giant ship and yelled "Go get 'em, *Antietam*!" This made such a hit with the ship's young fliers that several of them crashed the party that Admiral Draemel gave in our honor. Their ship's newspaper was named *Go Get 'Em Antietam* and the officers hung a large "Hollywood" photograph of me in the ship's wardroom. Apparently, I was also popular with the workmen who built the ship. When they heard that I had refused to accept an expensive gift from the shipbuilders, they took up a collection among themselves and gave me a present, which is one of my most valued possessions. It is a beautiful big sterling silver tray engraved with my name and the occasion. Both Millard's grandfather and mine had fought in the Union army in the battle of Antietam in the Civil War. I knew that the only other battleship to be called *Antietam* had been launched toward the end of the Civil War and had never seen action. When I christened my *Antietam*, I prayed that neither the ship nor its men would be wounded or killed in battle. They never were. My carrier missed the fighting but was in at the kill when the Japanese surrendered in August 1945.

Millard and I went home to Oakington after the christening. World War II was coming to an end by the end of the summer of 1944. Germany had been defeated in their siege of Russia's three great cities, Leningrad, Moscow and Stalingrad and the allied forces had driven the German panzers out of France. General MacArthur and the United States army and navy and air force were driving the Japanese back home.

President Kennedy appoints Joseph D. Tydings United States Attorney for the District of Maryland, February 1961.

Eleanor Tydings meets and marries Rev. Dr. Lowell Russell Ditzen in 1966. Photo by *Robert Browning Baker,* Bronxville, N.Y.

Eleanor and son Joe at ball for Eleanor II at Oakington, 1950.

Rev. Dr. Lowell Ditzen, director of National Presbyterian Center in Washington
D.C., and Mrs. Eleanor Tydings Ditzen, 1966.

Lyndon Johnson presents a pen to Senator Carl Hayden at a bill signing ceremony
while Senator Joe Tydings and Vice President Hubert Humphrey look on.

Rev. Ditzen presides over General Eisenhower's last birthday party, 1968.

Rev. Ditzen and Eleanor T. Ditzen outside of the National Presbyterian Church, built largely as a result of Rev. Ditzen's efforts, 1966.

Rev. Ditzen, Eleanor Tydings III, and Eleanor T. Ditzen. Photograph by *Jean Firth Tyng,* Bel Air, M.D.

Bringing up grandchildren at Oakington: Joe Gillet, Emlen Tydings, Warry Gillet, Millard Tydings II, Suzy Gillet, and Mary Tydings.

Dr. and Mrs. Lowell Ditzen travel on one of many cruises, 1973.

A costume party at Oakington: Senator Joe Tydings, Mary Tydings, Eleanor Ditzen, Suzy Gillet Chewning, and Lowell Ditzen.

Joe Gillet wins silver cup at amateur Steeplechase Race, with his mother and grandmother, 1983.

Eleanor and John Schapiro dance at Suzy's wedding at Tallyho Farm, 1984.

Joe Gillet gives away his sister Suzy at her wedding to William Chewning, 1984.

Rev. Lowell Russell Ditzen married Mary Tydings to John T. Smith at St. Johns Church in Lafayette Square.

Rev. and Mrs. Lowell Ditzen, Nantucket, 1986.

Eleanor with Chewning great grandchildren, William, "Ashy," and Caroline.

Eleanor Tydings III makes her debut at a dinner dance at the Sulgrave Club in Washington D.C. in 1986.

Eleanor cuts the ribbon at the Washington Hospital Center honoring the Center Society.

ANNUAL RECOGNITION DINNER

WEDNESDAY, NOVEMBER 5, 1986

CHEVY CHASE CLUB

ELEANOR D. TYDINGS DITZEN

The Washington Hospital Center is pleased to honor Eleanor D.
Tydings Ditzen whose untiring efforts and leadership helped bring
about the founding of the Washington Hospital Center.

Washington Hospital Center honors Eleanor Ditzen.

Part VI

Chapter 25

1945

President Roosevelt dies, Tydings goes to Manila, Davies goes to London, Harry Truman is president, and the A-bomb ends the war with Japan.

I sat proudly and happily in the Senate Ladies Gallery and watched my husband being sworn in for his fourth term in the United States Senate. He had served twenty-two years in Congress, eighteen of them in the Senate. Since the power in that body was vested in the chairmen of the committees, and the chairmen at that time was chosen by their length of service, Millard Tydings's reelection had pushed him still higher in rank and power. It was a happy day for the Tydingses.

Unhappily, my father was suffering from another bad attack of his intestinal trouble and was unable to go to the Big Three Conference at Yalta in February with President Roosevelt. I knew that he had worked hard with the Russians to bring it to pass and it was a bitter disappointment to him that his doctors forbade it. Millard and I spent a short holiday with the Davieses in Palm Beach before the Senate got down to work, and Daddy returned with us to Washington for his checkup.

I remember a conversation between my father and my husband in Palm Beach. Daddy said that both he and the president were most concerned about keeping friendly relations with Russia so that they would help us to defeat Japan after the surrender of Germany, which seemed to be imminent. Millard said he was more concerned about the fate of Russia's neighbors, especially Poland, which the Russian troops had already invaded. Daddy said that Poland was also a major worry of the President, but that FDR was pleased with Stalin's friendly attitude. It was reassuring that Stalin had signed the

Declaration of Liberty at Yalta, which gave all peoples the right to choose their government. My husband looked skeptical but said nothing.

My father was apparently Roosevelt's chief (if unofficial) adviser on the U.S.S.R. The president had followed his advice at Yalta, choosing to occupy quarters adjacent to the Russians and not sharing them with Mr. Churchill and the British. Roosevelt had also talked first with Stalin and had managed to keep peaceful relations between the Russians and the western allies.

A big problem at Yalta was the form of government for Poland, and the boundary between Russia and Poland after the war. Dad told us that Stalin had agreed to a democratic form of government in Greece and Turkey, but the Russians wanted to control the government of countries on their western frontier. The president and my father had been able to hold off an open fight between Britain and the U.S.S.R., but relations were very strained between them. Many of our American officials were angry over Russia's behavior in Eastern Europe. Roosevelt argued that the problems should wait until the war with Japan was over. Then they could be settled at the postwar conference. The president looked so ill in his photographs that I wondered whether he would live that long.

In March, Daddy told us that the president wanted him to go to London as special ambassador to solve the problem of war criminals. He had wired FDR from the hospital in New York that his doctors said no.

During those winter months, I was still working in our shabby old hospitals and in the Red Cross blood banks and trying to stem the increasing number of resignations in our Nurses' Aide Corps. We were still desperately needed in the hospitals. The nurses who had gone to war had not come home yet.

I heard the president address Congress on the state of the union and was more than shocked at his changed appearance. People remarked upon how thin and ill he looked, but nobody guessed that he had only a little more than a month to live. President Roosevelt wanted Millard to go to the Philippines to assess the war damage inflicted by the Japanese. The idea terrified me. My husband would be flying over enemy-held islands across the Pacific. He might be shot down. He tried to reassure me that he would be wearing the uniform of an Army private and would be of no importance to the enemy if he should be captured.

"But you will still be a United States senator and an ambassador and they would recognize you!" I wailed.

He grinned, "That's not all, I'll also hold the rank of a full general, Treasure, and you'll be the only gal whose husband has been all those things at once!" I glared at him.

"All I want is my husband home in one piece!"

Franklin Delano Roosevelt died on April 12, 1945 while resting at Warm Springs, Georgia. Shortly before Roosevelt's death, President Quezon of the Philippines died and his successor, President Osmena, had arrived in Washington to seek help for his war-torn country. We gave a dinner party for him at Tregaron.

The world was shaken by Roosevelt's death. Vice President Harry Truman was sworn in at once. He assured my father and Millard that he wished to carry out Roosevelt's wishes. We thought it fortunate that Vice President Harry Truman could take over that high office. My father and Millard were his friends and admirers. Like my husband, he had served in France in World War I and was a middle-of-the-road Democrat, perhaps with a bit more liberal political leanings than Millard had, more like Joseph Davies! Harry Truman was a man of fine character and much more attractive-looking than his photographs. Bess Truman was a nice person, and their daughter, Margaret, was a charmer. A colonel who had been a White House military aide for three different administrations told me that the Trumans were the nicest, most devoted family to occupy the White House in his experience. President Truman sent my husband to the Philippines as Roosevelt had wished.

Millard flew across the Pacific early in April. General Douglas MacArthur was commander in chief of our Allied forces in the Pacific and had taken the Philippines from the Japanese. He had graduated from West Point with high honors and his father had been a friend of my grandfather, Colonel John H. Knight. The colonel, a law partner of the senator from Wisconsin, had been helpful in obtaining an appointment to the military academy for Douglas. When he graduated, the West Point yearbook said that his three great ambitions were to be the top man of his class, the youngest chief of staff to the Army, and president of the United States! He achieved the first two.

I heard General MacArthur address Congress when President Truman recalled him in 1951. I have always felt he would have come out of the situation better if he had worn his uniform, boots, cap and decorations on that occasion. I also felt that his tearjerker line that "old soldiers never die, they just fade way," didn't help him much. They just emphasized his age, as his hair already did, and that he too would soon "fade away" to the hardships of life in the royal suite of the Waldorf Hotel in New York, complete with a private elevator!

My husband considered the general a brilliant man. When Millard arrived in Manila, he went at once to see his friend. MacArthur had received him warmly as "my old comrade-in-arms." Then the general launched into a long oration, striding up and down the room, constantly whipping a match over the seat of his pants to light his corncob pipe. The pipe would not stay lit. Millard's imitation of this monologue was so good that a few friends who heard it one evening said it should be recorded. Arthur Krock (*New York Times* man in Washington) phoned me the day after to insist that he do this, but my husband wouldn't cooperate. He was very careful of his gift of mimicry. It is a dangerous thing, especially in political life, he said.

I still remember my husband's imitation of MacArthur: "As you know, Millard, I have been a starved front over here! (scratch, puff). Eisenhower has had it all in Europe (scratch, scratch, puff), everything he wanted, while I had to do without! (scratch, puff, puff). Now that the war is over in Europe, it is my turn! (scratch, puff). At last they are going to give me everything I need! (scratch, puff). The Japanese are damn fine soldiers! I have had to dig them out of their foxholes, island by island, with my bare hands (gesture with hands), one by one! (scratch, scratch, puff—and a dramatic pause). Now, Millard, at long last I am going to have all the men and ships and armaments that have been denied me! I am going to invade the main Japanese island this summer! (here he forgets to scratch and puff in his excitement, and pounds the desk). I will mount the greatest land, sea and air invasion this world has ever seen! (pounds desk again), and I want you, Millard, to be with me on my command ship! It will be the greatest experience of your life! We were together in World War I, and you should be in at the victory with me in World War II!"

Millard replied with proper appreciation that he would have to hinge his acceptance on developments in the Senate. I asked my husband whether the general had worn his military hat during this meeting. Millard thought he had. The general was very handsome with it on. Without it, he combed what hair he had from a part just above one ear across a naked dome to the other ear. I thought a toupee would have been better.

Later, after the war, my friend Kathleen McNutt gave us a delicious description of the general and his second wife when she was in Tokyo during the period when MacArthur was virtually King of Japan. Douglas and the first Mrs. MacArthur had been divorced long since, and she had married and divorced the actor Lionel Atwell; since then, 200 pounds later, she had married the Marine bandmaster. The general's second wife was a charming little southern lady a good deal younger than himself. When MacArthur became military governor of Japan, she became virtually the First Lady of Japan, if never of the U.S.! She gave the general a son and unstinted adoration.

Kathleen and her husband, Governor McNutt, were invited to a reception at the MacArthurs' official palace. They were ushered into a huge ballroom where many people were standing around the walls awaiting the arrival of the Great Man. After some time, little Mrs. MacArthur came tripping in. She greeted each guest individually, explaining breathlessly to each: "The Gin'ral's coming! The Gin'ral's coming!" Finally, she turned to the double doors and exclaimed joyously, "The Gin'ral's here!" The great doors flew open and uniformed guards marched in. Kathleen said there actually were no trumpets, but there might as well have been! The general himself in full armor (uniform, cap, and decorations) strode around the room, saluting each guest and saying nothing. Then he strode out, and his wife fluttered after him. The party was over.

Just after Millard left for the Philippines, our dear friend Princess Kawananakoa had died, on the same day as President Roosevelt. We were both distressed over the loss of our friend. Millard flew to Manila on April 15 and stopped off in Hawaii to visit the Royal Mausoleum and lay a wreath on that noble lady's tomb. He returned to Washington only a week later, on April 22. The terrible devastation and dreadful conditions on the shattered Philippine islands had so shocked and horrified him that he hurried home to ask for aid for our suffering allies.

My husband was tired when he arrived home and had lost weight, which he could ill afford to spare from his tall, slim frame. He was impatient to report to the president and the Senate what he had seen. His address to the Senate on April 23 was so eloquent that it left many of us who heard him with tears in our eyes. He reported that thousands of Filipinos had died under the guns of our enemies, the Japanese. Their homes were destroyed, their cities a shambles. The Philippine people had fought the Japanese from house to house until only the walls were left standing. There was only one building left standing in Manila where General MacArthur had living quarters and his headquarters.

Millard described the dedicated loyalty of the Filipinos to Americans in hiding from the Japanese occupation. They had protected our people, often at the cost of their own lives, and there was not a single case of their betraying an American to the Japanese. My husband asked the Congress for hundreds of millions of dollars in reparation and war relief and tariff relief. The Senate gave him a standing ovation, and Congress and the president gave our island allies all that Millard Tydings asked for to help them recover from the war.

My father came home from the New York hospital where he had been since FDR's return from Yalta. He told me that the situation with the U.S.S.R. seemed to be deteriorating since Roosevelt's death. He had written the new president from New York offering to tell him about FDR's negotiations at Yalta, and Mr. Truman had answered cordially.

Meantime, our ambassador to Great Britain, Averill Harriman, had hurried home to see the new president, and the British foreign secretary, Anthony Eden, quickly followed. Both men were bitterly anti-Russian. They told the president that the U.S.S.R. was not living up to its Yalta agreements. The Russian foreign minister, Molotov, had arrived in town en route to the San Francisco Conference for a United Nations and had lunched with Daddy the day after the commissar saw President Truman. Apparently the meeting between the Russian and Truman had not been friendly. Molotov said the president had been almost insulting, accusing the Russian government of breaking its word on the Yalta agreements. Molotov was furious.

My father told me he had done his best to reassure Molotov that the president was a fine, fair-minded man like his predecessor, and that the United States would never gang up with Great Britain against the U.S.S.R.. On the contrary, Daddy told Molotov, the president's chief advisers, Secretary of State George Marshall, Admiral Leahy, and FDR's old friend, Harry Hopkins, were all more than a little suspicious of Churchill's post-war imperialist plans. The president, like these men and my father, was anxious that nothing stop the creation of the United Nations at the San Francisco Conference. He had wisely appointed a distinguished liberal Republican senator, our friend Arthur Vandenberg, as our representative there. Daddy said that Molotov had calmed down somewhat.

May was the month of garden parties. Marjorie gave two big ones at Tregaron and we gave our Senate luncheons at Oakington. Both places were famous for their gardens and the masses of azaleas, flowering trees, tulips, and the long wisteria arbors at Oakington. This year both Molotov and the new Russian ambassador, Gromyko, came to a Tregaron party with their wives. I thought Gromyko looked like a young Californian who was trying to get elected to Congress, Richard Nixon, but Gromyko was better looking. I did not like Nixon at all because of his vicious mudslinging campaigns to try to win election. He was accusing his opponent, Jerry Voorhis, of being a Communist. He was not.

Millard and I were commuting between Oakington and our Washington jobs. Among our weekend guests were Senator and Mrs. Worth Clark, a most attractive young couple. He was a member of a committee that had to do with the atomic bomb. We dined frequently informally with the Davieses at Tregaron.

Daddy told us that he had met with President Truman at the White House several times in May after he was out of the hospital. Truman, like Roosevelt, wanted him to take charge of the war crimes trials or to go back to Moscow as ambassador. Daddy thanked him and explained that he was in such poor health his doctors would not let him accept either appointment. The president had listened to Davies' account of FDR's Russian policy and approved of his predecessor's desire to meet with Stalin privately. The president said he wished to do so before the meeting of the Big Three leaders. Ambassador Davies passed the message on to Molotov and a cable came back promptly from the Soviet leader to the White House agreeing to meet with the president privately before the Tripartite Conference. The president told my father that he did not want to set the date for the latter until after the atomic bomb tests in New Mexico. So Daddy was one of the few Americans who knew about the bomb tests.

After a daylong conference with the president, which continued through a family supper at the White House, Mr. Truman asked my father if he would be able to go on a short trip to see Prime Minister Churchill in England. It would be a very special mission to sound him out about the difficult situation worsening between Britain, the U.S., and the U.S.S.R., and the president's desire to keep friendly relations until the peace conference. He also wanted Davies to explain the president's wish to confer alone with Marshal Stalin before then. He was sending Harry Hopkins to talk to the Russian when my father went to England. Daddy would be away only a few days and his doctors gave their permission for him to go. He flew across the Atlantic on May 24 and arrived at Churchill's country home two days later. Daddy's mission was to attempt to appease the prime minister's bitterness against the U.S.S.R. and to promote friendly cooperation with Russia.

The president was concerned lest the strained relations between Britain and the Soviet Union could hurt the forthcoming peace conference of the Big Three or the creation of the United Nations at San Francisco. Truman, like Roosevelt, thought that a meeting of Stalin and himself alone before the Tripartite Conference might resolve some of the questions at issue between the allies. Ambassador Davies, however, could not shake Churchill's anger against and distrust of the Russian government, nor could my father change the Englishman's strong opposition to a separate meeting of President Truman and Stalin, or his bitterness against General de Gaulle, Marshal Tito, and Stalin. He told my father that he feared an iron curtain across Europe. The prime minister insisted that U.S. troops must remain in Europe indefinitely. Churchill even accused the United States of making a deal to ditch Great Britian.

"Are you trying to say," he said to my father, "that the United States will withdraw from participation in European affairs? Then England will stand alone against Russia!"

My parent handled him with kid gloves. He coolly reminded him of the great Russian contribution to the war and the suspicion Stalin had felt after his secret service had recorded a conversation before the war between the prime ministers of France and England, both of whom wanted to get Russia and Germany into a war to destroy each other! My father is my authority for this. It may have been the reason for Stalin signing the pact with Germany at the start of the war. My father told Churchill that many people believed that if England found no great rival power in Europe to offset Russia, Great Britain would try to use the manpower and resources of the United States to support the leadership of Britain in Europe. The ambassador said that without continued unity of the Big Three, there could be no reasonable prospect of peace.

My father and Winston Churchill talked for two days until 4:30 every morning. Mr. Churchill consumed quantities of brandy and Daddy drank quantities of mineral water. At Churchill's request, he spent a third day in London talking with Foreign Minister Anthony Eden. The conversations went amicably enough on the surface, in spite of Churchill's firm opposition to any meeting of Stalin and Truman alone. Instead, he wanted to travel with Truman to the Tripartite meeting and confer with him before Truman met with the Russian leader. The prime minister sent a harsh telegram to the president the day Daddy left, refusing to attend a tripartite conference after a Truman-Stalin talk! However, he did tell my father that

Britain would take no action regarding the Soviet Union without consulting the United States.

Although the trip to England was a short one, my father was ill when he returned, and was in the hospital again for a while.

Air Marshal Tedder, when visiting Tregaron in June, told me a story that reminded me of my father's tale of the two nights with Churchill. The air marshal told me that Stalin was furiously angry with Britain and the United States for opening the promised second front in Africa instead of in Europe, the prime minister had gone to see him to try to calm him down and Tedder had gone with him. He told me that Stalin was so mad that he kept Churchill cooling his heels for over twenty-four hours before he would receive him. Finally, when an equally angry Churchill was about to return to England, Marshal Stalin saw him. The air marshal said the two heads of state had talked all night and parted fairly amicably. He said that the prime minister consumed a gallon of whiskey and the Soviet leader consumed a gallon of vodka! A good story, but doubtless greatly exaggerated.

Whenever I look at the photo of my father and Mr. Churchill taken at Chequers, I can imagine these two brilliant, strong characters representing their two great nations at that meeting, locking horns! I can't help but remember that my father was of Welsh descent. The two men came from very different backgrounds and had very different forbear and philosophies. Winston Churchill was a descendant of the great Duke of Marlborough and devoted primarily to his king and empire. Father was a cousin of Lloyd George, the great Welsh leader, a freethinker of North Wales. Joseph Davies was politically progressive, a liberal Democrat, and as devoted to his country as Winston Churchill was to his. Neither of them was a tall man. My father was very much handsomer. He often referred to Great Britain as "Perfidious Albion" and did not entirely trust either Churchill or the British government. He told me that Churchill believed that by serving the British Empire, he was best serving peace and that President Harry Truman believed the same thing with respect to serving the United States. I don't think either Davies or Churchill cared much for the other, although my father was an artist at pleasing people. I'm sure he did a fine job of buttering up the prime minister. Daddy said that Churchill was so concerned with preserving the British Empire that he would be willing to sacrifice the peace and go to war with Russia.

Hitler committed suicide and on July 5 Berlin surrendered to the

Russians, and on July 7 Germany surrendered, unconditionally, on all fronts.

My father attended the Potsdam Peace Conference in Germany as president Truman's unofficial Russian adviser before joining Marjorie, Millard, and myself at Camp Topridge. We were eager to hear about his experiences there, and about his meeting beforehand in Frankfurt with General Eisenhower. When I asked him about this side trip, he only smiled and said it was a political mission. I have reason to believe that he was sent by President Truman to sound out Ike on his political aspirations.

We listened enthralled to Daddy's description of the Potsdam meeting. It was near a town called Babelsburg, which I thought well-named for a big conference. My father found the feeling among the western diplomats to be one of distrust and dislike of the Soviets, with few exceptions, notably Secretary of State James Byrnes and his assistant secretaries, James Dunn and William Clayton. The Russians had taken over most of the Eastern European countries and were forcing Communist governments upon them.

The president, Davies, Byrnes, and Dunn managed to keep the conference running smoothly. Marjorie told me that our ambassador to Moscow, Averill Harriman, was so angry my father had arranged an early first meeting of the president and Stalin alone that he complained bitterly to both Daddy and the secretary of state. Daddy and Secretary Byrnes both told the irate ambassador that Ambassador Davies was acting on the president's orders. My parent went to see Truman and offered to go home at once, only to be ordered firmly to "stay put" and continue his good liaison work with the Russians.

I have the two official photos of the Potsdam Conference. In one of them, Prime Minister Churchill sits at the great round table. In the other, Prime Minister Clement Atlee sits in his place. Winston Churchill had been defeated for reelection. In both pictures, president Truman sits between my father and the Secretary of State Byrnes. The official interpreter, Charles Bohlen, sits slightly behind and between the president and my father. Across the round table are Josef Stalin and Admiral Leahy. The sessions were held in the Cecilienhof, a grand palace built in 1917. The grounds sloped down to the lake. Father said there were no screens in the windows. The mosquitoes were quite bad and everyone was scratching!

As history relates, nothing much happened at the Potsdam conference, but at least there was no open break with Russia, which was an achievement at the time.

World War II ended in August with the formal surrender of Japan after our air force dropped atomic bombs on Hiroshima and Nagasaki. Millard and I were at Topridge with the Davieses when the war ended, and we celebrated together. My "rowboat," the great aircraft carrier *Antietam*, rode in triumphantly with our victorious navy at the Japanese surrender. I wondered whether my husband was regretting that he was not there with MacArthur, but I didn't ask him. Later that night when we were alone, I was pretty sure he was not!

In September, I had an interesting conversation with Dr. Edwin Hubbell, the great scientist. He and his wife had been at the Aberdeen Proving Ground all during the war, and he was now put in charge of the enormous new telescope at Palomar in California They had recently returned to the east and were dining with us. Dr. Hubbell was prophetic. He said that inside of a very few years every great country would be making atomic bombs. "The scientific formula is known to scientists all over the world," he said. "German scientists and experts have already disappeared into Russia; some have even gone to Argentina. The United States should make the gesture immediately to our allies to give them our secrets." Senator Tydings disagreed. He said he thought our bomb secrets should be given to none unless to only the United Nations. It was hard to take in the immensity of the thing. I also asked Dr. Hubbell what he saw when he first looked through his great telescope at Palomar and saw so much farther out in space than anyone ever had.

He replied: "I saw the same thing!"

"And if you could see a billion light years farther?"

"I would see the same thing," he said.

The year ended with a frightening thing. In November, my son's school had its big football game, in the middle of which my son suffered a ruptured appendix. The school called to say he had been rushed to Johns Hopkins Hospital where our friend, Dr. William Rienhof, had operated on him. We hung up the receiver and the telephone rang again. It was the surgeon, and he sounded so broken up that he must have been crying.

Millard took the receiver from me, I was in such a state that I couldn't speak. The doctor said that he had done the best he could, but it had been the worst case he had ever seen. He feared Joe might not pull through. Maybe if the senator could get some of a new wonder drug recently on the market, it might save the boy's life. Only the Army had it. Millard immediately called General Marshall, who said they had not enough for their men, but the drug was being made by a Baltimore drug concern. My husband reached the head of the company and was assured the medication would be rushed to Johns Hopkins by special messenger. I wanted to go there immediately. Then I remembered what I had to do that evening.

I was scheduled to make an important speech to the hundreds of our city's Red Cross nurses' aides in a large theater. Like the soldiers, now that the war was over, the girls wanted to resign and go home! They were already dropping out and our hospitals were hurting. The army nurses had not come home yet and the situation was desperate, but I had a plan to persuade them to remain on duty. When the call came about my son, I began to weep in futile agony. Millard was wonderful. He told me I should keep my commitment. He would cancel his engagement and stay in close communication with the hospital and the doctors. If there was any change for the worse, he would come and rush me to Baltimore with a motorcycle escort.

That speech was the hardest thing I ever had to do, but I knew it had to be done. It would not help my son any to have his mother weeping over him. The "miracle drug" worked and by the following weekend, Joe was sitting with the McDonogh team watching the last game of the year! His grandfather, his dad, and his mother were there. And most of our nurses' aides had accepted my plea and stayed on the job.

When the war was over, the lights went on all over the world. I stood at the window of our Washington apartment and watched the lights of the Connecticut Avenue bridge come on with thanks to our Lord in my heart. Then I smiled when I remembered my grandmother Nellie and her golden spoon!

Chapter 26

Washington Comes Back to Life

1946: Richard Nixon is elected to Congress and Joseph McCarthy is elected to the Senate; Millard celebrates Philippine Independence and watches atomic bomb explosion at Bikini.

In 1946, all sides of the world were staggering out of the nightmare of the Second World War and facing a shaky, grim peace. America had not endured enemy attacks or been bombed or invaded, but had suffered the loss of many of our men. Now the boys would be coming home!

After the midterm election, the Republicans won control of both houses of Congress for the first time in thirteen years. We had had no Democratic vice president since President Roosevelt died, and Senator Arthur Vandenberg had become president pro tempore of the Senate. Congress convened in January and Millard had been appointed, the previous fall, to serve on the joint committee of the House and Senate for control of atomic energy. The committee held meetings with various important scientists to inform itself about atomic energy and the A-bomb, and my husband took a study course on the subject at the Bureau of Standards. What he learned upset him so that he had nightmares of Atomic War III. I asked him to get me copies of all the material he could on the subject and it helped us both to be able to discuss it with each another.

We talked about the faint possibility of achieving world prohibition of all A-bombs. Millard thought that wouldn't do much unless all nations agreed to a ban on all types of armaments under international inspection. I asked if the new United Nations could do that, and he said it was too young an organization to be effective. He wrote and delivered a powerful speech on the subject in the Senate on January 28. I sat in the gallery and listened. I had heard him

261

make many wonderful speeches before, but none so fine as this. He had worked writing it day and night, but he never read a word. He spoke from the heart. As he spoke, the galleries began to fill up and most of his colleagues were in their seats listening. The word had gone out that Tydings was really "going to town on this one" and many members of the House of Representatives and aides and secretaries were standing listening. He was making a plea for peace on earth. Peace, or the end of civilization and the mass murder of World War III.

He described what he had seen in the death and destruction of World War I in France where a friend of his boyhood had died in his arms. He told of the "ruin, ruin everywhere!" he had seen the year before in the Philippines, Tokyo, and Berlin. Whole cities destroyed and millions of lives, young and old, snuffed out by the mass murder of modern weaponry. He described it all in harrowing detail, and he had come to the conclusion that there was only one way the world could be saved. The nations of the world must band together and enforce disarmament—not only of atomic weapons, but of all weapons, down to the arms a man could carry, as President Roosevelt had wanted my father to persuade Hitler to do in 1936. Even that would not be good enough. There should be a ban on those guns also, for everyone except a nation's own police or security force.

Millard paced the floor in his overwhelming emotion, using his voice, expressions, and gestures to emphasize his appeal. He wanted the Senate to call upon the president to convene a world conference at once to consider his proposal—total world disarmament under international inspection. The United States was all-powerful at the time and our country was the only one that had the atom bomb. This would not always be the case.

Everyone in the Senate chamber roared their approval, when he sat down. Many of his fellow senators praised his speech and so did the nation's newspapers and publications, great and small. I was almost crying, I was so proud of him. When he concluded, he was exhausted. I took him home, made him eat a light dinner, and put him to bed. He slept soundly all night for the first time in a long while.

The atom bomb was so horrible and it so frightened everyone that people joked about it. I remember three such stories:

An old lady asked a scientist if atomic explosions could destroy the world. The expert, bored with having heard the questions so many times, replied, "Well, after all, Madam, it isn't as if our world was a major planet!"

Another story related a conversation between Sam Goldwyn, the movie czar, and a friend. The latter asked anxiously if Mr. Goldwyn wasn't worried about the atom bomb. To which Mr. Goldwyn replied, "Don't worry, old man, MGM has the A-bomb locked up tight! We're doing a really big movie on it!"

Millard's story of what actually happened at the first meeting of the Atomic Energy committee with a great atomic scientist is the best. It was a cold, dark day with dismal rain falling outside. Armed guards were posted outside the committee room and all around the Capitol. The atmosphere was gloomy. The famous scientist made his report to the senators and answered many questions. Finally, just as he was leaving, one senator asked timidly, "Tell me, Doctor, is it possible to blow up the earth?" The scientist paused at the door and said, "Why, no, Senator," then hesitated, and as the solons present heaved a sigh of relief, he completed his answer, "as of today!"—and walked out.

Another topic of conversation in Washington was the marriage of Dwight and Mamie Eisenhower. While the famous general was commanding the forces of Europe, his wife lived in a small apartment at the Wardman Park, where we lived. We all heard about his affair with the beautiful English girl, Kay Summersby, who was in the British armed forces and was his London chauffeur. My sister, Emlen, met her in Germany with Daddy in 1945 when he was on a mission to see the general, in route to Potsdam. They were guests at Eisenhower's handsome residence. Miss Summersby had graduated from being Ike's army driver to being unofficial hostess in his house. She sat at the end of the dinner table opposite Ike and accompanied him upstairs at the end of the evening. My sister was disgusted. "What a bad example this behavior on the part of the commander in chief must have been to the rest of our armed forces over there," she said. Her husband was a U.S. officer in England, too!

When General Eisenhower came home to the United States, his wife refused to meet his plane. General Marshall and my father tried to persuade her to do so, but she had had an unhappy time living alone in a small apartment while her husband lived in palaces with the pretty Englishwoman. When he returned, she met his plane and left at once to stay at her mother's home in Colorado for some time.

On January 3, General Eisenhower's first night back in Washington, I was seated next to him at Mrs. Laura Gross's dinner party at the F Street Club. He was a bit late, and we were already seated when he arrived. I welcomed him as he sat down, and he responded even more warmly. He was a sparkling charmer on the crest of the wave that evening and very much the conquering hero. We laughed and talked and paid no attention to the other guests sitting beside us. I told him about my idea of a way to keep my Red Cross Nurses' Aides working in our hospitals. I had talked with the superintendent of the city's public hospital (then called Gallinger), which had a nursing school. Our aides would be permitted to attend lectures there in return for working in their hospital wards. At the end of some weeks, we would "decorate" them for contributing their services and completing the course. I asked the general if he would give me permission to use military insignia to decorate the young women.

"Honey," replied Ike, "you can have the stars off my shoulders or the stars in my eyes!" Then he asked me when I would lunch with him at the Pentagon. I didn't tell him that his commanding officer had already invited me!

It was the beginning of a good friendship, but the next morning the general's aide phoned me to say that the general was distressed that there was a law against his letting me use military insignia for my Red Cross ladies. An hour later, a dozen red roses arrived for me from Ike and a note that he hoped I would settle for the stars in his eyes. He didn't mention his invitation! That was all right, but that was as far as I would let it go. After some weeks, Mamie Eisenhower came back to Washington and settled with Ike into the handsome house the Army provided for its chief of staff. She became happily engaged in redecorating the place and frequently asked my advice about it and about clothes. There is nothing like a shopping spree to cheer up a female and/or save a marriage! My stepmother and I and our husbands gave a dinner dance at Tregaron in honor of the Eisenhowers. We dined, danced, and sang together. Ike and Millard led square dances. The Davieses became close friends of Ike and Mamie also and were the godparents of the first Eisenhower grandchild.

When Daddy and Marjorie were in Florida, we lived at Tregaron, and the parties of our friends were gay and fun affairs. Lavish parties were becoming common again in postwar Washington. The society hostess Perle Mesta, who had moved into Herbert Hoover's former home on S Street, gave lots of dinner parties with music for dancing or a fortune-teller or a magician to entertain her guests. I remember dancing often with Ike when he sang his two favorite songs into my fascinated ear—"My Spurs Go Jingle, Jangle, Jingle" and "Lili Marlene." I danced with Millard and a few other men. One was young General Hoyt Vandenberg, chief of the air force, whom I met later at a truly gay leap year dance at the Sulgrave Club. We were all celebrating the end of the war.

Evelyn Walsh McLean, of course, had the distinction of giving the biggest parties before, during, and after it, with enormous seated dinners and luncheons and her mother's gold dinner service at the biggest table for the guest of honor. She would have both dance music and movies after dinner. She had sold her country place, Friendship, and had a big house in Georgetown, which she gave the same name.

Her most magnificent parties were in honor of Vice President Alben Barkley and President Truman. I remember the Trumans' young lady daughter at the party for her parents. She was a lovely blond and paid me a pretty compliment when we were introduced. I said I did not know her and was delighted to meet her and she replied quickly: "Oh, but I know YOU, Mrs. Tydings! Everyone knows you! You are the most etc., etc., woman in Washington!" It was a stupendous compliment, charmingly spoken.

These parties were all more enjoyable now that my husband no longer appeared to be upset when men looked at me. But the most exciting one for me was a dinner when Sir Winston and Lady Churchill arrived in Washington for the first visit after the war. He had just made his famous "Iron Curtain" speech at Fulton, Missouri, which helped to alert our people to the danger of the Soviet Union's dangerous and ambitious behavior by swallowing up the governments of many countries on Russia's western border, as well as East Germany and half of Berlin. It was a great speech, but I wasn't as impressed by his Iron Curtain words as I was by the line predicting that "Armageddon would come in on the gleaming wings of science!"

After Churchill's speech, Mamie Eisenhower phoned me to ask us to a small dinner at their house, and I gave my usual iffy answer. I would have to check with Millard's office. "There won't be anyone there except your father and Sir Winston and Lady Churchill, their daughter, his aide, the secretary of war and ourselves," said she.

"We accept!" I gasped. I admired Mr. Churchill and I quickly figured that according to protocol, I was sure to sit beside the Great Man, himself. Fortunately, there was no conflicting political date in Millard's calendar. I was in almost as much of a tizzy that evening as I had been before my first date with Millard Tydings. I got the lipstick on my nose and the powder on my gown and jammed my zipper.

Lady Churchill was tall and quite lovely looking, in a black lace dinner gown. Sir Winston looked definitely seedy and had a cold and spots on his more than slightly antique dinner jacket! Otherwise, he was his chubby, fascinating self. Neither their daughter nor the aide turned up, and neither Marjorie nor the secretary's wife was in town. My place card, correctly, was beside Sir Winston. Just as I was about to sit down, Mamie called from the head of the table, "Oh, Eleanor, you can't sit there, you would be next to your husband! Please go and sit next to your father." I was furious. Why should I be denied a seat between Millard and Churchill and placed next to my father! Thanks to my upbringing, I seethed in silence and obeyed. Such is the reward of virtue that had I sat beside Mr. Churchill, I would have been next to his deaf ear.

As it was, I was directly opposite him across a narrow table, and he could hear me and see me. I quoted his recent Iron Curtain speech in Missouri to him, and he purred and beamed at me. Then I told him a true story about the young American army fliers' first night in England, told to me by their commander. The fliers were billeted in what had been a girl's school and before that, an ancient monastery. It was a cold, gray day of sleet and fog, and the damp, depressing atmosphere of the old school only increased the fliers' sense of gloom. But seconds after they had been assigned to their quarters (tiny, monkish cells), all hell broke loose! There was a deafening clamor of bells and the boys were roaring with laughter. In each room there was a bellpull with a card tacked beside it reading: "If you feel at all indisposed, kindly ring for a mistress." The boys were singing, "The bells are ringing, for me and my gal!" The gloom had vanished.

Mr. Churchill said mine was the best story he'd heard of the war. Then he asked Ike to tell his story, which was apocryphal but amusing.

Ike's story was a contrived tale of an English soldier in Moscow with a British mission. It was about an English soldier being shown around Moscow by a Russian soldier.

Russian soldier: "This street is Sir John Dill Street, comrade, formerly Goring Street. And this Avenue is Eden Avenue, comrade, formerly Ribbentrop Avenue. Here we are at Churchill Square, comrade, formerly Hitler Square."

English soldier, producing a cigarette: "How about a light, comrade, formerly bastard?"

Although Washington was in a festive mood that spring, all was not just dining and dancing. Important business and big decisions were going on in both houses of Congress. Two most important issues were before the Senate. Millard had become one of its most powerful members, not only because of his seniority of service in that body, but because of his friendship with President Truman and support of most of the presidents' legislative programs. The Legislative Reorganization Act would streamline both the Congress and executive branch of the government. The National Security Act would create a single Department of Defense under civilian leadership with a joint committee comprised of chiefs of the Army, the Navy, and Air Force. They would all come under a civilian secretary of defense and an armed services committee of the House and Senate. Millard would be chairman of the Senate Armed Services Committee if and when the Democrats regained control of the Senate.

He was holding committee meetings to investigate and provide "advice and consent" on the appointment of the president's choice for assistant secretary of the navy, Edward Pauley, an oil millionaire from California. Secretary of the Interior Ickes and many Republicans were bitterly opposed to Pauley's nomination. The criticism of Mr. Pauley became so intense that my husband finally felt he had to tell the president to withdraw Pauley's name before he was smeared any worse. Truman reluctantly did so. Secretary Ickes resigned his Cabinet seat soon afterward, but remained one of my husband's most bitter enemies. The Navy also fought the unification of the Armed Services, and a new senator from Wisconsin named McCarthy did so in behalf of the Marine Corps. My husband had no trouble winning on this issue in spite of them.

Times were changing in our country as the Republican successes in the recent election indicated. Some national polls were showing a change in the American attitude toward the Soviet Union. United States citizens had never liked Communism, but so long as the Russians had fought on our side in the war, they had accepted them as allies. Now the stories of the Soviet Union's takeover of Eastern European governments and their barricade of East Berlin, and stealing our atom bomb secret, were making the Russians increasingly unpopular in our country. The Republicans in Congress were quick to seize upon this and attack the Democratic administration for being "soft on Communism." Two Republican-chaired committees in the House had investigated charges of Communism in the State Department and cleared the department. The chairman of one had declared that the U.S. State Department was infiltrated by Communists. President Truman got the message and set up a Loyalty Oath Program for all government employees.

I do not recall that this interested my husband or myself particularly. We were both concerned with our special interests. Millard had been appointed a member of a special joint commission on atomic energy in the fall of 1945. Now he was a member of the Joint Atomic Energy Committee of the House and Senate. The committee was to form policy on domestic developments and control of the bomb. Millard told me he was not so much interested in the domestic aspect of the bomb as he was in its international dangers. His experiences seeing the war damage of Europe and the Philippines made him more than ever determined to try to prevent a future war of atomic weapons. We could control them at home, but the real danger was abroad. He was worried over the poor prospects for a peaceful world.

That June, the navy held a ceremony to return Marjorie's yacht to her after its distinguished tour of duty as a weather ship on the Murmansk Run in the North Atlantic. It was a miracle that the ship was not destroyed. Instead, she sank two enemy subs and was proudly wearing the decorations that the navy had painted on her! When she had gone into the navy, all her towering masts and sails had been taken down and furnishings removed, and guns had been mounted on her teakwood decks. She was returned to Marjorie with her former beauty restored, wearing a million dollar suit of new sails and scrubbed clean as a whistle!

Also in June, Joseph Davies Tydings graduated from McDonogh School and led the Cavalry mounted on a curvetting black stallion. Both were very handsome! I heard that McDonogh had won more prizes at the big Madison Square Garden Horse Shows than any other military prep school over the years. Joe's record at McDonogh was almost as good as General MacArthur's had been at West Point! I am very proud of my son's career, but more proud of the inflexible honesty of his character. Like Millard, things are either black or white to him where principle is concerned. There is no gray area where one could shade one's conduct a bit.

Joe was a serious, ambitious young man. From his earliest years, I had told him stories about his grandfather Davies, his stepfather, the senator, and various other distinguished ancestors. Since my father had no sons, he had a great deal to do with Joe's formative years. Millard had neither the time nor the blood tie, but he spent as much time as he could with his adopted son, and his example had as much to do with Joe's character as my father's had. We had sent him to McDonogh when he was nine because Millard was sure World War II was in the offing and felt military training would help prepare Joe.

On my son's first visit home from school, he announced proudly, "I've learned one thing at school. That is, there's no such thing as a genius!" When I demurred, he said, "It's just the boy who works the hardest." He has lived up to this belief all his life.

The last of June, Millard left me to fly around the world on an inspection trip of war damage with Senator Stuart Symington and representatives of the U.S. military. They were to attend the celebration of Philippine independence at Manila on July 4. A few days before that, they would be the first civilian observers to witness the atomic bombing of a flotilla of old battleships, carriers, and destroyers at Bikini Atoll on the Kwajalein Island. My husband would never forget that truly awful experience. Of course, they would be flying in a government plane on government business, so I couldn't accompany them. When I found out about the atomic bomb test, I was very worried, even when Millard assured me they would not be near the explosion. However, his letter describing it gave me cold chills. Their plane was very close to it. I can still visualize the glorious sunset on one end of the island and the horrible bomb blast the next morning. My husband wrote me that the former was God the Creator at his best, and the latter was Man the Destroyer at his worst.

There were seventy-three ships tied up at the Bikini Lagoon, with animals, germs, and dummies on board. There were seventy-two unmanned planes circling around above them. They were painted red, as was the battleship *Nevada*. A B-29 bomber named *Dave's Dream* carried an atom bomb called Gilda. The observers' plane was a C-54 nicknamed *Folklore One*. Millard and Stuart were awakened in the early morning and strapped into "Mae West" jackets and parachutes. On the plane they sat on life rafts. *Folklore* followed *Dave's Dream* over the island (at a safe distance) to Bikini, and the observers were instructed to put on goggles and not remove them until told to do so. Millard said they were all frightened when the countdown began, not knowing what to expect. There was a shout of "bombs away," a dazzling flash of light and fireball, and then a towering column of smoke and the mushroom cloud we have all seen in photographs. The great cloud vanished in about twenty minutes and so did one of the steel towers. There was fire and smoke on some of the ships. The battleships *Arizona, California, Nevada, Oklahoma,* and

West Virginia rolled over like children's toys in a tub and sank. Thirty more cruisers and destroyers were badly damaged. I never heard whether any living creatures on board survived.

After that the ceremonies at Manila on July 4 must have been rather an anticlimax for my husband, even though he was the man who had worked for years to achieve Philippine independence. I would have been happy to be in Manila that July 4 to celebrate with Millard. General MacArthur, Governor Paul McNutt, President Manuel Rojas, and other Philippine leaders were all speakers at the ceremonies. Senator Tydings was the first and received the longest and mightiest roar of applause, so I was told. Rain had been predicted, but had held off until Millard's speech was over. The American flag was flying over the proceedings until President Rojas stopped speaking and slowly raised the Philippine flag. Equally slowly the Stars and Stripes descended until, halfway down, the two flags paused side by side for a minute. Then the Philippine flag went on up and our flag came down and the United States fleet in the harbor boomed a twenty-one gun salute. The band played the two national anthems and, as Millard said, "There was a new nation on earth."

While Millard was bombing Bikini, celebrating in Manila, and observing the tragedy of a shattered postwar world, I was busy working for my dream of a Washington Hospital Center. Bessie Huidecooper, Elysabeth Barbour, and I had held meetings, and doctors, hospital experts, and city leaders came to them to help us. Elysabeth and I had lobbied the bill in the House of Representatives after Millard had shepherded it through the Senate. He had literally left us on the steps of the House office building with "the baby on our laps!" We had dear old Sol Bloom, Democratic congressman from Chicago, and the Maryland delegation on our side, as well as Mr. Wigglesworth, the Republican chairman of the Appropriations Committee. Sol Bloom said ours was a noble cause, so God was on our side and we would win.

My friend Elysabeth was a very beautiful brunette and agreed to follow my plan of action. "If he is a Republican, Liz, you speak first, and if he's a Democrat, I will," I said. "It will take only two seconds to find out if the gentleman prefers blonds or brunettes!" The plan worked and Millard's bill passed the House and was signed into law by President Truman in 1946. Unfortunately, in spite of this magnificent gift of land and building and equipment from the government, it took almost ten years to persuade the sponsoring hospitals to give up their own rat-ridden domains. As chairman of the Hospital Center Corporation, I did all I could, with the invaluable help of dear Bessie and Elysabeth, to persuade the original consenting hospitals to give up their identities. Children's Hospital refused to go along, and the present Hospital Center consisted then of Garfield, Emergency, and Episcopal. (Note: Childrens Hospital was finally built on the land given to the Hospital Center but it is not part of it.)

After passage of the bill, I took our children to visit their paternal grandparents in Ashville for a few days, and then to visit my mother on the Brule River in the north woods of Wisconsin. I did not know at that time that an unscrupulous soldier of fortune was electioneering in that state for the United States Senate. His name was Joe McCarthy. I loved Wisconsin with its splendid great lakes and myriad of lovely smaller ones splashed all over it. It is still hard for me to swallow the fact that it could have bred such a scoundrel or that he would prove to be such a nemesis in my life and Millard's.

I met a tired, dispirited husband and breathed a sigh of relief when he returned from his world-inspection trip of the war damage and stepped off the plane on August 4. A horde of reporters was on hand to fire questions at him, but he put them off and escaped with me to the peace of Oakington, where he slept long hours for several days. Then he reported to the president, and ten days later we joined my father and Marjorie on the *Sea Cloud* for a cruise up the East Coast. This was, as always, a very happy and restful vacation for us. We landed at all the most beautiful places and played golf with friends. We were anchored at several resorts where small boats came out to stare at us and the yacht. Some had seen Millard on deck from afar and thought he was President Truman! I was not pleased, I thought my husband was a much handsomer man than Harry Truman.

Chapter 27

I Fly to England and Wales
with Father

On the cruise, Daddy told us that he had been invited to receive an honorary degree from the University of North Wales in October. Marjorie couldn't go with him because her daughter Eleanor needed her support in Paris. Another unhappy marriage and divorce. They wanted me to go with my father and Millard urged me to go. He wanted me to see the ruins of war in London and I would be away only a week or so. After an idyllic ten days together at Oakington, I reluctantly kissed Millard and the children good-bye and joined Daddy in New York to fly to England. It was my first flight across the Atlantic. On my return trip, I actually had a real upper berth like those on a train to sleep in, but I didn't sleep much in it. I was afraid that the plane might fall, so I didn't dare remove my clothes.

In London, Daddy was too ill to attend many of the affairs in his honor, but recovered sufficiently to go to Wales.

Besides myself, a distant cousin of ours, John Davies "J.D." Stamm, went with us as his valet, secretary, public relations man, advance man, and courier. He certainly was a beast of burden at the New York airport. My father, obviously unwell, was in a foul humor, the worst I had ever seen. Poor J.D. was laden down with the ambassador's overcoat, a case of books, a heavy briefcase, a case of medicines, and an umbrella.

"J.D.," ordered my father, "you forgot the Sunday papers. Go out and get me the *New York Times*, the *Herald Tribune*, and the Washington papers."

J.D. looked desperately at me. "Give me the overcoat, the umbrella and the medicines," I said. J.D. did so gratefully, dashed

272

away, and returned staggering under an enormous load of newspapers. My father was totally unconcerned.

I had summoned a porter with a cart and we managed to board the plane. I will never forget J.D. wobbling on board still carrying the overcoat, the medicines, the umbrella, the briefcase, and the newspapers. I had the books. Daddy and I left J.D. in London and motored up to North Wales. He had recovered from his ill humor and had been greatly pleased by the banquet given in his honor in London by the Welsh Societies. On our drive north, he reminisced about his boyhood in Anglesey and regaled me with tales of ancient Wales. I suspect that there is an Anglesey druid or two somewhere in my father's genealogy as well as the Norman count who came over with William the Conqueror!

My father stayed well through the ceremonies and the festivities in his honor at the university.

On October 23, 1946, I wrote my sister Rahel:

"This time yesterday I was in New York City and today I am in London, looking out of a window of Claridges Hotel at a row of bomb-damaged houses. Driving from the airport we passed acres of unbombed suburbs and my first impression was one of surprise that London had suffered less destruction than I had imagined. That is partly due to the fact that the Germans concentrated on the part of the city around St. Paul's Cathedral. Back of the famous 'Cheshire Cheese,' there are blocks and blocks of ruins. Then, too, the English have already cleaned up so well that the empty spots every block or so look rather like those New York City craters, which are at the stage between bulldozer and builder.

"There are many, many fire-and-bomb-gutted houses, among them the handsome ones facing Regent Park. We drove past Barbara Hutton's mansion there and it remains untouched. She has given it to Uncle Sam for our embassy, but our people haven't moved in yet. I remember how pretty she looked when she told me several years ago of her wish to give her house for our American embassy. I thought it a marvelous idea until she told me what armies of servants it took to run the place, and I wondered how on earth most American ambassadors could possibly afford to live there on their modest salary!

"Claridge's looks much as it did when I was last here in 1935, only slightly more bare and chilly. There are no palms in the lounge and there is very little, if any, heat in the hotel. Our rooms and baths are still luxurious but the bath towels are threadbare and the toilet rolls are like our toughest brown wrapping paper. In the dining room, the menu is limited, to say the least, only fish or fowl, no bread except at breakfast, never any oranges, and practically never any meat. The vegetables are so pale and tired looking that I'm sure the cooks must be too. Everything tastes the same, which is to say that means that nothing tastes at all. Poor London is very shabby; everything, including the women, simply screams for paint, but it is not their fault; there is no paint! I must say that everyone I've seen is cheerfully and gallantly putting up with all the shortages and working away under such trying circumstances that my hat is off to them. We Americans could certainly take lessons from them in patience and politeness.

"The English queue up endlessly for everything and wait for hours for buses, taxis, movies, and food. Nobody ever pushes or shoves.

(One week later:)

"Since I started this letter, we have dined at the American embassy; lunched with Lord Beaverbrook; attended Sunday services at the poor bombed Guard Chapel; motored to Bangor, Wales; collected Father's degree; visited some ancestral graves; and driven back to London.

"We dined with our ambassador, Mr. Averill Hariman, the night after we arrived. Mr. Harriman is a tall, quiet gentleman and very nice. Neither his wife nor his daughter was in London, so he only had a few friends in, among them young Mrs. Randolph Churchill and Mr. Brendan Bracken, a cabinet minister in Churchill's wartime administration. Both are charming people. Mrs. Churchill is twentyish, blond, and beautiful. Mr. Bracken is fortyish, red-headed, with a Churchillian profile (not figure!), and an encyclopedic mind. Both he and Dad being uninhibited conversationalists, the repartee was great fun. Young Mrs. Churchill is apparently not only the protégé of Beaverbrook and close to her father-in-law, Winston Churchill, but also a great friend of Ambassador Averill Harriman. The next day I went with Father to lunch with Lord Beaverbrook. England's great newspaper tycoon is a rugged old gentleman with a twinkle in his eye and a good solid American accent! All his years in England have not changed the basic Americanisms of his native Canada. His apartment was quite shabby and when I glanced from the window I could see a vast area next to the building had been leveled by German bombs. It was not hard to imagine this Canadian John Bull pacing the floor undaunted by the German blitz.

"I think Beaverbrook was as amused as I was at the thrust and parry of this talk with Dad. He was trying to extract Father's ideas on the Paris Conference muddle and on Henry Wallace's recent speech condemning Secretary Byrnes's policies, and my parent wasn't coming across with any information. Instead, he was trying to pump our host about the British political picture of today and tomorrow! Dad was the better excavator of the two. Lord B. said of course the Labor Party had put the 'Left-Wingers' in control and they would probably be there for some time; that Churchill had been too conservative in his campaign speeches and postwar political policies, so he was defeated; that Communist party members had far more seats in the House of Commons than ever before, but they had no real power in the government. He said Mr. Hugh Dalton seemed the most politically promising member of the cabinet. So far as the Paris Conference was concerned, both Lord B. and Dad agreed that the international picture looked dark but that it could and would be straightened out. Both thought Stalin wanted peace, not war. Lord B. said he heard that since the war, there had been a strong military movement to oust Stalin, which the latter had crushed. Father looked interested but made no comment.

"Lord B. insisted upon sending a reporter from one of his papers to interview me, in spite of my protests. He said he had one young writer who was one of his smartest and best and asked would I see her. Of course, I politely acceded and imagine my surprise when this superlative newspaper gal turned out to be none other than my little friend, Mrs. Randolph Churchill! We had a 'dish of tea' together and a good gossip that afternoon. She drew all manner of information from me about my husband, our children, and our Grand Champion boar hog, Glory Bound. However, when the article appeared, it barely mentioned Millard and not a word about the kids or Glory Bound! It was all about me, very complimentary with a flattering photo which was copied in the Washington papers.

"Last Sunday, Cousin J.D. and I attended the eleven o'clock service at the Guards Chapel and watched the changing of the guard at Buckingham Palace on the way. The old palace stood imposing as ever, but typical of postwar London, its facade was bomb-scarred and dirty. The military band was fine and the guard stepped out as smartly as ever, but in battle dress! Gone were the splendid uniforms and tall bearskin hats of yesteryear! We strolled across the square to the chapel and a lump came into my throat, for there the enemy had scored a direct hit, and during a Sunday morning service! All that was left was the fine altar; the rest of the chapel is a steel quonset hut and the congregation sits on camp chairs. The army band played martial hymns splendidly and a tall young chaplain with rows of campaign ribbons on his surplice preached a very fine sermon on lending.

"Daddy and I drove to Wales one fine morning (the sun actually shone!) in an antique limousine with a chauffeur who looked and talked exactly like Charles Laughton! He turned out to be a demon driver but was in complete ignorance of the fine art of tire changing and of the inner mysteries of an automobile engine. Five minutes out, our antique vehicle stalled, right in the center of one of London's busiest intersections. There we sat for what seemed an interminable time, trying to imitate Charles's impervious dignity and turn a blind eye to the dirty looks and honks of traffic. To the police and to us, Charles explained with unruffled poise that 'she's flooded in 'er carburetor, sir, and we'll just have to wyte a bit.' And 'wyte' we did till 'she' and Charles decided to move on.

"The English countryside was lovely, very like our home county. It was a sentimental journey for daddy to the land of his fathers and his youth. Some of his boyhood was spent in Wales and he still speaks that strange Celtic tongue. As we approached the castle-crowned heights of the Welsh border, the scenery became more rugged and beautiful. We passed many a fortress high upon the crags of the lovely valley of the river Dee where the Welsh fought endless battles against the British invader. We climbed over the highest mountains which guard the approaches to the sacred Isle of Anglesey.

"We crossed the broad Menai Straits to Anglesey, a big island with a tradition of special sanctity for the Welsh people. Its ancient name is Mon Mam Cymru, which means Mona, Mother of Wales. It was the stronghold of the Druid priests who taught laws of conduct as well as religion long before Christianity. They worshiped the sun as the Giver of Life, the One God, and they taught a code of ethics not unlike Christianity. All this and many legends Daddy told me. He said that Mon Mam Cymru had come by its name properly, for geologists claim that the rock of Wales was the oldest part of the land-mass of England, and that Anglesey was the original nucleus against which the mountains of Carnarvonshire piled up. Then in turn the old rock of Paleozoic Wales became the block against which the newer geological deposits of Britain were built up. Anglesey is so old that her rock ribs are worn down into a low, gentle terrain of great fertility and many farms.

"We visited a little old Norman church on a hillside where some of our ancestors are buried. I stood and looked over a low stone wall, across green fields rolling down to the straits and at the mountains beyond and I thought this a most perfect spot for the living as well as for the dead. Atop the heights of Bangor, across from Anglesey is a college of the University of North Wales. It is very beautiful with Gothic spires and halls. It was pouring rain and bitterly cold the evening we arrived and the old Castle Inn where we stayed was picturesque but extremely chilly. I had the royal suite, which had an odd-looking heater in the fireplace. With this I experimented in vain.

"We dined that night with chilly ceremony in an enormous room at the college, with My Lord Pro Chancellor, My Lord Vice-Chancellor, and a score of university lesser lights and wives. They served us the best dinner we had in England. Father sat on the Lord Pro Chancellor's right and J.D. and I were tucked away in the middle of the table. As my place card read 'Mrs. _____,' I gathered that Dad had neglected to mention that he was bringing me, and the University was quite in the dark as to who I was.

"I was just beginning to feel pleasantly relaxed and full of chicken, when Father, responding to the vice chancellor's toast, proceeded to drag me into his after-dinner speech! He not only introduced me to the assembled dons as the granddaughter of my Welsh poetess grandmother, but far worse, he called upon me to say a few words myself.

"Nothing could have caught me more off guard. I glared at Dad behind a polite smile, and did my best. I said something about the superiority of Wales and the Welsh and the future of world peace depending upon such people as these. I was so humble that I guess they felt some sympathy for the poor American female. At any rate, they gave me a hand, Daddy beamed, and apparently, I hadn't let the Welsh grandmother down!

"Next morning we went back to the college. J.D. and I sat in the front row of a great hall jammed with people and watched Dad march up with the dons to the platform and receive his honorary degree. The college robes were magnificent, brilliant turkey red with hoods lined in a sort of orchid-mauve color. The City Council marched in, too, in furred robes, with great silver chains clanking around their necks. All sat in rows with the dons on the platform. A large choir sang magnificently—in Welsh—but in a most unusual manner, not like we do, but better, and ended up with the Star Spangled Banner in honor of Dad.

"His speech had been the subject of curiosity on the part of the press, which was convinced that Father was in Europe on some secret mission. So he stuck to 'peace and the Lord's Prayer' (as he said!) and there was no news for the reporters.

(Three days later:)

"When we reached London we were all tired and Dad was not feeling well, so he began pulling wires to fly home as soon as possible. However, he insisted that J.D. and I dash over to Paris for a couple of days. After assuring ourselves that Father would be all right, we hopped across the Channel for one day and two nights in gay Paree. We dined and danced with some of J.D.'s friends and I wandered the streets soaking in the city. It was a beautiful sunny day, and it seemed to me that Paris had not changed a bit. I wandered around the shopping district and the shop windows were intriguing as ever—until one asked the prices! Most things were as expensive, or more so, than in New York.

"The food was as marvelous as ever—no London rationing here! Black markets flourish openly in France, whereas they are practically non-existent in England. As I strolled across the Place Vendome, the illusion was almost overpowering that I was back in the gay twenties, hurrying to meet a Yale beau and go dancing in the Bois. For a minute I was twenty again!

"I stopped in the long corridor of the Ritz where all the shops display their choicest wares in showcases lining the walls, and paused to inquire about prices. As I sauntered on I heard one young salesgirl say: 'Qu'elle est belle, n'est-ce pas?' (She's pretty, isn't she?) and my spirits soared! 'Oui, mais je crois qu'elle est plus distinguée que belle!' (yes, but I think she's more distinguished than pretty) came the response. My champagne bubbles collapsed. J.D. was walking toward me. 'Well, old gal, how're you doing? You look as though your feet hurt!' And I was back—fair, fat, and forty! We went to the reopening of a famous restaurant that night but it was like a crowded night at any of our New York nightclubs. I was eager to get back to London and Dad and still more so to get home to Millard and our Little El. Love, Eleanor."

Our Joe enlisted in the U.S. army that fall and went into basic training before being sent to Germany to serve on the Allied-Russian line. He wrote to his grandfather, "The army really feeds you. We have meat three times a day and generally all we can eat. I have been going through intense physical training for eight weeks and have still managed to eat enough to gain ten pounds. My squad won in competition as the best drilled squad in the platoon, then the company, and finally in the whole battalion. I received a letter of commendation from my battalion commander and in the final parade I and the three best men from my squad will bear the colors and form the color guard. I hope to see you and Aunt Marjorie soon. Your grandson, Joe."

November 29, 1946 was my father's seventieth birthday. Marjorie and I always planned family celebrations in his honor on that date. We decided to stage this party for him at Oakington. Daddy and Marjorie, Rahel, Emlen and Bob Grosjean, and Cousin J.D. Stamm and his wife were all to be houseguests. Five years before, for Daddy's sixty-fifth, we had put on a show in his honor with poems and a chorus line of us girls singing "My Heart Belongs to Daddy." I wanted to do something memorable this time. After our return from London, there was very little time to plan anything but I wrote an outline for three acts depicting highlights in Daddy's life. My sisters and the Stamms protested, and I insisted that they could ad-lib their parts without a written script. They didn't arrive until late afternoon the day of the birthday party and I handed them a description of what each one was to do. They all protested again that they couldn't, and then did their parts beautifully!

The first act was based on an old photograph of Joseph Davies, age five, sitting in the middle of the front row of his classmates, holding a slate! J.D. Stamm, wearing shorts and holding the facsimile of a slate, took this part and recited a hilarious poem. My sister Rahel played the part of her grandmother Rahel, but did not preach. The next act was Father as a candidate for the U.S. Senate in 1918. Bob Grosjean did this well, making a campaign speech for Woodrow Wilson and the League of Nations. Emlen acted the part of our mother. The last act was Daddy in Russia. Millard was the ambassador in a cutaway and striped pants going to see Stalin, and I was Marjorie planning a dinner party for the top brass of the Red Army. It was a great success with Marjorie and Daddy an appreciative audience.

Chapter 28

The Red-Baiting Begins

1947: Congress passes the European Recovery Act to stem the spread of Communism in Western Europe; Richard Nixon holds hearings on Communists in the U.S. government; Millard's health begins to suffer; Millard in Greece and with Sergeant Joe T. in Heidelberg.

Nineteen forty-seven was the beginning of another kind of war—the war at home started by politicians who were trying to portray all liberals as Communists and traitors. Debates raged in Congress over Communists at home and abroad and what to do to help our European friends. The Republicans seized upon the former and were trying to make it into an issue to defeat the Democrats in the 1948 elections. A new generation had arrived on Capitol Hill in the persons of a California Congressman named Richard Nixon and a senator from Wisconsin named Joseph McCarthy. They had both won elections by unusually vicious campaigning, and Mr. Nixon had quickly become chairman of a House committee investigating Communists in the government.

In Europe, the major cities were in ruins and Russia was taking over the governments of Eastern Europe, the Baltic States, Greece, Italy, and Turkey and refusing to take her troops out of Azerbaijan. The U.S. was facing the necessity of forming a new foreign policy to try to save the democracies and to prevent a possible Third World War with Communist Russia.

People were celebrating the end of the war and the winter was full of social events. We dined and danced at the White House, at most of the larger embassies, at Tregaron, at the Demarest Lloyds's baronial mansion, and at Evelyn Walsh McLean's Friendship. We gave a few parties and dined at the homes of Senators Cabot Lodge, Robert

280

Taft, Burnet Maybank, and Peter Goelat Gerry. At one such party, I urged the chairman of the board of General Motors to manufacture tiny automobiles like the wonderful, tiny Bantam car I drove during the war, which everyone had wanted to buy or steal from me. I told him that we were going to become a country of two-car families, a big one for the man and a little one for his wife. The chairman listened to me all through dinner and finally said: "Would you mind putting all this in writing, Mrs. Tydings, and mailing it to me?" I was disgusted. I said coldly that I was a busy woman and really didn't have the time. So the Germans jumped the gun on us and made a fortune in the U.S. out of their ugly little Volkswagens! General Motors would have made many millions if the chairman of the board had taken my advice!

When the Senate went home for Easter 1947, we spent two weeks at Mar-a-Lago in Palm Beach to give Millard a rest from his efforts to push through President Truman's legislative programs. President Truman and Millard saw eye to eye on most legislation except a few domestic measures, which Millard thought to be against states' rights. In March, the president had asked the Senate for $500 million to help Greece and Turkey fight the Communists. At that time, Millard had reintroduced his request for a conference on world disarmament, this time under international inspection by the United Nations. The only weapons would be in the hands of small national police forces and the U.N. Security Council. It was an impossible dream: Everyone was for it, senators, scholars, citizens, but nobody worked for it!

The significant event that session was when Congress passed the National Security Act of 1947, which created the CIA and unified the military command under a civilian secretary of defense. James Forrestal, who was secretary of the navy, was made the first secretary of defense. I sat beside him at a dinner and found him to be rather dour. Millard said the man was depressed because the act did not give him any real control over the quarreling branches of the armed services. However, at a dinner at the British embassy I saw another reason for Mr. Forrestal's behavior. His wife had obviously had too much to drink and tried to make a speech. Her husband had to leave the table and take her home. Millard and I were saddened when poor Forrestal committed suicide by jumping out of a high window at the Bethesda Naval Hospital.

Although my husband supported the National Security Act and was the top-ranking member of the new Senate Armed Services

Committee, President Truman did not support Millard's disarmament plan. He said Millard's proposal was not practical, considering world conditions. Instead, he had appointed Bernard Baruch to chair a commission on the control of atomic energy, and so informed Millard indirectly, through Senator Vandenberg and the State Department. Millard dropped the subject and didn't speak about it again in the Senate until 1950. But he did support the president's foreign aid proposals and the European Recovery Act, saying on the radio that they would cost far less money than a policy of unpreparedness, and would help to deter Communism. He also supported the Marshall Plan, unveiled by General Marshall (now secretary of state) at a speech at Harvard.

In June, I was the speaker to two large groups of women in Maryland. As usual, I discussed Millard's position on the state of the world and our new foreign policy of containing Communism in Europe.

Shortly after my speech, we received a shock when my stepmother sent for us to come at once to Bermuda. My father was very seriously ill on the yacht. We flew there at once with two of Daddy's close friends. Millard did not leave until my father was out of danger, but I stayed longer. I had been badly frightened that I might face life without Daddy. He recovered slowly but steadily and we sailed home together in time for our big garden party at Oakington for Maryland Democratic leaders.

That summer, we went again on a long cruise with my father and Marjorie up the New England coast. When we returned to New York, we lunched at the Plaza Hotel with the Lord Chancellor of England and his wife, Lady Jowett. The lunch party was great fun with the three men swapping anecdotes. His lordship recited a quite shocking limerick: "There was a young man named Magill who swallowed an atomic pill. One genital organ was found in Glamorgan and one on a tree in Brazil!" There was no air-conditioning yet in the Plaza and the windows were open to the August breezes. I am sure the passersby must have heard our laughter.

The great painter of English royalty, Frank Salisbury, who had painted portraits of Daddy and Marjorie and my sister, Rahel, was in New York and my father wanted him to paint me, so I stayed there for a few days while he did one of my head and shoulders, wearing a blue velvet ball gown. One of his patrons saw it and admired it. The artist told us she said that the subject was not only beautiful but looked like a fascinating person. Salisbury told her she was right, all very pleasing to an old lady like me!

Came September and President Truman sent my husband, as a member of both the Appropriations and Armed Services Committees, on a fact-finding trip to Europe. He was to travel for two months around England, France, the Low Countries, Germany, Austria, Switzerland, Greece, and Turkey. He was to assess war damage and estimate the cost of the European recovery plan. He talked with military and economic leaders everywhere. General Omar Bradley told me Millard was the best-informed man in the world on these matters. I thought he was doing much the same sort of mission that my father had done for President Roosevelt twenty-some years ago. Naturally, Millard wanted to see our son Joe, who was stationed in Germany and he sent word to General Harmon asking that Joe be given leave to meet him in Heidelberg. Joe was stationed near Cobourg, Germany, one of Harmon's cavalry, riding horse patrols on the Russian border. It was typical of both my husband and my son that neither one ever considered using the power of Millard's position for more than a day's leave for Joe. They lunched together, saw the town, and Joe went back to camp. Of course, the story leaked out that Joe was the senator's son and the other soldiers couldn't understand why he had not taken advantage of this relationship or why he had never mentioned it.

"Why didn't you stay longer with your old man?" they asked.

"He didn't ask me to and I didn't want to," replied my son. When he left the camp to come home, one of his mates told him that this incident had made him the most popular man in the regiment.

Later that summer, Joe volunteered for a secret mission to take five hundred horses down to Greece to help fight the Communists in the mountains. "We never lost a horse," Joe told me. "One died, but one was born on the way." He also told me he had enough of horses to last a lifetime! One of his pals was a young giant, six feet six, named Tex, who took every opportunity to get drunk. As my son didn't drink, he usually took care of getting Tex out of brawls. When the shipload of horses arrived at Piraeus, Greece, there was a British ship in port and the English sailors had taken over the bars. One night there was a battle royal between the English and the Americans ashore in a bar. Joe managed to extricate a very drunken Tex from the fight and get him back on their ship. This was no easy feat! It necessitated carrying the huge Texan across a narrow gangway, which was the only means of reaching the ship. Halfway across, Tex came to and protested. He didn't want to go back to the boat.

"What did you do?" I asked Joe.

"No problem, Mother, I just held him by one foot and dipped him in the harbor!"

My husband's adventure in Greece was not as amusing as Joe's. One of the officers who accompanied Millard described in hair-raising detail how he refused to follow orders and insisted on climbing high in the mountains to the Communist-held border. They visited a tiny village consisting of one small general store and a few humble dwellings. There were no inhabitants around and the store had been emptied of its wares. The Greek guide said the enemy must have kidnaped the villagers. They were afraid the enemy might be nearby and dragged my husband from an inspection of the little store. There he found nothing but one small can of corn. It came from the Harford County, Maryland, cannery of a distant cousin! He presented the much-traveled little can to his relative upon his return.

I met his boat and was too happy to have him home safe to scold him for taking such a chance of being shot by the Communists. He was also met by a horde of newsmen all firing questions at him, which he refused to answer until he'd had time to make his report to President Truman, describing the devastation, illness, and starvation he had found all over Europe. My husband said these poor people were in dire need of help, and that it was in our own interest to help them. Conditions were especially bad in Greece. Never a rich country, its ports had been badly damaged during the war and its fishing fleet sunk. There was no fuel, no food. In Italy, there were more people than there was land and very little food, but the Italians were hardworking and had good leadership. Austria, France, and the Low Countries were better off, but all needed food and economic aid to stave off the Communist threat. Millard wrote a series of articles for prestigious journals describing what he had seen and what must be done.

The weekend of the Maryland-North Carolina football game we had friends at Oakington, and my daughter came home for the weekend from Garrison Forest school outside of Baltimore. Our close friends, Violet and Jim McLean, who lived on a nearby farm, had two handsome boys her age. Young Peter had offered to drive her back to the school, and we gave permission. The two teenagers left Oakington in the boy's car in plenty of time to arrive at the school by seven. We were entertaining at dinner and hardly noticed that a light snow had begun to fall. We knew young Peter and did not worry that they would not reach the school by seven. By ten o'clock the snow had turned into a real blizzard and I called the school. The headmistress was most concerned. The children had not arrived. I telephoned the McLeans and they were as worried as we were. Peter's car had no top. They might have been wrecked. "Mac" McLean said that if we hadn't heard in thirty minutes, he would set out to search for them.

It was eleven when Millard phoned the state police to ask for their help. They assured him that they would scour the roads between Oakington and the school. Millard's conversation when they asked for a description of the kids and the car is amusing in retrospect, but it didn't seem so at the time.

"My little girl is a pretty, blond, sixteen-year-old with dimples, he said. The boy? He is a tall, good-looking, youngster with curly dark hair. The car? It is a red jeep with 'Termite Number Two' painted on the side. No, there is not the slightest chance that they have eloped!"

Soon after that, we heard from the school that the two wanderers had arrived, very cold and very scared! They had lost their way on the country roads in the storm.

"Honestly, Mother, we couldn't find our way and we just got lost. It wasn't any fun at all!"

The school scolded and punished our little girl with the loss of two weekends at home, but Millard and I did not. We believed her story. Our children never lied to us. I told them when they were little that I would fight for them to my last breath if they were ever in trouble, but I would not be able to if they ever lied to me. They never have.

It was a glorious autumn at Oakington. Millard raked leaves and made bonfires to his heart's content, and drove old golf balls into the bay from our high bank. I thought he seemed rested from his strenuous year. My mother and our sisters visited us at Oakington for Thanksgiving and we had our usual beautiful family Christmas there with a big tree and parties and the house decorated with our own holly and greens. Little El's stocking was hung by the chimney with milk and cookies left on the hearth for Santa Claus. I filled a big stocking for Millard and hid my sadness over the absence of my son. After Christmas, we closed Oakington and moved back to Washington where we danced the New Year in at Evelyn Walsh McLean's party. Many guests were talking about Millard for president or vice president in 1948. Millard just smiled and said it was nice to be wanted, if only by a misguided few!

Nineteen forty-seven ended joyfully with my son returning home from Army service in Europe. His two-year enlistment had ended in the summer, but he didn't arrive home from the Allied-Russian border until December. I waited impatiently. There had been incidents of Russian soldiers shooting at our boys, and the U.S. soldiers were under strict orders not to return Russian fire no matter what the provocation!

We were not sure of the exact date when Joe would get to Oakington, but I had his most recent girlfriend visiting us there. Millard and I were breakfasting in my bedroom when Joe unexpectedly walked in, big as life, and twice as handsome in his cavalry uniform, boots, and spurs! The girlfriend down the hall was caught with her hair done up in curlers. Mother was at Oakington too, and great was the rejoicing. We had a big party of old and young friends that night.

A few days later, in January 1948, Millard, Joe, El, and I went to visit Daddy and Marjorie in Palm Beach. I thought I was a good dancer and could follow any man's dance steps, but I soon discovered that I couldn't keep up with my son when he was galloping about doing a German polka! His boots and spurs didn't help! I took him down on Worth Avenue to be photographed, and he almost stopped traffic. Every female on the street was gaping at my good-looking soldier in his dashing cavalry uniform. He was an Army veteran, just twenty years old when he got out of the Army. He enrolled as a freshman at the University of Maryland and joined the Young Democratic Clubs of Maryland.

Millard could spend only a short week at Mar-a-Lago and it was not enough. He was more tired than I realized. The past two years had been strenuous ones for him, but he was always such a power-house of energy that I didn't notice his fatigue. In January 1948, we returned to a busy life full of demanding activities in the city and in our state. We gave a big party at Tregaron for Elysabeth Barbour and her bridegroom, the British air marshal, and went to another one of Evelyn Walsh McLean's big bashes.

In February our skies were suddenly obscured by a very dark cloud. My husband was stricken with pneumonia. The doctor and I thought that after ten days in bed it would be a good idea to take him to Hot Springs, Virginia, to recuperate. I knew that if he was in Washington he would be hard at work on Capitol Hill. That trip to Hot Springs was a bad idea. No sooner had we arrived than Millard's temperature shot up wildly. He had lobar pneumonia. The hotel doctor sent us back to Washington in an ambulance. It was a painfully agonizing trip of five hours for us both. Millard was in the Bethesda Naval Hospital for five weeks.

It was a grim time, the first since our marriage that he had been ill. Like most men, he was not a good patient. I visited him daily and he would moan and groan and I would fear he was not long for this world! I would weep all the way home. Then one day when I arrived at the hospital, his door was partly open and I heard nurses' voices and peels of laughter. They were joking and laughing. I walked in and my husband instantly lay back on the pillows and closed his eyes and groaned. I laughed and kissed him. "You old fraud! You needn't put on your suffering, moaning, groaning act with me anymore!" He laughed too and I felt enormous relief. I wept no more for him and did not feel guilty when I went to one big party.

When he was in the hospital I went to a leap year dance, the only big party I ever attended without my husband. I was so worried and depressed that Elysabeth and her air marshal insisted that I dine with them and go to the party at the Sulgrave Club. It was fun. All my young married women friends composed a long and extremely active stag line and cut in on the men—their husbands and others— and the men were danced off their feet! The more attractive ones loved the evidence of their popularity and we "stags" organized a constant flow of partners for the less attractive husbands. Emily Lodge took me out on the dance floor and introduced me to an extremely handsome young general. He was a very good dancer and promptly danced me over to a secluded corner away from the stag line when the music stopped.

"I'm sorry, I didn't catch your name!" he said, smiling down at me.

I laughed. "What difference does it make?"

"It does, a lot, to me," he insisted, but I enjoyed keeping him guessing. Finally, I told him my name. He had danced me into the adjacent card room and he stopped dead and dropped his arms. "My lord, you can't be the senator's wife!" he gasped. "You are much too young!"

I was flattered. "I am his wife and he is young too!" I was indignant and pleased at the same time.

He groaned. "You are the wife of my boss! That is too d—n bad!"

Elysabeth cut in just then but not before he whispered a plea in my ear. "I must see you again! Please cut in again!" I did not. Later, I found that he was married to a pretty but disagreeable woman. He telephoned once, but I never talked with him again. When he died of cancer a few years later, I was sorry and sad.

I spent almost all my time at the Naval Hospital with Millard while he was there. One evening when he was greatly improved, I

was driving back to town in a hurry to a dinner party in honor of
our friend, Bishop Donald Aldrich, the Episcopal bishop of Michigan. He had been chaplain at Bainbridge Naval Training Station
near Oakington during World War II. I was late for the dinner and
was exceeding the speed limit more than a little. A siren sounded. It
was the police.

"Pull over, lady! Let's see your driver's permit." The officer looked
me over as well as my license. I was wearing a velvet coat laden with
white fox that had belonged to my stepmother. I was all gussied up
for the bishop!

The Officer: "Eleanor Tydings. You any relation to the senator,
Madam?"

Me: "I'm his wife, Officer, and I know I was exceeding the speed
limit. You see, the senator is ill at Bethesda Naval Hospital and I'm
on my way from there to a dinner Admiral Dickinson is giving for
Bishop Aldrich and I'm supposed to pick up my father, Ambassador
Davies, on the way."

It worked. The officer chuckled: "Ma'am, that's the best excuse I
ever did hear! You don't need a ticket, you need a police escort. Just
follow me." And away we went.

When Millard was still in the hospital, Daddy wrote to me from
Mar-a-Lago. "Dearest Eleanor," he wrote on March 29, 1948, "your
news that Millard was better and had his last penicillin shots gave
me great relief. I had worried about him terribly . . . I know of no
better place to recuperate than our *Sea Cloud*. Let us know when
you can join us. I was much interested in the political news you sent
(about the rising fear of the Communist threat). Of course, public
opinion is volatile. It changes very rapidly, as we have seen in the
last nine months. But the time is running short. If what I hear in this
neck of the woods from everyone is any index of the trend of opinion,
it looks to me as though opinion is crystallizing definitely along these
lines: 1. People are confused. They want to know more of what the
real trouble is, outside of propaganda. 2. They don't want war. 3.
They are for the Marshall Plan if it is not used for military purposes.
They are against it if it is necessary for that purpose. 4. They want
an administration with a will for peace instead of a will for war.
They are suspicious of military propaganda of fear. They don't want
military men to run the government. 5. The South is very sour on
the president. All in all, it seems to me that if we get by the election
this year, without actual war, there will be a chance to cool off and
get down to a practical basis for composing differences through evo-

lutionary processes, on a sane balance-of-power base, which will give the United Nations a chance to survive and continue to develop into the great organism we hope it may become. Provided it is not stifled aborning. Love from us both.''

Chapter 29

Millard's Powerful Committees: Armed Service, Atomic Energy, and Foreign Affairs

Millard was under strict orders from his doctors that he could work at his office only two hours a day a few days a week. He could do no commuting between town and country save on weekends. I did my best to hold him down, but the strict regimen didn't last long in spite of entreaties and threats. Nadine Livingston's great cooking soon began to put back the weight he had lost, and he insisted on attending the Maryland State Democratic Convention in June. He was once more named favorite son, this time for vice president on the Truman ticket. He told me that he had accepted so that he could help swing the votes of our state for Truman.

He was on the Democratic Steering Committee in the Senate and was carrying much too heavy a workload. He resigned from his position on the Appropriations Committee and substituted a place on the Foreign Relations Committee, usually a much easier job. He could not know at that time what the Foreign Relations Committee had in store for us.

There was great rejoicing when I drove Millard home to the farm in April. The woods surrounding the broad lawns were carpeted with daffodils, and the big old tulip magnolia trees were in full rosy bloom, a royal welcome for my lord of the manor. In May, my father and Marjorie took us on weekend cruises on the *Sea Cloud* and this fortunately held down our social and political activities. On the first of July, we went to the Democratic Convention in Philadelphia. Millard seemed his old vigorous, athletic self and I was happy. The

Southern delegates were all angry at President Truman because of his pro-civil rights stand. Millard knew Maryland was still ultraconservative and much opposed to civil rights, so he was caught in the middle with states' rights. I did not urge him to come out for Truman's pro civil rights position because I knew he wanted to help carry our state for the president.

The convention was great fun for me. I wrote my father and Marjorie from the Bellevue Stratford Hotel in Philadelphia:

"Senator Richard Russell offered to deliver the votes of the solid south to Millard if he would run for president. He said that Millard could win the nomination against President Truman. Millard said he would let Russell know before the convention assembled, and we discussed it pro and con. There weren't many pros. Millard doesn't want the presidency and I don't want it for him because I have been so worried over his serious illness this spring. I am afraid the campaign, if not the job, could kill him. He thanked Dick and the Southern delegates but no thanks! Nor would he be a candidate for vice president. I drew a sigh of relief. The Maryland delegation joined him in supporting Senator Alben Barkley for vice president and of course Harry Truman for president.

"The first evening in Philadelphia we went to a big party given by Perle Mesta. We did not stay late and awoke early next morning. I left Millard sleeping, to go out for a walk. The day before, on top of the hotel's big porte cochere, we had seen a huge cardboard Republican elephant. Now it was gone and I saw that workmen had already put up an enormous Democratic donkey in its place. I crossed the street to take a better look. Thanks to clever electric wiring, the elephant had swung its trunk and shot sparks from its eyes. But our donkey surpassed its rival. I was laughing so hard I had to sit down—something had short-circuited and while our donkey shook its ears and tail, the electric sparks came from the wrong end!

"This convention is more exciting than I anticipated. There was a fight between the Northern and Southern delegates over President Truman's civil rights plank in the party platform. The Southern delegates put on a big show, waved the Confederate flag, sang 'Dixie,' whooped and hollered. We took no part. I am pro-equal rights for all and so is Millard, but he doesn't want to infringe upon states rights or to force the plan on the American people. He says it will come in time.

"We have been pursued by the news reporters and radio interviewers, which was fun at first, but it became tiresome answering so many silly questions like 'Will the Senator run for President?' 'Are you going to have any more children?' and 'What will you do with them in the White House?' That last irritated me, so I responded that at least I wouldn't hang up the baby's diapers in the East Room as one president's wife had. More publicity, of course.

"I haven't told of the many messages I was given and told to relay to you. Everyone wanted to know how you are, and where you both are, etc., etc. I was so buttered up, Marjorie, over the Coloradans who thought I was Mrs. Joseph Davies!

"This convention was exciting because right up to the end, anything could happen! A radio commentator asked me in an interview what I thought of this convention. I said that I thought it was a good example of the Democratic form of government in action, when everyone had a chance to have his say and certainly everybody said it! Again all my love, Eleanor."

The children and a few of their friends spent part of August with us and my father and Marjorie at Camp Topridge. It was a happy summer for us all. Mother and my sisters came to Oakington for a long visit at Thanksgiving, and the children went with us to Mar-a-Lago for Christmas. The Democrats had won back control of the Congress in the November election, and Millard seemed his old healthy self and was looking forward to the next session of the Senate. During that session, as chairman of the committee, he would control all armed services appropriations and be in position to do a great deal to facilitate the rehabilitation of Europe.

The last tiny cloud in my sky that year was so small I didn't even recognize it. In 1947, a Republican congressman named J. Parnell Thomas had chaired a committee in the House of Representatives to investigate "un-American activities in the United States." A member of this committee was a new congressman named Richard Nixon. In 1948, Nixon became chairman of a committee emulating Thomas's tactics. Witnesses were treated like guilty defendants on trial with none of the constitutional safeguards of our courts. Nixon had gotten the message that now that Russia had the bomb and had grabbed so much of Eastern Europe, it was no longer our ally and all Communists were anathema. A number of actors and actresses came to Washington to protest the Committee's Hitlerian tactics, among them the great actress Helen Hayes.

We had paid little attention to Nixon until he began to make headlines investigating a distinguished scholar and friend of President Franklin Roosevelt named Alger Hiss. More importantly, we did not realize that a wave of hatred of the Soviet Union and all Communism here and abroad was about to sweep over the United States. A self-confessed Communist named Whittaker Chambers, formerly of *Time* magazine, testified before the Nixon committee that Hiss had passed secret government papers to him to give to Russia. I went to hear Chambers's testimony with Martha Taft and was not impressed with Mr. Chambers or Mr. Nixon. I wouldn't believe Chambers on a stack of Bibles, I told Martha. She agreed.

Nineteen forty-nine was another busy and a happy year. We did not know at that time that it was Millard's next to last year in the Senate. He wrote some amendments to the National Military Establishment bill, which he had pushed through Congress in 1948, and he helped pass the bill creating a Department of Defense. The position of a civilian secretary of defense had been created the previous year, and Millard's new bill solidified the secretary's complete authority over all military leaders and departments.

When my husband was not working on Capitol Hill, he was happily playing golf at Burning Tree Club, shooting ducks at Oakington, and generally enjoying life. He had refused to run for Democratic leader of the Senate. He was already chairman of the Democratic Steering Committee, chairman of the Armed Services Committee, and a member of both the Foreign Relations and Atomic Energy committees. He had the committees he wanted.

I was happily occupied also, still trying to bring the Washington Hospital Center into being. Elysabeth, Bessie, and I were running into unexpected opposition from original supporters on the boards of Children's and Emergency hospitals. We had been trying to settle on the location where The Hospital Center should be built. We wanted to locate it near the prestigious stretch of Massachusetts Avenue known as Embassy Row, but the Norwegian Embassy, the Papal Nuncio's residence, and neighbors of the Chief of Naval Operations residence were all bitterly opposed to locating the hospital there. The government then suggested that it be built on the Old Soldiers Home property, almost the geographical center of the city. We agreed.

On a winter day of 1947, a little group of us stood on the empty space where the great hospital center would be built, and I broke the first ground with a shovel. Bishop Dunn was there and Doctors Worth Daniels and Jarman and all the other wonderful friends representing the three hospitals—Emergency, Episcopal, and Garfield. It was cold and windy but we were all so happy we didn't notice it.

It was the beginning of the realization of a long-awaited, long-worked-for dream. It would one day be one of our country's greatest hospitals.

My father was almost free of his duties as unofficial presidential adviser, and his health was much improved. He frequently played golf and poker, and enjoyed acquiring new clients for his law firm. Millard was happy playing occasional golf and making speeches on and off the Senate floor in support of U.S. aid for the war-devastated countries. In anticipation of the 1950 election, we began attending more political affairs in Maryland, although the media pundits declared Millard a shoo-in for reelection. They said that nobody could beat Tydings in Maryland. Our son, Joe, was playing football and lacrosse at the University of Maryland and was elected president of the student body, the first freshman ever to be so honored. I considered this a good omen! His opponent was a lad named Kefauver and there were large "Tydings for President" signs on the Maryland campus.

One night after a strenuous football practice, my son and several of his teammates decided to visit the kitchen at Tregaron. Clad in dirty blue jeans and sweatshirts, these young giants looked like thugs as they approached the back entrance of Tregaron, across the driveway from the dacha where Daddy was holding his weekly poker game with President Truman, Chief Justice Vinson, and a few chosen pals. He had instructed the servants that his grandson and friends were to be allowed to "raid the house icebox" any evening before midnight. But the Secret Service had not been so informed, and so on this night, as they approached the house, a dozen armed agents sprang out from the bushes and the astonished football players found guns against their chests. Fortunately, a butler carrying a tray of refreshments emerged from the house at that minute. He dropped the tray in horror and cried, "Don't shoot, boys! For god's sake, don't shoot! It's the ambassador's grandson!" Of course they didn't, but Joe and his friends were pretty shook up!

That spring, Marjorie gave a dinner at Tregaron for the foreign minister of France. I remember vividly the deep emotion exhibited by the French minister when he expressed his joy over the creation and apparent success of the United Nations and the membership of his country in that body. There were tears in his eyes when he told me that it was the crowning happiness of his life that now there would be peace on earth.

The Davies-Tydings family were all well and happy except for my dear sister Rahel. After having borne a little daughter and waiting patiently for several years for her husband's return from the war in the Pacific, Rahel finally got her husband, General Fitch, back from Japan. He had been Adjutant General on MacArthur's staff, living in luxury in Tokyo in a handsome residence with a retinue of servants and a pretty Japanese lady! Even when General Marshall offered to fly my sister there to be with him, her husband cabled her not to come. He had not been back very long when Rahel found, to her grief, that he truly was "the meanest man in the United States Army." This was his reputation among his fellow officers. He was sadistic in his treatment of my sister, her little girl, Suzanne Walker, and his own baby girl, Jennifer.

My mother and I were very worried over Rahel's unhappiness. I told my father and Marjorie about it, and they sent young Suzanne to boarding school in Switzerland. They also invited Rahel and me to go to Paris with them in June to see Marjorie's daughter Eleanor de Bekessey. Millard urged me to go and promised to join us later. The four of us sailed on the *Queen Mary.*

Rahel and I had a good time in Paris. We were installed in a luxurious suite at The Ritz and were provided with a chauffeur and our own limousine. Also, my father gave us new wardrobes from the best Parisian dressmakers. There were many parties, among them one at the famous restaurant Maxim's. We were wearing our newest evening gowns. Rahel's was much too tight in the bodice and it took the combined efforts of Marjorie's personal maid and myself to get her into it. Both of our gowns were elaborate big-skirted organza creations, and Rahel's was trimmed with flying feather birds! As I descended the stairs to the entrance of The Ritz, I glanced back over my shoulder to see my sister catch her heel on the top step and come flying through the air into the arms of two astonished gentlemen. Fortunately, Rahel was wearing a new white fox cape, for the bodice of her gown had popped open! She was obliged to sit all evening bundled in fur in the middle of June (there was no air-conditioning) while the rest of the party danced. She dearly loved to dance. The place was packed with notables, among them the young Agha Khan. It was too crowded to dance much, which was no great comfort to her.

Millard arrived in Paris in time to attend a most interesting and beautiful party. It was a special gala celebrating the opening of Marie Antoinette's little theater near her "Petit Trianon" at Versailles, which had been completely restored. It was a most memorable occasion. The little theater could accommodate only a small number and invitations were much sought after by the haut monde. We were met upon arrival that evening by footmen in satin knee breeches and white wigs who were carrying torches. After the ballet, refreshments were served from a small Grecian temple.

When Millard and Daddy returned to Washington, my husband insisted that I stay on in France with my stepmother. Rahel went to pick up her child in Switzerland, and return home. Marjorie, her daughter Eleanor, and I went on a motor trip through the chateau country of the Touraine. It seemed to me that Paris and the chateau country showed few signs of the German occupation. The shops in Paris were just as fascinating as before the war. We were guests at lunch at two beautiful old chateaus near Paris, one belonging to a descendant of the Marquis de LaFayette, and one where a beautiful room housed the library of Marie Antoinette. We had tea at another larger chateau called Vaux-le-Vicomte, which had been occupied by General Goring during the war. The owner told us she had lived in the attic and run the household for him. This chateau had acres and acres of the finest, most extensive gardens in France, laid out before those of Versailles by King Louis XIV's secretary of the treasury. The king was so impressed with the grandeur that he decided his minister was appropriating too much of the nation's wealth for himself. The king ended his minister's career and his life! The monarch then had the man who designed the minister's gardens at Vaux-le-Vicomte create the great gardens of Versailles.

One day we lunched with a friend of mine, Mr. Carvallo, at his chateau in Loire River country. It also had fabulous gardens, including vegetable gardens laid out like flower beds. I had met Monsieur Carvallo in Washington and had arranged for him to lecture and show slides of his chateau gardens at both the Sulgrave Club and the University of Maryland. I believe he had inherited a mustard fortune from Pennsylvania, but maybe it was running out!

Before we returned home, my father joined us in London and we attended another interesting dinner and reception given by the lord chancellor and Lady Jowett at their splendid apartment in the House of Commons. The Davieses were the guests of honor. We also went to a Buckingham Palace party and to tea at the country home of Salisbury, the great portrait painter, who had painted a wonderful one of my husband the year before, when he was in London. The artist had a beautiful wife and two daughters whom he had painted many times when they were small children. So he had learned to paint portraits very rapidly and had done the one of my husband and one of me in only two or three sittings. The original of Millard's is in my home. The one in the Maryland House of Delegates is a copy.

We spent the rest of the summer at Oakington, and the children sailed all around the bay. When they went back to school, we had more political parties. Our friends Ralph and Betty Hines came to visit during duck-shooting season, and we stayed with them in Southampton to shoot pheasants. My husband enjoyed the shooting; I enjoyed the people and the parties. Little El's debut ball was to be in 1950, and Marjorie and I were busy planning for it.

Then suddenly in October, the Communist threat intruded into our happy lives. In China, Chiang Kai-shek's army was defeated by the Communist Mao Tse-tung, and Chiang Kai-shek escaped to Taiwan. Madam Chiang was from the wealthy Soong family, and when China fell, her brothers, who were ambassadors and bankers, left China with the many millions they had gleaned from the Chinese people. Millard had seen their magnificent homes with hordes of servants when he was in China.

Chapter 30

Millard's Campaign, 1949–1950

Those wonderfully happy, exciting years of my forties rolled along all too swiftly. Of course I thought they would go on forever! I was intelligent enough to appreciate them. Was I spoiled? Of course I was! There was nothing I didn't have. Fortunately, I had inherited a good health, and life had brought me nothing but love and good fortune. I told my husband that if I died suddenly, I had no complaints to make! I had already had everything in life that anyone could ever wish for. He told me he felt the same way! It did not occur to me then that all this happiness and good fortune could not go on forever. My golden spoon had been pretty good up to date and nobody lives a life free of sadness and trouble.

Millard and I had discussed his retirement from public office many times. We had painted happy pictures of all the pleasant trips and activities we could enjoy. The all-important decision to run for reelection came when he was given a place on the Senate Foreign Relations Committee. His trips to all the war-torn countries and to the atom bomb test at Bikini had made him the expert on the subject of war torn countries. His passion in life was his determination to achieve his world disarmament plan and he thought he had achieved a position of sufficient power to do so. Even had this not been so, he would have probably been forced to run for reelection by the vicious attacks that became known as McCarthyism. So the "mills of the gods" ground on! We didn't know they would grind us up too!

Those first few months of 1950 I was beginning to step up the number of my speaking engagements around the state in preparation for the election campaign. We were getting such good reports of how much the ladies liked them—and me—that I was encouraged to go on with my speech format. From an Annapolis (Maryland) newspaper, *The Evening Capital*, on May 19:

Mrs. Tydings A Guest at Club Installation

"Maryland women are more intelligent and better informed than the women of many states," Mrs. Millard E. Tydings told members of the Severn Town Club last night at Carvel Hall. The charming wife of the state's senior senator was guest speaker. . . .

Mrs. Tydings said that today more than ever before in history, and in this country more than anywhere else in the world, responsibility has fallen to the women.

Mrs. Tydings said women must see to it that the people who represent them in the federal, state, and local governments are wise enough to steer the ship.

She urged the club members to read and listen carefully, sift facts, and demand the truth.

She said that when her husband became a member of the joint congressional Atomic Energy Committee, she started reading on the subject "in self-defense." The bombs dropped on Hiroshima and Nagasaki, she said, were "just kindergarten attempts."

Mrs. Tydings stated that while the U.S. is spending 13.5 billion dollars on its armed forces, Russia, according to intelligence sources, is spending what would be equivalent to 60 billion dollars. Russia, she continued, has 100 divisions ready for action and another 100 in reserve; this country has less than ten.

Apparently, I had done my homework!

Joseph McCarthy was just another rude newcomer in the Senate and no one paid any attention to him until he made his February 9 speech in Wheeling, West Virginia. Even then, I never mentioned him in letters to the Davieses. They had hosted one last gay dinner dance for us and our friends at Tregaron and then sailed off on a cruise ship around South America. In a letter I wrote them, I enclosed clippings:

The front-page headline of the *Washington Post*, February 1, read:

Bomb After H May End All, Tydings Says

In a Senate speech Senator Tydings says that new scientific weapons may turn the road of life into a Highway of Death. His speech came shortly after President Truman again rejected Tydings' proposals for a "dramatic" United States move such as a face to face meeting of the Russian and Western heads of state to discuss "world disarmament under international inspection."

The *New York Times* headline read: New Bid To Russia Urged By Tydings.

Neither Millard, nor I, nor anyone saw any storm clouds on the political horizon of his career. Quite the contrary. My husband was a leader in the U.S. Senate, conceded by the press to be one of its most brilliant and able members, beloved by Marylanders, and known and admired all over our country. His inspection trips abroad as chairman of the Armed Services Committee had made him almost as well known in our allied countries as at home in America.

Our major concern was Millard's disarmament resolution in the Senate. The time may not have been right in 1946, but it was certainly more so by 1950. In 1949, Russia exploded her first atom bomb. When Congress convened in 1950, Millard was again appealing to the president to call a disarmament conference with the leaders of Russia and our allies. "If Russia would not agree to disarmament under international inspection, then we must certainly increase our own armed forces," he said.

Still the president and Secretary Acheson argued against it. The Russian acquisition of the A-bomb, however, had awakened most of the citizens of the United States. It had also given them nightmares!

Millard Tydings had led the move to put Truman on the Democratic ticket in place of Henry Wallace at the Democratic Convention in 1944. They had always been friends. The press praised Millard's resolution as a wise and brilliant plan to bring about world disarmament under international supervision. So did General Eisenhower (who later changed his mind) and General Romulo of the United Nations (who did not) and many other brilliant and distinguished men, Republican and Democratic alike, at home and abroad.

Senator Tydings's eloquent speeches were ignored by the White House until the president sent a message to Senator Arthur Vandenberg, the president of the Senate, to kill the bill.

At that time, I thought that our countrymen's fears might turn them to the national leadership of Senator Tydings. In Washington, he was considered a leading candidate for the presidency and virtually unbeatable in the 1950 Maryland Senate election. By an ironic turn of fate, after having been named by the news media as one of the best U.S. senators, Millard's career would be ended by a man who had been voted by the press as "the worst senator on Capitol Hill!" He had been elected to the Senate in 1946, strangely enough in the state of Wisconsin, where I was born. His name was Joseph McCarthy.

Besides the columns in the *New York Times* and Washington papers, Millard was getting lots of time and attention on the radio and in the Southern, Western, and New England press. On February 13, 1950, I wrote to my father. "Secretary of State Acheson answered Millard with a statement that you couldn't deal with the Russians at all except by *force*! Of course, Millard's proposal takes care of that too. Millard says if the Russians won't play ball, then let's get ready, America! There is just no alternative except to sit and wait for the A-bomb war. I pray Millard's proposal works out."

A letter February 18, 1950, to my father:

> Time, events, and Millard march on! This past Thursday he cut loose again with another major speech on the Senate floor urging a disarmament conference. This time he wrote it so that the press boys had it in ample time. His mail has been flooded with support for his plan. After he had delivered the speech, many senators stood up and offered him their congratulations and support.
>
> Millard is working at a terrific pace. Constant problems keep coming up before his three big committees. The *Baltimore Sun* has written a fine editorial about him. We think the times are moving toward disarmament peace negotiations. There is no alternative except to sit and wait for incineration!

What were the decisions that were Senator Tydings's responsibility as senior member and chairman of the three powerful Senate committees on foreign relations, the bomb, and armed services? He was the only expert on all three to serve on all three. The war had left destruction and shattered governments all over the world. The United States had survived virtually unscathed and was the only creditor nation on earth. It was a total change in world conditions. It was up to the United States to finance reconstruction and to help rebuild the shattered economies abroad.

Millard was working to keep up our military defenses, to fulfill obligations of the Marshall Plan, the North Atlantic Treaty, the new-born United Nations, and to bring about world disarmament. He had to decide upon the H-bomb and protect the many military air and naval installations and bases he had secured for Maryland. All of these problems were his when he was obliged to chair a Senate subcommittee investigating Senator Joseph McCarthy's charges of "card-carrying communists in the State Department, known to the Secretary of State (Dean Acheson)."

The psychological climate in the United States at this time had changed to one of doubt and fear. We had won World War II, invented the atom bomb, and for a short time we were smug and comfortable citizens of the strongest country in the world. Russia had been our ally in the war and many of our people had worked hard for Russian war relief. Then Russia gobbled up half of Germany and all of Middle Europe. Worst of all, she had her own A-bomb! She was no longer an ally but a potential and fearsome adversary. Our people had hoped for peace and a reduction in taxes. They did not want to face a rise in defense expenditures!

There have been periodic waves of mass hysteria in the world throughout history. Bernard Baruch gave us a book entitled *Extraordinary Popular Delusions or the Madness of Crowds* by Charles Mackay. There was the "Mississippi bubble," "The Tulip Craze" (when Europeans paid thousand of dollars for a Dutch tulip bulb), the "Florida Boom," and many others. The Nixon-McCarthy period was another such. Perfectly intelligent people swallowed their words as gospel and destroyed the careers of many fine men, both in and out of government. One of these was that of Senator Millard Tydings of Maryland.

Millard and I, and most of Washington, had been concerned preeminently since 1946 with his speeches on world disarmament. It never occurred to anyone that McCarthy's wild statements in February 1950, in West Virginia, could have the slightest effect upon the Maryland elections. The press boys and the smart money were betting heavily that nobody could defeat Tydings for reelection.

Chapter 31

A Clown Who Challenged a Hero: The Story of Joseph L. McCarthy

I first heard of the new senator from Wisconsin when my husband voiced scathing criticism of him. This was surprising as Millard rarely, if ever, criticized a colleague. When asked, his harshest comment would be: "Oh, he's all right, but you'll never catch him out in front of the trenches!" Of course, when McCarthy first arrived in the Senate, neither Millard nor I knew much about his past history or how he had arrived as a member of "the greatest legislative body in the world," the so-called "most exclusive gentlemen's club!" He certainly didn't belong in it and became its most controversial member, feared and eventually ostracized.

At first glance, Joseph McCarthy would seem to be an example of the old American prescription for success. He had "pulled himself up by his bootstraps." Although his methods of achievement were highly unethical, immoral, and often illegal, he deserves credit for grit and drive. Born into a large Irish-American family, he watched his parents struggle to support it. Leaving school and home, he worked as a clerk in a nearby town until he was twenty years old. He then went back to high school and managed to graduate in a year by cramming. He went through college the same way, learning to be a hail-fellow-well-met and a platform speaker on the way.

A lawyer named Eberlein befriended him when he was studying law and took him into his office. Mr. Eberlein confided to his protégé that his lifelong ambition had been to be elected judge of the circuit court. McCarthy went about allegedly campaigning for his boss. However, the day after the latter filed for the office, McCarthy did likewise, and McCarthy, not Eberlein, was elected judge. He was on his way. As a judge he pushed cases through speedily and was accused of selling "quickie divorces" over the counter to anyone.

The Korean War came along, and Judge McCarthy wrote a letter on his judicial stationery to the Marine Corps. He said he wished to join the Corps, if not as an officer, then as a private. He announced publicly that he *was* enlisting as the latter, and it made for great popularity.

Of course, the Marine Corps made the judge a lieutenant in intelligence at once and he was never a buck private as advertised. They sent him out to the Pacific where he never came within battle range of the enemy. Realizing the importance of flying missions on his record, he begged rides in the tail-gunner's seat of planes, which were only going on reconnaissance flights. On these trips, he happily fired many rounds of ammunition at a totally nonexistent enemy! He had himself photographed in the plane and sent the pictures home to the local papers. He used them in his campaign for the U.S. Senate when he returned home. The desired impression was that of a brave soldier who had flown many missions to fight the enemy! He also exhibited a pronounced limp in one leg, which he claimed carried twenty pounds of shrapnel. For this the Marine Corps awarded him the Purple Heart, after his election to the Senate. Actually, the only injury he sustained during the war was a sprained ankle when he was thrown into the ship's swimming pool crossing the equator.

He returned home to his judgeship, a self-proclaimed war hero, and called himself "Tail-gunner Joe." He never relinquished his job as a judge when running for the Senate, but kept his salary and used his judicial stationery! The Wisconsin Bar Association protested this to the State Supreme Court. The Wisconsin Constitution made it illegal to run for one public office while holding another one. Judge McCarthy defeated the incumbent senator, Bob LaFollette Jr., a fine man of an illustrious Wisconsin political family. Senator LaFollette committed suicide because of McCarthy's vicious attacks. McCarthy used the old technique of destroying his opponent with lies and mudslinging, which had elected Richard Nixon to Congress and the Senate and, eventually, to the presidency.

Senator Tydings's battles with Senator McCarthy in the Senate began in 1949 with the Armed Services Unification bill. McCarthy had violently opposed it. He felt it might injure the power and prestige of his beloved Marine Corps and proposed many amendments, none of which passed.

There was also a fight on the Senate floor when Senator McCarthy moved for the impeachment of Mr. Francis Matthews, the Secretary of the Armed Forces. The Secretary had ruled against the Navy (and Marines) in a matter of Navy carrier planes versus Air Force long-range bombers. Admiral Denfield, testifying before my husband's committee, actually accused Secretary Matthews of plotting to wipe out the Navy and the Marine Corps! McCarthy backed Denfield and ran full tilt into a fight with Senator Tydings. McCarthy lost this one too.

The senator from Wisconsin's stand on the Malmedy Massacre investigation (also before my husband's committee) was the worst of all. In 1944, a German SS battalion took 150 American soldiers prisoner and proceeded to machine-gun them to death. After the war, forty-three German officers responsible for the Malmedy murders were sentenced to death. There was an outcry in Germany against the trial and the sentence, and from many Americans of German descent in Wisconsin. Senator McCarthy daily denounced the Senate Committee investigating the Malmedy affair and viciously attacked its chairman. Senator Hunt of Wyoming resigned and Senator Baldwin of Connecticut retired from the Senate, disgusted by McCarthy's despicable tactics. So the senator from Wisconsin won the Malmedy fight and so did the enemies of our country. Later, it came to light that one of McCarthy's assistants was a pro-Nazi.

The first time I saw him was in the supper club of the Shoreham Hotel soon after his election. We were guests at a party given by Mr. Glenn Martin, the great airplane manufacturer of Baltimore, in honor of his mother. As we trailed through the tables, I saw a newspaper friend sitting with a man I had never seen before. As I passed their table, this stranger jumped up and threw his arms around me and hugged! I was amazed and annoyed.

"So you are Millard's wife!" he bellowed. "I am one of your husband's greatest admirers and I hope to see a lot of you!" I disengaged myself and walked on, thankful that my husband did not see him. Millard would have taken a very dim view of this greeting.

One of Senator McCarthy's first unsavory activities in the Senate was a matter of public housing. He succeeded in becoming a member of a subcommittee investigating the need for it, and maneuvered a friend into chairmanship of the House committee involved. The sum of $37,500,000 was given by the Reconstruction Finance Corporation to manufacturers in Milwaukee and Ohio of cheap, prefabricated houses. One of the companies was Lustron. The president of it lived in one of his own prefabricated houses, built of such flimsy material that it promptly burned down. That was the end of any public housing appropriation in Congress. Senator McCarthy was paid $10,000 by one company for a booklet on housing, and he received $20,000 from the other, besides "party and whiskey" money on the side! The R.F.C.'s $37,500,000 quickly evaporated.

The Wisconsin senator was popular with most newspaper reporters. He was always good at providing a story for them, usually in time to go to press for the next edition, and popular because of his backslapping and picking up the tab for drinks and food. He also picked up (financial and political) support from Colonel Robert McCormick, owner of the *Chicago-Tribune*, and from such radio right-wingers as Gerald K. Smith and Fulton Lewis Jr.

According to columnist Jack Anderson, Senator McCarthy was looking for a big issue that he might possibly ride even so far as the White House. Early in January 1950 he met with three powerful and intelligent friends—an executive of the Foreign Service School of Georgetown University; a professor of political science at Georgetown; and a republican lawyer. At this meeting the possible issue of "Communism in government" was discussed.

President Truman had initiated a loyalty oath for all government employees, and Secretary of State James Byrnes had listed possible security risks in the State Department. Of these, only 57 were still there. All these had been first investigated and exonerated by the FBI and then by four separate congressional committees under Republican chairmen. Congressman Jonkman, Republican chairman of the most recent committee, had reported: "If there is any branch of the government that is completely free of Communism, it is the State Department!" Senator McCarthy decided to put his staff to work digging out the old files on these cases, just in case!

On February 9, 1950, Senator Joseph McCarthy addressed a gathering of Republican women in Wheeling, West Virginia, and made headlines in papers all over the country. Said he, "I have in my hand a list of 205 card-carrying communists in the U.S. State Department known to Secretary of State Acheson!" The Senate demanded to know where McCarthy got this information. He ranted and shouted for hours on the Senate floor but refused to give it. The publicity forced the Senate to vote for an investigation and the Foreign Affairs Committee appointed a subcommittee chaired by Senator Tydings. When Millard told me this, I was very disturbed. He already had too many heavy responsibilities. He had asked to exchange his membership on the Appropriations Committee for one on the Foreign Relations Committee. As a member of the latter, he would have less seniority and hence carry less of a load. However, as chairman of the Armed Services Committee, he still had to supervise the appropriations for all the armed services. Besides that, he had been made chairman of the Democratic Steering Committee in the Senate.

I remonstrated. My husband patiently explained that the chairman of Foreign Affairs, Senator Tom Connally, was old and ill in the hospital; and Senator Green, the next ranking member, was over ninety. Millard was the next in line. If he didn't do it, he told me, "a lot of innocent people are going to be crucified. McCarthy is a vicious demagogue and an unscrupulous liar." I stopped arguing with him. Perhaps I would have gone on had I any idea that my husband would be one of the crucified.

Chapter 32

The Tydings Committee Hearings and Little El Debutante, 1950

March 8 was the first day of Millard's Foreign Relations subcommittee hearings investigating McCarthy's charges. I wrote to my father:

> Millard says, "If only Big Joe were here! He is missing all the fun!" As in truth, you are. I am sending you a batch of clippings about the first two days of Millard's Foreign Relations Committee hearings. It is quite a theatrical production, with press reporters and photographers in the big caucus room of the Senate office building. Of course I have been there both days, perched on a big chair reserved for me behind the committee table.
>
> Brian McMahon of Connecticut and Theodore Green of Rhode Island are the other Democrats on the subcommittee, and Cabot Lodge of Massachusetts and Bourke Hikenlouper of Iowa are the Republicans. Millard is a great chairman. He looks so handsome and distinguished in contrast to Senator McCarthy! I am so proud of him, my senator!
>
> McCarthy made a late entrance both days to testify and talked to the press and posed for their photographers. I don't like his looks at all. He is blue-jowled and unkempt, and always looks as though he needed a bath and a shave. Emily Lodge and I were highly amused because he adopted a Napoleonic pose for the photographers (hand over heart), but his hand kept creeping up to scratch his armpit.
>
> Millard didn't let him start off but took the play away from him. He asked McCarthy for the names of the State Department employees whom McCarthy had accused but identified only by case numbers. McCarthy ducked the answer to that and to the chairman's question as to whether he knew the names. McCarthy's trick is to avoid any answers and just constantly bellow accusations of Communist traitors in the

State Department and of a "whitewash" by the Democrats on the committee. He couldn't—or wouldn't—answer Millard's questions. Millard says McCarthy hasn't read his own cases.

Herbert Elliston (editor of the *Washington Post*) wrote a fine editorial and told me that Millard was doing a great job and that he heard nothing but paeans of praise for him on all sides.

Emily Lodge sat beside me the first day and she kept repeating comments about how brilliant Millard is and what a stupid oaf McCarthy is, while her husband (Cabot) was trying to defend the Wisconsin senator! At Millard's second committee hearing, there were even more spectators, all the top press boys and socialites. It was a battle between Millard and McCarthy—of dignity on Millard's part and shouting on McCarthy's! The magazine polls all say Millard is the best-dressed senator and he is living up to his reputation. This is in such sharp contrast to McCarthy. The senator from Wisconsin always looks as though he had slept in his clothes.

On March 15, I wrote to Marjorie:

Millard's subcommittee hearings have been packed with press and spectators for two days. It is apparently considered a "great show," a battle between two senators—of wit on Millard's part and of vituperative bombast on McCarthy's. He railed against communists in the State Department and the attempted whitewash of the charges by Chairman Tydings and the Democrats.

Yesterday, I lunched in the Senate dining room with Martha Taft and the wife of one of the great atomic scientists and also one of the town's nicest (if less intelligent) grande dames. It was most amusing with the grande dame making the funniest remarks about McCarthy, Martha Taft defending him, and the scientist's wife denouncing him. I let them talk. I didn't!

The Guggenheims, just back from their South Carolina plantation, gave a party for Mitzi Sims. Bob G. was telling stories and said: "Oh, for the good old days when Red was a color and Hiss was a sound!"

And Millard told this one. "What is the shortest route from Baltimore to Washington?" "Go to Harvard and turn left!"

The comedian George Jessel told Millard that he gets the biggest laughs in his show with this one: He (Jessel) introduces a pretty girl in his act, saying: "This young lady is the prettiest, smartest girl in all of Iowa, and that is the real McCoy, folks, not the McCarthy!" But I like this one even better: An old lady is overheard saying, "But if Senator Tydings knows that Senator McCarthy is a Communist, why doesn't the senator put him out of the State Department?"

Claire Boothe Luce was to be the speaker at the Women's Congressional Club at the end of April and I was pressed into doing
her introduction, much against my will. I was not one of the lady's
admirers! Millard looked at me suspiciously when I told him. He
made me promise to give her "a proper introduction" and I promised reluctantly. I had planned something witty with some subtle
cracks. However, I behaved and kept my promise. I gave the lady a
nice introduction and sat down feeling quite virtuous, but became
irritated when she started her talk with a nasty remark about it.
"Whenever anyone introduces me with such complimentary remarks, as Mrs. Tydings has, I know they do not tell the truth," she
said. I spent the time she was speaking composing my final remarks
after her talk, not complimentary at all. However, I didn't have to
demolish her, she demolished herself. Her entire talk was a bitter
criticism of the members of the Congress, the husbands of her audience! Millard laughed over that, which was a blessing, for the poor
man had enough troubles investigating McCarthy's charges.

The Senate subcommittee hearings were a contest between the
cool brilliance of the chairman and the bellowing stupidity of the
senator from Wisconsin. I invited family and friends to attend many
hearings and to lunch at the Capitol. Millard played his role splendidly as "star of the production" and McCarthy was the loud-
mouthed buffoon. But he was no fool. He was playing a role with a
certain amount of success, which was becoming apparent with the
daily newspaper accounts of his lies and accusations.

He was in the headlines daily and thousands of Americans believed every word he said and were sending him money to help him
fight his battle against Communists in the government. It was not a
moment too soon. The Wisconsin senator was in bad financial trouble with his hometown bank. A real estate lobbyist friend had signed
a note for $75,000, which McCarthy had borrowed. The lobbyist re-
fused to pay it and McCarthy couldn't. Enough money apparently
poured in from his admirers for him to hire a staff of assistants as
"investigators" and to pay off his debts! The man in charge of this
group was named Don Surine. He had been a former employee of
the FBI and was fired for his connection with white slave traffic in
Baltimore! Senator McCarthy was now making thousands of dollars
speaking to groups of concerned citizens all over the country. He
was even being paid to appear at private parties! He had certainly
"struck it rich!" He had found a popular issue and the Republicans
were embracing him as their white-haired boy.

The rich and powerful "China lobby" in Washington also poured money into McCarthy's pockets and then into the Maryland election campaign against Millard. This was a group hired to promote more financial aid from our government to General Chiang Kai-shek. It represented Nationalist China and the enormously rich family of Madame Chiang, the Soongs.

Senator McCarthy had been testifying before Millard's committee when I chanced to overhear an exchange between him and Senator Taft. I was partially hidden from them in the crowd, behind a pillar. Taft was clapping McCarthy on the back and telling him to "keep on throwing mud at Tydings, maybe some of it will stick!" He didn't know he was overheard. I never did like Bob Taft, now I despised him.

Chairman Tydings interrogated McCarthy persistently on the names and identities of the accused. McCarthy hedged, roared, and refused to give any names. Of course, he could be sued for libel if he named them anywhere save on the Senate floor. After several days, he named Judge Dorothy Kenyon of New York. She had never been in the State Department. Next, he named four others he called "pro-communists." One was Owen Lattimore, a distinguished professor of international relations at Johns Hopkins University in Baltimore. He had never been in the State Department either. McCarthy then named John Stuart Service. As a foreign service officer of the U.S. stationed in Calcutta, India, he had never been in the State Department either!

Senator Tydings continued to press McCarthy for the names of the rest of his hundred or more "cases." Finally, at the end of March, the senator from Wisconsin said that he would telescope all of his charges into one against a single man, Owen Lattimore, who had been "the boss of Alger Hiss at the State Department!" McCarthy even asserted that four Russian spies had landed on the American coast and had gone to Lattimore for orders! "It is all in the State Department loyalty files of the FBI," he said, "and this committee can subpoena them anytime!"

Millard had been trying to get the president to release the files to the committee but Truman held back too long. When the committee was finally given the FBI files, Senator McCarthy shouted that they had been rifled of all pertinent material by the government! When J. Edgar Hoover, the chief of the FBI, eventually denied all McCarthy's charges that files had been rifled and that no State Department men had ever been found to be Communists by the FBI, the publicity had been very bad against my husband. The news-reading public was beginning to believe that Millard was whitewashing traitors in the government and doing so in the Senate Committee Hearings. The Republicans began to recognize that the wild man from Wisconsin might have blundered upon a successful ploy against the Democrats. They began to "rally round." After all, they had been out of power in the government for eighteen years!

A vivid picture in my memory is one of Senator McCarthy slouched in his seat beside the committee, looking unshaven and unshorn as ever, his cotton socks drooping around his hairy ankles. From time to time he would reach into his pocket, pull out what looked like a medicine bottle, and take a long swig of a brown liquid medicine—for his war wounds he would say. It was whiskey, and in the end it killed him.

Meanwhile my husband voted on the Senate floor for the draft and, over Republican opposition, a billion dollar global arms aid bill for our North Atlantic Treaty allies—Greece, Turkey, Israel, and North Korea. "We will never again have the luxury of time to prepare while our allies hold the enemy," he said.

The Democratic counsel for Millard's investigating committee, Mr. Edward Morgan, had tracked down the information about McCarthy's eighty-one cases, which had all been exonerated by congressional committees with Republican majorities. McCarthy never gave their names or his alleged information about them to Millard's committee.

My husband was worried over McCarthy's continued attacks upon the Democrats and upon himself as chief target. They were being published nationwide. The right-wing Republican newsmen were broadcasting them on the radio. Millard was unable to fight back because of his position as chairman of the investigating committee. By the first of May, he was attempting to close the hearings for lack of evidence to back up McCarthy's charges. The Republican members of his subcommittee would not agree. So my husband went to his friend, Sam Rayburn, the Speaker of the House. He wanted some help from Congress to counter McCarthy's charges or he wanted to turn the charges over to a bipartisan committee. The speaker passed the word and some Congressmen did speak up but not very effectively. My husband's mail was increasingly critical of him and "pro McCarthy." He then conferred with Senator Scott Lucas, the Democratic leader of the Senate. On May 3, the two of them and seven other Senate Democrats put on a brilliant show of combined oratory, attacking McCarthy. It was a splendid display of forensic fireworks! I sat in the Senate gallery and, along with the rest of the crowd of spectators, I thoroughly enjoyed it. Millard and his Democratic warriors demolished McCarthy and showed him up for the unprincipled liar he was. The galleries cheered and the press played it up well, but that was only one day's news! We were encouraged that not one Republican senator rose that day to speak on McCarthy's behalf.

The next day was my son's birthday and we celebrated at a party my mother gave for him that evening. Joe said Millard's Senate speeches had been a great birthday present for him! Millard finally persuaded the president and the Justice and State Departments to let his committee have the FBI files. He spent long hot days and nights that summer in Washington, studying the thousands of pages. He was determined to put an end to his subcommittee.

On July 19, he called a meeting of the full Foreign Relations Committee of the Senate. He told me that it was a battle royal but eventually he persuaded the senators to put an end to the subcommittee. No evidence whatever had been produced of McCarthy's charges. The committee voted to "transmit" the matter to the full Senate, which terminated Millard's subcommittee in full. As chairman, he would give the Senate his report.

He had read the thousands of pages of the FBI reports. The members of his subcommittee had read some of them, but none of them had read them all. My husband was the happiest man in Maryland when he told me that evening that at last he was free of the strains and frustrations of the subcommittee. We danced around the big hall at Oakington and broke out a bottle of champagne.

I had sat proudly in the Senate gallery that day listening to Millard's report to the Senate, happy in the conviction that no one could see or hear him and not realize what a liar and charlatan McCarthy was! The columnist Marquis Childs wrote that my husband's speech "was a masterpiece of analysis and denunciation. Senator Tydings's imitation of McCarthy shouting charges which had all been disproved and the Marylander's theatrical and magnificent prose were worthy of the Barrymores at their best." Millard brought a small Victrola to the Senate floor with a record of McCarthy's own voice uttering statements that he later denied having made. It was said to be one of the greatest orations ever delivered in the United States Senate. He concluded that McCarthy had perpetrated a fraud and a hoax on the American people and he "left it up to the consciences of the United States Senate" as to what they were going to do about it. William S. White of the *New York Times* wrote a great piece under the headline "Tydings Charges McCarthy Perjured Himself." Newspapers all over the country praised his speech. No Republican senator rose to defend McCarthy. We rejoiced and celebrated at Oakington with another bottle of champagne!

That spring my daughter was graduated from Garrison Forest School. My stepmother and I had long planned her debut ball at Christmas on December 27 at the Mayflower Hotel. It was to be the biggest and the best! (Of course, my stepmother and Daddy would give the party.) Mrs. Dwight Davis was giving a dinner party for young people in Eleanor's honor before the ball and the Davieses were going to give a dinner of 100 of our mutual friends at the Mayflower in honor of the Tydings's wedding anniversary.

We had engaged the entire first floor of the hotel beyond the Connecticut Avenue lobby. The long hall was to be decorated with giant poinsettia plants down its length and the ballroom with big Christmas trees. Meyer Davis's full twenty-piece orchestra with Meyer himself would play there. Across the hall a smaller room was to have a Cuban rumba band. We would receive in the Chinese Room adjoining the ballroom.

Of course, the news of this party was bound to leak out and it was widely reported in the papers and on the front page of the *New York Times* with Little El's photograph.

Chapter 33

The Dirtiest Political Election
Campaign in History

I wrote to Marjorie at the end of July:

"The deadline for filing for the Democratic primary has finally come and gone, to our great relief. Only three democrats filed to oppose Millard for the Senate; nobody ever heard of two of them and the third is a nonentity. We have to go to a big political powwow in Southern Maryland on the thirteenth, so maybe we can both come to camp after that.

"I have just spent two sizzling hot days in Washington with Mrs. Hetzel (social secretary for debutante parties) about the Mayflower ball for Little El, at Christmas. I also saw two florists about it. It will be a most gorgeous party and all our friends are talking about it. Millard and I went to two political meetings and a funeral in the two days I was in town. He feels much cheerier and now thinks he can get away on August 17 to come up to camp. I will bring all lists and data re the debut ball when I come up. Joe and El and her beau, Sam, are working on the sailboat (as usual) and I can hear the three of them laughing! They are going to spend the weekend at the Walker's place, Webley, on the Eastern shore, doing sailing races and regatta parties. I can't tell you how happy I am to have the primary worry off Millard's shoulders, and now he can have a wonderful rest at Topridge!"

A letter to my mother reported:

"Everything looks up! Yesterday I spoke to over a 100 women at the luncheon meeting of a suburban Baltimore Women's Club. As usual, my talk was nonpartisan, 'Life in the National Capital'—every other word about Senator Tydings! I described my first view of the

315

Capitol when I was little, and that Millard Tydings has defended what it stands for. It was the biggest success of any talk I have made. They clapped and clapped! Everyone came up to me to say they were all for Millard. I will use the same talk at all the other Maryland Women's Clubs—Western Maryland, Central Maryland, Southern Maryland, the Eastern shore, and Baltimore City. Joe drove Millard to Southern Maryland today and just phoned that the meeting with several hundred tobacco farmers was a great success.

You asked about our Joe—he is in the organized reserves, which are subject to call before the regular reserves. He is in the Airborne Infantry. I hope and pray he will not be called up."

The first serious political warning to me came in mid-May when my old friend, Ralph Hines, telephoned from the Eastern shore where he and his wife, Betty, were weekending with friends. He wanted to see Millard at once and came to Oakington alone on Sunday. We were entertaining the members of the Senate at lunch that day. Ralph was very upset. He and Millard spent the afternoon alone while Ralph reported the disaffection he had found among the Eastern shore friends of ours who had been taken in by McCarthy's lies. Millard was tired and retired early. Ralph and I talked until midnight, reminiscing about our youthful love affair. He told me again what a blow it had been to find I was going to marry Tom Cheesborough. Ralph had not married until after the war. He had been in the navy then and was very happily married now to Betty Pirie, sister-in-law of Governor Adlai Stevenson. I tried to reassure Ralph that Millard was sure of being reelected, but I was pretty shaken up over his report. He departed the next day, and ten days later we went to his funeral in New York! He had fainted on the stairs of their New York house and fallen backward, striking his head on the marble floor. It was a blow to us both for Millard was fond of Ralph too.

On August 1, we opened Tydings headquarters in Baltimore and Millard's campaign started officially, although it seemed to me that it had been under way for a long time. By the eleventh of August, the campaign was in full swing and Millard could not go to Topridge with me. I stayed for only a few days, and then went back to Maryland. When I was at Topridge, Marjorie told me how my father had been able to help our mutual friend, General Eisenhower, to make a fortune on the book of his memoirs. Ike had told Daddy that he had been offered about $200,000 for it by a New York publisher. My father had told him it was too little and went himself to New York to see Simon and Schuster, the publishers of *Mission to Moscow*. They paid Ike a $1 million for his book, and Joseph Davies got him another fortune from its syndication in newspapers. The stories of Mamie's wealth were far from accurate, and the General had no private means, so this was a most fortunate circumstance for them.

Ike was a strange man. Later, after the Davieses' divorce, he never came near Daddy when my father was old and ill. President Eisenhower played golf while my father's funeral services were being held at the Washington National Cathedral. Ike never spoke to me either, after I had been chairman of Governor Stevenson's campaign for the presidency in Maryland. Politics makes enemies more often than bedfellows, I think, although there certainly never was the faintest possibility of the latter where Adlai and I were concerned!

When I went to Camp Topridge, the prospects looked fairly good for Millard's reelection. When I returned home, in less than a week, there had been a distinct change in the Maryland political climate. Senator McCarthy and company had been busy. I wrote to my father on August 19:

"Forgive scrawl! I have just written 500 notes longhand to every woman in my files in Maryland asking them to listen to Millard's opening broadcast of the campaign (both radio and TV). His August 31 TV-radio speech was wonderful. It was about his conduct of the subcommittee investigating Commies in the State Department. J. Edgar Hoover had finally endorsed Millard and stated that the FBI files on these people had been "raped." We have an ad in next Sunday's paper from 600 leading lawyers in Maryland endorsing Millard. He will be on TV-radio next on his armed preparedness record and the bad record of the Republicans. McCarthy has actually voted against every appropriation for military preparedness for us or the countries of the free world! Most of the Republican senators voted against aid for Korea the very week before the fighting broke out, and they have the gall now to criticize the Democrats for not voting for more aid!

"McCarthy talks on the air Thursday, and on Friday Millard broadcasts a question-and-answer program. The Catholic War Veterans were to have sponsored one of his talks but have reneged! Isn't it too bad that our dear friend Catholic Archbishop Curley of Maryland isn't alive?

"Millard has been so chained to Capitol Hill that he hasn't been able to go out on the stump. We hope that he may be able to get away after Labor Day for a rest. Joe is driving him all over the state. I think we can still win, but the lies, half-truths, and brickbats from the Butler (Republican candidate) crowd are unbelievable! Many of Millard's old friends and supporters have been taken in. We opened Tydings Headquarters in Baltimore Monday. Millard has sent out 5,000 letters about his Thursday broadcast. Joe is writing 500 of his university pals. As president of the statewide Young Democrats, he has organized groups in every county. He has one boy in the hospital with a broken leg helping him to write notes. I pray Millard's health will hold out.

"Last night I spoke at a rally in Baltimore. Today I go to Prince George's County for a big meeting, and tonight to one in Montgomery County. Tomorrow I have all our Harford County women Democrats at Oakington. They are going to be precinct workers and motor corps. This is a sample! My hand is so swollen I can't write anymore. All these letters could have been typed, but our advisers think longhand is more effective. I think the counties are with Millard, but Baltimore is our weak point. Most of the labor unions are unfriendly and our Tydings Republicans are being seduced by McCarthy's lies."

My father replied to this with a warning that it would not be wise to let anyone outside the family know that I was concerned about the election.

There is nothing like the loaded wagon in the political game," he advised. "Some weak-kneed friends and supporters are apt to run for cover. The work that you have done, and are doing, is most effective and I am sure that it will tell in the result. Moreover, the seeds of goodwill, friendship, and democratic spirit, and the friends you have made over the past years all over the state, will bear fruit.

"The outstanding fact is that Millard's stature in the national field and, in fact, in the international situation, is stronger than it has ever been before. There are very few men in the country who have the public acceptance he has, being the great national and international figure that he is. That will be a matter of pride, and is a matter of pride, when it comes down to cases for the people of Maryland.

"I am very, very proud, not only of Millard, but of you and Joe for standing up to this situation. Go over the ramparts confident of victory and with your swords gleaming. Millard always does that. It will win. You are a very fortunate woman, my dear. You can well be proud of your little family. I take the greatest pride in them, and in one of the finest wives and mothers in the world—you, my first-born."

As the campaign continued, I wrote again to Daddy on September 9:

"Millard joins me in gratitude to you both for your generous campaign contribution. It was a grand present and cheered us up a lot. I enclose our first big ad in the *Baltimore Sun* papers. I have organized a Women's Committee for Tydings with an office in our Baltimore headquarters at the Emerson Hotel and I have sent out four thousand letters to women all over the state, many of them written longhand. I am dated up for talks all over Maryland."

At the same time, I wrote to thank Marjorie:

"Campaigns are so expensive and this one is a real beast. I think it is actually worse than 1938! Then we were only "tools of Wall Street" and "princes of privilege." Now we are "red Commies" and "Truman's rubber stamp." It is a desperate attempt by the Republicans to get rid of one of the most powerful Democrats in the Senate by slander and mudslinging! I should think our erstwhile Republican friends would be ashamed of themselves. Maybe it is the power of evil itself manifested in this man McCarthy and his henchmen.

"Today I was guest of honor at a big Democratic meeting in Aberdeen. All the Harford County candidates were there and all spoke for Millard. We have a Tydings booth at the county fair Wednesday through Saturday. Mac and Violet McLean and all our county pals are running it. The booth has a six-foot photo of Millard (the one that was on the cover of the news magazine), flag and bunting, garden decorations, and free Coca-Cola for all who register for Tydings! It is really fun and an experience and education for our young Joe!"

We were greatly encouraged when Millard won the primary election in September by a handsome majority and we were encouraged, in spite of some of the outrageous tales being told about us by the Republicans. These upset my husband more than they did me. As long as I had him, my parents, and my children, nothing could really hurt me, but he was angry and hurt. The stories were that I wanted to be the vice president's wife, or the chief justice's wife, or an ambassadress, and so my husband was "doing the president's dirty work hiding communists in government." Our friends, and even our enemies, knew these things were not true, and if the dear constituents didn't know that, they didn't deserve to have a wonderful man like Millard Tydings for their senator!

Maryland Republicans had nominated a little-known Baltimore lawyer named John Marshall Butler for the Senate. This gentleman had never run for office or distinguished himself in any way. Senator McCarthy did most of his campaigning for him. More important, the senator had secured the financial support of three of the largest fortunes in the U.S. for Mr. Butler. Two were Texas oil billionaires and one was a Pennsylvania tycoon. They spent a fortune against us. Millard spent $75,000, the largest sum by far he had ever spent in a campaign. In one of his past reelections he had had no opponent from either party!

In October, a letter to my father read in part:

"Today we had a great ad in the papers: 'Could a new Senator do this?' List of Tydings's achievements for Maryland. Among them facsimiles of two letters to Senator Tydings from the president of the B&O and the president of the Longshoremen's Union thanking Millard for blocking the St. Lawrence Seaway Project, which would have ruined the Port of Baltimore. I still think Millard will win. McCarthy is coming to Maryland to speak against him on Thursday.

"El is so excited over all the debut balls being given in Baltimore and Washington almost every night. Of course, she is thrilled over the splendid one you and Marjorie are giving for her at the Mayflower Hotel on our wedding anniversary. I am too. It is dear of you to be giving the big dinner in our honor that evening."

On October 4 I wrote to Daddy:

"I wasn't able to attend the Democratic Convention when Senator Tydings's and Governor Lane's nominations were certified because I was the speaker at a big Women's Club in Baltimore. They say Millard made a ripsnorting speech, which I was sorry to miss. He is hoping the party rift over the gubernatorial fight between Governor Preston Lane and George Mahoney is somewhat smoothed over and that Governor Lane will have a fighting chance of winning. The governor is so unpopular because he instigated the sales tax in Maryland. I like him and find him attractive, but apparently the voters don't! Being on the ticket with him doesn't help Millard any. He knew the governor would be defeated and Millard tried to persuade him *not* to run."

I wrote to thank Marjorie for inviting Little El to go on a European trip with her granddaughter "Whizz" (Marjorie Durant) and Lady Connie Lewis as chaperone:

"Eleanor's letters from Paris and Venice are ecstatic! She loves being with 'Whizz'. Jim and Ellen Bruce have rooms reserved for you and Daddy and Millard and me at the Belvedere the night of the Baltimore debutante cotillion in December. El is also going to Charleston, S.C., for the historic St. Cecilia Ball as guest of dear Judge 'Uncle Dick' Whaley. She should be thoroughly 'out' in society after you give the ball for her in Washington this Christmas and we give the fancy dress dance at Oakington for her next June! I am glad she is going to Charleston because her Cheesborough ancestors are buried there in St. Michael's churchyard.

"Did Daddy tell you about what the president did to Jim Bruce? He was our ambassador to Brazil and then about to be appointed our ambassador to France when the president gave it to his brother David instead! Then Jim was appointed ambassador to Great Britain, and the British had formally accepted, and their baggage sent over, when Truman reneged a second time. Millard went to see the president about it and actually accused him of breaking his word! The president admitted it but said the secretary of state wouldn't hear of two brothers (Jim and David) having the two big neighboring and most desirable diplomatic posts (France and England). The president said he was sorry. He should have been. Jim Bruce actually raised the money in New York, at Millard's request, for Truman to go on TV-radio the last two weeks of his presidential campaign. There were no funds available at the time."

I wrote a letter to Marjorie in late October:

"My El is all a-twit over the wonderful European trip you gave her and her prospective debut ball in Washington in December. She says all Baltimore parties for that evening have been canceled and the kids there and in D.C. are counting the days till your party! We are concerned over the bad turn of the fighting in Korea, with the Chinese troops attacking ours. The veep called off his big dinner for the president and Millard and Daddy think the ball may have to be called off. Millard talked to General Collins (Army Chief of Staff), who is just back from Korea, and he said, 'Don't call it off! There will be sharp fighting but no massacre, nor any Dunkirk!' I fear that there might be criticism from partisan press and politicians.

I am still trotting around Maryland, flattering the ladies and kissing the babies. It is fun, but I am getting tired and will be glad when it is over. Last week I drove into Baltimore to talk to a big club of ladies who couldn't have been nicer, caught the 5:15 train to Western Maryland and arrived at 11:45 p.m. A nice doctor met me and drove me to his home to spend the night. There was a crowd of people there to greet me and it was 1:30 in the morning when I got to bed. The doctor and his family lived in a square, porch-girdled house with only one bathroom with no lock. The mother-in-law and a large family of children lived there too. I spent a somewhat tense morning in my room trying periodically to make it to the bathroom and usually walking in on someone—the last attempt on the doctor himself, enthroned! That discouraged further efforts on my part until mother-in-law appeared and chaperoned me to the bath!

"Made two speeches out there and back to Baltimore to make another talk. Yesterday, I had the Democratic candidates' wives and the Democratic National Committeewoman and lady members of the legislature for lunch at Oakington. No souvenirs removed save one silver salt spoon, so I figure we came out of that fairly well! I hope it does some good for the cause! If Millard doesn't make it in November, it won't be my fault!"

Senator McCarthy was also making money speaking to groups of concerned citizens all over the country. He was even being paid to appear at private parties. He had found a fabulously popular issue and the Republicans were embracing him as their white-haired boy. Contributions continued to pour into McCarthy's office whenever he attacked Millard as a pro-Communist traitor. Although most of the news reporters and columnists realized what a liar McCarthy was and despised him, they had to print any sensational charges made by a senator. Thousands of Americans hated Communism, read McCarthy's attacks on Tydings, and believed them.

McCarthy did even more damage to Millard by mailing out a pamphlet accusing Millard of shielding communists in the State Department. The pamphlet featured a composite photograph of Senator Tydings with his arm around the leader of the American Communist Party, Earl Browder. Millard had never even met Browder. McCarthy had used a photo of Millard with his arm around my shoulders, cut me out, and replaced me with Browder. The effect, of course, was one of intimacy between the two men. It was delivered the day before the election!

I did not think many Marylanders would believe these lies, but the effect of the pamphlet was compounded by the fact that Millard was on the ticket with an unpopular governor who had raised taxes. After the war, most state governments had to raise money by sales taxes and the governors of all who did so were defeated. These reasons were enough to greatly cut into the vote total for Tydings. Then, too, our old friend, Archbishop Curley of Maryland, had died and there was a new Catholic Archbishop in Maryland whom we didn't know very well. This prelate was in Rome as it was Holy Year. He told Millard afterward that he would have supported his candidacy had he not been out of the country. Many of Millard's other older friends and supporters had died, as well. Then too President Truman was most unpopular at the time because of the Korean War, which had made many people resentful of him and the government. After we became involved in this most unpopular war, Millard had introduced a $1 billion Global Aid bill for our allies on June 25, and the Extension of the Draft the very next day. He had also expedited the shipment of supplies to our army, but McCarthy made speeches all over the country saying Millard had shipped nothing but baling wire.

Some weeks before election day, my husband told me that he was not going to be reelected. I couldn't believe it and argued with him. He was perfectly calm and collected, but loving and consoling. He put his arms around me. "Don't feel badly, darling. I am telling you now because I didn't want it to come as a shock as well as a disappointment to you. You know, I really am tired of my Senate job. We have talked about when I would retire and we could do all those things we have wanted to do and never had time for. Now we don't have to make the decision ourselves, the constituents will do it for us!" He was smiling. "I know the signs so well and my friends from every part of the state have passed the word along. Don't cry, Treasure! We're going to enjoy our life and our love together!"

I was crying with sheer rage, but I dried my tears and hugged him and assured him my tears were just because I was so mad at McCarthy and Butler and all the stupid people in Maryland! Then I took the dogs and went for a long walk along our bay shore at Bar Point where Swan Creek joins the Chesapeake. I wrestled with myself all the way and sat down on the stump of a long-dead chestnut tree and wept. I couldn't bear to have my wonderful husband so betrayed and deserted by his beloved Marylanders. He had fought on and off the battlefields of France and in Washington for them and for their interests all his life. When I had finally mentally destroyed McCarthy and all the rest of those horrible people, I calmed down and came to terms with the change in our lives. After all, none of the important things had changed. Millard and I had each other, and the children, and Oakington, and my darling mother and sisters, and Daddy and Marjorie. But I stayed mad at Maryland for a long time!

Election night was worse than I had anticipated. It was no surprise that Millard was not reelected. He could have been defeated by a much larger margin considering all of the outrageous, illegal, and disgusting campaigns against him, most of which we knew nothing about at that time. Only later did it all come out when a Senate committee investigating it brought it to light and condemned it. We were prepared for a decisive victory by the Republican candidate, John Butler, but his victory speech on the radio was insulting and truly sickening. We had our old friends Mac and Violet McLean for dinner that evening and Mac drove us in to Baltimore headquarters to hear the returns. At about 10:00 Millard went on the air to concede the election and made a (for me, heartbreaking) brief, beautiful talk. He thanked the people of Maryland for their support for so many years and congratulated the winner. It was a beautiful, gracious speech, never mentioning the dirty campaign or criticizing Butler, but wishing him well. It was a great little "hail and farewell" and there wasn't a dry eye among those present. I was more proud of him than ever!

Mac was driving us home when Millard turned on the radio and we listened to the lowest of the campaign's low blows. We listened to Butler deliver a monstrous, despicable diatribe against Millard Tydings, accusing him of disloyalty to his country! It was a vicious, inexcusable attack upon a defeated candidate. We could hardly believe our ears and rode in silence for a few minutes. I was so shocked with pain and rage that I could barely manage to control myself. Then suddenly, my husband gave a sharp command. "Stop the car, Mac! Pull off the road!" Our friend quickly obeyed.

"What's the matter, Senator?" he asked anxiously.

"Didn't you hear that crash off the back of the car?" my husband asked. None of us had heard a thing. Our friends looked at him blankly, but I thought I caught the glimmer of a twinkle in Millard's blue eyes. "That was the load of thirty-some years falling off my back!" he said with a grin.

The McLeans laughed, but I couldn't. That night he held me in his arms until I cried myself to sleep, but he never even gave the slightest sign of hurt or disappointment.

The only indication of the deep pain he must have experienced came on a Caribbean cruise that my generous stepmother insisted upon giving us in December. I realized too late that it was a mistake. People recognized Millard and stared at us, and we knew they were talking about us. On this trip, I realized how much and how bitterly my husband was suffering from the wicked campaign and defeat of 1950. Doubtless, also, he was feeling the intense fatigue from the long, hot summer he had spent in D.C. reading the thousands of pages of FBI reports of the McCarthy "cases" of "Communists in the State Department." My husband withdrew completely inside himself behind a wall that I could not breach.

Part VII

Chapter 34

Life after the Senate

1951 to 1954: Millard begins a lucrative career as a lawyer; my father has surgery for cancer; the 1952 convention; the Davieses' separation; Eleanor Jr. marries Francis Warrington Gillet.

When we returned from the Caribbean we had closed the door upon 1950 and we were busy with our new lives. Perhaps I had not lost my golden spoon after all! Millard and I had each other, the children, Oakington, my parents, my sisters, our friends, and Marjorie.

Our Little El was a college student and a budding concert pianist. She was presented at the Baltimore Cotillion by Ambassador James Bruce and at the St. Cecilia Ball in Charleston, South Carolina, by Uncle Dick Whaley, the chief justice of the Court of Appeals. My mother introduced her to the elder generation at a beautiful reception at the Sulgrave Club, and her grandfather and Marjorie gave a dance for her at Christmas at the Chevy Chase Club.

Sadly, our war in Korea had taken a turn for the worse just before the 1950 election, and Daddy and Millard had ruled against the spectacular ball that Marjorie and I had planned for my daughter for so long. Instead, the Davieses gave a smaller dance for my daughter at the Chevy Chase Club, the guests limited to debutantes and young men in uniform. Telegrams to that effect were sent to all on the original guest list.

We had given up our apartment at the Wardman Park and rented as our Washington residence a beautiful house owned by dear friends, Colonel and Mrs. William Ritchie. It overlooked Rock Creek Park near Mother's house on Kalorama Road.

Millard joined my father's prestigious Washington law firm and immersed himself in making a good deal of money for the first time in his life. He was also a member of his Baltimore law firm and allocated all Maryland clients to it. His Washington clients included many foreign governments. Among these, of course, was the Philippines, whose new freedom was the result of Millard's efforts. Because of his reputation, the prince regent of Iraq asked for Millard's assistance in getting rid of the British domination of Iraqi oil. Millard was very excited over this and made many trips back and forth to Iraq. It all came to naught, however, because the Prince Regent and the royal family were all murdered during the Iraqi revolution.

Because he was so busy and often out of the city, he missed a great deal of the strain I was enduring that year because of the Senate investigation of the Maryland senatorial election. The wives of the committee members and the investigating staff members themselves were constantly bringing me news of what the committee was discovering about the outrageous campaign tactics of Senators Butler and McCarthy. It would have been much easier if I had lived miles away from Washington and could have metaphorically crawled into a hole and forgotten about the whole thing. The Senate committee, chaired by our friend Senator Mike Monroney, unanimously condemned Mr. Butler's campaign as a dirty backstreet affair. If such a campaign were allowed to be repeated, the committee report said, it would "do more to undermine our form of government than anything else." Butler had broken the laws of Maryland by naming an out-of-state campaign chairman—Jon Jonkel, one of colonel McCormick's boys from Illinois, who was later fined and sent to jail—and for accepting out-of-state campaign contributions. Mr. Butler was a lawyer and he broke the laws of his state.

One story that came out during the committee investigation was about a Baltimore printer who was given a contract of many thousands of dollars to print and mail Butler campaign material. When his bill was not paid, he appealed to Mr. Butler. The latter wrote the printer a letter guaranteeing that he would be paid in full, if necessary by Butler himself. The candidate signed it. It was against Maryland law for a candidate to spend more than $3,000 on his campaign out of his own pocket. When Senator McCarthy found out about Butler's letter, he immediately dispatched his man, Don Surine, and another of his goons to recover it. These men kidnaped the printer and by strong-arm tactics, tried to force him to give up his letter. The printer, however, had given the letter to his lawyer! Senator McCarthy's men had to let him go home at daybreak, bruised and battered. He was not the only person kidnaped and threatened by McCarthy's men. The previous year during Millard's subcommittee investigation, Senator McCarthy's men had a room in the basement of the Senate office building where some of the committees witnesses were taken and browbeaten to prevent their testimony.

All of these stories kept my resentment and bitterness at a white heat. The effort of presenting a cool, controlled, and smiling front to my family and friends brought me an agonizing case of shingles, and I itched miserably until spring took us home to Oakington.

In March 1951, my newly wealthy husband took me to a New York boat show, where he realized his lifelong ambition and bought a beautiful forty-five-foot motor yacht. He named it *Elona*—"Iona" being Spanish for wild duck, and "El" for me. We had great fun in it, cruising our beautiful Chesapeake.

Then in April, my father, my daughter, and I sailed for Europe on the *Liberte*. Marjorie had urged him to arrange for Eleanor to be presented at the first court that King George and Queen Elizabeth were holding since before World War II. Marjorie was going to be visiting her daughter in Paris, and Millard was busy commuting to Iraq. I had not realized until this trip how much my father's health had deteriorated. He was a very ill man and like all very sick people, his disposition had become more irascible and short-tempered, as we saw on this trip. When we arrived in London, Daddy told me that all was not well between him and Marjorie. He had forbidden her daughter, Eleanor, to visit in his home in Washington. He considered her multiple marriages a disgrace to the family. At this point, she was divorcing her fifth husband and about to take on her sixth. He said that he and Marjorie had had a very serious quarrel but that there was no question of their divorce. They would go on with the appearance of marriage, but would go their separate ways! I was sad about this, but I couldn't believe it was anything but a temporary problem. I told him he was wrong to forbid her child to visit Tregaron.

We celebrated my birthday onboard ship with many lovely gifts from Dad, Eleanor, and Marjorie. In a letter thanking her for flowers and boxes of lingerie, I reported how amusing it was to watch my father eat out of my child's hand! "She can even disagree with him and stand her ground without any thunder and lighting!" Marjorie's old friend, the Duchess de Chaulnes, was on board. Her story was a sad one. She was a charming American heiress who had met the young French Duke, fallen in love, and married him. After the wedding, they went to Paris and he promptly deserted her for the young mistress he had wanted to marry! Although heir to one of the great titles of France, he was dissipated and quite unbalanced. He and his girlfriend were found dead in a love nest. But "Toosie" de Chaulnes had his son and remained in France. The son was a skinny young man with a heroic record in the French Underground in World War II.

On May 6, I wrote Marjorie again from the old Mansion House of the mayor of Cardiff, Wales, where Dad, Eleanor, and I were installed like visiting royalty:

"I am a dead duck after the past five days of gaiety visiting the Garretts (Ambassador George and Ethel) in Dublin. There was a banquet at the Angel Hotel the night we arrived here in Cardiff. Dad had forgotten about it and we had already eaten dinner on the train. We had to wade through umpteen courses and sat through seven speakers, including Dad. They called on me and I had to rise and shine! I was so tired my head was aching and goodness knows what I said. Today the mayor is giving a lunch party at the mansion and tomorrow afternoon I must address several hundred women. Tomorrow night there is another banquet where Dad is to speak. When we return to London next day, we are in a whirl of parties ending up with luncheon at Chequers with Prime Minister and Mrs. Attlee before taking off for Lisbon."

I wrote next to Marjorie from Lisbon:

"It was an interesting experience our last day in London lunching with the Attlee's at Chequers. It was a perfect day to drive through the lovely English countryside. Chequers was much more attractive than I had expected. It is a big old brick Elizabethan house with a formal walled terrace, marvelous bay windows, and potted chimneys. The Attlees were very nice and showed us all the treasures of the old house. There is a magnificent library of ancient books, Cromwell's sword, slippers, and life mask, and the ring Queen Elizabeth I gave the lover whom she beheaded! We saw the bedroom Dad slept in, and the room where Prime Minister Churchill slept and where they talked all night together. We were served a delicious lunch by five uniformed WAVEs. It was all very pleasant and interesting. Dad was in great form and he and the prime minister swapped stories.

> The Prime Minister: A man died and applied to St. Peter for admission to Heaven.
> St. Peter: Who are you, sir?
> Man: A psychiatrist.
> St. Peter: Come right in, dear chap, we certainly need you here. The Almighty thinks he's General Eisenhower!

"While in London, my daughter had been presented to King George VI and Queen Elizabeth. It was an afternoon affair. Eleanor looked ravishing in "changeable" blue taffeta, ankle-length, with little puffed sleeves. She wore a most becoming little white feather hat with a tiny white aigrette. I wore blue lace and a small blue hat with gray paradise feathers. Eleanor was instructed on how to make her curtsy to their Majesties and told not to smile at them. You might as well tell the sun not to shine, I thought! I was taken to a bleacher arrangement of benches around the throne room and seated with the British milords and miladies. The reason I was the only American besides the ambassador's wife so honored was that an old friend who was Queen Elizabeth's Equerry escorted me there. I couldn't see my daughter's face when she curtsied but I could see the king beam (the only time), and I knew my Eleanor's dimples were flashing and her blue eyes sparkling. The Queen smiled at her too and the Britishers on my bleacher bench wanted to know who was that beautiful child. I told them!"

Back home in June, Millard and I gave a costume dance for Joe and Eleanor at Oakington. On the invitations, Eleanor called it a "Gone with the Wind" party. We had a dance pavilion set up on the bay lawn, indirect lighting on terrace and garden and wisteria arbor. The clock was turned back to Civil War times that night. Baltimore and Washington costumers completely ran out of young men's Confederate uniforms! The Cheesborough cousins came up from Carolina and we had a house party of young people. Friends in the county entertained us at dinner before the dance and my children had a dinner for the young people at Oakington. We had the best orchestra in Baltimore. Eleanor was a dream in pale yellow taffeta, off the shoulder, with a hoop skirt and fichu of her great-grandmother's lace. Joe was handsome in his Scottish kilt tartan, jacket, and sporran. I wore blue organdy with a bustle, and Millard was the perfect antebellum Southern gentleman in pale gray frock coat and lace ruffles! Several of our friends came from Washington and Baltimore and the home county. Of course, Millard's sisters and mine and their husbands were there. My father wasn't well enough to come and Marjorie was still in Paris. We had left him in Europe the month before, and I knew he expected to join Marjorie there. I learned later that she had refused to see him. It was hard for me to believe. They had been so much in love with each other for so many years!

In August 1951, Senator William Benton introduced a ten-point resolution to impeach Senator McCarthy. "He has no friends and is certainly not a member of this club of the United States Senate," said Senator Benton. Some of the ten points were: 1. Perjury before the Tydings Committee; 2. Accepting $10,000 from Lustron; 3. Calling General George Marshall a traitor to his country; 4. Illegal action in Maryland campaign against Millard Tydings; 5. Deliberate misuse of FBI files; 6. False accusations re: Malmedy Massacre; 7. Keeping a man charged with perjury in his employ.

Senator McCarthy was courting the daughter of a senator who told Daddy that she had disliked and feared McCarthy so much that she wouldn't see him. McCarthy had told her: "I'll end up either in the White House or in jail!" *Life* magazine had an editorial against McCarthy, but by that time he was chairman of his own subcommittee investigating Communism in government and was flying high. Eighty-five senators had voted to approve the creation of this subcommittee and only one senator, William Fulbright, voted against it. The eighty-five were afraid of McCarthy. One-third of the Senate was up for reelection in 1952, and they feared that the McCarthy campaign tactics of innuendo, insinuation, libel, scandal, and suspicion, which had defeated Millard Tydings, would be used against them. In 1952, McCarthy was reelected by his constituents in Wisconsin. So mass madness in our country was still prevalent.

On December 19, 1951, since she had not told me about her separation from Daddy, I wrote to Marjorie at Mar-a-Lago:

We are going to miss being with you and Daddy very much this Christmas. Maybe next Christmas you will spend with us at Oakington. It is heavenly beautiful today—a fairyland—sheathed and glittering with ice and snow. There will be eight kids in the house for Christmas—Rahel's two, my two, and the Eagers's two (Millard's sister Kathleen Eager), and assorted pals. I am going to hang up stockings for all of them and fill them with little gifts. Lots of friends are coming for dinner Christmas Eve. We will sing hymns and carols afterward and go to midnight church. There will be 24 grown-ups at dinner. Last evening we went to a dinner the Bonnets gave at the French embassy in honor of the Veep and Janie Barkley. I sat next to Senator Wayne Morse, the left-wing Republican from Oregon. He is an admirer of Millard's. He told me that he is going out to Wisconsin to speak against Senator McCarthy and said we should too. I told him that we had been advised not to go. "Hell," said he, "you'll never defeat a political dictator by sitting at home." Maybe, but my husband had suffered enough.

Nineteen fifty-two started out happily for our family. My husband did not have to work so hard and we had more time together. He was enjoying his law practice. We all enjoyed cruising the bay on our lovely new yacht. Joe had done well at the University of Maryland and had gone to work part-time in Millard's Baltimore law firm. He had organized Young Democratic Clubs in most of the Maryland counties and doubled the number in Baltimore. We were all proud of him and of his little sister, who was at Goucher College in Baltimore and studying piano at prestigious Peabody Institute. She was a good musician.

Millard went to New York early in 1952 to try to persuade General Eisenhower who was president of Columbia to run for president of the U.S. in November on the Democratic ticket. After President Harry Truman had won the 1948 election, we both believed that Eisenhower had a good chance of becoming president in 1952. Ike and Mamie were good friends of ours, so Millard had enlisted leading Democrats, including all of the big city bosses, to support Ike. Millard told him that if he would run on the Democratic ticket he would surely be elected. My husband came home thinking Ike was going to accept his proposal. The general had said he wanted a week to think things over, but he chose to run as a Republican. Wealthy Republicans in New York had won him over.

That spring, my father went through a serious operation in New York City for that dread illness, cancer. The doctor told us we might have him only a few years at best. This was crushing news to my sisters and me. Life without Daddy was unthinkable. I refused to accept it.

As if that wasn't bad enough, the great love affair between him and Marjorie was apparently a casualty of his illness. She had told me when she sent us on the postelection cruise that life with my father was becoming increasingly difficult. His disposition was more and more disagreeable. I had remonstrated, of course, telling her that men were all poor patients when ill and that he loved her devotedly. She had not argued the point and I had thought all would be well.

My relationship with my stepmother had been friendly enough that spring. We had been to several of her dancing parties and a dinner dance to celebrate my birthday. In early June the Davieses came to Oakington for the weekend. Nothing seemed to have changed except that Daddy's health was obviously failing. In Washington, I lunched and dined alone with him more often. Toward the end of June, I was surprised, when Marjorie phoned Rahel instead of me about Father's cancer operation. She and my sisters had never been as close friends with Marjorie as I had been. I was still more surprised when she did not invite us to stay in her big apartment when we came up to New York to see Daddy in the hospital. I did not see her except when we were visiting him in the hospital. She would personally bring him his midday meal from the Colony Restaurant. She always left quickly and was equally cool to us and to father. His nurse said she was the coldest person she'd ever met. She had never before been cold to me.

While we were in New York, Rahel and I were invited to a supper party at her apartment and to a Long Island affair afterward. We went to the supper but I declined to go to Long Island. I wished to spend the evening with Daddy in the hospital. Governor Paul McNutt was indignant when I took a cab alone and was not offered one of Marjorie's fleet of limousines. He wanted to escort me but I firmly refused. Things were bad enough without making them any worse.

When my father recovered somewhat, I went home to Oakington and on July 19 Millard and I went to the Democratic Convention in Chicago. Millard was head of the delegation, as usual, as Maryland's favorite son. He was still being talked of for president or vice president.

I wrote Daddy a long letter from the Blackstone Hotel:

"When we arrived at the B&O station in Baltimore, all the Maryland delegates and alternates joined us, escorted by a parade composed of mostly flag-waving females and two live donkeys. With them was Maryland's perennial Democratic candidate, George P. Mahoney, with an armful of black-eyed Susans and a sheepish expression.

"The mayor of Baltimore, Tommy d'Alessandro, asked me if I knew that Mrs. Roosevelt had come out for Senator Kefauver night before last when she addressed the convention. He said she had received a real ovation because she was wearing a Kefauver hat! Her frizzy new hairdo had reminded the mayor of Senator Kefauver's coonskin hat!

"I have been regally ensconced at the convention in Jim Bruce's box with Mrs. Cordell Hull. Senator Kerr's wife was in the next box. We were only about two feet from the Alabama and Oklahoma delegations. I brought my biggest hat to Chicago, and *Life* magazine's photographer has made my life miserable. He picked me out to photograph before he knew who I was because of my beautiful hat, he said. I finally told him and the other photographers that if they would let me alone, I'd make a deal with them and let them photograph my daughter when she arrived.

"The entire Alabama delegation has been introduced to me by either Senator Lister Hill or Senator John Sparkman. They have made me an honorary member of it. One of them, at one point in the North-South battle, told me they had decided to nominate me for president! Aren't southerners something! No wonder I married two of them!

"The first afternoon of our arrival (Sunday) we went to a party in honor of all the candidates at the LaSalle Hotel (where the Maryland and South Carolina delegates are staying). The president of the Maryland Young Democrats told me that Joe had made a fine speech at the big rally. There was a fight over some very controversial (North versus South) amendments to the National Young Democrats constitution. Joe led the fight to table the amendments and forestall a row before the convention, and Joe won it.

"The Convention Hall was, as always, a great sight, with glowing colors, brilliant lighting, balloons and people. Two lady delegates from Oklahoma wore hats trimmed with miniature oil wells and log cabins. The Kefauver coonskin hats were everywhere.

"That morning I talked to Peg Kenney (husband John is Averill Harriman's assistant deputy administrator and they were working hard for Harriman). She was bitter against the president and Les Biffle and all those who had urged Averill to run and were running out on him to work for Stevenson. She told me about the meeting after the session was over the night before when the Young Turks fought against the Stevenson swing, when the delegates voted to seat Virginia.

"Millard and I went to a dinner party at the Blackstone, that Jim Bruce gave. It was very gay and there were lots of Democrats we knew. I was wearing a black dress and the big hat I wore to Buckingham Palace with you and Marjorie. We all danced and table-hopped. Some people from Colorado at a nearby table beckoned Millard over and asked him if I wasn't Mrs. Joseph E. Davies. Isn't that amusing? Millard said, 'No, that is my wife!' He didn't say who he was and they were wild with curiosity. Someone finally told them. The same thing happened at the convention four years ago.

"On Monday noon I had scarcely seated myself in our box when Kathleen and Paul McNutt came by. Their box was near ours. Kathleen and Mrs. Carpenter, [mother of Betty Hines (Ralph's wife) and of the ex-Mrs. Adlai Stevenson] were in a nearby box and she was going over to speak to her. So I went too and Mrs. Carpenter urged me to stay and talk to her about Betty, which I did. I was the only person with her there when Stevenson gave his address. I was completely won by his speech! It was tops, I thought, and a real literary jewel. He said most of life is education and could think of no finer or tougher education than life in the White House!

"Mrs. Carpenter said her daughter Betty Hines was coming Wednesday and invited us to a supper party at her apartment that night. I accepted for Millard and Joe and me and we went. Betty didn't come, after all, but Mrs. Adlai Stevenson was there. She is lovely looking and gave me a warm greeting. She asked if my daughter was coming and if her eldest boy could take her out. I said Eleanor Jr. would be there only Thursday and Friday and we would be at the convention.

"When El arrived, she and I dined with the Edison Dick's and a group of Adlai's close friends and supporters at a handsome club Thursday night (Millard couldn't leave the convention). It is a beautiful club on the University of Chicago campus, all Gothic architecture. (Eleanor roomed with the Dicks' daughter at Garrison Forest School). Friday morning El and I drove to the convention with Millard and some people who were hoping for a deadlock so they could push Barkley for president. That afternoon Henrietta (Mrs. Lister Hill) sat with us and we kept the vote tally and figured in advance that the end of the first ballot would be almost a dead heat—300 votes apiece for Kefauver, Russell, and Stevenson. We were right."

I continued a letter to Daddy from the Nississhim Lodge on the Brule River—Sunday, July 27:

"There was never another moment to write in Chicago, so here I am on the porch overlooking the river and it is blessedly cool. El and I flew here yesterday (Saturday) to visit Mother and Millard returned home on the train with the Maryland delegation. The last days of the convention were hectic. The battle between the North and South had raged over the loyalty pledge before we left. Senator Burnet Maybank was at first truly sunk and told me the solid south would walk out. You probably saw the Young Turks, (Michigan governor and Franklin Roosevelt Jr.), grab for power on the rostrum when they tried to force the fight over Virginia. I was disgusted. They were trounced and the convention voted to seat Virginia on Millard's motion. Then they seated the other Southern states. Millard was a leading peacemaker. North and South firebrands had been leading the two battle factions.

"Senator Kefauver begged Millard to run his fight for the presidency and offered him anything in his administration, but Millard refused. He really wanted either Barkley or Stevenson. I was for Barkley or Russell or Stevenson! When Barkley spoke on Wednesday night, I thought he would be nominated for president. Millard said he had never heard such an ovation given at a convention. It was perfectly thrilling and a marvelous crown to Senator Barkley's career. Janey Barkley looked more beautiful than ever in her life in a dark dress and big hat and an armful of roses. Barkley's speech was great.

"A highlight of the convention was Estes Kefauver's dramatic entrance with Senator Douglas (wearing his coonskin hat). They tried to interrupt the voting to give up Estes' votes to Stevenson and marched up the center aisle the full length of the hall. It is so much harder to take a blow like that if you are as tired and exhausted as Kefauver must have been. His face was worn and strained. That last night when the fight finally ended, the president and Adlai spoke early in the morning. I had an air-conditioning cold coming on and we had to wait over an hour after the nomination for the president and Adlai to arrive. It was a dreadfully long wait, but Adlai was worth it. His speech was marvelous. It electrified everyone. I haven't a doubt that he will win the election. Anyone who could write and deliver that speech is not only superlatively brilliant, but a very, very fine man! I wouldn't have missed it for anything. Warmly, Eleanor."

In the fall, El went back to Goucher College, and I agreed to become chairman of governor Stevenson's campaign in Maryland. He wrote me after Eisenhower was reelected:

"During that wet and rushed journey to Baltimore, I heard much of your gallantry in action, and was reliably informed that you were the best campaigner in the state, and certainly the most indefatigable one. I think Millard had better look to his laurels!

"I am so relieved to hear that he is mending now and I yearn to see you both under somewhat more tranquil circumstances than the last couple of visits. I shall mark well the invitation to Oakington for duck hunting another year, with children and even grandchildren!"

Daddy was going to New York every week for chemotherapy which made him miserable. Marjorie was seldom in town except for the big parties she gave. We were always included and played the public roles as well as we could. The old warm relationship between my stepmother and me had changed, and I was sad about it. Millard reminded me of his warning that if their marriage ever broke up, so would my friendship with Marjorie. She was basically a cold person, he said. Great wealth brought great power and great egotism. I had not believed him and now it was difficult to do so. I had loved her for a long time.

Ike defeated Adlai Stevenson in November. Eisenhower had been embarrassed shortly before the election, when his vice presidential nominee, Senator Nixon, was accused of having a large yearly income, or slush fund from a group of California millionaires. We heard that Ike was so angry when he heard about the slush fund that he had written Nixon a letter "accepting" his withdrawal. However, after Nixon went on television and wept and asked whether he should also give back his "little dog, Checkers," the sentimental American public rushed to support his candidacy and Ike's letter was never sent. Neighbors of the Nixons during his Senate years have informed us that they never had a dog!

Those were good years, the first half of the 1950s. Millard and I had more time together and with our children. They were growing up to be fine people, blessed with good brains, bodies, and looks! Love may have died at Tregaron but it was breaking out all over at Oakington. Both our children were eager to marry their chosen ones, but Joe had to wait until he could earn enough to support a wife. Eleanor's beau, Francis Warrington Gillet III, was a lieutenant in the U.S. Army, and he, like Eleanor, had an allowance from his parents. We announced their engagement at a dinner party at Oakington on Christmas Eve.

Millard and I commuted regularly to Washington for his law business and my hospital business. The former was booming, but the latter seemed stymied in spite of the passage of the Hospital Center bill. Some of the hospital leaders were reluctant to give up their old rat-ridden institutions (and their power over them) by submerging their individuality. Fortunately, our friend, the former Republican congressman Charles Dewey, became president of Garfield Hospital and led the Hospital Center back on track. Bessie, Elysabeth, and I worked to help him achieve this. Our social life rolled on as usual, and we dined and danced with our friends in official and unofficial Washington.

Millard was happy in his new career and so was I. The Davieses marriage seemed to be going on as usual. Marjorie was away a great deal of the time. However, when she was in Washington, we dined and danced at her parties, and I assisted at her teas and garden parties. Our relationship of twenty years might have cooled off some, but I thought the basic affection was still there, although she did not come to Oakington for weekends or for our spring Senate Sunday luncheons with Daddy.

She invited the children, Millard, and myself to spend the last half of August 1951 at Camp Topridge. My husband, my daughter, and I took our boat, *Elona*, up the East Coast and the Hudson River to Lake Champlain. We had to take our little yacht through thirteen locks between New York and Lake Champlain. El and I were the crew and manned the decks with long poles to fend off other boats and the walls of the locks. Captain Tydings sat at the controls on the flying bridge. It was great fun. Joe brought a friend to Camp and El's fiance, Warry Gillet, was also invited.

I had warned El to be careful of any lovemaking as I well knew the espionage system, whereby the activities of all guests were served up daily with Marjorie's breakfast by the longtime butler and household manager, the elderly Taylor. The children's behavior was exemplary, although there was a slight ripple when Joe and a college friend upset the sailboat with Deenie aboard.

That visit at Topridge should have warned me that the Davieses' alienation was complete. For the first time, Marjorie was obviously trying to avoid me. I was sensitive to the change, but I still couldn't quite believe the rift between my father and Marjorie. Those two people had loved each other so much, and now that he was old and suffering a terminal illness, she was cold to him. What I didn't realize was that she was older too, and more self-centered. Besides, she had arthritis!

I heard later that she was also under the evil influence of her secretary, Margaret Voight. Mrs. Voight had arrived at Topridge some years before, the wife of a German footman, who was fired during the war for his Nazi leanings. Dear old Miss Wells, who had been Marjorie's secretary for years, had retired and Marjorie was looking for someone to replace her. Mrs. Voight was acting as secretary to my father, who offered Marjorie her services. Mrs. Voight was an insignificant, little mouse of a woman whose exterior belied the burning ambition within her. She knew that as long as my father and Marjorie were together, she would never be able to exercise the control over his wife that she eventually achieved.

She told Marjorie that (a) cancer was contagious, (b) that it affected the brain, and (c) that cancer victims became homicidal! Unfortunately, Marjorie was growing more and more deaf, but she could hear Mrs. Voight and she listened to the constant daily poisonous drippings from the woman's tongue. Of course, none of us knew all this at the time. It has only been since Marjorie's death that I have been told about it by other members of her household.

The combination of my father's illness and his increasing irascibility was sad, but I had all my family together and it was our last happy summer together at Topridge.

Eleanor's choice of a husband was an extremely good-looking young man, a graduate of Texas A&M and Johns Hopkins University. Tall and dark like his handsome father, Francis Warrington Gillet Sr., of Baltimore, young Warry had been brought up by servants in a motherless household, and had been spoiled by both the domestics and his doting father. Warry Senior had been a famous ace in World War I in the Royal Flying Corp of Great Britain at the age of eighteen. He came from an old and well-known Baltimore family whose ancestry dated back to early colonial days. Upon his return from World War I, he had married one of Baltimore's great beauties, a granddaughter of old Governor Warfield, who was also the grandfather of Wallis Warfield, the duchess of Windsor. But the Gillet bride, Louise, deserted her husband and two-year-old son, Warry, Jr., and ran off with a married man from South Carolina. The ensuing divorce scandal rocked social Baltimore with a court battle over custody of little Warry. The judge gave custody to his father.

The dashing war hero was a much sought-after bachelor until long after his son married my daughter. He had two brothers as good looking as he was who were also successful in business. One of them married Governor Swann's daughter, and she warned me against the marriage of my child to Warry Jr. She, her husband, and their daughter were extremely fond of Eleanor and foresaw trouble ahead for my child. However, there is little one can do against a young person in love who has a mind of her own! We held off the marriage until Warry had graduated from college and had become a lieutenant in the Army. That was as much as we could do.

My daughter's wedding took place at Oakington on September 23, 1953, on the bay lawn with the altar in front of the old English box hedge. The wedding was planned to be outdoors like my sister Emlen's wedding at Oakington in 1939. It would be our second family wedding there. We had the same big marquee on the lawn and the same old Italian credenza chest for an altar in front of the wall of two hundred-year-old boxwood. Eleanor's wedding gown was a lovely classic white taffeta with a tight bodice and a long train. There were six bridesmaids and six ushers—all extremely good-looking young people. Everyone said my golden-blond daughter and her tall, dark-haired groom were the handsomest couple ever. Millard and I enjoyed the exaggeration and agreed. In the excitement of planning the wedding festivities, I had forgotten to buy a "mother of the bride" dress. At the last moment I found a long emerald green tulle gown and a big hat to match, which looked marvelous with my emerald necklace.

The forecast had been for rain, and the weather was as threatening as it had been for my sister's wedding. But the rain held off until after the bride and groom had departed late in the evening on their way to a Caribbean honeymoon. Warry was in Army uniform when they left, as they were to return first to his post in Columbia, South Carolina.

The ceremony was performed by the Gillet's Presbyterian pastor and by our old friend, Episcopal Bishop Donald Aldrich, who had been chaplain at the Bainbridge Naval Base during World War II. After the war, Dr. Aldrich became chaplain at Princeton University and then bishop of Michigan. We were all very fond of him. The night before the wedding, the bridegroom's father gave a big dinner for the couple at the Mt. Vernon Club in Baltimore, and there were dinner parties in their honor every night for a week. Both my parents were at the wedding, but Marjorie was in Paris with her daughter. My father was ill, but he was able to escort me down the aisle. My cousin, John Davies Stamm, said to me later: "You and Uncle Joe were great theater, Eleanor!" As J. D. later became a theatrical producer in New York City, that was praise from an expert.

Millard looked ten years younger than he had a year before as he proudly escorted our child and gave her away. I thought there never had been a more beautiful young bride and groom than our Little El and young Warry. My most vivid memories of that day were my husband escorting my lovely bridal child, and of my father, in top hat, cutaway, and gold-headed cane, escorting me across the lawn. Robert Livingston had even dressed up the dogs for the occasion. The two Chesapeake retrievers and the two Great Danes all wore big white ribbon bows.

Many distinguished guests came to Oakington from Washington, New York City, and Baltimore. My stepmother was not among them, but she sent Eleanor a handsome check. Young Senator John Kennedy was married that same day to Jacqueline Bouvier, Mrs. Hugh Auchincloss's daughter.

Later that fall, Governor Adlai Stevenson and his sons came to visit us at Oakington, which we all enjoyed. Joe took the governor's young sons to parties in Baltimore, and we had one at Oakington for us. Millard and Joe and Adlai shot ducks from our offshore blinds, and even though he had lost the election, we found the governor had not lost his wit or charm.

Ben Tydings Smith with grandfather, Senator Joe Tydings, 1988.

Eleanor T. Ditzen and Eleanor Tydings III.

Eleanor with Hillary Rodham Clinton and Tipper Gore, 1993. *White House Photo.*

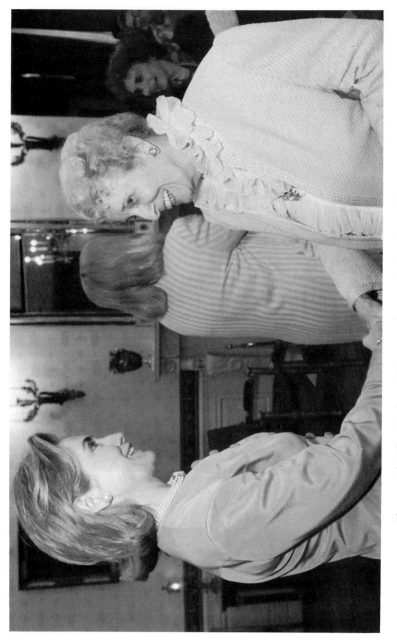

Eleanor with Hillary Rodham Clinton at a Senate Ladies luncheon. *White House Photo.*

Eleanor Schapiro takes her granddaughters for a ride at Tallyho Farm, 1992.

Eleanor Ashton Chewning winning one of many ribbons and silver cups at pony shows, 1995.

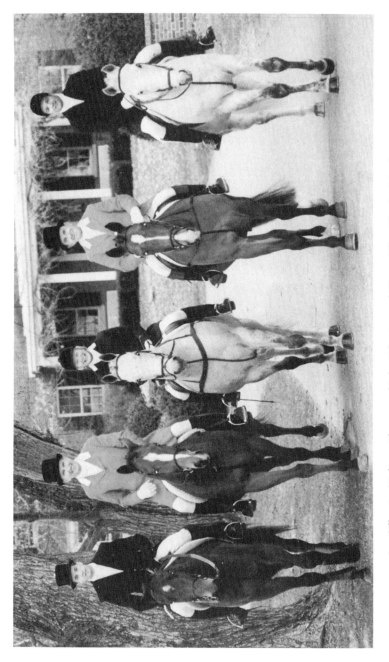

Joe Gillet, Joe Tydings, Eleanor and John Schapiro, and Warry Gillet, Thanksgiving hunt, 1992.

Senator Joe Tydings, Eleanor T. Schapiro, Suzy Gillet Chewning, Warrington Gillet, and Eleanor T. Ditzen with great-grandchildren.

Eleanor Ditzen and great-grandson William Chewney, 1995.

Group picture of Eleanor and progeny at 90th birthday party, given by her son, Joe Tydings, and daughter Eleanor and John Schapiro. Left to right, standing: William Chewning, Suzy Chewning, Warrington Gillet, Emlen Tydings, Alexandra Tydings, John Schapiro, Joe Davies Gillet, Eleanor Tydings Schapiro, Senator Joe Tydings, Mary Tydings Smith, John T. Smith, Eleanor Tydings III, Millard Tydings II, and seated in front is Eleanor Tydings with her Chewning great-grandchildren.

Eleanor Ditzen celebrates her 90th birthday at a dinner dance at the Sulgrave Club on April 27, 1994, with Dr. Richard Stoltz.

John Schapiro giving a birthday toast to Eleanor.

Senator Harry Byrd of Virginia, Eleanor Tydings, and Ambassador Douglas MacArthur.

Eleanor Tydings Schapiro with four of Eleanor Ditzen's great grandchildren. Left to right, William Chewning, Benjamin Tydings Smith, Eleanor Ashton Chewning, and Caroline Blair Chewning.

Eleanor with grandsons Joe Davies Gillet and Warrington Gillet.

Eleanor Ditzen with granddaughter Eleanor Tydings and grandson Millard.

Eleanor Schapiro, Eleanor T. Ditzen, and Senator Joe Tydings.

John T. and Mary Tydings Smith.

Senator Joe Tydings with his youngest daughter, Alexandra.

Eleanor Ditzen dances the Charleston.

Chapter 35

Millard Runs for the Senate
again in 1956

*Millard wins primary election and is stricken with encephalitis. I
replace him as a candidate for the Senate and am defeated by one
vote.*

On February 9, 1954, I was lunching with Daddy at Tregaron alone
when I was taken ill, and was taken to Emergency Hospital in an
ambulance. I was quarantined there with what the doctors diagnosed as typhoid fever. I was very ill in the hospital for several
weeks. When I was delirious with fever, they said I kept insisting
that they bring Joe McCarthy to see me so that he would catch my
germs.

In March when I recovered sufficiently to cruise down the inland
waterways on the *Elona* with Millard, I met Mother in Columbia,
S.C., and spent a few days with Eleanor. In July, the Army ordered
Warry to Frankfurt, Germany, and Little El stayed on Oakington.
There were parties and picnics and cruises on the *Elona*. After El
went to join her husband in Frankfurt, Germany, Millard and I spent
August cruising up the coast visiting friends on the way. On the way
home, we left Nantucket harbor in the teeth of a hurricane, when
bigger yachts were scurrying in for shelter. My husband and skipper,
a true son of the Chesapeake Bay, brought us to Long Island unscathed.

Then we received the sad news of the death of our friend Sue
Bryan. We had dined with her and her husband at Mt. Pleasant before we left. It was a shock to us both. We put on all the speed *Elona*
could muster and arrived home for the funeral. I missed Sue terribly
and I know Millard did too.

343

That fall, another sad event shadowed our lives when Marjorie's New York lawyer, Mr. Freeman Daniels, phoned Millard to tell him that Marjorie was going to file suit to divorce my father. Mr. Daniels thought that Millard might wish to break the news to Daddy and represent him legally. Most of that year, Millard and I had been with him at Tregaron. Marjorie had appeared only for a few social events. Daddy came to Oakington for a few weekends with close friends like Chief Justice Vinson. It should have been no surprise when she had her lawyer phone Millard. My father's reaction to the news of Marjorie's intended divorce action was a towering anger. Of course, he asked Millard to represent him in this new unpleasantness. Millard and "Matt" Daniels did their best, but it was far from easy with people whose love had turned to anger.

Once again, I was slated to be nurse, companion, and guardian for this parent as I had been for my mother in 1935 and the succeeding years. Daddy wanted Millard and me to be with him continually. I told him we would spend the winter with him and that we would like to have him with us at Oakington the rest of the time. As it turned out, we tried that winter, but it was not possible.

We moved into Tregaron to try to help Daddy. I did my best, but soon found that it was not enough! For example, my father insisted upon being served the same breakfast, lunch, and dinner every day! And he became angry when I tried to keep the domestic wheels running smoothly by employing the services of a maid for our rooms.

In spite of Marjorie's recent coolness, the divorce posed a problem for me in the matter of the close friendship that had existed for so many years between us. There was no question of where my number one love and loyalty was. I was my father's daughter. I could not be solicitous to, or intimate with, the woman who had hurt him so. Furthermore, she had not honored our friendship with any kind of a gesture or explanation or farewell. It was sad that a friendship such as ours should be totally lost, but she did not call me and I did not call her. She had so often said that I was closer to her than her own daughters, and she had been a delightful part of the happiest times of my life! I did not see her again for many years.

In March, Millard and William Castle were made honorary members of Washington Hospital Center, which was finally under construction. Millard was almost as pleased as I was that he was so honored. However, it was the least they could do for him. If it had not been for him, there might not have been a Washington Hospital Center.

Millard and I had planned a dinner dance at the Sulgrave Club in honor of my sister Rahel and her new husband, Fontaine Broun, upon their return from their honeymoon. We had hoped that my father would feel well enough to come, but it was fortunate that he did not. That evening the *Evening Star* broke the story of the Davieses' divorce. All our guests were abuzz with the news, which took the edge off the Brouns' homecoming party.

Marjorie had been moving everything out of Tregaron—the furniture, rugs, draperies, linens, and even chandeliers and cooking utensils—because my father would neither give the place to her nor sell it to her! Millard and I advised him to let her buy it, and either go to live at his club or take an apartment, but he said it was his home, and he intended to live and die there. It was nothing short of a miracle that Millard and Matt Daniels were able to hold a lid on the situation and keep the vituperation of the two people concerned under control and out of the newspapers. Long before, I had told them each separately that if they ever turned on each other, it would be an epic battle. My words had certainly been prophetic! Marjorie, however, did not invade my father's rooms—the furnishings in his bedroom suite and the dacha she left intact. Also, she left their Russian collection to be divided by Mr. Daniels and Millard. She sent a list of the things she most wanted and she received them. The great glass cabinets full of Russian china that walled the sunroom and drawing room were left almost intact.

After she had removed most of the furnishings, it fell to me and Rahel to furnish the huge house. It was evident to us that if my father was going to live there, this must be done. We persuaded him to employ a decorator to provide draperies and carpets for the big drawing room downstairs. I furnished Marjorie's upstairs bedroom suite and a guest room. The rest of the downstairs was taken care of with some of my sister Rahel's furniture, some of ours, and a few Cheesborough heirlooms I had bought when Mrs. C. died. Since Emlen lived in Germany and Rahel had a new husband and family, it was evident that I would have to supervise the running of the household. Daddy had never done so in any of his homes! It was a testimony to his normal sweetness and kindness that the best people of the Tregaron household staff wished to remain with him and not go with Marjorie. He refused to let them and told them that he could not do for them in their retirement what she could. He kept only his chauffeur and valet, and I hired a succession of cooks, maids, laundresses, and butlers for him.

The only happy result of my father's divorce was his renewed romance with my mother! Her love for and devotion to him had never ceased over the twenty years since their divorce. She was a charming, wonderful woman who had had at least one opportunity to marry again, but my father was her only love. When she heard about Marjorie's divorce plans, she became noticeably younger and more beautiful!

While my father was going through his divorce, my son was planning his marriage. Joe had told us that he and the lovely, young Virginia Campbell were engaged and that her parents approved, although she was only eighteen, so we did also. Joe was twenty-six. I gave him my Cheesborough engagement ring, which was made up of diamonds from his two great grandmothers, one the wife of a Confederate colonel in the Civil War and one the wife of my grandfather, a Union Army Colonel. This ring, sadly, was lost or stolen many years later. Their engagement was announced on May 14, 1955, at a party given by her parents, Captain and Mrs. Frederick MacGregor Campbell, at their home in Lewes, Delaware. We had met them only once when they came to Oakington for lunch and we liked them very much. She was a great golf player, very pretty and young looking. He was a big man, even taller than Millard, and I immediately thought, "He is John Ridd, in the book *Lorna Doon*! He was the son of a Scottish sea captain and the president of the Delaware Bay Pilots Association.

Three weeks later, in June 1955, Joe graduated from the University of Maryland Law School and went to work full time in Millard's Baltimore firm. Ginny also had a job in Baltimore, teaching kindergarten. They had a beautiful wedding in August on the lawn of her parents' home. It was a blistering hot day and after the ceremony and reception, the groomsmen threw Joe into a surrounding creek, clothes and all. Then they tossed each other in! My father had given Joe his wedding suit—cutaway and striped pants, made to order. We sent it to the cleaners at once and it survived its bath. My father was feeling badly, but drove with Millard and myself all the way to Lewes and back to Washington. Millard was Joe's best man, and I sat with Daddy in the front row. We both suppressed chuckles when the bridegroom knelt at the altar. There was a large hole in the sole of the bridegroom's shoe!

Bob Grosjean was managing a factory in Frankfurt, Germany, for General Foods, and I wrote Emlen weekly during that time, partly to keep her informed about daddy, and partly to blow off steam about my difficulties. By Christmas 1955, Daddy's health was worsening. I quote a letter to Emlen:

"December was a busy month for me. Eleanor and Warry are back from Europe and are settled in the guest cottage at Oakington. Their baby is due in February. Great excitement! The house looked beautiful at Christmas, but I was disappointed because Daddy wasn't well enough to come to Oakington. We offered to go in town to be with him, but he said he only wanted to be alone. He did go over to Rahel's for dinner, but I gather that was pretty much of a frost! He does not like Rahel's husband, Fontaine Broun.

"We phoned them a merry Christmas. Mother was with us and El and Warry, Joe and Ginny, and Millard's sisters on Christmas Eve. Eleanor played the piano and I my violin and we all sang carols as usual and went to St. John's Church service. I had filled stockings for everybody and hung them on the south parlor mantel. Now I am really broke!

"We gave a Christmas party to celebrate our twentieth anniversary on December 27th at Oakington. Thirty people at dinner. Rahel and Fontaine and Ginny's parents came for the party and the Charlie Gillets and Warry Senior. Lots of cocktails and champagne and dozens of roses from my husband made it all very festive! He made the most beautiful toast to me. I do wish you could have been there.

"Mother left for Florida after Christmas and we moved into Tregaron for the winter. Of course, I'll go home in February when El's baby is about to arrive. El came in for New Year's Eve at Mother's. Daddy came to family dinner, but only took soup and went home afterward. He had been to play cards at his club that afternoon, which exhausts him. I hear from the club members that it is most embarrassing because he can't remember the cards or even assemble a bridge hand. He had one of his 'heart attacks' last week. He went to the Clark Cliffords' New Year's Day party with us and fainted as we were leaving, but is planning to go to the National Women's Press Club banquet!

"The Tregaron household is a mess. First he says I am to run it, check up on and pay all bills for him. Then he says not to! I will try to stick it out as long as he needs me."

Another letter to Emlen, February 16, 1956, from Tregaron:

"You can't imagine how difficult it has been here! With Daddy discussing his death and his will endlessly! Poor Millard gets it both here and at the office. Daddy never makes a decision about anything. He sometimes talks to us about leaving everything to us three, but then tells others that (a) he is leaving it to his Scholarship Foundation of Wisconsin; (b) he is leaving it all to the National Cathedral; or somewhere else. I am about convinced that he will leave us all out of it! Dr. Daniels says loss of memory, uncontrollable temper, and unpredictable actions are common in old age. It is so tragic to see this happen to someone you love. I have struggled to keep the household here running peacefully."

I wrote to my mother in Florida:

"A week ago I came out to Oakington to await the arrival of my first grandbaby. It is almost as exciting as having my own first child! El is so happy and looking so lovely! Millard is coming out here Friday and is going up to New York on business on Sunday. He told me a week ago that he is being urged to run for the Senate by most of the Maryland Democratic leaders, but that he has definitely decided not to. Then last weekend the Kent County paper had a wonderful editorial urging him to run and a petition signed by all the bigwig Democrats of the Eastern shore urging him to do so. Then Harford County, Central and Southern Maryland papers followed suit and we were besieged with telephones and telegrams and politicians!

"Senator Butler is so discredited and unpopular that they say anybody can beat him. Millard is receiving bushels of mail and constant phone calls begging him to run. He says he doesn't want to go back to the Senate and must decide by filing day. Joe says I should try to dissuade him, that his health couldn't stand the campaigning he would have to do. He is sixty-six. I am afraid that if he ran and anything happened to him, I would be to blame! I am torn about what to do."

I wrote to Mother on February 25:

"At eight o'clock this morning our Little El became a mother, I became a grandmother, and you became a great-grand! I spent the night with her at the Havre de Grace Hospital, trying to help her until Doctor Foley took her to the delivery room. Miss Susan Eleanor Gillet arrived around eight, to be called Sue, for lovely Sue Bryan. She has dark hair and looks like the two Warry Gillets. I phoned her father who was asleep in the guest cottage. He was irritated over being awakened for an insignificant little female and said he'd go in later! I said, 'You'll get yourself out of that bed and come NOW or I'll send the Havre de Grace police after you!' He came and his father came the next day. Neither of them seemed very excited over the tiny female who looks so exactly like them!

"The evening before Millard went to New York, Joe came and we three discussed his candidacy at length, listing all the pros and cons. Millard said Joe was right; that it would mean a very strenuous, exhausting campaign fight and he definitely would not agree to run. Then when he came back from New York, he announced that he had changed his mind! He had thought about it all the way on the train. Joe objected, as did I, but he had made his own decision. He said he would beat Butler, who had so terribly smeared him."

Now I was on the campaign trail again. I organized a Women's Committee for Tydings, with a distinguished Baltimore woman as chairman, and other citizens who are county, town, and precinct chairmen. Joe had been elected to the Maryland House of Delegates and knew the members of all the Young Democratic Clubs in the state. Many of them went to work campaigning for Millard, but the one who dashed all over the state every day, every week of those two months, and made speeches, shook hands, and rang doorbells was Millard himself. Only rarely did the candidates cross. I was not too worried about him. He had his yearly medical checkup when he went to New York and the doctor said he was like a man in his forties. He grew thinner and I knew he was tired, but he seemed to be feeling well and enjoying himself. Millard and his driver quite literally went from one end of the state to the other.

His driver told an amusing story about trying to find a place in the mountain wilds of western Maryland. He said that the senator was reading the papers in the backseat when they came to the end of the paved road. "Where to now, Senator?" he asked. Millard looked up, indicated a dirt road branching off. "Take that road," said he. The road grew increasingly rough. Millard went on reading. Finally, it dwindled almost to nothing. The driver stopped. "Now, where to Senator?" Millard looked up from his reading, "Take that way to the left," he replied. Eventually, when the driver was becoming convinced they were hopelessly lost, they drew up at a mountain cabin where an old man sat on the front porch, chewing tobacco. The old man got to his feet and beamed: "Lawd God, Millard boy, I ain't seen you in thirty years! Come in and have a drink!" He was the Democratic leader of that part of the mountain country.

The last week of a Maryland campaign was always devoted to Baltimore. Millard was speaking in Prince George's county at the Fairgrounds and planned to meet me at our Baltimore headquarters. His driver arrived, but Millard was not with him. "The Senator is ill, Mrs. Tydings," the driver whispered to me "and I have put him to bed in a room at the hotel. Nobody knows this. You had best go quickly." I found Millard lying on the bed, running a high fever. I telephoned Dr. Rienhof at Johns Hopkins, and he at once sent over a batch of antibiotics. He told me to dose him, take him home, and keep him in bed a day. He would probably be all right on Monday. I did this and he seemed well enough to go back to Baltimore on Monday. He was tired, but his temperature was normal.

We arranged to divide up the evening speaking engagements. I would go to half of them on one side of town and he would go to the other half on the other side of town. This way, we would meet by 11 P.M. and drive home to Oakington. I was driven to my meetings by a tall, young Italian-American war veteran who was one of Mayor D'Allessandro's protégés. We became good friends. He had a fine war record in our invasion of Italy in War II. As he spoke Italian fluently, his officers would send him ahead of our armed forces to spy on the enemy. He barely escaped with his life more than once, and had been decorated for bravery.

One evening as we drove through the deserted warehouse district of Baltimore on our way to a political meeting, he pointed out a large man sitting on the steps of a big, dark warehouse under the faint light of a street lamp. "Look, Mrs. T., there's old moneybags, George Mahoney, with the election pay-off money!" said my escort excitedly. "Just give me permission, Lady, and I'll take it from him so fast he won't know what happened. The senator won't have any more worries about financing our campaign!" George Mahoney, a wealthy Baltimorian, was Millard's democratic opponent in the primary.

More amused than shocked, I said, "Certainly not! What a dreadful idea!"

"Oh, please, Mrs. T., they're all crooks and I know our candidate needs the money!"

Of course, I firmly refused to allow it and my friend was forced to drive on, greatly disappointed.

I regaled Millard and my children with this colorful tale of my political experiences and after that they called my Italian-American war hero "Mother's Mafia man!" He became a distinguished citizen of Baltimore.

Millard and I finished the week campaigning in Baltimore and he won the primary election against Mahoney. Everyone said this was tantamount to election, since Senator Butler had been a total flop in the Senate. We went to Hot Springs, Virginia, for a week's rest. Millard was tired but there were no more episodes such as he had suffered that day in the Baltimore hotel. We ate and slept and strolled the paths around the hotel. We didn't even play golf! Millard told me he had no intention of doing any more of the strenuous campaigning he had been doing in the primary. He would speak at only a few banquets in key points around the state. That was all.

We returned to Oakington and Millard continued with his rest cure. One morning I left him lying on the bed and went to Aberdeen to do a few errands. He had told me he was going to drive into Baltimore later in the morning and see some Democratic leaders and lunch with George Mahoney. I said I had read in the paper that Mahoney had gone to Florida. I returned from Aberdeen an hour later and found my husband on the bed where I had left him.

"I thought you were going to Baltimore," I said.

"I did go! I had lunch with George and talked to a lot of important Democrats!"

"But Millard, you couldn't have had lunch. It's only noon now."

"Well, I did!"

I went downstairs to where Robert Livingston had been polishing floors all morning. I asked him if the senator had gone out in his car since I left the house. "No, ma'am, he hasn't left his room! I would have seen him if he had gone out. His car has not left the garage!"

I was very upset over this strange occurrence, but said nothing further about it. That night, Millard began to complain of a terrible pain in his head, all around his left eye. I gave him aspirin tablets and tried an electric pad and an ice pack. Nothing did any good. By 11 P.M. he was in such agony that I phoned Dr. Rienhof. He came out at once from Baltimore with the top eye doctor and the leading nose and sinus specialist. They couldn't diagnose the pain and sent for an ambulance to take Millard into Johns Hopkins Hospital. The next morning I visited him there. He was dressed and chatting with nurses and friends on the floor who were patients. The pain seemed greatly diminished.

I told his doctor at Johns Hopkins, Ben Baker, what had happened the night before and in Baltimore. He told me he feared that my husband might not be able to go on with his campaign. A personal friend of my husband who was a psychiatrist came to see Millard in the hospital, and spent an hour or more chatting with him. He reported to me that Millard's mind was as brilliant as ever.

Then, a few days later when I thought all was going smoothly, Dr.

Baker phoned me that Millard had gone quite berserk the night before, out of his mind. They had moved him up to a top floor room where he was installed with nurses around the clock. My poor husband was groaning from the awful pain in his head when I arrived. There ensued a terrible ordeal for us both. The press descended upon the hospital daily, in a mob, asking for information about the senator and demanding to see him. I drove from Washington every morning and would have to talk to them all and put up a happy, nonchalant front. I told them he was only suffering from fatigue from the campaign—that it was not a stroke or a heart attack, as rumored. Then I would visit my husband and find him in the same dire straits.

All the top doctors at Hopkins examined Millard. They thought it might be a brain tumor and wanted to do a spinal tap and brain x-ray test to find out. If it was, they would have to operate. At Daddy's request, Dr. Baker sent for a Boston specialist to consult on the case. This gentleman arrived and immediately ordered the brain x-ray and spinal tap. It was not a brain tumor.

The next day, I sat in conference with ten doctors who told me that my husband was suffering from encephalitis and that he could not continue to run for the Senate or even go to the Democratic convention. This would be a great blow to my husband, I knew, and I argued in vain with the doctors. They were adamant. The hospital could no longer keep him there anonymously. Too many of the staff—nurses, doctors, and patients—knew he was there. I must either take him home with trained nurses or put him in the Hopkins special hospital for brain disorders. I took him home with his devoted Hopkins nurse, Miss Waterman. She took care of him during the day, and a night nurse came from the hospital in Havre de Grace. I was on 24-hour duty.

My father had been wonderful during the weeks Millard was at Johns Hopkins Hospital and I was living at Tregaron with him. He would often drive me to see Millard and talk with the doctors. I will never forget when Dr. Baker told us what encephalitis is. "It is a virus infection of the lining of the brain," he said. I asked if the patient would recover eventually with quiet and good nursing care. The doctor tried to let me down easily, but finally told me gently: "The best you can hope for is that the senator will get worse slowly." I was stricken. I refused to believe it and Daddy encouraged me not to. The marvelous invention of tranquilizer pills finally took the unbearable edge away from Millard's suffering, but he was still miserable with the violent itching and burning of his eye and the area around it. He remained an invalid until after Christmas.

When we returned to Oakington, I at once summoned his chief political advisers to tell them the sad news. Colonel E. Brooke Lee of Montgomery County, Congressman Sasscer of southern Maryland, "Boss" Birmingham of Baltimore County, Governor Preston Lane of western Maryland, Mayor D'Allessandro of Baltimore, U.S. Solicitor General Perlman, among others, talked with Millard and then with me. The nurse heard them talking outside Millard's room afterward. Most of them, she told me, obviously wanted to take Millard's place as the Democratic candidate for the Senate! Colonel Lee and Mayor D'Allessandro urged me to run. I couldn't possibly with my husband so ill, I told them. They said Joe Tydings couldn't run as he was not yet of legal age to do so, and only a Tydings could beat Senator Butler. I was adamant. They then insisted that we keep it secret that Millard could not be a candidate until after the Democratic National Convention in Chicago in August. Otherwise, the Democratic party in Maryland would be in chaos and Mahoney would immediately capture the candidacy.

From then on, reporters were literally storming the gates. I had to keep telling them that the senator was perfectly all right, just taking a rest cure at doctor's orders. I am not a good liar and I didn't like any part of it. I finally told my son I couldn't go on doing it. Joe met with me and the leaders and we composed an announcement that Senator Tydings was withdrawing from the race shortly before the convention. Once more Colonel Brooke Lee and the Mayor of Baltimore urged me to be their candidate and I refused.

Millard was to have addressed the United Womens Democratic Clubs of Maryland at their yearly convention at Ocean City, and I went in his place. I had been doing my best to pinch-hit for him, speaking at all the important Democratic affairs. The day before I was to speak at Ocean City, I drove far down into southern Maryland to "give the charge to the knights" at the big summer tournament there. These tournaments had been popular in Maryland for three hundred years! The knights on horseback joust for the honor of crowning their lady queen at a ball in her honor. The jousting consists of riding at a gallop through three arches and spearing large rings hanging from them with their lances.

There was a luncheon given for me beforehand by the president of the District Fire Department. After lunch, I was presented as speaker from a platform on the grounds by the grand marshal of the tournament. This gentleman wore a red sash over one shoulder and rode a prancing steed. He was accompanied by three young ladies (former queens) who were his "aides". I made my little talk:

"It is an honor to be invited to give the charge to the knights on this, one of Maryland's historic occasions. It is not for nothing that Maryland is known throughout the length and breadth of our land as the state of the Cavaliers as well as the Great Free State. The first settlers who came here landed and settled in southern Maryland and with them they brought the courage of high ideals, which they had inherited from the highest Christian concept of conduct known as chivalry. The words "cavalier" and "chivalry" come from the same Latin root meaning a horse or soldier on horseback—hence a knight on a horse.

"At home in Harford County, my knight is convalescing from a long and painful illness. He fought for his country on the battlefields of France in War I and through a lifetime in your service in the legislatures of Maryland and the Congress of the U.S. Six years ago he was dealt a foul blow and struck from his post by a man allegedly a gentleman who employed the most despicable tactics to rob you of the experience and noble qualities of a very great man. The present republican U.S. senator of Maryland is famous throughout the land for striking the lowest blow yet in a political campaign—the use of a composite photograph and lies to smear the reputation of a fine man named Millard Tydings.

"The democratic candidate for the U.S. Senate will be voted upon Monday in the democratic convention in Baltimore.

"Millard Tydings expected to be your standard-bearer in the fight to rid Maryland of this man continuing in office, and Millard Tydings could only have been prevented from doing so by illness. Millard is a son of old southern Maryland. His father and his forefathers were born in this very county."

It was a long drive down there and it was eleven at night when I arrived home at Oakington. Millard was asleep but his nurse, Miss Waterman, was waiting up for me in great excitement. Had I seen the Baltimore *Evening Sun* paper or heard the radio news in the car? They were full of my candidacy for the Senate! The Democratic National Committeeman and Committeewoman of Maryland and the Mayor of Baltimore had come out for me and so had many other party leaders. Mayor D'Allessandro wanted me to call him at home no matter how late it was! I called him and held firm to my decision not to run. He persuaded me to meet with him, Colonel Lee, Congressman Sasscer, and other leaders at his house at Ocean City the following morning, before I addressed the United Democratic Women's Clubs. I agreed to do so and I tried in vain to reach my son for advice. Millard told me to go ahead and do what I wished. It was fine with him! My father had urged me to run. What should I do?.

The next morning (Saturday) my driver delivered me at the Ocean City boardwalk near the mayor's house. Boss Birmingham, the boss of Baltimore County, was waiting. He had planned to be the candidate himself and had arranged a dinner in his own honor in Baltimore for Monday night before the state convention. He had given up the idea for lack of support and had endorsed my candidacy in the newspapers. Parading along the boardwalk toward me came a great crowd of women, waving banners and carrying huge signs saying "Eleanor for Senator!" I was surprised and for a moment I thought, "What is Eleanor Roosevelt doing running here in Maryland?" Then the leaders were upon me, hugging and kissing! A lot of them were the mayor's Baltimore henchwomen. At the mayor's house I found Congressman Sasscer and Colonel Brooke Lee and Millard's other leaders sitting around a table with a large map of Maryland and lists of the various districts and their votes.

I finally told them I would accept if the state convention drafted me. I had friends looking for my son all over town, as I knew he would be there for my speech. The gentlemen told me that wouldn't do. I must announce my candidacy now. I telephoned my husband for advice. It was one of his better days. He laughed and said to ask Brooke Lee if it really was in the bag for me to win, as they claimed. I did and the colonel said that nothing was ever a sure thing in politics but this was the closest thing to a draft he had ever seen.

My son still had not been found, and I thought that if I ran it would please Millard. On the other hand, what about his illness? I told myself there were always nurses to be had.

"What about it?" the men asked impatiently.

"All right!" I said. The press boys were waiting outside. It was done. I was a candidate for the United States Senate. I knew of no other woman who had ever done so before in the history of Maryland.

I went to the convention hall and saw my son at the entrance, looking at me anxiously, "What have you done, Mother?" he asked.

"I am going to run," I told him cheerfully.

Mr. and Mrs. Mahoney were seated on the speakers' platform looking extremely dour. I bowed and smiled pleasantly and proceeded to give the best short speech of my life, so the newspapermen present told me. There wasn't a dry eye in the house (including the Mahoneys') when I finished my brief recital of the agony of my husband's illness and my final prayerful decision to try to carry on his work for Maryland. The crowd gave me an ovation.

A nice, experienced Maryland newsman stopped me on the way out. "Mrs. Tydings, that was the finest political talk I have ever heard," he said. Joe drove me home to Oakington. and we sent out telegrams to Millard's friends and supporters around the state. Millard was in bed asleep. His nurse was very excited. She was, by this time, one of the family.

That was Sunday. It was a wild day, but Monday was wilder. Millard made telephone calls for me to his friends. I spent the morning telephoning and planning my talk for the banquet in my honor that evening (Boss Birmingham's party!). Then there was a news conference and a session with photographers. Did I think I could win? they asked. "Of course, or I wouldn't be a candidate," I said. Could they see the senator? "No," I replied, "he is not up to seeing a crowd." At four o'clock I was dressed in a simple black afternoon dress. The nurse gave me a tranquilizer pill.

At the banquet there were only a very few women, mostly men. I sat and automatically applauded the distinguished guest introductions, including my own! The mayor kicked me! "Stop applauding for yourself, and stop talking about Millard!" he said sternly. "You're the candidate. Talk about yourself!" They had introduced me, the guest of honor and I was still in a daze. I got up, laughing. "I have been applauding all of you distinguished Marylanders for so many years that it has become a habit," I told them. All the males in the audience and a few females gave me a big hand.

Afterward, I was whisked to the Belvedere Hotel and taken up to a private suite where Boss Birmingham's lady friend awaited me. The mayor said she would keep me informed about the convention below and I was left there. This was a mistake. I should have been downstairs to see and be seen and to greet the delegates as they arrived. I had always been better one-on-one. Of course, hindsight is always better, and, after all, I had never run for office before. Left with the Boss's lady friend, I telephoned Daddy and Mother.

The former was visiting the latter at Brule. They knew nothing of the events of the past few days, and, of course, they were thrilled. "That's my son-daughter!" Daddy kept repeating. I told them not to get their hopes up, there was many a slip. I would call them back.

My Italian war hero then came in to report that there had been a fight right away over whether there would be a "unit count" vote or a popular roll-call vote. The chairman of the convention was unfortunately a Mahoney man and he gavelled through the unit count system vote, whereby each county has so many votes. It might not have made much difference, but Colonel Brooke Lee and others thought it would. The colonel counted votes and I lost by only two in the vote count!

Mahoney had been working overtime since the announcement that Millard was no longer the candidate. He had secured the pledged support of many of our friends before my announcement. "We wuz robbed, Mrs. T!" my war hero snarled. "The bastards bought the bastards! They ran out on us! If only you had let me take care of old moneybags that night, maybe they couldn't have bought the SOBs!" Or if I had been present and not sequestered with Boss Birmingham's girlfriend!

As the vote was taken alphabetically, we suffered a setback right away when one of the Baltimore City districts deserted us and went for Mahoney. It was a sell-out just before the meeting convened. My Italian war hero was right. He groaned that he and the mayor should have killed the bastards! Several counties pledged to me that voted late (alphabetically) flopped to Mahoney when they saw he was ahead.

My son escorted me down to concede Mahoney's victory and pledge my support. I had two short speeches already written and memorized—one for victory and one for defeat. In case I won—"I accept with all humility my nomination by the Democratic Committee of Maryland for the U.S. Senate. For many years I have been closely identified with political life in our state. I am deeply concerned with the welfare of the people of Maryland and the other united states and with world peace based upon justice and the safety of the free world. I will do all in my power to win the election for myself and the other Democratic candidates, and I most humbly ask for the support of you and your friends that we may have a Democratic victory in November."

But I ended up giving the speech I wrote in case I was defeated, with Joe Tydings standing next to me: "The delegates have spoken and have chosen Mr. Mahoney to be our Democratic candidate for the U.S. Senate. I will do all I can to help him to win the election. I request that the delegates present make his election unanimous." Short and sweet but actually my defeat was "a win" for me. I would have had to resign if I had won because Millard's illness worsened so terribly. There would be no Senator Tydings on Capitol Hill until one whose first name was Joe! My son drove me home and another chapter in my life was over. I had feared for Millard as an invalid with a wife in his Senate seat. So the Lord was looking after me once more, I decided. I did not know then how very much. My grandmother's golden spoon was working!

I wrote Mother that I was never at any time the least bit upset. I had spent a sleepless night worrying about what I would do if I won! How could I leave Millard and campaign every day all over the state against Ike's ticket? I was relieved that I wouldn't have to. A number of nice editorials were written about me in the Washington and Baltimore newspapers. And that was that!

That November we celebrated Daddy's birthday at dinner at Mother's house. Millard seemed to almost be his old self again. The treatment had gotten the pain under control. His mind seemed clear, but he had not regained his usual strength. My father urged him to try to control the pain by a visit to the Arizona Inn in Tucson. We spent a quiet Christmas at Oakington with our children and the beautiful new grandbaby, Susan Eleanor Gillet (Suzy), and left for Tucson four days later.

The winter had seemed to increase Millard's pain and malaise. It lessened a lot when we were out in Tucson. The dry climate seemed to help my poor husband. He had friends there who entertained us and he enjoyed himself, but for the first time I was shocked by his loss of memory. He would start to tell a story and forget it in the middle; or he would repeat it to the same people a short time later. It broke my heart to see the smiling glances exchanged by these people. Why is it amusing when a great mind starts slipping, I wondered. I was glad to get home to Oakington where I could protect him from general knowledge of his mental illness. I couldn't bear to have it known that his wonderful mind was sick.

Chapter 36

My Father Dies

1957 and 1958: my father becomes weaker and strangers try to turn him against his family and get his fortune; he celebrates his last Christmas with us and dies in the spring.

The trip to Tucson did nothing to help Millard, and back home our lives became increasingly bleak. At first it seemed that he might get well. He was able to walk over to the guest cottage to see Eleanor and baby Suzy and would spend long periods watching the child. Finally, we were able to let his nurses go, but my husband still suffered with the pain in his head. I took him to New York to see a doctor about alleviating the head pain by cutting a nerve. He said it could not be done.

My father's health was also deteriorating rapidly, and "the vultures were flying in for the kill." I can think of no more fitting description for what was happening at Tregaron the year before his death. His favorite activity was entertaining people from large, important schools, churches, and charities and discussing what he was going to do with Tregaron and his Russian collection. Of course they were all after his money, also! His fortune was a bit overestimated in the public mind, largely because of his lavish gifts for good works. He was a proud man and wished to be known as a multimillionaire in his own right, quite apart from his wife's fortune.

When he was with his children, he would assure us that we would get Tregaron and everything else he had (except for mother's income, which was secured by a large insurance policy on his life). I am sure that up until the spring of 1957 my father's meetings with the fortune hunters were merely a game to him! Too infirm to play cards at his club anymore, he thoroughly enjoyed "giving away" Tregaron and his Russian collection. But the game became more serious when certain people attempted to turn him against his children.

The happy years were over for me and the dark ones were growing darker. My father was failing and Millard was not improving. My husband preferred to just sit and watch television or listen to the radio in the darkened library. Doctor Baker had told me that I could not sit beside him all the time or I would end up in a mental sanitarium. I had to resume my active life. So after the election, I accepted the job of cochairman of the United Nations Association of Maryland. I also took over the chairmanship of the Women's Auxiliary of our wonderful new Washington Hospital Center. The latter involved weekly meetings in Washington. For awhile Millard was able to go to the city with me and we would stay with my father at Tregaron. He was usually glad to have us. When he was in one of his bad humors, we would stay with Mother. She was always happy to have us and always her usual sweet self.

He could carry on a highly intelligent conversation for short periods of time, which helped. At home, I would arrange for short visits with his friends, and I worked for hours on end in the garden. The exercise kept me healthy and, I think, kept me from a nervous breakdown. My beloved husband's mind was succumbing to the old trouble—the jealously of our early married years. Now it was much worse. His sickness made him imagine all manner of lovers for me. Bob Livingston first told me of his awful obsession. Whenever I left the house, the senator was sure that I was going to meet some man! Bob would find him endlessly looking up numbers in the telephone book! When these spells were upon my husband, he would sit in stony silence, glaring at me. Other times, he was his old dear, loving self. I never knew when his bad spells would come. Of course, I told him how ridiculous such imaginings were, how much I loved him, and how silly to think a woman of fifty could be having an extramarital affair! Both my children were often in our house and would often scribble phone numbers on a pad by the hall telephone. Millard thought these were numbers of my gentlemen friends! I tried in vain to reason with him. "Darling, I rarely ever leave your side. I don't have time to have an affair, even if I wanted to, which I don't!" He was sure that I was meeting army officers from the Aberdeen Proving Ground. I didn't even know any!

We went to an anniversary dinner party for old friends at the Sulgrave Club in Washington. Millard accused me of leaving the party after dinner for a rendezvous with some man. I was so desperate that I asked our hostess to telephone Millard and tell him that I had never left the party for an instant before going home with him. He refused to listen. The only time I ever left my husband was when I was asked to drive someplace in Maryland to tell people about the United Nations and get them to join the Maryland Association. Once I went with my cochairman, an old friend who was very much in love with his wife, but Millard accused me of having an affair with this man, and so I finally gave up even this small outside interest and devoted myself to my husband and my father.

Sometimes Millard would drive into Washington with me to spend half the week with Daddy at Tregaron. It seemed my father also needed my constant supervision. He had been invited to visit a famous religious institution out west and receive an honorary degree. On his return my father told me that the president of the institution had promised that if Daddy would will his Russian collection to them, they would build a fine museum to house it and would hang a portrait of my father at one end and a portrait of his mother, the Welsh Baptist congregationalist minister at the other! My father was having the painting of the Last Supper by Leonardo copied as a gift for this institution. I listened sympathetically. I could imagine my Grandmother Davies revolving in her grave at the idea of a portrait of her gracing that museum!

Daddy told me about a brilliant young New York lawyer, a trustee of this university, whom he had invited to visit him at Tregaron. This Mr. X arrived soon afterward, and Millard and I met him and disliked him at once. His flattery of my father disgusted me. He told me Daddy was so devoted to him that he had given him a blank check with which to pay for the copy of the "Last Supper". Mr. X said it cost over $20,000!

We also had servant problems at Tregaron. Father's manservant-valet, Barry, was always hanging around, spying on us when we were there. He was a slimy individual whom I had never liked. My father was fond of him and I knew that he had given Barry an expensive automobile and goodness knows what else. Barry was now hiring and firing the help and generally acting like a little czar in the household. He obviously did not want the Tydingses around! We heard that when we were not there, he was entertaining his friends at parties downstairs with Daddy and his nurses behind double doors upstairs. For some time he kept us away by saying the cook and maid had left and he couldn't find others to make the house comfortable for us! He became quite impudent and rude to me.

In March 1957, I began writing a series of agonized letters about Daddy to my sister Emlen in Frankfurt:

"Daddy is more confused than ever. He gets furious if anyone disagrees with him. He says he is working hard to get his book finished. His secretary says he can't dictate at all anymore. He makes very large money gifts to charity or to any cause or person who asks for it! I was foolish enough to accept the chairmanship of a big banquet given by the Democratic National Committee. Daddy bought a thousand dollar table from Paul Butler, then denied having done so! He eventually paid for it and afterward said he had not, as he hadn't been invited, and he refused to go. I gave the tickets away the day before the banquet and then he changed his mind and wanted to go to it! So he used Mother's ticket. He has even been cross with her lately. Miss Turnbloom (his secretary) says he has a phobia that he has no money and is refusing to pay his bills.

"In August he planned a big party at Tregaron for a Welsh choral society that was giving a concert at Constitution Hall on Sunday. He is honorary president of this group and was to speak at the concert. I am very worried about his trying to do all this because he isn't strong enough. I think he has suffered several small strokes. We had an awful time trying to get him to make coherent plans with Mr. Ellis, the caterer, for guests from all over the U.S. and Canada whom he was entertaining at the reception at Tregaron. I stood beside him in the receiving line when all these people arrived, by the busload, and he introduced me as his beloved wife! I tried to correct this, but it didn't last long. Daddy suffered a total collapse soon after the party started and had to be carried upstairs by my son and Dean Frank Sayre. Barry got him into bed. Of course, his new friend Mr. X was there, and Dean Sayre was furious when he discovered later that Mr. X had gone up into Daddy's room and locked the door! Of course, when Doctor Daniels arrived, he had to unlock it and come out."

After that, my father had nurses around the clock and Mr. X was constantly coming down from New York City to visit him. The nurses told us Mr. X and Barry were plotting to turn my father against his children so that he would will everything to Mr. X's religious institution and to Barry!

At the time of my father's collapse, he was working on his autobiography, *In the Days of Their Power and Glory,* and on a memoir entitled *Missions for Peace.* After his collapse, I continued to write Emlen weekly to keep her informed about his condition and about what was going on at Tregaron. On October 23 I wrote:

"Mr. X telephoned me at Oakington and said he had seen Daddy and he seemed better, but Mr. X was concerned because Daddy talked so terribly about his children! Daddy told Mr. X that we were trying to take his money away from him! Isn't that horrible? Doctor Daniels says it is a persecution complex, a common phobia of senility."

My next letter to Emlen, October 26:

"Mr. X is as smooth as goose grease! He said his organization wanted us to know that my father had given them Tregaron and the Russian collection and that Daddy had been phoning him daily, insisting that he (Mr. X) come to see him. He said Daddy was determined to complete these gifts at once; that he knew his daughters didn't want him to, but if they didn't go along, he'd 'fix them!' I was shocked. I told him that we girls had been brought up never to question any gifts our father made; that if he wanted to give anything away, it was all right with us! Mr. X then actually asked me to tag everything at Tregaron for his organization! He said he wanted it on paper that we'd never protest any gifts to them! I hedged on both counts.

"Daddy's afternoon nurse, Mrs. Clayton, told me that Mr. X had been with Daddy for three hours the previous day and had worn Father completely out.

"All of us are very upset over the situation. Barry and Mr. X are working together to poison Daddy against us! Barry talks horribly against us to the nurses. He told them we don't care anything about our father! The nurses distrust and fear Barry. Nurse Clayton told Mr. X he could only see Daddy for half an hour, but that then he stayed for three hours. Daddy was upset last week. The nurses said: 'Barry had told him that Millard and I and all the children were coming to live with him. Poor Daddy is obsessed with worries about his household expenses and refuses to pay any of his bills!' "

Rahel and I and our husbands decided that under the present conditions at Tregaron, we should borrow the money at the bank and pay the bills ourselves. Daddy's estate would pay us back some day! This we did until his death in May 1958.

On November 1, 1957, I wrote Emlen again:

"Doctor Daniels has told the churches that Daddy is not strong enough to be bothered with any business or charity matters. He agrees with Millard and Joe that I am not to take anything (not even my personal belongings!) out of Tregaron. I am being polite to Barry. The night nurse says that there are all kinds of comings and goings at Tregaron at night, and she is scared. I have had double locks put on Daddy's doors, and the nurse keeps them locked. Daddy has ordered that no light be left on indoors or outdoors at night in the interest of economy, and the place is like a haunted house after dark! It is not only scary but dangerous to go into such a big pitch-black place at night. Anyone could jump out of the shrubbery and attack you! Then, if you can control your shaking hand to turn the key in the lock, you enter a huge, dark hall with only one little light somewhere upstairs, or perhaps none at all! It is not pleasant.

"If I am alone, I dash upstairs and lock myself in my room. I always carry a flashlight. I am wondering whether some of the Russian collection is being removed. (We found out later that many important items had been.) There has been no inventory made of it since Daddy's divorce from Marjorie. I have informed Barry and the new butler that I will be at Tregaron at least half of every week from now on.

"Yesterday I drove home to Oakington after three days at Tregaron. Daddy had been his old self, and we had a happy time together. He seemed so much better. The nurses say Barry behaves like a dictator when we aren't there and says awful things about us. He is furious when any of us is there. He even said you couldn't stay there when you come over from Germany!

"It seems that Barry controls the telephone switchboard and keeps everyone away save Mr. X! He also eavesdrops on me. I caught him at it twice this week.

"The barefaced effrontery of Mr. X and Barry makes me furious. Daddy is just well enough to make it impossible for us to raise a finger to get rid of them. We just have to sit tight and wait. Love, Eleanor."

Whenever I would come to Tregaron after one of Mr. X's visits, I would find Daddy weak, depressed, and cold to me. Once Mr. X subjected Daddy to three days of three-hour sessions while I was at Oakington and when I arrived I was shocked over the change in him for the worse. When I left, I felt he was much better and stronger physically. The doctors told me we could protect him by moving him to a private sanitarium. Of course we would never do so.

A few days later, I wrote to Emlen again:

"Miss Matthews, Daddy's secretary, is so afraid of Barry that she has asked me to move her from the basement office in the dacha (which has only one narrow stair exit) to the big house, and I agreed. Larry had given her a newspaper clipping about a peculiarly horrible murder and told her she had better watch her step or that might happen to her! She is now cataloging books in the library in the main house.

"On November 5th, when I went in to see Daddy, he started complaining about Joe. I guessed at once that this was because Joe told Mr. X that it would be illegal for us to tag any of Daddy's possessions for gifts. I listened as long as I could and then told our father that what Joe told Mr. X was at Millard's and my direction. I told him we couldn't and wouldn't give anything to Mr. X, and that Mr. X was asking us to tag and sign things behind Daddy's back. He is pretty clear in the mornings, and he listened to me. Then he tore into me, Joe, and Millard. He said we lied or twisted the truth, that Mr. X was the finest man he knew, and he would give away anything he wished to. I said that was fine, that what we objected to was the horrible things Mr. X said Daddy said about us!

"The situation got out of hand and broke me into bits but didn't seem to upset Daddy! Maybe I sowed a seed of suspicion in Daddy's mind against the enemy. After all, it's the first blow struck so far for our side.

"Mother just phoned that she saw Daddy after we left, and he seemed sunk in despondency. She told him his old friend, John Marshall, wanted to see him, and he said he didn't want to see anybody.

"Miss Ford says that Barry told her he was going to get rid of the afternoon nurse and get a nurse who is a friend of his. So you see, they are getting desperate. They must realize that Daddy is getting weaker all the time and that soon we will be able to throw out Barry.

"Barry actually came into my bedroom at Tregaron and told me I had better stop criticizing him behind his back and that he could tell a few nasty stories about me and he might sue me for libel! I looked him coldly in the eye and said I didn't know what he was talking about. When he started to bluster at me, I stood up and pointed to the door. 'You will leave this room, Barry, and don't ever come here to me with such threats again!' and that was the end of that. Since then, he has stayed out of my way."

In answer to Emlen's letter, I wrote:

"I can understand your concern and distress. I assure you I am in a state of high nervous tension and insomnia over this devilish situation. As Mother says, it is like a slimy snake that you seize, and it slips right through your hands! My life is a nightmare of eighty-mile drives between Oakington and Tregaron through vicious traffic with misery at one end and complete frustration at the other. While there is some degree of peace and relaxation at Oakington, I worry about Millard all the time when I'm not there with him.

"When I was at Oakington last Sunday, some man phoned Tregaron and Barry put the call through to Daddy. The man told Daddy he was his old classmate from the University of Wisconsin and wanted to come out to see him. Apparently, Daddy told him to come and the man turned out to be a perfect stranger and a bum who tried to persuade Daddy to give him money and made horrible remarks to the nurses. He had to be escorted out of the house. Naturally, we were all upset and decided we had to get Doctor Daniels to put a stop to all direct phone calls to Daddy to protect him from crooks, and cranks and that I should suggest to Daddy that Barry take a well-earned vacation now, since the nurses are doing everything for Daddy. Doctor Daniels is now giving orders for all incoming calls to be taken by Miss Matthews or the nurses."

Later in the month I wrote:

"The nurses report that Daddy is quite cheerful and amiable and is suffering no pain, thank goodness. They say that he is very weak and tired. Joe and I spent less than a half hour with him before dinner, and he was so happy to see us that he asked us to come to his room later. We did, but he was exhausted so we didn't stay but a few minutes. He was more affectionate than he has been for some time. He told Doctor Daniels that he had the most wonderful, devoted family who came to see him every day; the Tydingses even came all the way from Oakington, etc. That is the first time he had said anything nice about us in quite some time! I am sure it is because Mr. X and Barry can't get to him to continue the poisoning. Daddy was much sweeter to us and like his old self. He didn't want us to go home and begged me to return soon. He was also most loving to Joe. Miss Ford said he didn't want to put on a silk shirt because he says it was too nice, and he wanted to give it to his grandson!

"Mr. X wrote to Daddy last week that the president of his school was coming to Washington and would Daddy see him and be photographed presenting him with the Russian collection. Miss Matthews answered the letter, telling Mr. X that Daddy was not feeling well enough to see anyone at this time and she would let him know when he was! Barry came in a few days later and said Mr. X had telephoned him to inquire about it. Miss Matthews asked why Mr. X hadn't called her and then there was a row between them. Barry threatened to go to Daddy and leave, and Miss Matthews said to go ahead! She is most disturbed and feels there is a plot afoot with higher stakes than the Russian collection! The nurses keep Daddy's door locked all the time and he seldom, if ever, leaves his room."

A letter of November 29 to Emlen continues the tale:

"I just got back to Oakington from Daddy's birthday party, and I have good news to report. Millard and I arrived at Tregaron Tuesday afternoon to find Daddy in a most affectionate mood. He was in bed but insisted upon getting up and coming downstairs for dinner with us! It was the first time he had been downstairs for dinner since August! He was so happy to see us—didn't talk much—let us do the talking. This morning El brought baby Suzy into town for Daddy's birthday party that took place at 11 A.M. in the library. We had a table with tea and coffee, cookies, and a birthday cake.

"Another table was full of birthday presents. Mother and Millard, and Rahel and her girls, Suzanne and Jennifer, and El with little Suzy were all there. Dean Sayre and Doctor Daniels both came and we all sang "Happy Birthday," and Daddy got all choked up and was very pleased and very happy. His eighty-first birthday party was a howling success! He was so pleased that you telephoned him. Mr. X sent him a plant, and Daddy looked at the card and said, 'Mr. X! Who is Mr. X? I don't know anyone of that name!' Miss Ford said afterward she never watered the plant, and it died! All is quiet, at last, on the Tregaron front, and the new Swedish couple is very good. Nurse Ford informed me gleefully that Barry wears a toupee—that he has two, one with a grease spot in front and one with a worn spot in back, and both are very dirty!''

December was a happier month for me because of the dedication of our wonderful new Washington Hospital Center. Full and flattering tributes were paid to "the founders": Lady Elysabeth Welsh, Mrs. Bessie Huidecooper Fay, and, of course Senator Millard Tydings and myself. Our names were on a bronze plaque in the hospital foyer. The hospital has a thousand beds, and everything in it is the very latest and best equipment. Bessie Fay gave a beautiful dinner party Sunday night, and there were more parties on Monday. It was all very gay. Because of the pressures of taking care of my husband and my father, I had by then given up all my work with the hospitals and the Red Cross, and Rahel had taken my place as head of the Women's Auxiliary of the Hospital Center.

Emlen came from Germany to see Daddy just before Christmas, and while she was at Tregaron, we were able to have Daddy agree to sign papers giving his bank the conservatorship to pay his living expenses at Tregaron. Christmas at Oakington was much as usual. I was very tired and Millard sent me roses and I was happy! Our children sent me flowers, too, and my mother was with us. We celebrated with our Christmas dinner at Oakington on December 23 with our children and the Warry Gillet Seniors and some Baltimore and Harford County friends. It was a happy party. We trimmed the tree and did our carol singing. Christmas morning, the two grandbabies, Joe and Ginny Tydingses, blond little Mary Tydings, and little Suzy Gillet were brought over, and we all opened our presents around the tree. Then Mother and Millard and I drove to Washington to be with Daddy for his last Christmas.

As my father grew weaker, my sisters and I worried about what had happened to his will. I knew he had made a will, because in 1956, before both he and Millard had become seriously ill, he had asked Millard to advise him on the wording of one paragraph. Naturally curious, I had asked Millard about it, and he had told me with an amused smile that the old gentleman had let him see only one clause referring to his scholarship foundation! Now, with my father terminally ill, my sisters and I asked his law partners if they had his will. They said they did not, that our father had removed it some time ago, as well as all copies. There were three safes at Tregaron, but there was no will in any of them! We wondered if he had destroyed it and written another one.

One evening in the early spring of 1958, I had left Millard at Oakington and arrived at Tregaron in time for dinner and to spend the night. Daddy was too ill to have dinner with me, so Rahel and Fontaine had dinner with me there, and went home early. I was alone in the library and as usual, there were no lights on in the great entrance hall or the upstairs hall. The servants were in the other end of the house. I delayed going upstairs to my room to write a memo to myself of the next day's appointments. I rummaged in the Russian desk, which was supposed to have belonged to Catherine the Great, but could find no scrap of paper to write on. Irritated, I yanked at the last drawer and inside was a heap of old Christmas cards and invitations. I reached in to pull one out to make notes upon and found a large manila envelope underneath it all. It was sealed and labeled *PRIVATE PROPERTY OF JOSEPH E. DAVIES*. I was so excited that my hands shook. I dropped it back in the drawer and stood listening intently. Had I heard footsteps in the hall? If this was the 1956 will, which would surely leave everything to my father's family, wouldn't it be important to keep it out of the hands of people who had a later will that might leave them his fortune?

I shivered and walked over to the library door, closed, and locked it. Then I drew a deep breath of relief and checked the draperies at the French doors leading onto the terrace. I closed the curtains tightly and opened the envelope. Sure enough, it was my father's will, dated early in 1956, and witnessed. One glance told me all I wanted to know. His daughters and our mother were the beneficiaries. I picked up the telephone and dialed.

"Hello, Rahel! Will you and Fontaine come back here to Tregaron right away? It's very important!"

"Oh, Eleanor, it's too late! We're all undressed and going to bed," she said.

"I don't care how late it is! You'd better get dressed and come over here. I've found something pretty important to us both, and I'm alone here in the library!"

"We're coming!"

They came and Fontaine corroborated my recognition of the original will, properly executed by my father in 1956, when he was well and still of sound mind. Fontaine instructed Rahel and me to go to the bank in the morning and put it in a joint lockbox. That night I slept (as usual behind locked doors) with the will hidden under my mattress. Next morning, Rahel and I took it to the bank.

Our beloved father died in early May 1958 at Tregaron. It was some consolation that his last years did not bring him great physical suffering. I can still see him as he looked until 1955, wearing his top hat and tails, red satin-lined cape swinging, and with his ever-present walking stick! I can hear his hearty laugh and see the warm brown eyes beaming at me. I will remember him that way, and I will never cease to miss him.

My father's funeral was one of the largest and most impressive ever held in the National Cathedral. He had many friends who had not seen him in those last sad years, and they came to do him honor for the last time. An enormous Welsh choir sang, and Dean Sayre planned it all to be, as he said, a joyful and triumphant occasion. The flowers were magnificent—huge floral arrangements from many heads of state including Russia, England, Belgium, and France. The honorary pallbearers included senators, ambassadors, and justices of the Supreme Court. The president of the United States, Dwight D. Eisenhower, was too busy playing golf to come, just as he had been too busy to ever come and see my father when he was ill. I grieved for Daddy, but a great load was removed from my shoulders and I was free to devote all my strength to my rapidly failing husband.

After the funeral, we entertained a number of pallbearers and close friends at Tregaron—I don't remember much about that. I was so crushed over the loss of my father that I couldn't participate later in the division of his personal effects with my sisters. We divided all the Russian things by drawing lots for first choice, second choice, etc. I had persuaded Daddy some time before to give his wonderful collection of Russian icons, some very old, many bejewelled, to the National Cathedral's museum. My sisters and I had a fine wrought iron screen made to order in Hungary to cover the window of the big display case. My father's ashes are in the National Cathedral, and a tribute to him is carved in the stone buttress beside President Woodrow Wilson's casket. It reads:

Joseph E. Davies
1876–1958
Son of Wisconsin
Civil Servant, Ambassador
Adviser to Presidents

Chapter 37

Millard's Terminal Illness and Death—My Heartbreaking Years

1958 to February 1961: Millard's encephalitis makes him mentally unstable and he threatens divorce; his sisters try to take Oakington; Millard dies of pneumonia in the winter of 1961.

The burden of my father's last year was over, but worse lay ahead for me. Millard's condition was not improving. Fortunately, we did not have to wait for Daddy's estate to be settled. His daughters were the beneficiaries of it. We also had handsome insurance policies on his life and we had our trust funds.

Bob Grosjean's father in Belgium advised me to take Millard to see a famous specialist in Zurich, Switzerland, and we sailed soon after Daddy's funeral on the *S.S. United States*. I planned the trip through American Express. We would visit countries Millard had not seen, and would have a limousine and chauffeur at our disposal. We motored through Spain and Portugal. Millard was very ill in Madrid and I feared we might have to go home at once, but he recovered enough to visit our friend Connie Thaw Landa at her chateau on the Island of Mallorca. Here, with rest and proper diet, Millard became well enough to continue our trip by motor through the Pyrenees and southern France to Zurich.

Mr. Grosjean's doctor there examined Millard and encouraged him a little, but did not give me much hope. He prescribed strange oral doses of iodine in water. We stayed awhile in Zurich and then went on to join Emlen and Bob and their two darling young girls at Zermatt, a charming little town at the foot of the Matterhorn (no automobiles there!). I was so happy to see them all! The two Grosjean teenage daughters were acting as extras in a motion picture being filmed there. Friends of the Grosjeans' invited us all to come up the street to their hotel for an evening of song and dancing with some of the movie people. We didn't stay long, as Millard was tired and so were the Grosjeans. They had been mountain climbing all day. Bob and Millard walked along the little street in the moonlight, we girls following, arms entwined, laughing and singing. Millard and Bob Grosjean went into the hotel ahead of us. We were about to follow when a young man whom the girls knew came up to the Grosjean girls. He was one of the movie actors and, after greeting them warmly, he waltzed each of them once around the hotel terrace in front of our hotel. Then he gave Emlen and me a whirl. It was just fun.

My happiness was short-lived. When I opened the door to our room, I found my husband seated by the window overlooking the front entrance and seething with rage. His poor sick mind had convinced him that I had committed every sin in the book, dancing once around the terrace with that boy! Nothing that I could say that night or that the Grosjeans could say the next morning could convince him otherwise. He told Bob that he intended to kill the young man! He would not speak to me, and the next morning the Grosjeans persuaded me to go up the mountain with them. The girls sent word to their actor friend not to come near us at the party that evening. This experience with my ill husband and his continued anger convinced me that we must give up our motor trip through England and Scotland and our planned visit to the Duke of Argyll. We went home to Oakington. Things did not go well between us that winter. His treatment of me see-sawed between love and hate.

The following spring, 1959, I suffered an acute gall bladder attack that necessitated an emergency operation at Johns Hopkins Hospital. My faithful friend, Bob Livingston, drove me there. Millard wouldn't even say good-bye to me, nor did he come to see me until I had been there over a week. I told him then that our old friend, Dr. Rienhof, wanted to have lunch with him that day at the Maryland Club. He said he would not go there because my conduct had so shamed him! He did go, however. Dr. Rienhof came to my room afterward, shocked and distressed over the mental deterioration my husband had suffered since 1956.

The doctor called a conference in my hospital room with the other doctors who had attended my husband when he was in the hospital in 1956. They all agreed that the only possible treatment that might arrest Millard's mental deterioration would be at the Payne Whitney

Clinic for Mental Disorders at Cornell Medical Center in New York. Dr. Rienhof persuaded my husband to go there to see whether they could alleviate the constant pain around his eye. Both Dr. Rienhof and I had corresponded with the doctor who was head of the clinic. I had written him in detail, describing the history of Millard's case.

We went up to Payne Whitney and a nurse took us up to the clinic on the top floor. She locked the elevator behind her when we got out. There were large, luxurious sitting rooms with people playing cards or looking at television. We were high up in the great medical center overlooking the East River.

The nurse showed Millard to his room. I was not surprised when I saw bars at the window, but I was when the nurse asked Millard for his belt, razor, and neckties and went through his suitcase! I was upset about this and went back to the doctor's office for another conference with him. He told me this was necessary. He thought they could help my husband. However, it was important that I not try to contact him in any way during the two weeks that he would be with them as a patient. That was the total length of time that Payne Whitney would keep any patient. I demurred. Millard and I always talked on the phone daily if separated, and we wrote to each other also. I refused to believe that our love affair was over.

"What if he phones me?" I asked.

"He won't be able to get to a phone," the doctor replied. I went back to Oakington alone, sad, and worried. Would Millard ever get well?

Millard's two sisters had been (so I thought) my warm friends for twenty-five years. I included them in all our parties and did everything I could for them both. When Millard was stricken, I wept with them and reported every word the doctors told me about his case. They knew all about the trip to Payne Whitney. So it came as a surprise and shock to me when Dr. Rienhof phoned me soon after I got home. "Eleanor, two women came to see me about Millard today," he said. "They told me they were his sisters. I didn't even know he had any sisters!"

"Certainly he does," said I. "They are both widows and old friends of mine—Mrs. Naomi Pickett and Mrs. Katherine Eager."

"Well, I want to warn you, sister," said Dr. Rienhof, "they are no friends of yours!"

I protested, but he insisted. That evening Millard telephoned me to get him "out of this place at once! Phone the doctor!" I said I would and promised to come after him. Then I phoned Payne Whitney and told the doctor that I was coming up to New York to take Millard home the next day (Friday). He said I must not do so; that he was helping Millard to greatly improve; that I would have to see and talk with him (the doctor) before I could take Millard home. The doctor would be away over the weekend and not be able to see me until Monday. I agreed reluctantly.

The next day I gave a long-planned ladies' luncheon party in honor of my mother, who was visiting us at Oakington with a friend from California. Both of Millard's sisters had been invited and had accepted, but they had then canceled. After the luncheon, I telephoned Payne Whitney to inquire about my husband and to tell them I was coming after him the next day. I was amazed to hear that he had checked out of the hospital that morning with his two sisters! I tried in vain to reach the doctor in charge. Then I telephoned Naomi and Katherine. Their phones (one in Havre de Grace, one in Washington) did not answer. The next morning, Millard arrived in a taxicab and walked into the library looking like a storm cloud. He accused me of having tried to have him "locked up for life!" Then he ordered me to "get out of his house!" I kept cool. I told him he had decided to go to Payne Whitney himself, on the advice of his doctors at Hopkins; that Payne Whitney only kept patients for treatment for two weeks; and that I was prevented by the Payne Whitney doctor from coming for him at once when Millard phoned me. I had planned to come the next day. I also reminded him that Oakington belonged to us both and I had no intention of leaving! Fortunately, Mother and her guest had departed before he arrived. He blustered angrily a few minutes more, then rushed out of the house. Bob reported that the senator drove off in his car.

I telephoned Dr. Rienhof. "Pack your bag and leave at once," he ordered me. "Go to Washington to your mother. It's no longer safe for you to remain. Poor Millard is a borderline case, and they are the most dangerous!"

I packed an overnight bag and drove to Washington. When I walked into Mother's house, I ran to her. "Mother, I have no husband and no home!" I was crying.

She took me in her arms. "You always have me and my home, darling," she said.

Bob Livingston gave me daily reports on the phone. When I departed, Millard's sisters had promptly moved into Oakington. Katherine Eager had tried to occupy my bedroom, which adjoined my husband's. Bob had informed her, with haughty British dignity, that she could not do so, that no one could occupy that room but Mrs. Tydings! Later, he told me that he found she had actually installed a tape recorder behind my bed to register every word I spoke if and when I returned! I had no intention of doing so, I told Millard the first few times he phoned to inquire when I was coming back. "You ordered me out and I don't know whether I will come back," I said. Finally, I simply refused to speak with him on the phone. I was too upset and miserable.

Joe told me that I should have a lawyer on account of Millard's threats to divorce me on nasty grounds of adultery. My friend Richard Cleveland became my lawyer. He was the son of President Cleveland and a member of the board of governors of old St. John's College at Annapolis, as I was also. He conferred with the doctors and they advised me not to live at Oakington House with Millard if nobody else was in the house at night. The Livingstons lived in a house fifty yards away. I continued to stay with my mother in Washington and to drive out to our house on the days Millard went to his weekly bank board meeting in Aberdeen, which he never missed, and when his sister Naomi was out (Katherine had become bored and gone home to Washington). That way I was able to retrieve some of my clothes and personal things. The Livingstons were taking good care of Millard. Joe was going to see him every so often and they would talk as though nothing had happened, my son told me. Then Millard discharged the Livingstons and ordered them off the place. On the advice of the lawyers, I could and did urge them to stay in their house there. After that, Millard and his old sister Naomi were alone in that big house, I was worried over who was cleaning and cooking for my husband.

The Livingstons did their best to watch out for him from a distance. Then one day in December 1958, they told me that if I would come back, they would sleep in the big house with us. The next day, they reported that Katherine and Naomi had taken Millard away in a taxi and that the house was empty. I talked to Dr. Rienhof and Dick Cleveland and they said to move back into it, so long as the Livingstons would stay there with me. Mother, Joe, El, and Warry went back to Oakington with me. It was December 27, our wedding anniversary. The place was all locked up with a chain across, inside, the front door! Warry Gillet climbed in a window and let us in. The house was icy cold and dark. I hurried up the big front staircase calling my husband's name. There was no reply.

Just as I reached the top of the stairs and was standing at my bedroom door, Naomi Pickett rushed out of the blue guest room down the hall. Bob Livingston was mistaken. She had not departed with her sister and brother. She apparently had risen from bed, for she was wearing a nightgown and a soiled kimono. Her hair and eyes were wild. She flew at me and screamed, "Get out of this house! You don't belong here!"

"Oh, but I do," said I, holding her by the wrists and pushing her back into the bedroom. "*You* don't! Now put your clothes on and we will send you home. You are a wicked woman, Naomi Pickett, and someday you will have to answer to the Lord for what you have done, not only to me, but also to your poor, sick brother!" I pushed her in the room and closed the door.

Warry took her back to Havre de Grace. For some years, she continued to buttonhole the citizens of the town with terrible tales about her wicked sister-in-law. I heard that everyone ran when they saw her coming! Finally, she moved into an apartment in Baltimore and died there some years later. My mother said, "There is a silver lining to all storm clouds, Eleanor. Now you no longer need to have those women on your hands!"

I did not know where Katherine Eager had taken my husband, and I worried constantly until Dr. Worth Daniels told me that Millard was a patient in Georgetown Hospital.

Mother stayed with me at Oakington until one spring day Millard arrived with his sister Katherine. He told Livingston he had come for his clothes. I was in my bedroom waiting for him. I showed him a letter from the Payne Whitney doctor saying that I had taken him there on the advice of the Johns Hopkins doctors and was to come for him the day after he left with his sisters. I asked Katherine Eager to leave the room and she refused to leave us alone together. "I'll protect you, Bubby" she said, glaring at me. My Eleanor walked in just then and said, "All right, Daddy, if she can stay, I can too!" So Millard told them both to leave the room, his sister protesting loudly. My mother saw her in the hall and gently reminded her, "Don't you know, Katherine, the Bible says that it is wicked to come between a man and his wife?" Whereupon, Mrs. Eager screamed and cursed at my mother. My husband refused to believe either my statements or the Payne Whitney letter and he sent for Livingston to carry his suitcases downstairs. I followed him sadly to the head of the stairs, crushed at my inability to communicate with the man I had loved so much for so long and still did. To my shock and amazement, when I looked down, I saw sitting in the big front hall of Oakington House a uniformed policeman. He had evidently accompanied Millard and his sister. I was outraged! I remembered his sisters words "I will protect you." What had she told that officer!

My indignation flared. I would give that Havre de Grace policeman a tale to tell! My sad tears were supplanted by a flood of angry ones. I flew down the stairs and embraced my husband as Livingston was helping him into his coat. "Don't leave me, darling! Please don't leave me," I sobbed. Behind the backs of Millard and Livingston stood my daughter, her mouth open, amazed at this highly uncharacteristic behavior on the part of her mother. I solemnly dropped one eyelid at her. She understood and carried on the dreadful, melodramatic performance. When Millard and his sister and the policeman went out the door to the automobile, my lovely blond child flew after them crying, "Don't go, Daddy! Don't go! Don't break Mother's heart!" My own mother stood in the hall in utter astonishment at our behavior. Afterward, she laughed with Eleanor, but I couldn't laugh. It may have been ham acting, but it was stark tragedy for me to have the beautiful love story of twenty-five years so shattered.

My ordeal did not end that spring. The saddest time of my marriage had another year to go. I ran into Millard at our dentist's office in D.C. and again at the Davies law office and begged him to come home to Oakington. I knew from Bob that after Millard left Georgetown Hospital, he had been living in Naomi's small apartment in Havre de Grace and that the woman was neither feeding the sick man nor taking care of his laundry. Both times Millard refused to return home with me, but gave me a full account of his latest illness. Then, all of a sudden, one morning when I was in Aberdeen, my husband arrived at Oakington in a taxi! Bob had served him breakfast in the solarium and had driven out the lane to intercept me with the news. I came in and greeted my husband quietly and affectionately as if he had never been away. Now I hoped I could take care of him, he looked so thin and ill. He did not berate me and I would sit with him by the hour, doing endless needlepoint while he watched television. Sometimes he was his old self. Other times he would suddenly stare at me malevolently and accuse me of infidelity and trying to lock him up at Payne Whitney. I took care of him.

In the late spring of 1960, Joe came to us and asked if we would mind if he worked for John F. Kennedy for president. It was one of Millard's good days. He told Joe to go ahead, that "your mother and I are taking no part in politics anymore." He was so thin and emaciated and looked so sad that I put my arms around him. "I am so thankful that is so and that we are together here at Oakington," I said. Joe and Senator John Kennedy had known each other in Palm Beach before the war, and had met again at the Democratic Convention in Chicago when Kennedy was a young senator. They had become fast friends. Now the senator had asked my son to manage his primary campaigns in Maryland, Delaware, and Florida. The old Maryland politicians had no idea that Jack Kennedy had a chance of winning, or they would have never let Joe do it!

My son did a fine job. He carried Maryland and Delaware for Kennedy and almost carried Florida. The Floridians wanted Joe to run for the Senate in their state! Millard and I watched Joe and his wife ride in the official Maryland car in the inaugural parade on television. Washington was buried in snow, and I had lent Ginny my mink coat and hat. They looked like movie stars on the TV screen. She was a beautiful girl and I was very fond of her. Joe Tydings was one of six honorary marshals of the parade. These six men were those who had managed JFK's key primary battles. As they drove past the presidential box, the president, in his box, stopped the parade so that the Tydingses could join him there. He sent them into the White House for lunch. His father admired Joe's top hat. "It was my grandfather's," said my son.

"Well," snorted old Joe, "I never liked your grandfather, but I have always been a great admirer of your dad, the senator!"

In 1960, I kept a diary of what I was living through. Life would have been tragic enough watching the man I loved die by inches. The machinations of his sisters made it pure hell for us both.

March 1: Millard refuses to send Naomi her monthly check. She needs it, so I am giving it to her. The more fool me.

March 21: Went to two Hospital Committee meetings (in D.C.) before lunch. M. didn't return until 6:30 P.M. He wasn't at the office. We spent night at Mother's. Millard is very upset again and accused me of spending nights at Charlie Bryan's with some imaginary colonel! If only dear Sue (Bryan) were alive, maybe she would set him straight on this.

March 23: Meeting of Board of Directors of Harford Day School. We must raise $100,000 to build it. I am afraid I am coming down with flu. Millard has gone in to see Naomi in Havre de Grace. Came home cold and furious with me again. Naomi does this every time he sees her!

March 24: Sick as a dog. Millard still very upset, which doesn't help.

April 3: Millard is in good spirits once more and very affectionate. Drove Mother to Joe's new house to see grandbabies. Dinner at Charlie Bryan's. Millard in great form! I couldn't believe it. These emotional swings between love and hate are killing me.

April 4: Millard went to Havre de Grace this A.M. and came back in another of his cold furies against me. More accusations of sleeping with officers at Bryan's. Wants divorce. I phoned Stella and Bessie (Bryan's maids for 25 years) and they told him I had never been there with any man save my husband. Millard apologized and was very sweet again.

April 6: Today is Millard's 70th birthday! Where are the Aprils of yesteryear? I worked in garden and picked daffodils. El arrived with babies, Suzy and Warry, for the birthday dinner. Little Suzy is growing up! I showed her the festive dinner table and the czar's silver plates, and she said she'd like to be a king! Millard not feeling so well, but sat through family dinner.

April 10: Millard very ill in bed with temperature. I sent for Dr. Loo and sat in Millard's room all day while he dozed and slept.

April 11: Millard is taking antibiotics. In very bad mood. Bad news from Hospital Center. Lobby Shop chairperson is resigning! All my buttering up in vain, in both cases.

April 12: Drove in to D.C. for Hospital Center meeting to get new chairman. Phoned Millard twice—icy replies.

April 13: Meeting of Episcopal Guild. Millard arrived by train and I drove him home. He will neither eat nor speak to me. I went out and raked leaves, then fed him dinner and let him put himself to bed instead of waiting on him as usual.

April 15: Worked in rose garden all A.M. Millard weak and ill— still beastly to me. Garden Club meeting here to discuss plans for garden pilgrimages to Oakington next month. Took grandbabies to Havre de Grace to buy shoes.

April 18: Drove to D.C. for Hospital Committee meeting. Awful traffic. Exhausted.

April 19: 10:00 Hospital Meeting Lobby Shop; 11:00 Hospital Meeting Executive Committee. Ironed things out. Drove to Baltimore and went on TV for garden tour. Home to Oakington. Bob says Millard has been upset and nasty about Joe and me. No wonder, he has been going to see Naomi daily and I think she has been poisoning him with all these awful lies about me.

April 20: Millard said he had been to see some black woman in Havre de Grace for proof of my adultery! Am very upset. Worked in garden all day.

May 1: Millard went in to Havre de Grace for lunch with his sister. When he returned was really berserk, raved and ranted about all the old lies his sisters have been telling him. Again he demanded divorce. I left him and worked outdoors until he had gone to bed. I knelt by his bed and prayed in vain.

May 2: Drove to D.C. for Hospital meeting and Senate Ladies lunch for Mamie Eisenhower. Mamie very sweet. We reminisced about our gay times after the war! Millard followed me to town and was very nice.

May 4: Awful day! Thank heavens Mother is at Oakington. Finally took Millard to see Naomi's friend, whose maid told the lies about me and the unknown lover at Charlie's! Confronted black woman, an impudent, slatternly creature. She said Charlie's Bessie told her! Took Millard to Charlie's. The Bryans' maid, old Bessie, denied ever knowing the Vogel maid and phoned the woman and bawled her out with Millard listening! No good. Old Charlie rebuked Millard for his treatment of me and an awful scene ensued. I had to physically push Millard out of the house. Is there such a thing as demonic possession? Must be "sister possession"!

May 5: Millard ranted and raved. I worked in the garden and Mother sat and sewed. This afternoon, he talked to Mother about divorce, but in the end came outside and kissed me under the arbor! Once again all is well. How can I stand it!

May 7: Millard went to Havre de Grace yesterday and again this A.M. to see Naomi and again he's raging at me. I discovered that Katherine Eager was there.

May 8: Went to church without speaking to Millard. When I returned, he informed me he'd followed me there! Am sure I would have seen him and that he was with his sisters. He harped on Anne and Lewis Clark's party until I phoned them and they told him no Colonel C. had been at the party. They didn't know anyone of that name and had driven Millard and me home themselves! I was done in and lunched on tray in bed. Millard came up and apologized and wanted to make love! Then left for Havre de Grace! Is he really brainwashed?

May 9: He is. He glowered at me all day.

Mother came to visit us, and after visiting Naomi, Millard had another attack of his awful hallucinations about me. He told Mother and me that he was going into Baltimore and get a lawyer and start legal proceedings against me on the grounds of adultery. My mother tried to reason with him, in vain. I didn't even try. He had always loved Mother dearly, but she couldn't move him. He was so enraged, I was afraid that this time he would do it. It would not only mean the shattering of my reputation, but the scandal would hurt my daughter and my son's promising career. In the event of a lawsuit, I would be forced to defend myself, and this would hurt Millard too. I would have to make public what I had worked so hard to keep secret, the sad truth of his mental illness. I phoned the Hopkins psychiatrist. He could not help me. In desperation, I phoned our doctor in Havre de Grace, but he said he could do nothing. "Please, God, help me!" I had tried so hard and I was so tired.

Miraculously, Dr. Loo and the Lord answered my prayer. The doctor called back and said, "I think I have a new, more powerful tranquilizer that might help the senator." Bob Livingston went immediately and brought it home. Subconsciously, Millard must have always loved and trusted me throughout his nightmares because he would always swallow any medicines I gave him. He took Dr. Loo's pills and slept in his chair for three hours. It was miraculous! Never again did he threaten to go to court against me. On the contrary, he couldn't bear to have me leave him for a minute, even to work in the gardens outside his window.

My diary continued:

June 7: Eleanor is 28 today. I remember so well the day she was born at Columbia Hospital in D.C. The "Bonus Marchers" were camped down in the swamps on the Potomac. There was depression, hunger, and suicide down there and General Douglas MacArthur was sent with troops to oust them. The nurses were afraid they might spread some kind of epidemic over the city. Washington had no adequate facilities to handle it. Eleanor Jr. was a beautiful baby, weighed eleven pounds and she had dimples!

June 14: Joe told me that our head farmer's wife says that Naomi is continuously phoning her to ask about Millard and tells her we are trying to kill him! She told Bob Livingston this and he told Millard. My husband phoned Naomi and told her to call him after this and not the farmer's wife. I could hear her screaming at him over the phone. Katherine Eager has written asking for financial help to pay for her daughter's wedding. Millard said he wouldn't do it! I finally persuaded him to send her $500 and I would give her the same. For his sake and the child's.

June 17: Drove to D.C. for hospital meeting. Drove home and found Millard so ill we took him to Havre de Grace hospital. Temperature up, but electrocardiogram okay. I spent thirteen hours at the hospital.

June 17: Millard still at hospital. Naomi apparently comes to see him every day and upsets him every time! So far she has missed my daily visits. I have ordered special duty nurses to stay in room when she comes and curtail her visits.

Millard was in and out of the Havre de Grace hospital with pneumonia several times the winter of 1960-61. His sisters sent a Baltimore doctor to examine his lungs, and their doctor advised an exploratory operation on them. Our doctors said it would kill him, and I refused to allow it. Of course his sisters said I was killing him. When he was well enough, I took him home and learned to use the oxygen tank treatment there. My wartime hospital experience was standing me in good stead. I was a pretty good nurse.

Oakington was buried in snow the first week in February 1961. Millard could not breathe unless he was sitting up in bed. I would sit beside him and hold him in my arms until he slept. That last night, it was midnight when he finally did so. Hours later, I was awakened and saw my husband sitting in his big chair beside the open window looking at his beloved bay. It was icy cold and he had no robe over his pajamas. I bundled him back to his bed and closed the windows. The next morning his temperature was soaring. The doctor came and said he should go back to the hospital. I begged to keep him at home. He hated the hospital. We would keep him in bed and take care of him. The doctor reluctantly agreed.

After lunch, the Livingstons urged me to go out for a walk and a breath of fresh air. I had not been out of the house for weeks. Before I went, I straightened Millard's bed, plumped the pillows behind him, and kissed him. He took my hand and smiled at me. "Take a nap now, darling," said I.

"You know you're a wonderful girl, El, I love you very much," he whispered, smiled at me, and closed his eyes. I put on galoshes and overcoat and went out the back door where the lane was plowed. I slogged through the snow halfway around the house when a thought flashed into my mind. What was I doing out there when my husband was inside, maybe dying? I flew back around into the house and up to Millard's room. He was asleep. Nadine Livingston was sitting by the window reading. She smiled at me. "The senator has been sleeping peacefully," she said. I took his wrist to check the pulse. There was none! Millard Tydings was gone. I had lost my dear love forever. It was February 6, 1961.

The week that Millard died, we had the heaviest snows in many years, and Oakington lane was walled with six-foot drifts. In spite of almost impassable roads, hundreds of American Legionnaires came to Oakington to pay tribute and a last farewell to their comrade-in-arms, "Chief" Tydings. I shook hands with them all and served refreshments. Millard lay in his casket in the great bow window of the solarium with the ice and snow of his beloved Chesapeake Bay and snow-covered lawn behind him. He looked young and hand-somewith his war decorations on his chest. Many of his colleagues in the U.S. Senate, both Democratic and Republican, came by train and car for the funeral. I sat beside him all that night and said good-bye to him.

The Episcopal Bishop of Maryland drove miles to give a service at Oakington. The big rooms of the first floor of our home were walled with flowers on lattices and tables. Joe phoned Millard's sisters in Havre de Grace to tell them we would send an automobile to bring them to the house, but they refused to come. Afterward, Reverend Jennings, our rector at old St. John's Church in Havre de Grace, which Millard's great-great-grandfather had built, did a brief service there. As it was a Sunday and there was no road service to clear the way to the church and cemetery, the town fathers manned the snow machines themselves to clear the way to our front gate. Our farmers had cleared our lane. A young Maryland opera singer came down from New York City to sing the Lord's Prayer at the church and the Army gave a military funeral at the cemetery. Millard Tydings was gone, my life was over, and my widowhood had begun.

The day of the funeral, Marjorie telephoned me from Palm Beach and urged me to come down for a "much-needed" rest. She talked as though we had not ignored each other for almost ten years. She knew, she said, all I had been through! Apparently, once again, I was reinstated as her child, and as though the intervening years since her divorce from my father had never been! I told her I had agreed to go to Europe with my friend Hallie Elkins Davis. I told Mother the same thing when she invited me to visit her in Florida. Actually, I did neither. Hallie was taken seriously ill, and I wasn't well enough myself. I stayed home at Oakington and played with my grandchildren.

I wept for a long time, and when the tears ceased to flow, I still cried inside for my lost love, lost romance and, perhaps, my lost youth. I was fifty-seven. My world had come to an end and for a while I was too tired to pick myself up and make the effort to go on living. I had lost the two men I loved best, my husband and my father, after years of heartbreaking illnesses, but I still had my children and my mother, not to mention the "grands." God had taken care of me and I had weathered the storms of the past five years. Now I should relax and try to enjoy the rest of it. But that was not going to be any time soon. I was too tired. I had forgotten all about the fairy story of my golden spoon.

Chapter 38

1961–1963

Mother's and my surgery; I go around the world; President Kennedy appoints Joe Tydings federal attorney, sends him to Interpol Conference; President comes to Oakington, and his assassination.

That spring of 1961 I worked in my garden at Oakington and entertained a few friends on quiet weekends. Mother visited me and so did my friend, Marjorie Post.

My Aunt Rebekah was planning to visit Mother at Brule until I came up later in July. Early in that month my aunt phoned and said that Mother was suffering great pain and was going downhill rapidly. I flew at once to Wisconsin and mother met my plane. She was very pale and thin. She told me she was suffering much pain and taking a great deal of aspirin for it. She was going into the hospital at Superior for x-rays the next day.

The doctor found trouble in her gall bladder and said she must have an operation at once. Brule friends from Duluth sent us to the leading surgeon at a fine hospital in Duluth. He urged Mother to go home to Washington for surgery, but she said she wished to have it there. She was eighty-three years old. She insisted that I go ahead with plans to have our friend Hallie Hutchinson come out to visit us. Mother was very fond of her.

Four days after her operation, Mother was sitting in her hospital room having a permanent wave! I did not approve of this, but it was too late to do anything about it. The next day Hallie and my two sisters arrived. I woke that day with only one-half the vision of my left eye. By noon that eye was completely blind. At the Duluth Clinic that afternoon, the eye specialist told me I had a badly detached retina, which necessitated an immediate operation.

I wired Joe to tell Dr. Rienhof that I was flying back to Baltimore

385

and Johns Hopkins Hospital early next morning. I left Mother with my sisters, and Hallie flew back with me. The surgeon told me there was only the barest chance of saving my eye, and I might lose the other one, but he would do his best. The operation was scheduled for the following morning. That evening my sisters phoned that our mother had suffered a major stroke and it was doubtful if she would live. With this last terrible blow, I went into surgery.

In 1961, a patient who had undergone eye surgery had to lie immovable for two weeks with head anchored between sandbags, not a very comfortable position! It had taken my surgeon over five hours to tie my retina together with plastic (according to my nurse) and the postoperative pain was pretty bad. I felt as though Joe Louis had smashed every bone in my face! My sisters phoned that Mother seemed to be improving, and they were flying her and her nurses home.

My old friend, Millard's law partner, Morris Rosenberg, phoned to tell me that Millard's sisters were about to attack Millard's will (and, incidentally, me!) in the courts. Millard had made a will, before his illness, that was more than fair to his sisters. Katherine Eager and her children inherited somewhat less from him than her older sister, Naomi Pickett. This was because Naomi's inheritance from her husband was less than Kathryn's from her late husband, the colonel. Both women were the beneficiaries of insurance policies from their brother. Naomi also received a small income from money that Millard left in trust for our grandchildren. What was left of his estate came to me. Of course, Oakington and the cattle herd were automatically mine. Apparently, his sisters thought Oakington was his. The will did not satisfy them. They wanted everything their brother had. They threatened to throw the book at me if I did not agree. When Morris told me this as I lay in the hospital, I told him in not very polite terms what to tell them! The sisters eventually calmed down and accepted their bequests.

Those days in the hospital when mother was stricken and possible blindness threatened me were rough. I suffered periodic violent pain in my eye for months, but miraculously I could see! The operation was successful. I divided my time between Oakington and Mother's house in Washington. My loneliness was devastating. I was in low physical condition and deeply depressed. On the long drive between Oakington and Mother's house in Washington, I found myself praying out loud, asking the Lord if there was anything left in life for me. I was sure there was not. I had lost my golden spoon.

Just before Christmas, my friend Polly Guggenheim, also a recent widow, urged me to come and visit her in her Washington mansion, Firenzi. Mother's house was a sad place, full of nurses and pretty much a hospital. She was partially paralyzed and had suffered more strokes. I accepted Polly's invitation.

My old friend Frances Rust suggested that we take a trip abroad together. My sisters and the nurses and doctor said I should go. We decided to fly around the world in 1962 and go to only those places we had not seen or those we wanted to return to. We traveled first-class, well chaperoned by the American Express Company, which supplied limousines, chauffeurs, and guides. We planned to visit our friend Consuelo Morgan Thaw (she was divorced from Landa) at Mallorca on our way home. We flew west across the Pacific and visited Hawaii, Hong Kong, and the Philippines. Joe had sent word to General Romulo that we were coming, and the Philippine government rolled out the red carpet for us. We were met officially and wined and dined by the president and the congress. I addressed the latter from the speaker's chair, and it was all quite exciting.

We went to India to see the glorious Taj Mahal and from there to Cairo and Istanbul. There I became very ill, and dear Fran nursed me for a week through a very high fever. It was early March, and cold weather and snowstorms were breaking all records around the Mediterranean. For days no ships, trains, or planes came in or out of Istanbul. We took the first plane out to Athens. I could barely crawl, I was so weak!

Fran had been a widow for many years, and a beau of hers, a handsome, retired army officer, General Bill Cowgill, met us in Athens. It was wonderful to have a gentleman escort from there on! He was very much in love with Fran, but they refused to ever leave me alone for a moment. Bill's favorite joke afterward was that he had heard of girls who traveled with their personal maids and silk sheets, but he never heard of any who traveled with their private bartender! Bill was about six feet five and we never found a bartender who would not allow him to take over the mixing of our drinks!

In Athens, we drove out to the oracle of Delphi. I asked our guide where the lady oracle was supposed to be. He showed me a crack in the stone floor and pointed downward. "In there, perhaps," he said. He left me looking down. "Tell me, Madam Oracle," I whispered, "is there anyone in the world to spend the rest of life with me?" Fran and Bill laughed at me, but I did not tell them what the oracle said!

From there we flew to Casablanca and motored to Marrakech where we stayed at Winston Churchill's favorite hotel. A handsome sheik in native robes sat in the bar and stared at us every evening. Fran and Bill said he was staring at me and they feared he would kidnap me. They teased me unmercifully! We spent a delightful week at Mallorca with Connie Thaw and spent a few days in Madrid. Then home. The trip had almost rejuvenated me.

I returned to Oakington to find my daughter's marriage on the rocks. She had three Gillet babies, Francis Warrington, Susan Eleanor, and Joseph Davies. Little Joe was her only blond child. The others were brunettes. She had been married the same length of time I had been when I divorced Tom Cheesborough—nine years. Her husband turned out to be the same spoiled young man we had been warned about. Eleanor told me that she hadn't been married to him a week before she realized that they didn't have many principles in common.

I decided I could not bury my beautiful daughter in the country, so I rented a furnished house in Washington, which had belonged to General George Patton. I moved Eleanor, her babies, and their nurse in with me and my new cook. The Livingstons were going to work for my ex-stepmother, with my blessings. She could do a great deal more for them than I could, and I was deeply grateful to them for their many years of service and friendship.

Jack Kennedy was president of the United States and a close friend of my son and his wife. He had appointed Joe federal attorney for Maryland, the only post in government my son wanted. The Tydings and my daughter were included in all the White House parties. Inevitably, some of the president's young men began to buzz around my Eleanor. When one dashing young man began to make some headway with her, I became alarmed. He had a wife and six children at home. Fortunately, Eleanor was keen about fox-hunting with the Elkridge-Harford Hounds in the western part of our Maryland county. A most attractive widower named John D. Schapiro was a member of this hunt. His father, Mr. Morris Schapiro, was a leading financier in Baltimore and a good friend of my late husband. John was a most cultured and charming man, and I approved of his courtship of my daughter. I told her she must not encourage him if she didn't intend to marry him. She denied having any intention of doing so.

One evening she and John returned to the Patton house later than I had come in from a dinner party. For a while I heard music and laughter below. Then there was total silence for some time. By this time, it was after 1 A.M. I lay awake and fretted for what seemed an endless period. At last I could stand it no longer. Going to the head of the stairs, I called down, "Eleanor, tomorrow is a school day!"

I couldn't think of anything else to say to a daughter who was thirty years old and the mother of three! I scurried back to bed and "played possum", snoring gently when she came up and looked into my room.

The next morning she brought me my breakfast tray and said indignantly, "Mother, how *could* you have called me that way last night?"

"Well," said I, "I didn't know what John would think of you, behaving like that!"

"But, Mother," came the reply, "I have never been so embarrassed! He had just proposed to me!"

"I thought you said you had no idea of marrying him," said I.

"Oh, Mother," said she in exasperated tones, "I've been trying to get him to propose to me for ages!"

I liked John and I was happy for them both.

President Kennedy had often stayed at Oakington House when he was campaigning in Maryland with Joe. After he became president, he did not visit us until May 1963. Bobby Kennedy and his family had visited my home at Oakington several times. My "Big House" was a "Guest House" for my son as his growing family occupied all of the house he had built on the place.

The last summer before his assassination, the president had appointed Joe the United States representative to the Interpol Conference in Europe (International Police). Joe's wife asked me if she could give a farewell party for him at the "Big House."

"Of course," I said. "How many guests will you have?" She told me about twenty-four; then called later and asked if they could have a few more.

"Certainly," said I, "who are they?"

"The president wants to come," she replied.

"The president of *what*?" I asked.

"Why, the president of the United States," she replied.

I was pleased. We had entertained ex-presidents, future presidents, vice presidents, senators, justices, ambassadors and cabinet ministers at Oakington House, but never a "sitting president!"

Great were the preparations that ensued. I let my daughter-in-law handle the menu, etc. I would slick up the garden. One day while I was crawling around it in dirty blue jeans, a gentleman came into it and asked to speak to Mrs. Tydings. He was the president of the C&P Telephone Company, no less! They were putting the "hotline" telephone for the president in my front hall! Then the FBI had to have a list of the tenants who rented houses on the place. These people would all have to be investigated! Also the servants in the house. Finally, a truck drove up with a special chair for the president to sit in at dinner. We kept his visit a secret. None of the other guests knew the president was coming. Some of them, from Baltimore, were what we called "Tydings's Republicans."

The president flew in about seven o'clock in the evening in his jet helicopter and landed on the lawn at the front entrance. A Secret Serviceman informed us when his plane was about to land, and Joe and Ginny left the guests on the terrace on the bay side of the house and went to greet the president. Their children, Mary and Millard, were running along beside them. I stood on the front porch and watched the smiling, young president walking across the lawn with his arms around Joe and Ginny and my grandchildren dancing around them. It is a mental picture I will never forget.

The president was en route to his wife, who was having her baby in Boston. He sat between Ginny and myself at dinner and talked about Senator Millard and about Joe running for the Senate next year. He was a great admirer of both Millard and Joe, he said. After dinner, the young people all sat on the terrace and sang, as we had done when I was a girl in Carolina. Joe had three of Baltimore's best musicians. Everyone was thrilled to be with the young president, and he, apparently, was thoroughly enjoying himself. He was supposed to leave at ten o'clock, the Secret Serviceman had told me, but he didn't go until after eleven. When he was leaving, Joe drank a toast to him in the Gold Parlor, and the president made a beautiful speech in return, toasting Ginny and myself and prophesizing that Joe would be as great a senator as his father had been. For over a week that wretched "Hotline to Moscow" telephone sat in our front hall, a mute (thank heavens!) reminder of the awesome responsibility the president takes with him wherever he goes.

In 1963, John F. Kennedy was assassinated. My children and I were stricken with grief, as was the rest of the country. I heard the news while shopping in Washington and hurried home to the Patton house. I knew that Joe and his wife were planning to go to Bobby Kennedy's birthday party at the White House that evening. Joe's wife heard it on the radio driving to D.C. from Oakington. She was hysterical when she arrived. I put her to bed with a sedative. Soon after, my son came in, red-eyed and sorrowful. He had planned to announce his candidacy for the U.S. Senate that week. Now, without the president's backing, he was uncertain whether he wanted to do so. In the end, he decided to make the race, and I was once again involved in a Maryland political campaign.

Meantime, my daughter had gone to St. Thomas in the Caribbean to get her divorce. Ginny Tydings's parents had given El their house on Water Isle. She took her youngest, little Joe Gillet, with her and left Suzy and Warry and their nurse with me.

Part VIII

Chapter 39

Green Pastures—My Golden Spoon Shines Again

1964 to 1987: my son enters the U.S. Senate; I meet and marry the Reverend Doctor Lowell Russell Ditzen; my mother dies; my new husband brings me happiness once more.

In 1964, the dark clouds that had enveloped me for so long lifted and the sun began to shine once more. In that year, my son was elected to the U.S. Senate and I met the Reverend Doctor Lowell Russell Ditzen.

I can now see that in 1964, the Democratic machine in our state was ripe for defeat by any good, honest young democrat. My son had these qualifications, and he also had good looks, brains, and his father's great name and reputation. Marylanders still regretted their loss of Senator Millard Tydings and were disgusted with the Republican who had replaced him in the Senate. Joe Tydings had already made a name for himself. He had been president of the student body at the University of Maryland, president of the Young Democrats of our state, a member of the Maryland House of Delegates, and Federal U.S. Attorney for Maryland, appointed by President Kennedy.

In the House of Delegates, he had introduced and passed the much-needed law to give equal accommodations in public places to all citizens. Until then, only white people were allowed in white hotels or restaurants. Also, while serving on the Judiciary Committee, he discovered that Maryland was one of a very few states that had no laws to protect its citizens against crooked savings and loan companies. He went to the governor and urged him to back such a law, but the governor refused to do so. When President Kennedy appointed Joe U.S. Attorney, he set about to clean up the crooked savings and loans and sent two Congressmen to jail, one from Maryland and one from the deep South. Ben Griswold, head of the oldest banking house in the state (Alexander Brown and Company), telephoned me the day of the verdict in the latter case and informed me jubilantly that my son "stood ten feet high in Maryland!"

My son had agonized over whether to run for the Senate after his friend President Kennedy was killed, but we all urged him to go for it. I worked to help him, writing letters and addressing women's groups. My daughter, who had gone to St. Thomas for her divorce, returned to vote for Joe, the day he won the primary election in May. The politicos said his large vote assured his election in November.

About ten days before the primary, my cousin Jack Cochran invited me to a dinner party he was giving before the Waltz Club dance. I told him I couldn't possibly accept on account of my campaign commitments. He said I needed a rest and that he would invite any bachelor in town whom I wanted for my escort. I replied that I knew them all and didn't want any of them! He phoned me a few days later to say he had met "a new man in town" who was tall, dark, and handsome, gave a great champagne party, and wore red-lined jackets! I laughed and asked who was this unusual person. My cousin somewhat sheepishly informed me that his name was Lowell Russell Ditzen and that he was a Presbyterian clergyman. "Oh, no!" I replied, laughing. In my experience, he didn't sound like a clergyman! Out of sheer curiosity, I accepted Jack's invitation to dinner and went back to Maryland to campaign until my cousin's dinner party.

The day of the party, May 15, I returned to Washington and the maid informed me that Dr. Ditzen had telephoned. The phone rang again and it was the reverend doctor. He told me that he was to have the honor of escorting me to Jack's dinner that evening, that he would call for me at 7:45, and that I would know him by "the pink orchid in his left antler!" This amused me. It was the kind of thing Millard might have said. I wasn't quite ready when the doorbell rang and I heard the rush of my grandchildren's feet down the stairs to greet the newcomer. I followed them at a somewhat more sedate pace. At the foot of the stairs stood a tall, handsome gentleman in evening clothes, holding little Warry Gillet, my six-year-old "grand" and laughing. "Methinks I hear the patter of little feet!" said he, putting Warry down and bowing over my hand. "And you are the lovely Eleanor Tydings whom I have heard so much about!" I thought this was overdoing it a little, but he seemed a pleasant person and he was certainly tall, dark, and handsome!

He was also a superb dancer, and he evidently enjoyed dancing with me for he tried to do so at every dance. He escorted me home and hesitated at the front door. We shook hands and said goodnight. Then suddenly he grabbed me and kissed me soundly! After which, to my great amusement, he gave me a horrified look, turned, and ran down the walk to his car! I laughed all the way upstairs. The next day I returned to my Maryland campaign labors and temporarily forgot about this unusual clergyman. Things were looking very good for my son's election. My future son-in-law, John Schapiro, called to invite me and my family, and anyone I would like, to supper on May 19, the evening of the primary election, at his historic house in Baltimore. I accepted for myself, cousin Jack, my friend Lucy Fain, sister Rahel, and her husband. No sooner had I hung up than I thought of Dr. Lowell Ditzen. Everyone said Joe's victory was a sure thing, and it would be fun to have the Reverend to celebrate with. Still, I was enough of a Victorian female to shrink from inviting a stranger to a family celebration. I phoned my sister and my cousin for advice, which was given freely and firmly: "Don't be silly. Go ahead and invite him!" I did, and he accepted. I told him that my family would be returning to Oakington to spend the night after John's dinner and celebratory dance I was giving at the Belvedere election night. Would he join us? He would.

That was a great and memorable evening. The azaleas, the tulips, and the wisteria were all blooming full glory at Oakington and there was a full moon. I didn't see much of Dr. Ditzen at the Belvedere, as I was surrounded by enthusiastic friends and supporters congratulating me on Joe's victory in the primary election. It practically assured the November election. Also, I was busy telephoning the great news to friends from coast to coast. It was midnight when we got home to Oakington. My friend Lucy Fain played the piano and we all danced. Then everyone went to bed save Dr. Ditzen and myself. I took him out to show him the gardens and the moonlit bay. We sat on the garden bench for a long time, telling each other about our lives. Then under the wisteria arbor he kissed me for the second time! I had never dreamed that I could ever fall in love again, but now it seemed I might! If I were to ever marry again, this man might be the third husband of the fortune-teller's prophecy.

That night and during the following months we became friends and he told me more about himself. After I heard him preach once, I went to hear him every Sunday at the old National Presbyterian Church on Connecticut Avenue. He was a dramatic figure in the pul-

pit in his long black robes with red velvet hood and slashings and
the white Geneva bands at his throat. His dark wavy hair was barely
tipped with silver at the temples and he had one of the most beautiful
speaking voices I had ever heard. It was very like my father's, as
were his black eyebrows, but his eyes, unlike Daddy's, were blue.
His sermons were the finest I had ever heard. I had never enjoyed
church so much because some sermons bored me. Lowell didn't
need to do much courting after I heard him preach. But of course
he did.

The Reverend Doctor Lowell Russell Ditzen, D.D., L.H.D., L.L.D.,
LITT.D., was born in Kansas City, Kansas. His father was a lawyer
who had been reared in an orphanage and had worked his way
through college and law school. Lowell's mother was a gifted musician, the granddaughter of a Swiss pioneer who settled on a large
land grant near Kansas City. She was a deeply religious woman who
died when Lowell was barely eight years old. Her widower married
twice more and there wasn't much home life for Lowell after that.
At sixteen, he went off to college and won most of the oratorical
contests of the Midwest. Then he won the "National Old Line," the
oldest oratorical contest in the country. He was president of the student body at William Jewell College and graduated with honors, in-
tending to study law and enter public life. He joined the young Republicans of Kansas City and became so disgusted with the crooked
political machine that he went to McCormick Theological Seminary
in Chicago and became a Presbyterian clergyman.

He was pastor of large churches in Chicago, New York City, Utica,
New York, and Bronxville, New York, was married while still in college and had four children. Two of them died tragically. Apparently
his home life was anything but a happy one. Dr. Ditzen immersed
himself in his church and the many beautiful books and sermons he
wrote. He won the Valley Forge Freedoms Foundation Award for
Best Sermon in the United States ten times. Admiral Arthur W. Rad-
ford presented the organization's tribute to Lowell at a Sunday service at the National Presbyterian Church in Washington soon after
we were married.

He had preached in Scotland, England, France, Egypt, and Hong
Kong. On a mission for the U.S. State Department, he had traveled
throughout India for several months speaking to civic, college, university, and religious groups. He had tried to deepen the level of
understanding between our two countries. Keenly interested in the
ecumenical movement, he attended the formative meeting of the

World Council of Churches in Amsterdam, Holland, in 1948, and international Presbyterian conferences in Switzerland, Germany, and Canada. In 1949, Dr. Ditzen was one of two Americans participating in the "Younger pastors of the world" conference in Switzerland.

Under his leadership, the Bronxville Reformed church had grown from fifteen hundred to more than three thousand members. He and his wife had legally separated before Lowell came to Washington as director of the National Presbyterian Center. The Center had been founded by a number of distinguished Presbyterians, among them Henry Luce, Paul Austin Wolfe, and Eugene Carson Blake. They asked Lowell to help raise the $7 million needed to construct the new National Presbyterian Church and Center and assume its leadership. He did. He was chosen, as the clerk of the Presbyterian Church said at Lowell's retirement, because he was "an able scholar, a creative person, communicative in both speech and writing, with distinguished pastoral and pulpit experience." Dr. Ditzen possessed and demonstrated all these qualities. He understood the significance of the American heritage and was a man of eminence and broad vision.

When I first met him, he was preaching in Dr. Elson's pulpit in the old Presbyterian church on Connecticut Avenue, taking a leading part in fund-raising for a new church and center, organizing conferences of national religious leaders, and working with Dean Sayre of the Washington Cathedral, Bishop Creighton of the Episcopalian Church, and many other denominational leaders. He was also teaching at American University, speaking all over the country, and moderating a popular television program in Washington every Sunday entitled "Issues." He obviously had no time for marriage, and after an unhappy marital experience, he had no desire to marry again. This made no difference to me. I was in no hurry to marry again either. I admired the man and was perfectly happy with his friendship and companionship. I was not sure he was someone I might enjoy spending my later years with! So we played golf and danced and I went with him often to hear him preach.

Soon after Joe Tydings won the primary election, my daughter and John D. Schapiro were married in the bridal suite of the ocean liner *United States* by our friend Doctor Lowell Russell Ditzen! It was a very beautiful and touching ceremony. Lowell had talked at length with both of them beforehand. Only our immediate families were present at their marriage. I was very happy for my daughter and happy that Lowell Ditzen had come into my life.

Early in 1965, I went out to Santa Fe, New Mexico, for a meeting of the board of governors of the new branch of St. Johns College, which was built on the slopes of Sun and Moon Mountains. The Annapolis campus of St. John's College is the third oldest college in the United States. It is a small liberal arts school based on study of The Hundred Great Books. I had met the president, Dr. Richard Weigle, and had joined the board in 1956. Two dear friends of mine lived in Santa Fe, Mrs. Gladys Dempsey, widow of Governor Dempsey, and Mrs. Patrick J. Hurley (widow of the general). I stayed with one or the other every year when I went to board meetings. When I went in 1965, Gladys Dempsey and I went to Mexico afterward. Dr. Ditzen followed us, and we had a delightful holiday touring that country and Yucatan.

He obtained permission from the church that year and secured his divorce. After the year required by the Presbyterian church before Lowell could remarry, he asked me whether I would marry him and I said yes. I loved him and was sure he loved me! Apparently my golden spoon had returned.

We planned our marriage for December 16, 1966, and made reservations for a two-week holiday at a fine Jamaican resort. The place required payment in full in advance. The money was sent. Lowell and I did not want any publicity about our marriage, so we didn't inform either of our churches until just before we were to be married. Then Lowell went to the presbytery about it, only to be told that he couldn't marry me because I had once been divorced, thirty years before!

I informed him indignantly that Millard and I had been married by none other than Doctor Albert M. McCartney, pastor of the National Presbyterian Church in Washington D.C.! The presbytery said that Dr. McCartney had kept no records of the marriages he had performed. I was furious. I informed my future husband that we were going to Jamaica legally or illegally, "in sin or not in sin!" Our holiday there was already paid for! It was not necessary, however, to go in sin, because I had the marriage book given me by Dr. McCartney in 1935, signed by him and by six United States senators! Lowell showed it to his presbytery and we were married by Dr. Edward L.R. Elson, pastor of the National Presbyterian Church, in the drawing room of my Tracy Place house. My son, Senator Tydings, gave the bride away, and Lowell's son, Stuart (who was even taller than Joe and Lowell), was the best man. The only other guests were family members and a few close friends. I had written a note to my ex-stepmother, Marjorie, inviting her to our wedding, only to receive a brief message from her secretary, Mrs. Voight, regretting my invitation.

Since Millard's death, I had seen Marjorie many times, and with my son and his wife, I had visited her at Topridge, but we had never resumed the close relationship of the past. I put it down to her increasing ill health and growing deafness. Now I know that it was also due to the machinations of her secretary, who wanted no such influence on her employer. She had a great deal to do with my father's divorce from Marjorie, as I discovered later. She died before Marjorie did, and, I understand, left a large estate.

A short time before our marriage, I gave a small lunch party in honor of Ruth Hurley. Ruth was an old friend of Marjorie's, and my stepmother came to the luncheon. I told her how sorry I was that she could not come to our wedding. "What do you mean, your wedding?" she exclaimed. "I never received the invitation. Of course I'll come!" Marjorie not only came to the wedding, but she invited me to have dinner alone with her shortly before it and gave me a most beautiful wedding gift. It was a magnificent big double clip pin of pearls and diamonds, shaped like a butterfly. My father had presented it to her on their tenth wedding anniversary when we three were breakfasting together in her bedroom. She had remembered how much I had admired it and wanted me to have it. It made me happy to have her at my wedding. After that, although she had been as affectionate as ever, I saw very little of her until her final illness and death at Mar-a-Lago. I had grieved over the death of the love between her and my father, and I grieved at her death. I had lost a truly wonderful friend. She was a great woman—not perfect, but none of us are.

After Lowell and I were married, many friends asked me curiously what it was like to be the wife of a minister after having been the wife of a senator for so many years. My reply was, "There's no difference, really. Both 'wife-hoods' involve just love and people. I like people and I love Lowell!" However, I do not think I would have found happiness with a less broad-minded, ecumenical religious teacher. Lowell Ditzen's vision was wide and wise and untrammeled by narrow theological concepts.

He once told me of a dream he had had when he briefly participated in a group studying extrasensory perception led by the psychologist Dr. Ira Progoff. The dream was so vivid that Dr. Progoff was much interested. He said it was a "major dream." Dr. Progoff had been a student of Jung's and was highly interested in all kinds of spiritual phenomena, among them important, or major, dreams.

Lowell dreamed that he was in a great hall and part of a vast conclave of all the leading minds of the world in every field—scientific, technological, aesthetic, political, religious, etc. This group of world leaders felt that they had an obligation to humanity to meet for yearly discussion and decide on a topic for study and possible implementation in the coming year. The topic had to be important to mankind at that time. In Lowells dream, it was the end of a long day and everyone including the chairman on the podium was tired. Many scientific theses had been read, not all easy to understand. The chairman was raising his gavel to adjourn the meeting when from one side of the hall a commanding presence entered and walked toward the podium. The figure was tall and slender and garbed in a white toga. Lowell said he thought his skin was dark but it wasn't noticeable because of his extraordinary eyes and the majesty of his bearing. The chairman's gavel paused in midair. The newcomer came to the podium and whispered in the chairman's ear. Then he turned to face the leaders of the world's thought and spoke only five words. "God and Man are One." A kind of electric current permeated the gathering as the white figure slowly glided from the hall.

Dr. Progoff wanted to put Lowell under hypnosis to try to reestablish spiritual contact with the remarkable figure in the dream. Lowell tried to cooperate, but it was impossible for Dr. Progoff to hypnotize him. The dream was only one of many things that made me decide to marry Lowell Ditzen.

Before we were married, I asked him if he would like me to leave my Episcopal church and become a Presbyterian. Of course I would have become a Holy Roller if he had wanted me to! He liked the idea so I said: "All right, I'll be a Presbyterian, but you have to register as a Democrat!" I knew he had been a lifelong Republican. He laughed and I became a liberal Presbyterian and Lowell Russell Ditzen became a good conservative Democrat.

Our first trip together around the world was with an ecumenical group known as The Temple of Understanding. My husband was interested in the interreligious aspect of this new group and wanted to help it. It had been the brainchild of a Connecticut woman named Judy Hollister. She wanted to get all the world's great religions together and build a meeting place in Washington where the leaders could gather for study, conversation, and, hopefully, deepening understanding and cooperation. There were several wealthy and influential people in the group.

Their first big meeting was to be held at Darjeeling in the Himalayas. Representatives of the world's religions would speak on the relevance of their faith to the world of today. As it happened, we were forced to meet in Calcutta instead because of excessive rains and washouts and a dangerous epidemic in the Himalayas. That was a disappointment! We flew west and visited Japan on the way. It was the first time I had been in Japan and I thoroughly enjoyed the beautiful temples and gardens. We were invited to a formal tea party there by Bishop Otani in the midst of his great monastery-like compound. This amazed our fellow Americans in Japan. No Westerners had ever been allowed inside the place. The bishop made a little speech and his tea was excellent. We attended services at two other great Japanese temples—one where a wedding was in progress, almost Western style. Everyone sat cross-legged on the floor at the other one. Neither Lowell nor I could achieve this yoga posture and spent the hour squirming around trying to arrange our legs in a halfway comfortable position. (We didn't succeed, but managed to get up without outside help!) One of my most vivid memories of Japan was of a small, natural chapel-like enclosure, walled by green shrubbery, in one of the vast temple gardens. In it was a lovely statue of the Buddha. The light filtered through onto his face and it seemed he smiled at me. "Life is good to you now, my child," he seemed to whisper. I wondered if he knew about my golden spoon!

One of our next stops was that most fascinating city, Bangkok. Here we met a dear, tiny little lady named Princess Poon, who was the head of the Buddhist sect.

In Calcutta, we were part of a sunrise service on the edge of a lake in the park. It was hot and the city was very dirty and full of pathetic paupers living on the pavements. The sunrise service was to have been photographed by *Life* magazine, but *Life* failed to appear. The whole affair was a flop in my opinion.

Our visit to Indian friends, the Birlas, in New Delhi, was more interesting. I laid flowers on the spot in their New Delhi garden where the great Gandhi was murdered. The Birlas were the Rockefellers of India. They had built an enormous Hindu temple in New Delhi, and in Calcutta, a modern hospital, a museum and civic center where we held our meetings. Both Mr. Birla and his wife were high-minded, charming people. Madame Birla explained to me that in their ancient Hindu faith they too worshiped one God, the Creator. All their lesser deities were only "faces of the one God," and these "lesser lights" had come down as imaginative myths through thousands of years. I had read the Upanishads at Vassar when I had studied the world's religions. I was fascinated by the thirty speeches I heard (in English) at the Birla museum on the relevance of their different religions to the modern world. I listened to them all. What impressed me most were the two great principles to which all these religions subscribed. Like our Christian faith, all worshiped one God, the creator, and all taught the Golden Rules of "Do unto others" and "I am my brother's keeper."

Unfortunately, while we were in India one person in our group took the latter too literally and ran off with the young daughter of one of the most supportive Americans with us. They intended to sleep under the tree where Buddha had his vision! It turned out all right. We never heard what happened there, under the tree, but the girl eventually rejoined her parents, who were most unhappy over the whole thing. They took her home and resigned from the organization.

Our last stop was in Rome. We were to have a private audience at the Vatican in the morning with Pope Paul. We flew into the ancient city in the early morning the day of the appointment, and I rushed to purchase a mass of rosaries to wear. I knew the Pope would bless us all, and I could bring the blessed beads back to my son, the senator, to give to his Catholic constituents.

We were put in the charge of a fat little priest who couldn't speak English. He stared at Lowell and gestured excitedly at him, pointing at Lowell's clerical collar. My husband repeated loudly, "I am a Presbyterian minister. I am a Protestant priest!" The Catholic just shook his head.

Finally the pope entered the room through a door behind a throne on a small dais. He wore white garments and was thin and pale. He made a nice, brief talk in English, then rose and came down from the dais and started shaking hands with us. To my horror, I could not remove my gloves with all the rosaries wrapped around them; it was unthinkable to shake hands with the pope with gloves on! The pope was looking at me with a suspicion of a twinkle in his eyes. He knew perfectly well what my problem was! I had an inspiration. I made the beautiful gesture of India, tented hands, fingertips touching. I bowed my head and said, "Your Holiness, I have been in the East and this is how they express reverence and respect." The pope gave me a faint smile and raised his hand. "Bless you, my children! I will pray for you and I hope that you will pray for me."

The audience was over. We returned to our hotel and Lowell exchanged the ministerial collar for something more comfortable. I looked at his coat lapel and burst out laughing. "So that was what that red-robed priest was pointing at! Darling, that is a Buddhist emblem in your buttonhole!" It had been placed there in Taiwan by one of our Buddhist friends. No wonder that priest was puzzled! So far as I know, it is the only Buddhist button in the world worn by a Presbyterian minister and blessed by the pope. I hope the pope was amused. I suspect he was!

Lowell and I attended a Presbyterian meeting in Geneva one year, and Lowell preached in Calvin's Church of Saint Pierre. There were many robed and turbaned representatives of the world's religions, each intoning a long prayer of his faith. I could imagine old Calvin revolving in his grave! I was told he had burned someone at the stake outside that church for doing less!

My darling mother lived until 1971. She had been an invalid for ten years. During her last years she was semi-comatose and had three nurses. When she was conscious, she was barely able to speak a word. She took an instant liking to Lowell. He would hold her hand and say prayers with her and she would smile so happily at him! We went to see her almost daily. For a long time she would smile at me even when she couldn't talk. Then she no longer smiled for anyone but Lowell. He was with her and held her in his arms when she died. He loved her as my father and Millard had and as all who knew her did. For me she was an ever-present source of love and support.

In 1974, Lowell retired from the church. He was tired after forty years of hard work in the ministry. He said he just wanted to "swing on the garden gate" with me! We did a good bit of joyous "swinging" in our twenty-three happy years together. His death in 1987 was another tragic loss for me. We had traveled around the world, by air and by sea, and sailed around all the continents save the polar wastes. We greatly enjoyed life together. Once again I had lost a dearly beloved husband and was left with grief and loneliness.

What happened next? Do you really want to know? Well, I picked myself up again, dusted myself off and lost about thirty pounds and a sagging chin! I made new friends and renewed old ones. My golden spoon polished up my old happy personality and I found three wonderful bachelor friends, one almost my age, one my son's age, and one even younger!

My son and daughter gave a big dinner dance in my honor, on my ninetieth birthday. At the dinner, a famous U.S. senator whose late father had been a U.S. senator, and a good friend of Millard's, was seated on my right. On my left was Douglas MacArthur, former U.S. ambassador and nephew of Millard's friend, the general. The fathers of both my dinner partners had been my friends too. I ended the evening dancing with my friend Dr. Richard Stoltz and did a high stepping dance of the 1920s called the Charleston. I told my children I wanted no more birthday parties. They laughed and told me they were already planning my 100th.

When this book is published, which I wrote so long ago, I will have another ball!

Epilogue

This concludes my report to you, my "grands" and "great grands," on my adventures and the events of my twentieth century. You can see that the old tradition of being born with a golden spoon in your baby mouth does not guarantee protection forever. Many enjoy it part of the time, but no one can count on it all of the time. I have enjoyed almost everything most of the time, but I suffered tragedy too. St. Paul's words are a good principle to live by: "Faith, Hope, and Love," and the greatest, he says, is Love.

Best of all I have learned to enjoy not just a family but a tribe! My two well-nigh perfect children have given me a wonderful son-in-law and some beautiful daughters-in-law, and eight grandchildren—all successful and beautiful and some gorgeous great grands! Who could ask for anything more?

Oh my goodness! My doorbell is ringing! I haven't even fixed my face! I hate to look in the mirror these days. "My face, I do mind it," even though "I'm behind it," but that doesn't apply to a female. The doorbell is still ringing—what am I supposed to do this evening? I wish I could remember. I hope it is dancing tonight.

Oh dear, that doorbell! Is it Bill or Delly or Millard or Lowell or Tom, Richard, or—Daddy! Just a minute please. I'm coming! We are going to a ball and I'm dancing to open the door!

Index

About the Author

Eleanor Davies was "brought up Victorian" by Emlen Knight Davies of early Maryland ancestry and a father, Joseph Edward Davies, whose parents came to Wisconsin from North Wales. His mother was an ordained Protestant minister and Joseph Davies became friend and adviser to three presidents and a U.S. ambassador.

The Davieses came to Washington in the Woodrow Wilson administration. Eleanor was a graduate of Vassar College and her husband and son were both U.S. senators (Tydings) from Maryland. She herself was a candidate for that high office for 36 hours. Friends say she "knew all the movers and shakers" in Washington and "where the bodies are buried."